REFINISHING

A Text-Lab Manual

Glencoe Automotive Technology Series

REFINISHING

A Text-Lab Manual

Josiah Newton
Auto Body Instructor (Ret.)
Indian River Community College
Fort Pierce, Florida

GLENCOE PUBLISHING COMPANY
Mission Hills, California

Glencoe Automotive Technology Series

Body Repair
Brakes
Engine Repair
Power Trains
Refinishing
Suspension and Steering
Transmissions
Air Conditioning and Heating

Send all inquiries to:
Glencoe Publishing Company
15319 Chatsworth Street
Mission Hills, California 91345

Library of Congress Catalog Card Number: 84-82192

Printed in the United States of America

ISBN 0-02-810050-6

2 3 4 5 6 7 8 9 90 89 88 87 86

Contents

UNIT 9 Custom Finishes and Effects 357

Preface

Refinishing: A Text-Lab Manual is a program designed to train students in the procedures for preparing a vehicle body surface and applying a paint finish. The program may be used with either beginning body repair students, or those who have had considerable body repair training. For students accomplished at doing body work, refinishing is a natural next step in their education. For those who do not do body repairs, refinishing is an occupation that stands by itself. This course of instruction is designed for the secondary and post-secondary levels of vocational education. It can be used in the hands of each student for traditional group instruction, or on an individualized basis.

Many students who would never consider a career in repairing automobile bodies will be pleasantly surprised to discover that refinishing is different. The body repairperson has a large tool box or shop filled with different types of tools or equipment, but the repairs he or she does on dented fenders, smashed fronts or rears, and damaged doors are predictable and occur often. The refinisher uses comparatively few tools, but the ideas and techniques available are unending. The body repairperson might be compared to the person who nails together a picture frame and stretches the canvas in place. The refinisher is the one who paints the picture. Both are important, but the refinisher unquestionably has more artistic license. The joy of creating in paint on automobile bodies has led many an artistic person into the creation of a thriving business in custom painting on cars, trucks, boats, or motorcycles. This book will awaken your students to the possibility of great personal satisfaction in the refinishing field.

ORGANIZATION

This text-lab manual consists of 9 logically constructed learning units. Each unit deals with a special area of knowledge or with the development of a specific set of skills. Important concepts are explained in simple language. Technical terms are fully defined when introduced. Illustrations are keyed to the text and appear as close as possible to the subjects being explained.

Safety is emphasized throughout the text. Special notes also are used to call attention to important procedures and areas where extra caution is necessary.

Each unit begins with a brief statement concerning the major topics to be discussed. A written test objective follows spelling out exactly what the student is expected to achieve. Below the objective is the preparation assignment, which lists the text pages that the student needs to study.

A manipulative objective, or objectives, follows the explanatory text material. Manipulative objectives are stated in terms of tasks to be performed. Step-by-step procedures follow the manipulative objectives, with directions for completing a repair operation or developing a specific skill.

Each unit, or major division within a unit, concludes with a written test. These tests are designed to closely approximate the auto body certification tests conducted by the National Institute for Automotive Service Excellence. The tests are multiple choice. Each test is labeled to match the written test objective found earlier in the unit.

Since skill development is stressed in this course of study, the text-lab manual gives the instructor maximum flexibility to work individually with students as necessary. The structure of the text-lab manual suits the nature of the refinishing shop class, where several projects usually are being conducted at any given time.

Unit 1 introduces the student to sanding tools and abrasives. It covers the use of sanders and grinders, both electric and air powered. The shop compressor, an often ignored piece of equipment (until it breaks down), is included so that your students will realize the amount of maintenance required to keep it in good condition.

Unit 2 covers a broad range of refinishing materials, such as paint removers, primers and fillers, and the different types of paint.

Unit 3 shows how to use spray guns and baking equipment used for drying paint. Detailed text and illustrations show the student examples of what can go wrong when spraying, and what to do to correct the problem. Use of an airbrush is also included.

Unit 4 deals with surface preparation, including sanding, priming, and filling of surfaces in various conditions.

Unit 5 is about lacquer refinishing, when to use it, and when not to use it. Mixing and spraying are thoroughly covered. Compounding or "rubbing out" is explained as a necessary step in lacquer refinishing.

Unit 6 covers enamel refinishing, including alkyd, acrylic, and polyurethane finishes. Detailed procedures show exactly how to prepare and spray the paint.

Unit 7 shows 30 of the most common paint problems and how to avoid them. Illustrations show the actual problems so the student can learn to recognize exactly what went wrong.

Unit 8 is about the exotic finishes: metalflake, pearlescent, spatter, and vinyl sprayon, with complete application techniques.

Unit 9 covers unusual and imaginative effects in custom finishes. Decals, striping, stenciling, lace effects, cobwebbing, custom woodgraining, and smoke are all explained in detail, with photos of actual finishes.

unit 1

Sanding Tools and Abrasives

Automotive refinishing is basically a two-step process. In the first step, the surface to be refinished is prepared: old paint is sanded, minor imperfections are sanded or filled, the surface is primed and, where necessary, sealed. In the second step, the new finish is applied in several coats and air dried or baked.

Most of the equipment used in the preparation stage is not unique to the refinishing field. Grinders, orbital sanders, and files are all tools used regularly in body repair and sheet metal work of all kinds. The equipment used in the painting stage, however, is associated mainly with auto refinishing. It includes the refinisher's most important tool, the spray gun.

This unit presents an overview of the first group of tools. It reviews the use of sanders and grinders and describes in detail the design, operation, and maintenance of the compressed air systems that are frequently used to power them.

OBJECTIVE 1-A (written)

After doing the reading and shop exercises, you will be able to answer correctly without reference material a minimum of 14 out of 20 test questions on the following topics:

1. Compressed air systems and their maintenance
2. Grinders and sandblasters
3. Sanding tools and accessories
4. Coated and paste abrasives

Preparation:

1. Study pages 1 through 37.
2. Attend classroom discussions on Objective 1-A.
3. Read the Safety Checklist on pages 37 through 39.

COMPRESSED AIR SYSTEMS

The vast majority of tools used in the paint shop are power tools. While these may be driven by either electricity or compressed air, compressed air is by far the more common power source. Air-driven tools are preferred for three reasons. First, since they have no motors, they are smaller and lighter. Second, since they are constantly cooled by the air that operates them, they do not overheat. Third, since they eliminate electricity from an

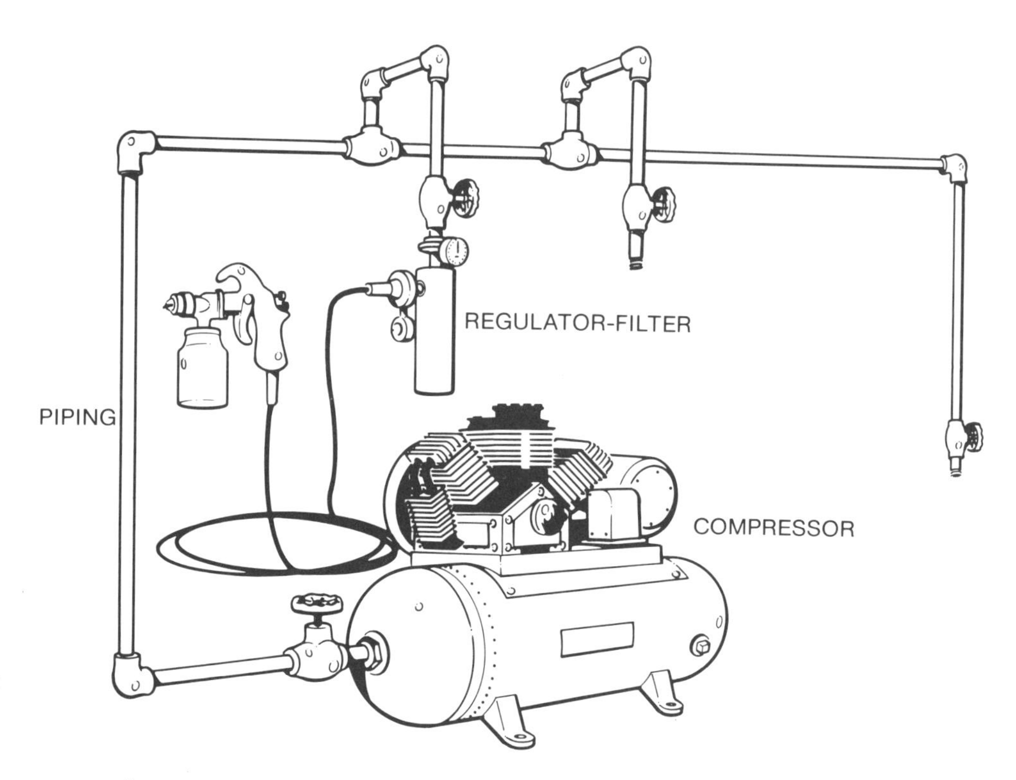

FIG 1-1
Three parts of a compressed air system.

area where paint and other flammable materials are being used, they are safer.

In its simplest form, a compressed air system consists of three parts: (1) a compressor to supply the air, (2) a piping system to carry it, and (3) a transformer-regulator to filter the air and control its pressure (Fig. 1-1).

Compressors

A compressor takes in air at atmospheric pressure and, using a piston in a cylinder, forces it into a confined space. This compressing of the air raises its pressure as expressed in pounds per square inch (psi).

Compressors are generally categorized by the horsepower of the motors that drive them. Individual models also vary in the number of cylinders they have. (There can be two, four, or more.) Together the horsepower and the number of cylinders determine the volume of air the compressor can supply. This figure is known as the compressor's capacity and is expressed in cubic feet of air per minute (cfm). The larger the motor and the more numerous the cylinders, the greater the compressor's capacity (Table 1-1). The greater the compressor's capacity, the more tools, equipment, and work stations the unit can supply.

Operation

There are two basic types of compressors used in auto refinishing. The single-stage compressor is used where demand for compressed air is small or only intermittent. Its cylinders are all the same size. Each compresses air once and sends it directly to the storage tank. A two-stage compressor is used in large-scale production work or where the demand for compressed air is steady. It can deliver a higher psi than the single-stage model. This increase is achieved by compressing the same air twice in cylinders of unequal size (Fig. 1-2).

Table 1-1 COMPRESSOR SPECIFICATIONS

Model Number	Motor (h.p.)	Displaces (cfm)	Delivers (scfm)	Pressure (psi)	Tank Size		Dimensions (in.)**	Weight (lb.)
					(in.)*	(gal.)		
Vertical, two cylinders								
33-1023	1½	6.9	4.8	140-175	20 × 48	60	34 × 21 × 70	690
33-1027	2	9.6	6.7	140-175	20 × 48	60	34 × 21 × 70	700
33-1033	3	15.0	11.5	140-175	24 × 48	80	34 × 25 × 74	940
33-1037	5	22.4	17.3	140-175	24 × 48	80	34 × 25 × 74	975
Horizontal, two cylinders								
33-1022	1½	6.9	4.8	140-175	20 × 48	60	53 × 21 × 45	690
33-1026	2	9.6	6.7	140-175	20 × 48	60	53 × 21 × 45	700
33-1032	3	15.0	11.5	140-175	20 × 63	80	68 × 23 × 49	940
33-1036	5	22.4	17.3	140-175	20 × 63	80	68 × 23 × 49	975
33-1041	7½	34.8	26.8	140-175	20 × 63	80	68 × 24 × 54	1260
33-1047	10	48.0	34.5	140-175	24 × 72	120	75 × 29 × 58	1500
33-1051	15	78.7	60.6	120-150	24 × 72	120	75 × 30 × 64	1600
Horizontal, four cylinders								
33-1054	15	86.0	63.6	120-150	30 × 72	200	82½ × 32½ × 68	2550
33-1055	20	107.0	79.2	120-150	30 × 72	200	82½ × 32½ × 68	2600
33-1069	25	123.0	93.0	120-150	30 × 72	200	82¼ × 32⅛ × $68\frac{5}{16}$	2715

*Diameter × length
**Length × width × height

The cylinders in two-stage compressors work in pairs. In a four-cylinder model, for example, air is first taken into the larger (low pressure) cylinders, where it is compressed to 60 psi. Then it passes through finned heat exchangers, called intercoolers, to the smaller (high pressure) cylinders. There it completes compression to 175 psi. A second cooling follows before the compressed air is fed into the storage tank through a one-way valve (Fig. 1-3).

FIG 1-2
Two-stage, four-cylinder compressor. (The DeVilbiss Company)

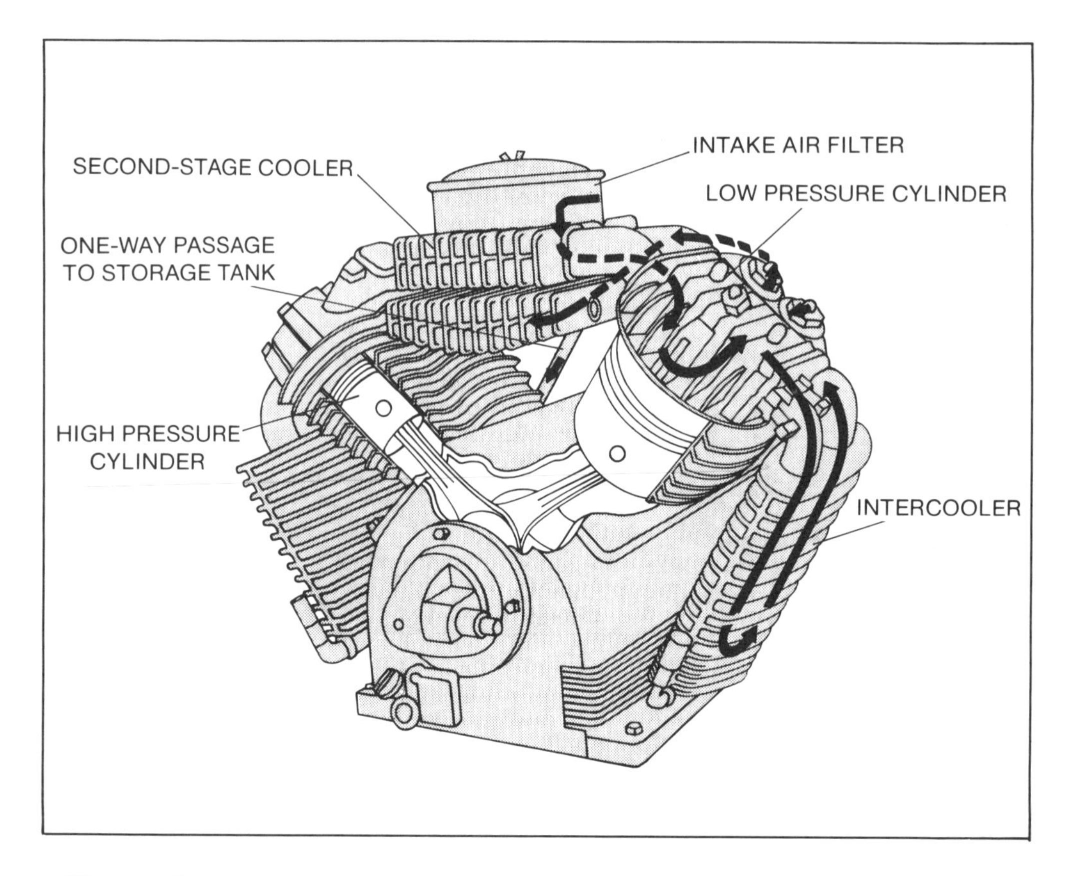

FIG 1-3
Two-stage, four-cylinder compressor operation.

The cooling stages in the process are necessary because compressing air generates a tremendous amount of heat. If not controlled, over a long period of time this heat could expand metal, break down lubricants, and generally shorten the life of the compressor's moving parts.

Safety Devices

In both single- and two-stage compressors, the process of compression and storage continues until an automatic cutoff switch shuts down the compressor's motor. Without this switch, the compressor would continue to operate until its tank ruptured. The switch's cutoff level is preset at the factory to the purchaser's specifications.

Should the cutoff switch fail to function, a backup system is provided. On the tank itself, there is a safety device called the pop-off valve. It automatically opens when pressure exceeds the preset level by a certain amount (usually about 25 psi). The valve bleeds enough air to lower the tank pressure to an acceptable point and then closes again automatically. If the malfunction continues, the valve will open and close repeatedly until the compressor is turned off.

Pop-off valves are also frequently placed at various points on the compressor itself. These valves operate to relieve excess pressure in the cylinder heads. The malfunction is different, in other words, but the safety principle is the same.

Maintenance

A regular maintenance program is the best guarantee that a compressor will not malfunction. On at least a weekly basis, six compressor components should be checked and, if necessary, serviced.

1. *Air filter.* All air is taken into the compressor through one or more circular filters mounted either on the top or the front of the unit. There are two kinds of filter assemblies. Some compressors have filter pots that take paper filter elements (Fig. 1-4). These resemble automobile filters and can be treated very much like them. They can be removed and tapped or blown clean one or more times before replacement is necessary. Other compressors have exposed filter elements. These are usually made of foam rubber and can be removed, washed or blown clean, and reused. Should the material start to disintegrate, however, the filter should be replaced immediately. If drawn into the compressor, particles of foam rubber could interfere with the operation of the pistons.

FIG 1-4 Filter pot. (The DeVilbiss Company)

2. *Crankcase.* Lubricating the crankshaft is extremely important in maintaining the compressor's efficiency and extending its useful life. Oil levels are monitored in one of three ways. Older compressors have dipsticks similar to those used in automobiles. Newer models have either a sight gauge (a window through which the oil level is read) or an oil port (a kind of reverse dipstick in which the oil level is read on the threads of the opening rather than on the shank of the object inserted in it) (Fig. 1-5). A good-quality oil (generally SAE 30) is recommended for use in compressors. It should be added as necessary and changed completely every 200 working hours. This is particularly important if the compressor is equipped with a sight gauge. In such a case, dirty oil could fog the window and result in a false reading.

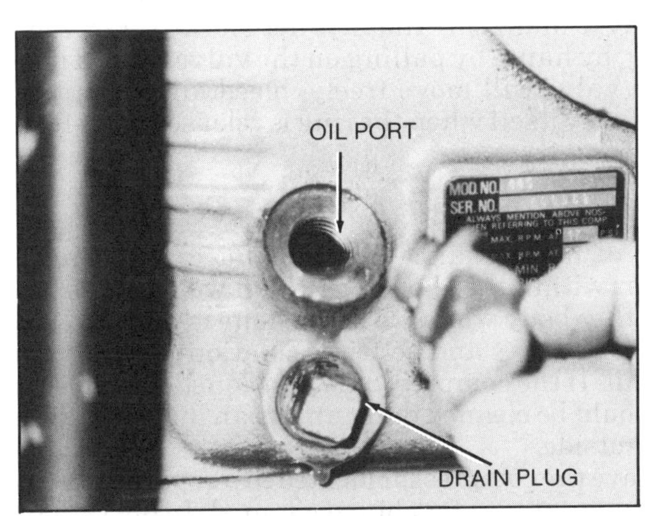

FIG 1-5 Checking air compressor oil. (David Keown)

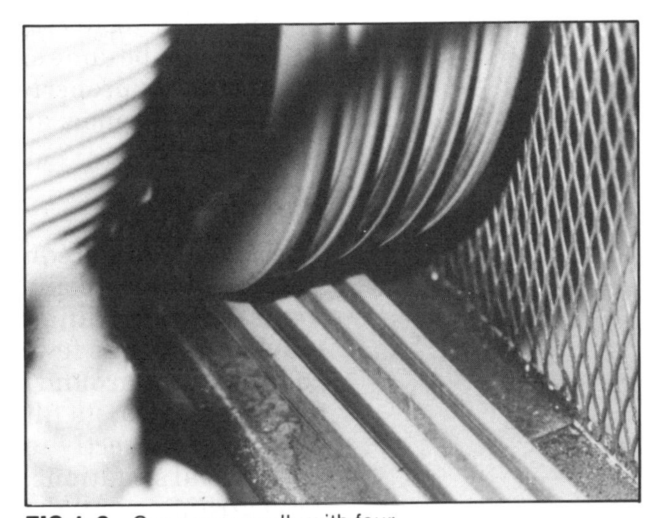

FIG 1-6 Compressor pully with four belts. (David Keown)

3. *Cooling fins.* Accumulations of dust and dirt decrease the efficiency of a compressor's cooling system. The intercooler fins and motor vents should therefore be blown clean with a duster gun or air hose. If the shop is especially dirty, this kind of cleaning should be done daily.
4. *Drive belts.* The compressors used in paint shops are driven by up to five rubberized belts operating in parallel (Fig. 1-6). These should be checked visually for tension and signs of wear. Slack of 3/8 inch or more requires adjustment. Such slack can be taken up by loosening the bolts holding down the motor and moving both motor and flywheel farther from the compressor. When cumulative adjustments exceed an inch, however, the belt (or belts) must be replaced.

FIG 1-7 Drain petcock on compressor tank. (David Keown)

FIG 1-8 A pop-off valve on compressor. (David Keown)

5. *Drain cock.* As compressed air cools, moisture condenses out of it and collects at the system's low points. Since water could damage the mechanisms of most air-driven tools or spot a new finish, it must be removed. In the case of the compressor, a petcock is provided for this purpose, usually on the bottom of the storage tank (Fig. 1-7).
6. *Pop-off valve.* As the major system safeguard, the pop-off valve should be tested regularly to make sure that it is not blocked or frozen. This can be done simply, by hand, by pulling on the valve ring. If it is operating properly, the valve will move freely, bleed air while it is being held open, and close by itself when the ring is released (Fig. 1-8).

Location

The extent and frequency of maintenance can be reduced by careful placement of the compressor within the shop. A location well away from areas where sanding and other body work are being done is best. Such a placement means fewer filter changes and better circulation of relatively cool, clean air around the unit. If the compressor is positioned in or near a dirty work area, its filter should be cleaned daily unless an air intake has been rigged directly to the outside.

The ideal situation is to have the compressor located in a separate room. This arrangement also has advantages for shop personnel. In operation, compressors are extremely noisy. Mountings can help to some degree, but only a solid barrier will reduce the noise to a comfortable level. (This is particularly true where the volume of work dictates the use of a second, backup compressor.) Location in a separate room shields those working nearby from the noise. If the compressor must be placed on the floor in the main work area, it should at least be partitioned off in some way.

Piping Systems

Compressed air is carried throughout the shop by a system of pipes—a main line and a series of branches. This system has three important variables: pipe size, pipe length, and slope. Together these assure that the air being delivered to the transformer is cool, dry, and the right pressure.

Pipe Size

The size of the pipe is determined mainly by the capacity of the compressor feeding air into it. The larger the compressor, the wider the pipe (Table 1-2). Friction is the reason for this variation. Friction between the compressed air and the inner wall of the pipe tends to reduce line pressure. A wider pipe allows easier passage and thus minimizes the pressure loss.

Table 1-2 MINIMUM PIPE SIZE RECOMMENDATIONS

Compressing Outfit		Main Air Line	
Size (h.p.)	Capacity (cfm)	Length (ft.)	Diameter (in.)
1½–2	6–9	Over 50	¾
3–5	12–20	Up to 200 Over 200	¾ 1
5–10	20–40	Up to 100 100–200 Over 200	¾ 1 1¼
10–15	40–60	Up to 200 100–200 Over 200	1 1¼ 1½

Pipe Length

The overall length of the piping system varies with the shop layout. Ideally, however, distances should be kept short. The reason once again is friction. The pressure loss from friction over a 5-foot length of pipe is bound to be much less than over a 20-foot length.

The only exception to the rule favoring shorter distances is the length of pipe between the compressor and the first transformer-regulator. This distance must be at least 25 feet to allow sufficient time for cooling and condensation. If it were shorter, the air passing through the transformer-regulator might still be warm enough to hold moisture. That moisture, condensing out later, could damage a power tool or spot a new finish.

Slope

The piping system finally must have a slope built into it. The main line should incline toward either the compressor or a drain leg at the end of the system called, appropriately, the dead-end drain. The purpose of this arrangement is to create a low point toward which any moisture in the system will run. Moisture drains back into the storage tank or into the dead-end drain, where it can be removed easily by opening a drain cock.

This same logic dictates other system features. The place where a branch for a work station joins the main line is called a takeoff or, less frequently, a drop. *Drop,* however, is not a term that should be taken literally. If the branch actually did drop from the main line, it would form a moisture trap. To avoid this problem, all takeoffs are made from above (Fig. 1-1). Where the pipe must dip (to detour around a rafter or a ceiling duct, for example), a petcock is installed to drain off any moisture that collects. These and all other drains in the piping system, including the dead-end drain, should be opened daily.

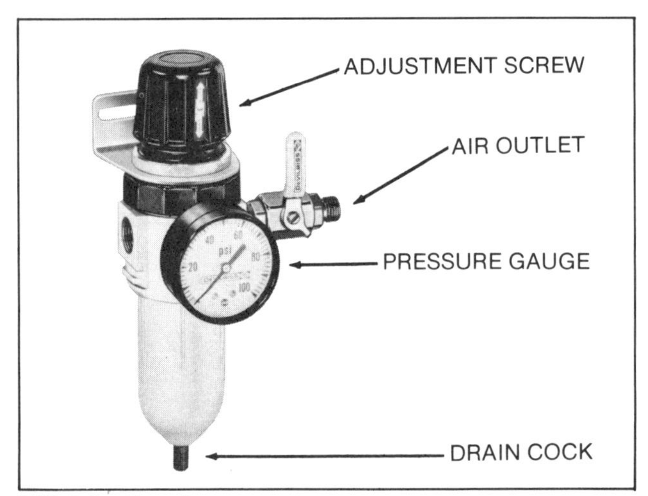

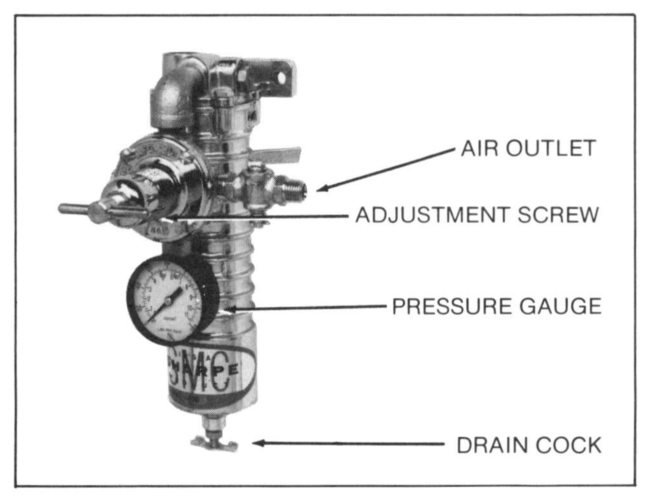

FIG 1-9 Transformer-regulators. (The DeVilbiss Company) (Sharpe Manufacturing Company)

Transformer-Regulators

What if some moisture does remain in the system? The last line of defense is the transformer-regulator. One of these devices is located at each work station.

The transformer-regulator serves a dual purpose. First, it regulates air pressure downward, reducing it from the maximum in the main line to a psi usable by individual power tools. Second, it filters out dirt, oil, and any moisture remaining in the compressed air. (*Note:* It is possible to have a device that does not perform this second function. In such cases, separate water and oil filters must be installed elsewhere in the system.)

Key Parts

Transformer-regulators vary to some extent in their design. Some models are smaller, more streamlined, and more lightweight than others. All, however, have four parts that the refinisher must be able to recognize and use (Fig. 1-9).

1. *Adjustment screw.* The mechanism that actually regulates air pressure is the adjustment screw. In its closed position, the screw feels loose and moves freely. As it is turned inward, however, it engages an internal spring and becomes tighter. The increased tension on this spring is what actually opens the air flow valve.
2. *Pressure gauge.* The increasing amount of air escaping from the valve is registered on a pressure gauge located adjacent to the adjustment screw. On transformer-regulators with more than one screw, there is more than one gauge.
3. *Air outlets.* Transformer-regulators can, and usually do, have multiple outlets. These pass regulated air through hoses to the tools being used. (Some transformer-regulators also have special outlets that pass air at line pressure. These outlets are easily identified because they lack adjustment screws.) Multiple outlets allow a transformer-regulator to supply air to several tools at one time, often at different pressures. Actual air flow is controlled by levers located on each outlet. Usually a quarter-turn of a lever is enough to start or stop the air flow, regardless of its pressure.

4. *Drain cock.* Like any other low point in the system, the transformer-regulator is equipped with a drain cock. As oil, dirt, and water are filtered out, they collect in the bottom of the device. Because of the transformer-regulator's sensitive location and function, these contaminants must be drained daily. In the case of a transformer-regulator supplying a spray gun, draining before each use is advisable (Fig. 1-10).

Pressure Drop

The most important thing to remember when reading a transformer-regulator gauge is that the pressure shown is *not* the pressure available at the power tool. Between transformer-regulator and tool there is a hose that presents the same problems as the compressor's piping system. Here, too, friction between the compressed air and the passageway it travels creates a pressure loss. Since accurate pressure adjustment is so important in refinishing (particularly in spray painting), manufacturers regularly provide tables of pressure drop as part of transformer-regulator specifications. These indicate the difference between the pressure showing on the gauge and the pressure actually available at the spray gun or power tool being used (Table 1-3).

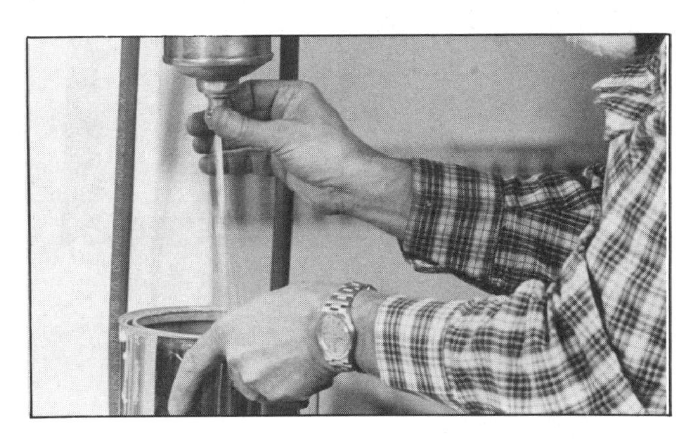

FIG 1-10
Draining a transformer-regulator. (The DeVilbiss Company)

Table 1-3 TABLE OF PRESSURE DROP

	Air Pressure Drop at Spray Gun (psi)					
Hose	5-foot length	10-foot length	15-foot length	20-foot length	25-foot length	50-foot length
¼-inch diameter						
At 40 psi	6	8	9½	11	12¾	24
At 50 psi	7½	10	12	14	16	28
At 60 psi	9	12½	14½	16¾	19	31
At 70 psi	10¾	14½	17	19½	22½	34
At 80 psi	12¼	16½	19½	22½	25½	37
At 90 psi	14	18¾	22	25¼	29	39½
5/16-inch diameter						
At 40 psi	2¼	2¾	3¼	3½	4	8½
At 50 psi	3	3½	4	4½	5	10
At 60 psi	3¾	4½	5	5½	6	11½
At 70 psi	4½	5¼	6	6¾	7¼	13
At 80 psi	5½	6¼	7	8	8¾	14½
At 90 psi	6½	7½	8½	9½	10½	16

It should be noted, however, that the charts themselves have a significant limitation. They account for only two variables—hose diameter and hose length. They do not consider other factors that may affect pressure, factors like the actual condition of the hose or the number and nature of fittings and connections. The tables, in other words, must be interpreted just like the readings on the gauges.

FIG 1-11
Line pressure gauges. (The DeVilbiss Company)

Because of this difficulty, many refinishers prefer to use an in-line gauge, at least when spray painting. The gauge is an attachment that fits between the tool handle and the air hose. It gives the refinisher an immediate and accurate reading of the pressure available (in this case, at the gun). Some companies now even manufacture spray guns with such gauges built into their handles (Fig. 1-11).

OBJECTIVE 1-A1 (manipulative)

Working as a team with one other student and with the aid of Job Report Sheet 1-A1, you will give the shop compressor its weekly maintenance check.

Time Recommended:

15 minutes

Preparation:

1. Review pages 1 through 10.
2. Study pages 10 through 14.

3. Read the Safety Checklist on pages 7 and 8, items 1 through 7.
   Note: The Safety Checklists are designed to be cumulative throughout the book. Before doing each shop exercise, review the applicable entries from the unit list. On at least a weekly basis, review all items in all lists covered to that point in the course.

Tools and Materials:

1. Compressor air filter (paper or foam rubber)
2. Duster gun and safety goggles or shop vacuum cleaner

Procedure:

1. Turn off the compressor's power.
2. Read any compressor nameplates. These may be located on the motor, storage tank, or other surface, depending on the manufacturer and model. Enter any relevant information in the specifications section of Job Report Sheet 1-A1. Continue entries as the various maintenance checks are made.
3. Inspect the compressor's air filter. Unscrew the wing nut and remove any washers. On compressors having exposed filter elements, lift off the filter lid. On compressors having enclosed filter elements, use both hands to pull off the filter pot.
4. Remove the filter element. Blow clean or replace as necessary. Reassemble air intake.
5. Check the compressor's oil level. Enter both the method of monitoring and the actual reading on the job sheet.
6. Add oil as necessary. If low, on sight gauges fill to the halfway point; on dipsticks, to the upper mark; on oil ports, to the bottom of the threads.
7. Using a duster gun, air hose, or vacuum, clean the compressor's surfaces. Give special attention to the cooling fins and motor vents.
8. Visually check the compressor belts for wear and slack. (*Note:* If the belt guard can be opened, use finger pressure to test for slack. Belts that give more than ⅜ inch need tightening.)
9. Locate the drain cock on the lower surface of the storage tank. (Usually this is in the center, but on older model compressors with siphon systems it could be at either end.) Open.
10. Close the drain cock when or if no moisture trickles out.
11. Locate the storage tank pressure gauge. Enter the reading on the job sheet.
12. Find the pop-off valve. Test by grasping the ring and pulling firmly up or out, depending on the orientation of the valve. Release.
13. Be sure all checked portions of the compressor are secured—the filter wing nuts tightened, the belt guard in place and locked, the drain cock closed.
14. Switch on the power.

JOB REPORT SHEET 1-A1

COMPRESSOR MAINTENANCE CHECK

Student Name ______________________________ Date ______________

Time Started ____________ Time Finished ____________ Total Time ____________

Specifications

Compressor type: Number of stages _____ Number of cylinders _____

Manufacturer: ______________________________

Motor: _____ h.p.

Storage tank: Maximum pressure _____ psi Actual pressure _____ psi

Air filter type ______________

Oil level: Type of indicator ______________ Reading ______________

Belts: Number _____ Belt guard: Yes _____ No _____

Drain cock location ______________________________

Pop-off valve location ______________________________

In the space below, sketch the shop compressor. Show and label these parts: (1) compressor, (2) motor, (3) storage tank, (4) air intake filter, (5) pop-off valve, (6) belts and belt guard, (7) tank pressure gauge, (8) drain cock, (9) oil gauge/port/dipstick, and (10) cooling fins.

Checkup Questions

1. When the pop-off valve ring is pulled, what happens? ______________________

2. Why might it be better to use a vacuum cleaner on the motor's cooling fins rather than a duster gun? ______________________

3. Describe the location of the shop compressor. Evaluate its good and bad points.

4. In the sketching instructions, the term *compressor* has two different meanings. What are they? ______________________

Date Completed ____________ Instructor's Signature ____________

SANDING TOOLS AND ACCESSORIES

In auto body work, preparing the surface usually means removing all or part of the existing finish. The most common method of removal is sanding.

On a panel severely damaged by rust and scale, for example, the sanding is done in stages. The refinisher starts by using a heavy-duty grinder and a coarse abrasive, or sanding disc. This combination removes most of the old finish and all of the damage. To smooth the marks left by grinding, the refinisher works with lighter tools and finer abrasives. He finishes the surface by hand, using a sanding block. The process, to summarize, moves from power to hand tools, from coarse abrasives to fine.

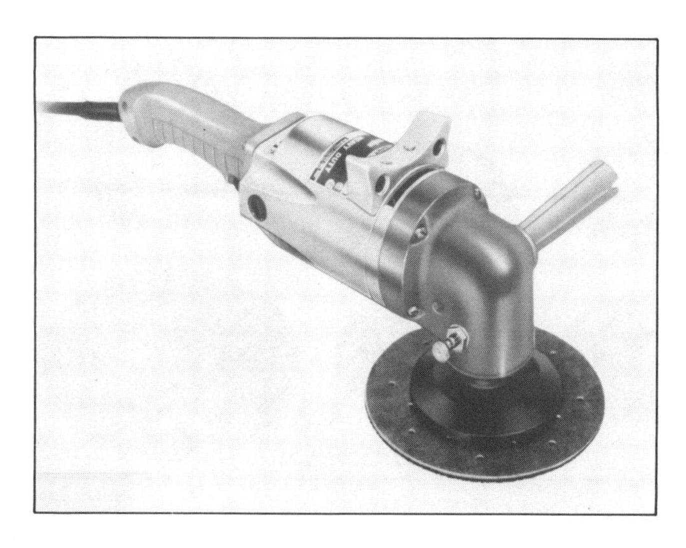

FIG 1-12
Grinder (disc sander).
(Milwaukee Electric Tool Corporation)

Grinders

The workhorse of the refinisher is the grinder or, as it is sometimes called, the heavy-duty disc sander (Fig. 1-12). The grinder is used to strip off rust and paint, to cut down welds, and to eliminate tool and other repair markings. Basically, it is a portable version of the bench grinder used in engine and other mechanical repairs. It comes in 7- and 9-inch sizes.

The portable grinder can be driven by either electricity or compressed air. Each version of the tool has its own advantages. The extra weight of the electric grinder can be used to provide the firm pressure needed for a smooth cutting action. The air-driven grinder, being air-cooled as well, can be used for longer periods of time without overheating. It is common for refinishing shops to have and use both tools.

Design and Assembly

The body of an electric grinder consists of a motor to which are attached two sturdy handholds—one at the base of the motor, the other at the side of the disc. The air-operated grinder has a simpler design. More lightweight, it is essentially just two handles attached to a shaft housing. In both tools, the trigger is usually built into the lower handle. As a safety feature, it is pressure sensitive. Pulling back with a finger starts the disc spinning; release, whether intentional or accidental, stops it.

To prepare the grinder for use on flat surfaces, the operator first threads a rubber or phenol backup pad onto the tool's spindle. (*Note:* The pad may actually be an assembly of two or more parts. The phenol, or plastic, pad is added for extra rigidity.) The pad provides a sturdy base for the sanding disc. The disc is mounted on the pad and locked in place with a disc nut. The nut is then tightened with a spanner wrench.

For sanding on curved surfaces or getting into tight spots, there are special grinder accessories (Fig. 1-13). Molded discs and mandrels that take cone-shaped abrasives adapt the tool for work on contoured body panels. The mandrel, for example, is used to remove paint or rust from panels containing 90-degree curves (fender flanges, door posts). Wire brushes make it possible to remove rust and scale from areas where grinding discs will not fit.

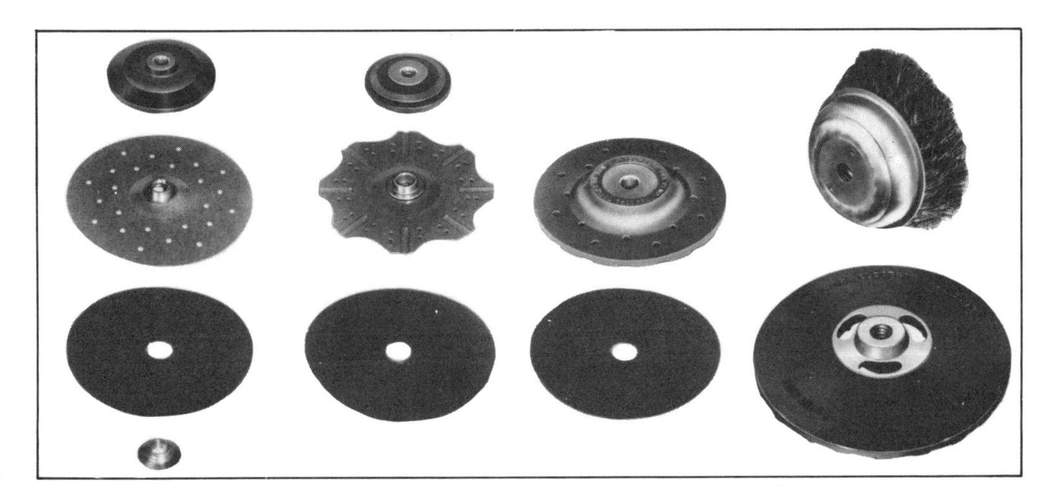

FIG 1-13
Grinder accessories.
(Milwaukee Electric Tool Corporation)

Grinding Technique

The typical 9-inch grinder is operated at speeds up to 5000 revolutions per minute (rpm). The comparable figure for the 7-inch grinder is nearly 1000 rpm more. Such speeds make it possible to strip the finish from an entire automobile in a short period of time. They also make it possible to damage the underlying metal, perhaps beyond repair, almost as quickly. For this reason, good technique is especially important when using a grinder.

A grinder should be held firmly with both hands. The basic movement is first from left to right and then from right to left. Called cross-grinding, this technique makes small scratches that cross each other at right angles. These scratches erase any trace of the grinder's circular action (Fig. 1-14).

When bringing the grinding disc into contact with a metal surface, the operator must consider three factors.

1. *Disc angle.* The disc should form a 5-degree angle with the surface. (This positioning means that only its outer 2 inches will be in contact with the panel.) If the angle is greater than 5 degrees, there is a possibility that the disc will gouge the metal surface. This additional damage will have to be sanded out with other tools. If the angle is less than 5 degrees, the disc will, for all practical purposes, be lying flat on the work surface. In this position, its high-speed rotation will pull and jerk the tool violently. This action could injure the operator or result in damage to adjoining parts of the vehicle. Long-term misuse of this type also tends to warp the backup pad and shorten disc life (Fig. 1-15).

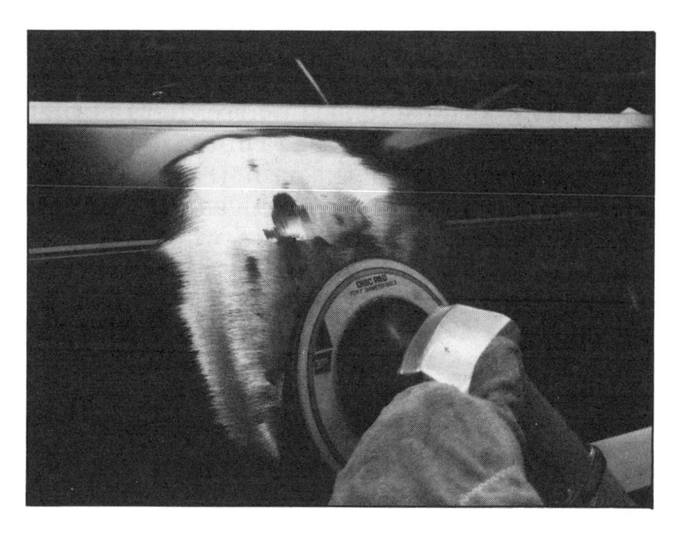

FIG 1-14 Cross-grinding scratches. (3M Company)

2. *Movement.* Under no circumstances should a grinder be held in one spot while it is turning on a surface. Constant movement from left to right and back again is necessary to avoid heat buildup in the metal. Excessive heat can leave burn spots—areas of bluish discoloration on the surface. In extreme cases, it can even expand a body panel, creating a bulge that will have to be hammered out later. *Note:* Constant movement is a precaution that applies across the full range of power tools discussed in this section.
3. *Hand pressure.* Ideally, the hand pressure behind the grinder should be just enough to flex the disc and backup pad into the proper 5-degree angle. This pressure will be less for an electric grinder (where the operator can bring the weight of the motor to bear) and more for an air-driven tool. Excessive pressure, on the other hand, will slow rather than speed grinding. It will also generate heat, which can shorten disc life and result once again in a burned or expanded panel. *Note:* Pressure is particularly important when starting and stopping the tool. A grinder, like all power tools, should never be started under load. It should be switched on first and then applied to the work surface.

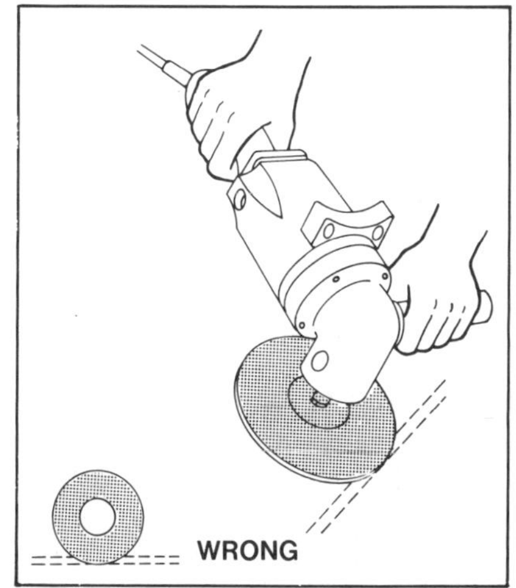

FIG 1-15 Using disc sander with wrong contact. Angle is too high with not enough of disc in contact with surface.

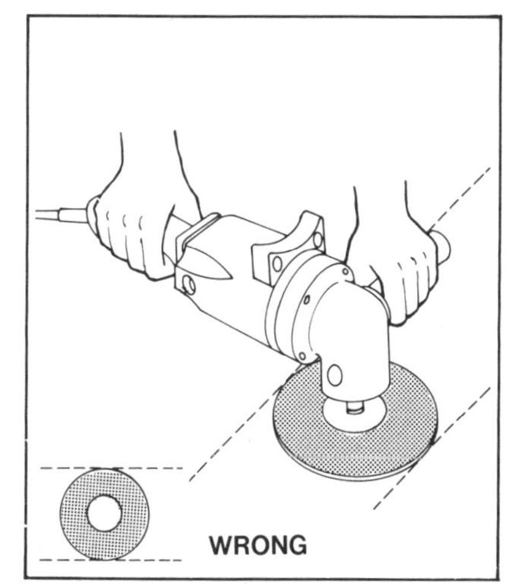

Using disc sander with wrong contact and wrong angle. Too much of disc in contact with surface.

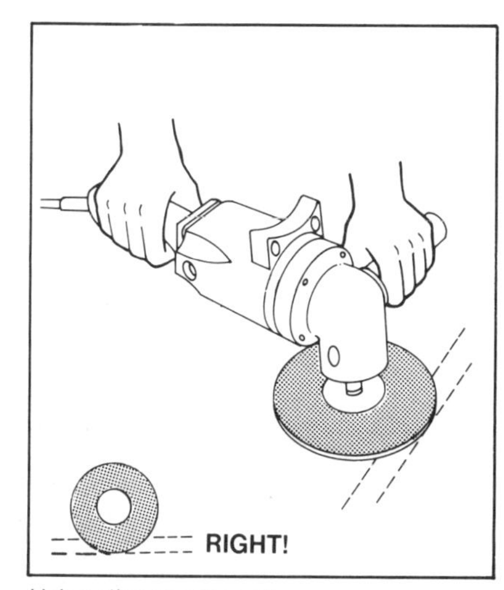

Using disc sander with correct angle and correct contact.

Sandblasters

A sandblaster is used mainly in two situations: (1) where there is rust damage to a surface and (2) where dents or surface contours make it impossible for a flat grinding disc to remove all of the paint (Fig. 1-16). The device uses compressed air to spray the metal surface with sand particles. Because of the extreme force with which the particles are propelled, they chip away the metal's outer layers, taking the old finish with them. The roughened surface that is left requires no further sanding to prepare it for application of the base coat.

FIG 1-16 Small sandblaster in use. (ALC)

FIG 1-17 Two different sizes of small sandblasting outfits. (ALC)

Design and Operation

The sandblaster used in auto refinishing is usually small, with a sand pot capacity of less than one bag, or 100 pounds (Fig. 1-15). The sand itself is a synthetic material made especially for sandblasters. Called silica sand, it comes in various grades ranging from coarse (#16) to fine (#30). The fine is used in refinishing.

A small sandblaster has three main components: (1) a sand pot (also called a hopper); (2) hoses (one for compressed air and one for sand); and (3) a spray gun (Fig. 1-17). The sand pot has a small opening at the bottom through which silica trickles into the sand hose. The hose connects the pot to the spray gun near its nozzle. The actual journey to the spray gun, however, is an uphill one that the sand cannot make by itself. The compressed air entering the spray gun at its handle solves this problem. With the transformer-regulator set at 70 to 90 psi, the air rushes through the gun with such force that it pulls the sand along with it. In other words, it draws the sand into the gun by suction and then expels it.

Precautions for Use

Because air-propelled sand is extremely abrasive, the operator should keep the sandblaster gun moving. Holding it too long in one place can pit the surface and make mechanical or hand sanding necessary. This result, in turn, would cancel out one of the major advantages of using the sandblaster in the first place.

The operator should also limit the amount of time any portion of a vehicle is exposed to the procedure. Sandblasting for long periods of time, even when it does not visibly damage a panel, can cause work hardening of the metal. In this state, a panel can no longer flex with vibration and normal vehicle movement. Instead it cracks, usually long after the repair has been made.

During sandblasting, surrounding vehicle surfaces must be protected. Bumpers and chrome fixtures that can be removed should be. All other moldings and trim should be covered with duct tape. Windows should be rolled up and masked along with windshields. *Note:* In this instance, paper is not an adequate masking material. Use weather or duct tape to protect a 2-inch border nearest the sandblasting area. Then cover the remainder of the glass surface with fabric or a welding blanket.

Under no circumstances should sandblasting be done near painting areas. The sandblasting process disperses fine silicone dust in the air. This dust can float onto a new finish or even find its way into a spray booth via the exhaust fan.

OBJECTIVE 1-A2 (manipulative)

Working as a team with one other student and with the aid of Job Report Sheet 1-A2, you will use a grinder to remove the paint from a practice panel. *Note:* Reserve the panel for use in Objective 1-A4.

Time Recommended:

30 minutes

Preparation:

1. Review pages 1 through 19.
2. Study pages 19 through 22.
3. Read the Safety Checklist on pages 38 and 39, items 8 through 11.

Tools and Materials:

1. Portable grinder
2. C-clamps, vise grips, or welding pliers
3. Spanner wrench
4. Safety goggles and respirator
5. Grinding discs (24D and 36D, both open coat)
6. Painted practice panel

Procedure:

1. Place the panel flat on a workbench and secure it using C-clamps, vise grips, or welding pliers.
2. Thread the grinder backup pad onto the tool's spindle. Place the 24-grit disc over it. Screw the disc nut in place and tighten with a spanner wrench.
3. Put on the safety goggles and respirator.
4. Grip the grinder firmly with both hands and trigger it.
5. Apply the tool to the panel, allowing the disc's leading edge to form a 5-degree angle with the surface. Begin moving the tool to the right as soon as contact is made. *Note:* No more than 2 inches of the grinding disc should be touching the panel at any time.
6. As the first stroke is completed, shift both the weight of the grinder and hand pressure to the left. What was the trailing edge of the disc should now be the leading edge. Move across the panel in the opposite direction. Continue in this fashion till all of the paint is removed.
7. Lift the grinder from the surface and release the trigger. When the disc has stopped spinning, replace the 24-grit abrasive with the 36-grit.
8. Repeat steps 4 through 6 with the new disc. Be sure to cover all areas reached by the initial grinding.
9. Return all tools and equipment to their proper places and reserve the panel for use in Objective 1-A4.

GRINDING

Student Name ______________________ Date ______________

Time Started ______________ Time Finished ______________ Total Time ______________

Specifications

Type of panel ______________________________

Condition of finish (Describe any damage.) ______________________________

____

____

Technique

Type of grinder: Electric ______ rpm Air-driven ______ psi

Checkup Questions

1. What was the difference between the 24-grit and the 36-grit grinding disc?

____

____

____

2. How did the panel look after grinding with the 24-grit disc? ______________

____

____

How did grinding with the 36-grit disc change this appearance? ______________

____

____

3. Describe the nature and location of any visible wear on either grinding disc.

____

____

____

4. The tool shown in use below is called a disc trimmer. Having used a grinder, can you guess why a refinisher might want or need this device? _______________

____

____

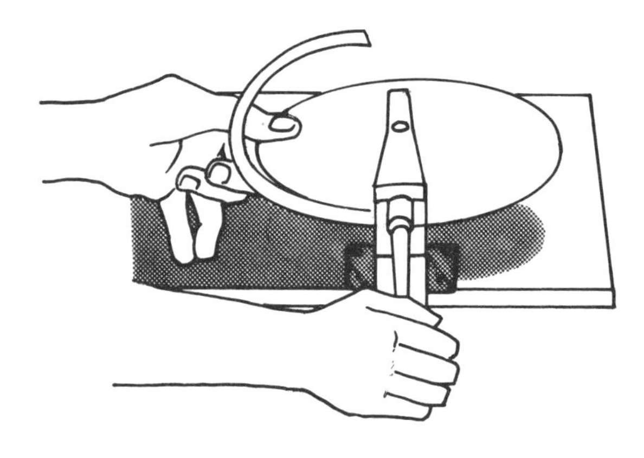

Date Completed _______________ Instructor's Signature _______________

OBJECTIVE 1-A3 (manipulative)

Working as a team with two other students and with the aid of Job Report Sheet 1-A3, you will use the shop sandblaster to remove rust from a vehicle or portion of a vehicle.

Time Recommended:

30 minutes

Preparation:

1. Review pages 1 through 22.
2. Study pages 23 through 26.
3. Read the Safety Checklist on page 39, item 12.

Tools and Materials:

1. Weather or duct tape
2. Welding blanket or heavy fabric
3. Silica sand (fine grade)
4. Sandblaster
5. Duster gun (optional)
6. Safety gear—hood or face mask, leather gloves
7. Screen for sifting (if sand is or will be reused)
8. Shop vacuum cleaner

Procedure:

1. Mask any chrome, glass, or trim within 12–24 inches of the rust. For large surfaces like windshields or adjacent panels, put 2-inch duct tape on the area that is close to the sanding operation. The remaining area should be covered with a welding blanket or heavy fabric.
2. Sift or pour a fine grade of silica sand into the sandblaster pot. (The type of equipment found in refinishing shops usually holds 10–30 pounds of sand, or less than one bag.)
3. Attach the sandblaster hoses—one from the transformer-regulator to the gun handle, the other from the bottom of the sand pot to the gun barrel.
4. Put on safety gear. *Note:* This precaution applies not just to the person actually using the sandblaster but to all observers within 10 feet of the work area.
5. Set the transformer-regulator at 90 psi or at the pressure recommended by the manufacturer.
6. For a small patch of rust, position the sandblaster gun 1–1½ inches from the vehicle surface. For larger areas of damage, hold the nozzle farther back. *Note:* In either case, do not point the gun directly at a panel. In this head-on position, particles of sand bounce back toward the operator with enough force to pit safety goggles. Rather, aim the gun at a slight angle—either to the left or to the right, from either above or below.

7. Trigger the sandblaster gun in short bursts no more than a second or two in length. Observe the panel carefully. As soon as the rust is cleared from one spot and the bare metal visible, move on to the next. Continue in this manner until all damaged areas are clear.
8. Use a duster gun to blow sand from the vehicle's surface and to dislodge any particles from under or around moldings and trim. For this procedure, the transformer-regulator setting should be the same as that used for sandblasting—90 psi. *Note:* As an alternative, the sandblaster itself can be employed as a duster gun. Simply disconnect or remove the sand pot hose so that the equipment passes compressed air only.
9. Remove all masking.
10. Sweep up all sand scattered during the sandblasting and store for reuse or discard. Then use the shop vacuum cleaner to remove any silica dust from the work area.

JOB REPORT SHEET 1-A3

SANDBLASTING

Student Name ______________________ Date ____________

Time Started ____________ Time Finished ____________ Total Time ____________

Specifications

Sandblaster: Manufacturer ____________ Model No. ______

Sand pot capacity ______ pounds Operating psi ______

Damage: Degree of corrosion ______________________

____

Panels affected ____________ ____________ ____________

____________ ____________ ____________

Technique

Safety gear:

Hood ______ Face shield ______ Safety goggles ______

Gloves ______ Coveralls ______ Other ______________________

____

Problems:

Work hardening ______ Reason ______________________

____

Pitting ______ Reason ______________________

____

Holes ______ Reason ______________________

____

Damage to safety gear ______ Reason ______________________

____

Checkup Questions

1. How long did it take the sandblaster to remove individual patches of rust?

   ____

2. How far were sand particles and silica dust dispersed from the work surface?

   ____

3. A duster gun is normally used at 35 psi. Why was a much higher psi employed to clean the surface after sandblasting (step 8)? ______________________________

   ____

   ____

Date Completed ______________ Instructor's Signature ______________________

Sanders

Sanders are perhaps the most versatile of the refinisher's tools. They can be used on any panel surface or material from paint, filler, and primer-surfacer to bare metal. They can be employed for a wide variety of refinishing tasks from smoothing the scratches left by grinding to shaping filler and featheredging.

Featheredging is one of the most important functions of sanders. It is the process of eliminating the dividing line between a repair area and the old finish. It involves tapering the edges of the old paint back away from the repair. What was once a distinct break between two surfaces is graduated so that it is invisible when the panel is repainted.

There are at least four major types of sanders, all having very different forms. Two factors, however, unite them as a family of tools. First, they are all generally smaller and more lightweight than grinders. (Some are even designed to be used with one hand.) Second, in the refinishing process, their functions generally fall midway between removal of the old finish and final hand sanding in preparation for the new.

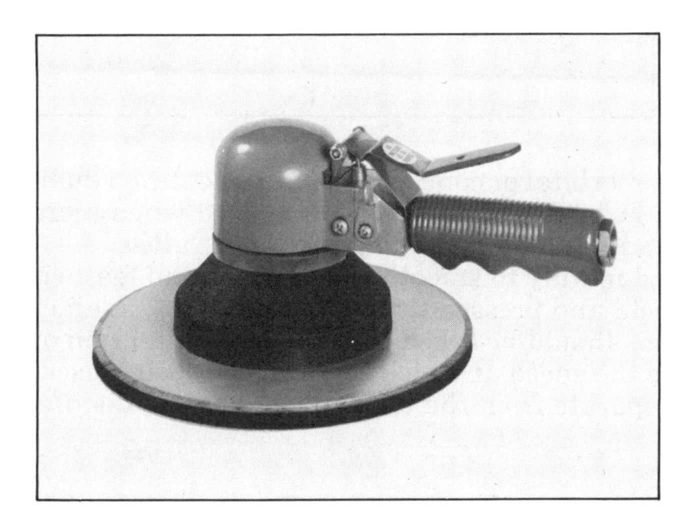

FIG 1-18
Orbital sander.

Orbital Sander

The only sander that takes a disc-shaped abrasive is the orbital sander (Fig. 1-18). In this sense, it can perhaps be considered a scaled-down version of the grinder. The sander's discs, however, are applied with adhesive rather than bolted in place. The pad is thus not penetrated by a spindle and nut. This arrangement lessens the chance of the user's damaging the work surface by metal-to-metal contact. It also allows the tool to be held flat to the surface.

Till recently, the disc adhesive came in a tube and had to be applied by hand. Today adhesive-backed discs are also available. These are simply pressed onto the face of the sander before use and peeled off when they become clogged or worn.

The orbital sander is named for the action of its disc. Rather than simply spinning in place, which might leave concentric marks on the metal surface, the disc turns in an orbit. Each revolution of the disc is displaced from the previous one by 3/16 of an inch. As a result, if the sander is kept moving, the disc never retraces its path along the surface (Fig. 1-19). This eliminates the possibility of its etching rings into the metal.

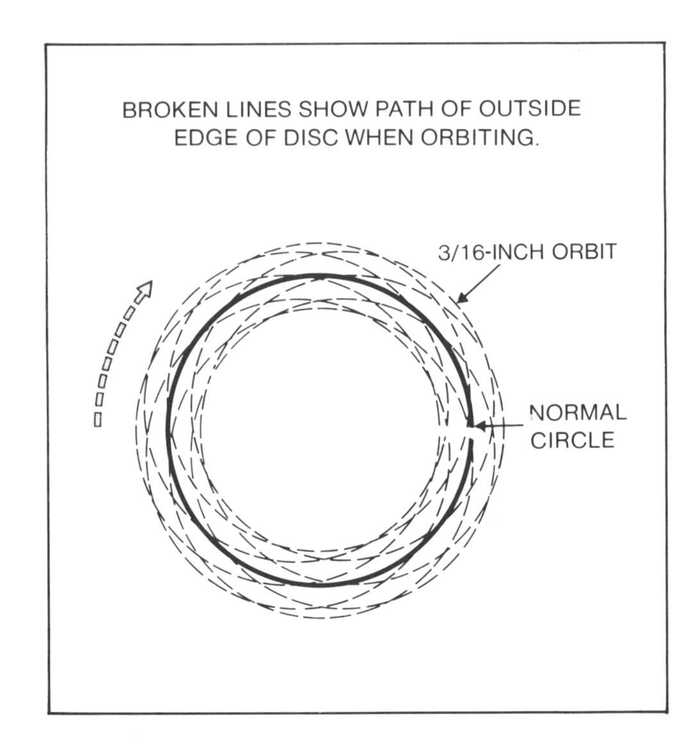

FIG 1-19
Sanding path of orbital disc sander.

A sander that allows either orbital or concentric action is called a dual-action sander, or simply a D.A. The circular action is used when more control is desired, as when sanding along a molding or near glass.

The orbital sander is used mainly to smooth rough paint and featheredge. It works best when held and pressed firmly, but not hard, against the work surface. *Note:* Care should be taken that the maximum rpm of the pad matches or exceeds the speed at which the sander is being used. Otherwise the disc could separate from the backup pad or even disintegrate under load.

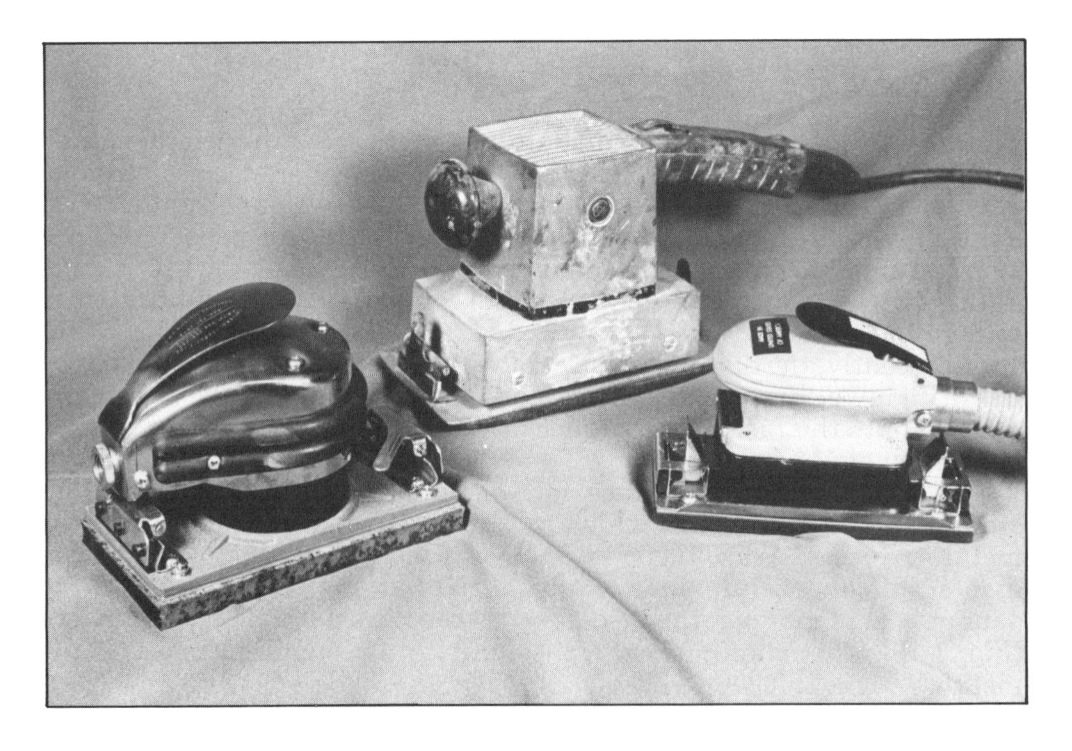

FIG 1-20
Vibrator sanders. (Courtesy of Indian River Community College)

Vibrator Sander

The vibrator sander has a flat rectangular pad that moves in tiny circles (Fig. 1-20). These small, rapid movements give the tool its nickname—the jitterbug.

The vibrator comes in 7-, 9-, and 17-inch sizes and can be used for smoothing virtually any reasonably flat area. The 17-inch size is particularly valuable for extensive sanding of body panels.

To use the vibrator sander, the operator centers a piece of abrasive paper cut to size on the backup pad. Clamps at the front and back of the tool are used to hold the paper in place (Figs. 1-21A and B). In operation, the vibrator is held in one hand (except for the 17-inch size, which requires two hands). The pad is laid flat against the work surface. In this position, only light pressure is necessary to control the tool. Like all sanders, the vibrator should be kept moving across the repair area from one side to the other without stopping.

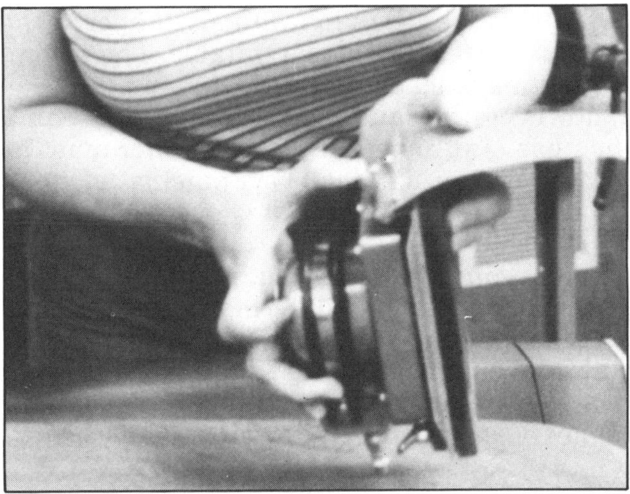

FIG 1-21A Attaching sandpaper to vibrator sander. (David Keown)

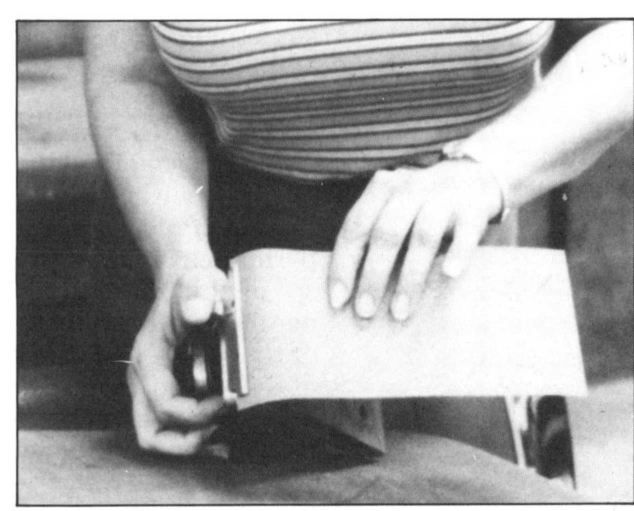

FIG 1-21B

Straight-Stroke Sander

The straight-stroke sander looks very much like the 17-inch vibrator. Each has a long, flat shoe and a handle and knob to guide the tool across the surface (Fig. 1-22). The straight-stroke sander, however, moves back and forth, in line with the direction in which the tool is being held. This fact accounts for its name.

FIG 1-22 Straight-stroke sander. (3M Company)

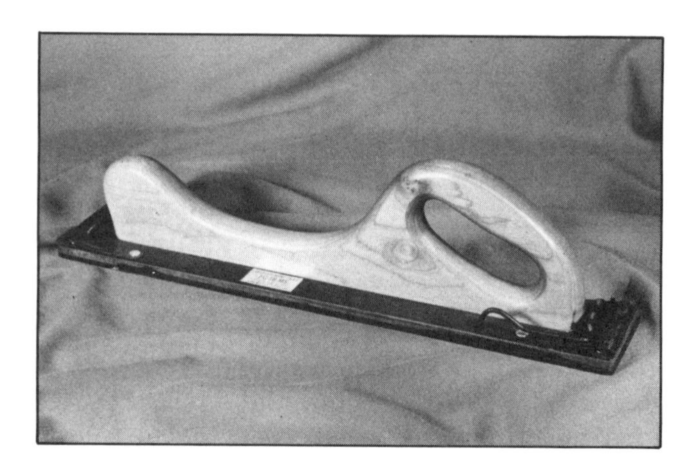

FIG 1-23
File board. (Courtesy of Indian River Community College)

The straight-stroke sander is used for initial featheredging of chipped paint and smoothing large areas of plastic filler. Smoothing filler is a job for which a file is often used, and a straight-stroke sander is in fact sometimes called an air file. The tool takes the same abrasive paper as the 17-inch vibrator. Adhesive-backed sheets are also available. The recommended air pressure for its operation is 90 psi.

For use directly on metal, however, the sander can be equipped with a standard-size file blade. When used in this manner, the sander must be operated with extreme care. Power driven, a file can very quickly cut away too much metal. The result could be a deeply scratched or perhaps even permanently damaged body panel.

For this reason, when complete control is required, many refinishers use a hand tool. The file board could be considered the manual equivalent of the straight-stroke sander. Like the sander, it has the handle and knob of a file and uses the same abrasive paper as the 17-inch vibrator (Fig. 1-23). Because the refinisher moves the board himself, however, he can cut away filler or chipped paint slowly, gradually, and with great accuracy.

Belt Sander

The belt sander, as its name implies, uses a belt abrasive. In function, it overlaps other sanding tools discussed thus far. It can be used to remove paint over broad areas, sand plastic filler, and locate low spots. In other words, it can function as grinder, sander, and file. It has, however, one feature that none of these tools possesses: it is fitted with a dust collector

FIG 1-24
Belt sander. (Milwaukee Electric Tool Corporation)

(Fig. 1-24). The bag shown in the illustration collects the dust; or the bag can be removed and the hose from a vacuum cleaner connected in its place. If a bag is used, it should be emptied when half full.

Because of its dust-collection system, the belt sander is especially helpful in two situations. First, it is invaluable in a small shop where distances between sanding and painting areas, including paint booths, are less than ideal. Second, it is an essential tool for sanding work on all fiberglass surfaces. The reason is that fiberglass filaments or dust can irritate the skin on contact and, if inhaled, adversely affect long-term health.

Belt sanders are driven only by electricity. They can be used to advantage on any relatively flat body panel and are especially effective when large areas must be worked very quickly. In operation, they are used much like the air file. They are placed flat to the surface and moved by using a handle at the back of the tool and a guide knob at the front. The strokes should be parallel to facilitate cross-grinding. (*Note:* It is also possible to sand curved surfaces by carefully using only the forwardmost edge of the sanding belt.)

Polishers

The polisher is not properly a sanding tool, but some models can be adapted for featheredging and other fine metal finishing. The polisher looks similar to a grinder and comes in the same 7- and 9-inch sizes (Fig. 1-25). The major differences are its smaller proportions and lower rpm. (The latter is very important, since it takes much less speed to burn paint than metal.)

FIG 1-25
Polisher. (Black & Decker U.S., Inc.)

For sanding, the polisher's regular polishing bonnet is replaced by a standard 7- or 9-inch sanding disc. In use, the polisher is positioned and moved so that only half of the disc is touching the surface at any given time.

For polishing, the tool is fitted with a lambswool disc or bonnet. The disc is bolted on. The bonnet is pulled over the backing pad and secured with a drawstring. When using the polisher with polishing accessories, the operator should cover only a limited portion of a panel—approximately 2 square feet. Constant movement and the polisher's low speed will compensate and minimize heat buildup in the small area.

For compounding, the polishing disc is replaced with a buffing pad. This can be either flat or bowl shaped. The bowl-shaped pad is the more frequently used. It gets its characteristic shape from a backing that pulls the pad's edges upward toward the operator. With the edges no longer contacting the paint, the operator is much less likely to burn the surface he is compounding.

Sanding Blocks

The final stage of sanding before application of a new finish is usually done by hand. This procedure serves two purposes. First, it smooths the scratches left by power tools and their relatively coarse abrasives. Second, it roughens the surface so that the new coat of paint can adhere easily. These two purposes may seem contradictory. In fact, they are not. The abrasives used in hand sanding are among the finest available. The scratch they leave is microscopic—sufficient to provide the roughness that the new paint requires but invisible to the eye.

Even a fine sandpaper can leave marks if improperly used, however. Hand sanding can result in depressions where pressure is more heavily applied—usually at the fingertips (Fig. 1-26). To avoid this problem, such sanding is done with a rubber backup pad called a sanding block. This sanding aid can be either hard or soft, depending on whether the surface to be sanded is flat or curved. The flat surface of the hard rubber pad is particularly useful for cutting down primer-surfacer and putty, thus making it possible to identify the smallest imperfections for filling. When used in this manner, a sanding block helps the painter improve the quality of his repair work considerably over that done with sandpaper alone (Fig. 1-27).

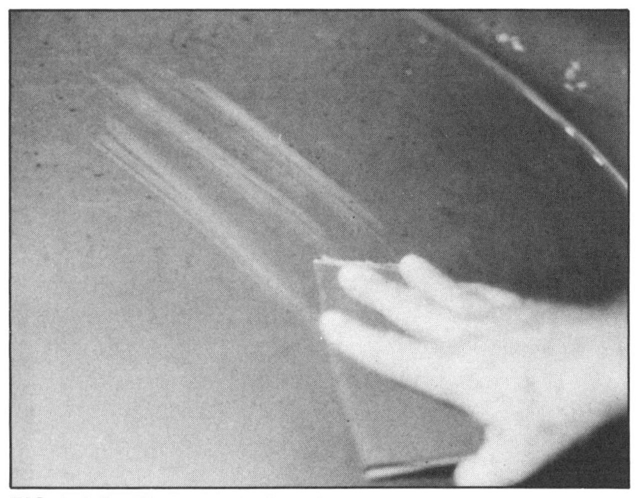

FIG 1-26 Finger marks from improper hand sanding. (David Keown)

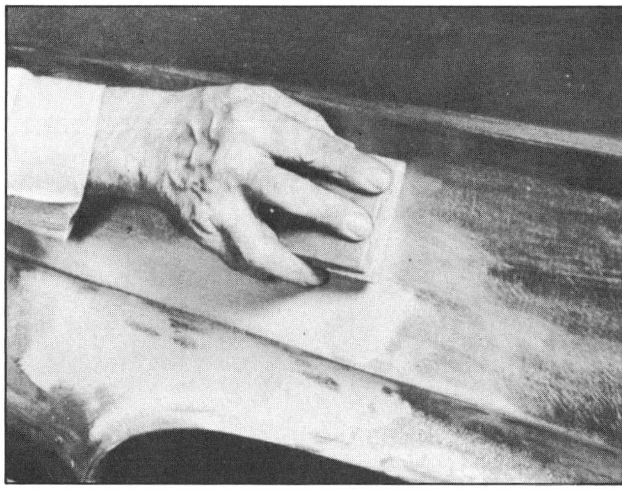

FIG 1-27 Hand sanding with block. (The Martin-Senour Company)

Duster Guns

FIG 1-28 Duster gun. (Binks Manufacturing Company)

With the exception of the belt sander, all the sanding tools discussed in this section produce a tremendous amount of dust when they are used. Much of this dust remains on or near the repair area, where it will ruin the new finish if it is not thoroughly removed. The remainder is dispersed around the shop, where it can work its way into tool mechanisms and interfere with the cooling and filtering functions of stationary equipment.

The tool specifically designed to remove dust from all of these surfaces is the duster gun (Fig. 1-28), also known as the blow gun. It should be operated at a maximum pressure of 35 psi when being used for shop cleanups. Higher pressures are reserved for specialized tasks like forcing water and sanding dust out from under moldings.

ABRASIVES

The term *abrasive* is thought of as being synonymous with sandpaper. In fact, it is a much broader term. It refers not just to papers coated with abrasive grit but to pastes in which abrasive grit has been suspended. The grit itself is not even a single material, nor is it actually sand. It can be any one of a half dozen minerals, both man-made and natural.

Coated Abrasives

The coated abrasives used in refinishing can take many forms—bolt-on discs for grinders, adhesive-backed discs for sanders, sheets and strips for files and vibrators, belts for belt sanders. Regardless of their form, however, all consist of three basic elements.

1. *Abrasive.* In auto refinishing, the actual abrasive is either of two man-made materials—aluminum oxide or silicon carbide. Aluminum oxide is the reddish-brown grit that most people associate with sandpaper. It is a tough material whose particles resist fracturing in use. As a result, it is capable of cutting through virtually any surface, including metal, rust, solder, and multiple layers of paint. Silicon carbide, on the other hand, is black. It is a brittle material that depends for its cutting action on the repeated fracturing and refracturing of its particles. This process constantly exposes fresh, razor-sharp edges that make it possible to finish surfaces to a high degree of smoothness.
2. *Backing.* There are four principal types of backings used for abrasives: paper, cloth, fiber, and combinations of these. The cloth and paper backings come in different weights, the lighter ones for hand sanding, the heavier ones for mechanical sanding. Even at their thickest, these backings are always relatively flexible. Fiber, however, is not. It consists of paper that has been compressed and hardened until it is nearly rigid. It is used either alone or in combination with cloth to make abrasive discs.
3. *Adhesive.* An adhesive is used to hold the backing and the abrasive together. Usually it is either resin, a natural substance, or glue, a man-made compound. The main difference between the two is that resin will not dissolve in water. It is therefore the ideal bonding agent for abrasives used in wet sanding.

All abrasives are graded according to a standard set of criteria. These include grit size, grit density, and water resistance. The actual grade assigned to a given abrasive is printed on its backing.

Grit Size

The grit particles used to cover an abrasive's surface can be ground to various sizes. These correspond to grades called grit numbers, which range from 12 to 600 (Table 1-4). Large grit particles produce coarse abrasives and are assigned low grit numbers. Small particles produce fine abrasives and are assigned high grit numbers. Coarse grits remove a large amount of material very quickly and leave a deep scratch. Fine grits remove extremely small amounts of material and leave behind a nearly invisible scratch.

Table 1-4 STANDARD ABRASIVE GRITS

600	Extra fine	Wet-or-dry sandpaper
500		
400		
360		
320		
280		
240	Fine	
220		
180		Dry sandpaper or sanding discs
150		
120		
100		
80	Medium	
60		
50		
40		
36	Coarse	Grinding discs
30		
24		
20		
16		
12	Extra coarse	

To illustrate, the standard sequence of grits for grinding discs is 16, 24, 36, and 50. In the full range of grits, these are all extremely coarse. However, 16 is coarser than 24, 24 is coarser than 36, and all three are coarser than 50. A 16- or a 24-grit disc might be used to remove paint from a body panel. A 36-grit disc would be used afterward to smooth the surface in preparation for the next stage of sanding.

At the other end of the scale are the grits most commonly used for hand finishing. These include 220, 240, 280, 320, 400, 500, and 600. All are extremely fine.

Between grinding discs and hand abrasives, the grits run the gamut from relatively coarse (60) to quite fine (320). These are the grits used mainly with sanders (Fig. 1-29).

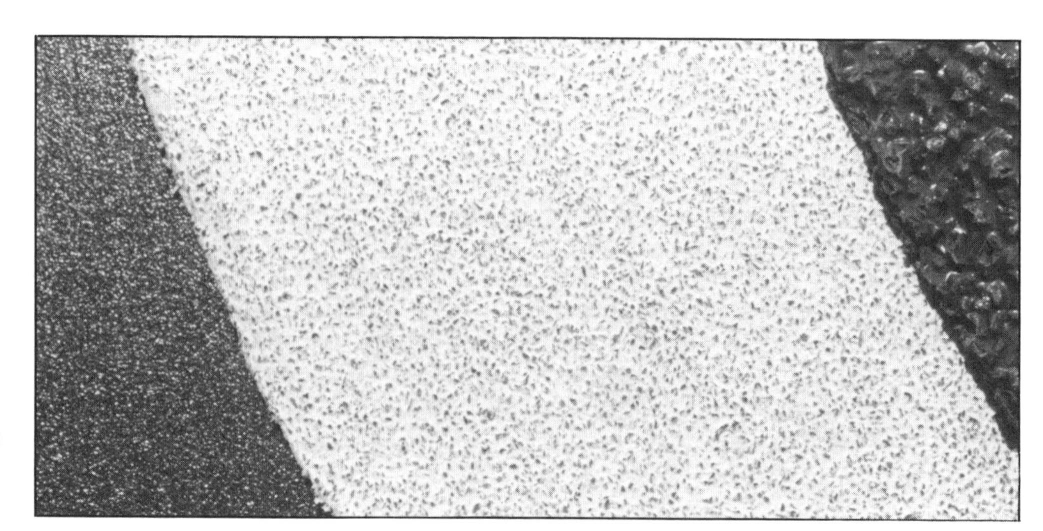

FIG 1-29
Extreme close-up of fine (320), medium (80), and coarse (24) grits of sandpaper. (Jay Storer)

Grit Density

Two abrasives having exactly the same grit number can still look and feel very different. This is because one may have its grit distributed thinly with wide spaces between the particles. Such an abrasive, one whose surface is only 50 to 70 percent covered, is said to have an open coat. An abrasive whose surface is solidly covered has a closed coat (Fig. 1-30). One of these two terms appears on the back of every abrasive disc.

Open coat abrasives are designed primarily for use on thick paint, brass, and solder. All of these are relatively soft materials that tend to cling to grit particles. Since there is less grit on the open coat (to which it could cling), the sanding debris is shoved against the exposed backing (to which it cannot cling) and falls away. This means there is less clogging to interfere with the cutting action of the abrasive.

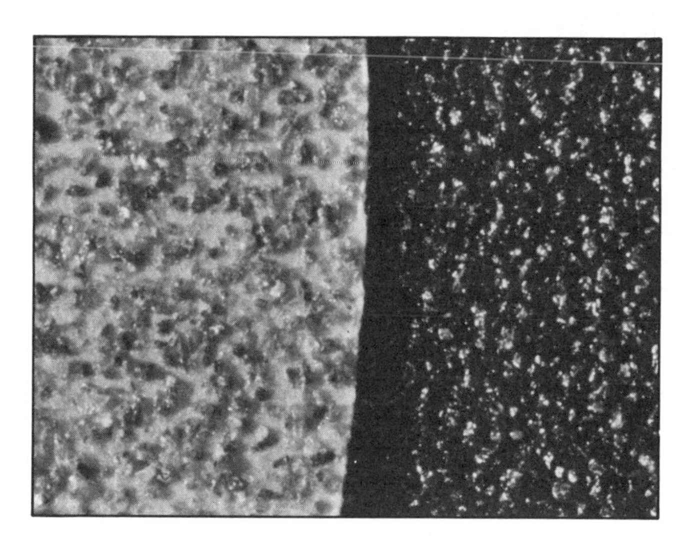

FIG 1-30
Close-up of two grinding discs, same grit, but one open coat (on left), the other closed coat. (Jay Storer)

Notice that there is a similarity between the functions of open coat abrasives and those of heavy-duty disc grinders. The fact is that grinders use only the coarsest abrasives, and these are manufactured almost always in open coat. Beyond the middle range of grits, open coat abrasives are seldom stocked by automotive jobbers. They can be obtained but must usually be special-ordered from a manufacturer. There are two reasons for this situation. First, by the time these finer grits are in use, the materials being sanded do not clog as readily. (These materials include metal, primer-surfacer, and body filler.) Second, at the highest grit numbers, the preferred finishing method is wet sanding. In this technique, a stream of water is used to wash away the sanding debris. An open coat is thus not necessary.

Water Resistance

Clearly, however, not all abrasives can be used for wet sanding—only those whose adhesives and backings are water-resistant. These can be recognized by the letter *A* following their grit numbers. This designation means that they can be used either wet or dry. Abrasives that are not water-resistant have a letter *D* as part of their grade designations and must be used dry. Thus a 36D grinding disc will, if immersed in water, shed its grit and eventually disintegrate. Part of a 400A sheet wrapped

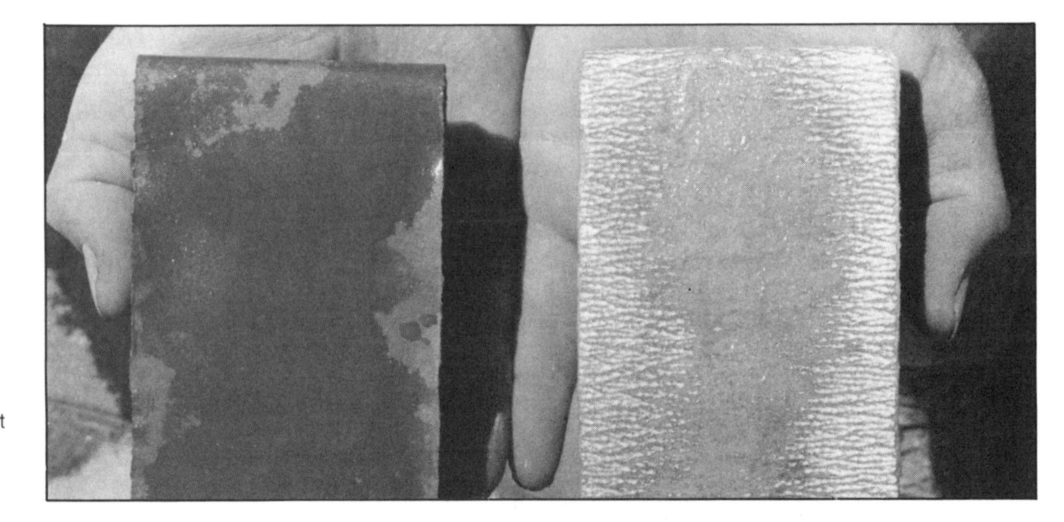

FIG 1-31
What happens when A and D papers are used wet/soaked: D paper at right is obviously disintegrating, minus most of its grit. (Jay Storer)

around a rubber sanding block and treated in exactly the same way, however, will not only stand up to the soaking but perform exceptionally well because of it (Fig. 1-31).

The actual process of wet sanding involves using a stream of water from either a hose or a sponge to wash away the sanding dust before it accumulates on either the work surface or the abrasive. Wet sanding does not produce results as quickly as dry sanding, but the ultimate finish is smoother. For this reason, it is the method of metal finishing most frequently used just before application of top coat. *Note:* Some refinishers prefer gasoline to water for wet sanding. Beyond the obvious safety hazard, this procedure can leave oily residues on the surface that can contaminate a new finish and interfere with adhesion. This form of wet sanding should be avoided.

Rubbing Compounds

There are some paint repair jobs that require a degree of finishing that not even the finest abrasive papers can deliver. One of these jobs is bringing out the sheen in a lacquer top coat. Another is removing water spots from a new finish. The abrasive used for both these tasks is called rubbing compound.

The grit particles in compound are much finer than those used in sandpaper. They are also made of a softer material (usually pumice). Most important, however, they are suspended in an emulsion of water and oil rather than glued to a backing. For this reason, rubbing compounds are frequently called paste abrasives.

There are two main types of compounds—hand rubbing and machine rubbing. The material used for hand work has coarser abrasive particles than the material intended for use with a polisher. The machine rubbing compound, in other words, is formulated to cut more slowly. This difference compensates for the increased speed of mechanical polishing.

Hand Compounding

To smooth a finish with hand rubbing compound, apply some of the product to a soft, clean cloth or brush and rub onto the surface in back-and-forth strokes. Friction will gradually cause the compound to dry out until it seems to roll itself up and disappear. Once it reaches this state, compound ceases to do much cutting. In fact, if it is applied and for some reason allowed to dry out before buffing, compound simply scatters like powder. Remember, all compounds do their cutting only when moist.

Contoured surfaces and edges require special care. When compounding along a crease, for example, always rub up to the crease first on one side, then on the other. This technique avoids cutting away too much paint at the center.

When compounding is finished, the surface will be clean except for a few streaks of the compound itself. These can be removed by rinsing or washing with water, since all compounds are water soluble.

FIG 1-32
Machine compounding. (E. I. du Pont de Nemours & Co., Inc.)

Machine Compounding

Machine compounding proceeds in much the same way as hand compounding, with three important cautions. First, under no circumstances should hand rubbing compound be used with a mechanical polisher. The coarser abrasive particles combined with the speed of the polishing disc would quickly burn or cut through a new finish. Second, whenever it is in contact with the surface, a polisher should be kept moving (Fig. 1-32). This, too, is a precaution against burning the new paint. Third, machine compounding should never be done near a spray painting area. The abrasive particles in compound are light enough to float in the air. Like the silicones in polish, they have been known to enter spray booths through filters and contaminate new finishes. (*Note:* Polish is simply the finest form of rubbing compound and thus the finest abrasive available.)

SAFETY CHECKLIST

Compressed Air Systems:

1. Before cleaning or checking any compressor component, switch off the compressor's power at its source so that the unit cannot start up by itself.
2. If wearing wet or damp clothing, do not work on the compressor. Also do not stand in the runoff from the compressor's drain cock or on any wet area of the floor. Remember, the compressor is driven by an electric motor. It eliminates the electrical hazard from the work area, not from the vicinity of the compressor.

3. Local safety codes usually require that compressor drive belts be enclosed in a cagelike structure called a belt guard. If this device is either not required or has been opened for belt service, use extreme caution when walking or working behind the compressor. Do not frustrate the purpose of the guard when it is in place by sticking tools or foreign objects through its grillwork.
4. Never use or store flammable materials like paint or solvents near the compressor. (Both the electric motor and the heat generated by the unit are the hazards here.)
5. When using a duster gun or an air hose to clean off the compressor's motor and cooling fins, always wear safety goggles. Never point either the gun or a hose at another person. Compressed air can force solid particles as well as air through the skin. Foreign matter propelled by compressed air could cause the loss of an eye. Compressed air itself, even at very low pressures, could puncture an eardrum. At higher pressures, it could enter the bloodstream as a bubble and cause death.
6. Never do anything that might damage a transformer-regulator's internal mechanism. In particular, do not force the adjustment screw inward to obtain more regulated pressure when the main line pressure drops or is cut off. When restored, the pressure could blow the diaphragm or damage the threads in the diaphragm cover. The correct procedure to follow is to turn the adjustment screw out until the problem is solved at the source—the compressor.
7. Never try to dismantle any portion of the transformer for cleaning or maintenance while it is under pressure.

Sanding Tools and Abrasives:

8. Always disconnect a sanding tool from its power supply before changing or installing an abrasive sheet or disc.
9. When sanding or grinding, always wear both protective goggles and a respirator (a face mask covering both nose and mouth) (Fig. 1-33).

FIG 1-33
Safety gear for sanding: dust mask, eye shield, and gloves (optional).
(3M Company)

The only exception is when using a tool like a belt sander that is equipped with a dust-collection system. Wearing coveralls or some other approved protective garment is also advisable. Shop clothing of this type serves two purposes. First, it protects exposed skin from sanding debris. Second, it controls flaps, ties, and cuffs that could get caught in the rotating parts of a sanding tool and cause a serious injury.

10. Always observe the manufacturer's psi recommendations for an air-operated tool.
11. Never use a torn, frayed, or cracked backup pad on a grinder or sander. Never exceed the recommended speed for a given pad.
12. When sandblasting, always wear proper protective gear. At a minimum, this includes a sandblasting hood or face mask and leather gloves. A long-sleeved coat or coveralls are recommended for additional protection and comfort.

OBJECTIVE 1-A4 (manipulative)

Working as a team with one other student and with the aid of Job Report Sheet 1-A4, you will use three different kinds of sanders to cover grinding scratches in a metal practice panel.

Time Recommended:

30 minutes

Preparation:

1. Review pages 1 through 39.
2. Study pages 39 through 42.
3. Read the Safety Checklist on pages 38 and 39, items 8 through 11.

Tools and Materials:

1. Masking tape
2. Metal practice panel (reserved from objective 1-A2)
3. C-clamps, vise grips, or welding pliers
4. Mechanical sanders (orbital, vibrator, straight-stroke, or belt—any three)
5. Selection of 800 abrasives (discs, sheets, stays, or belts as necessary)
6. Safety goggles and respirator (dust mask)
7. Duster gun
8. Disc adhesive (optional)

Procedure:

1. Use strips of masking tape to divide the panel into three equal parts.
2. Place the panel flat on a workbench and secure it using C-clamp, vise grips, or welding pliers.
3. Install the abrasives on the various sanders. *Note:* On a belt sander, a release lever exposes the belt track and allows the abrasive to be lifted on and off. Use Job Report Sheet 1-A4 to record the details of installation.

4. Put on the safety goggles and respirator (dust mask).
5. Use each tool to sand one-third of the panel. Remember to switch on the tool first and then apply it to the work surface. Remove the tool from the work surface before switching it off. *Note:* A belt sander is applied to a surface heel first and then toe. Otherwise, it is moved just like a straight-stroke sander—lengthwise across a panel in parallel rows.
6. After all sanding is complete, blow the panel clean with a duster gun. Use Job Report Sheet 1-A4 to describe the difference in appearance between (a) the panel's surface before and after sanding and (b) the sandscratch patterns left on its three parts.

SANDING

Student Name ______________________ Date ____________

Time Started ____________ Time Finished ____________ Total Time ____________

Specifications

Orbital sander: Manufacturer ______________ Disc size ______ inches

Electric ______ rpm Air-driven ______ Recommended psi

Vibrator sander: Manufacturer ______________ Size ______ inches

Electric ______ rpm Air-driven ______ Recommended psi

Straight-stroke sander: Manufacturer ______________ Size ______ inches

Electric ______ rpm Air-driven ______ Recommended psi

Belt sander: Manufacturer ______________ Belt width ______

Speed ______ rpm

Dust collection ______ Bag ______ Vacuum

Technique

Abrasive Installation:

Orbital Sander

Type of Abrasive ______________________

Method of Attachment ______________________

Vibrator Sander

Type of Abrasive ______________________

Method of Attachment ______________________

Straight-Stroke Sander

Type of Abrasive ______________________

Method of Attachment ______________________

Belt Sander

Type of Abrasive ______

Method of Attachment ______

Sanding:

Orbital Sander

Describe grip ______

Describe any problems in use ______

Vibrator Sander

Describe grip ______

Describe any problems in use ______

Straight-Stroke Sander

Describe grip ______

Describe any problems in use ______

Belt Sander

Describe grip ______

Describe any problems in use ______

Checkup Questions

1. How did sanding change the appearance of the grinding scratches? ______

2. Describe any differences in the marks left by each sander on the panel surface.

3. Which sander was easiest to use? Why? ______

4. Which sander was most difficult to use? Why? ______

Date Completed ______ Instructor's Signature ______

Student Name ______________________ Date ______________

DIRECTIONS: Circle the best answer to each question.

1. A compressor's weekly maintenance check includes all of the following EXCEPT
   A. cleaning the cooling fins.
   B. checking the oil level.
   C. opening the dead-end drain.
   D. testing the pop-off valve.

2. On the device at the right, which adjustment regulates air pressure?
   A. B. C. D.

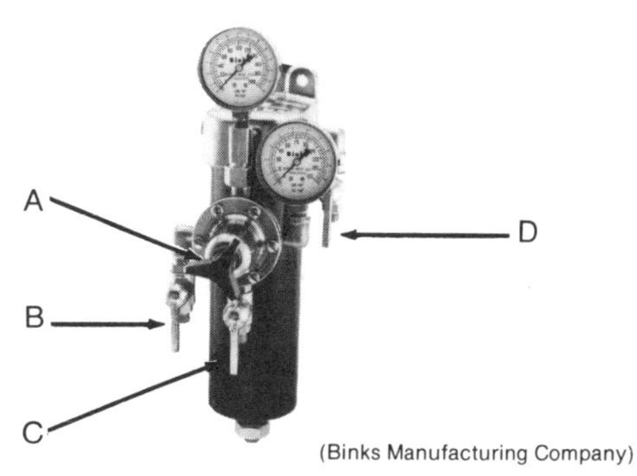

(Binks Manufacturing Company)

3. A buckled or expanded body panel can result from holding and operating a grinder
   A. flat to the work surface.
   B. at a 30-degree angle to the work surface.
   C. firmly with both hands.
   D. in one spot.

4. Using a sander to hide the dividing line between a repair area and the old finish is called
   A. cross-grinding.
   B. featheredging.
   C. wet sanding.
   D. air filing.

5. A compressor should be located in a separate room because compressing air
   I. generates heat.
   II. is extremely dirty.
   A. I only B. II only C. Both I and II D. Neither I nor II

6. The synthetic abrasive used in sandblasting is
   I. aluminum oxide.
   II. silicon carbide.
   A. I only B. II only C. Both I and II D. Neither I nor II

7. Which tool is especially suitable for sandblasting fiberglass panels?
   A. Vibrator sander
   B. Straight-stroke sander
   C. Belt sander
   D. Orbital sander

8. The pressure shown on the transformer-regulator's gauge is
   A. higher than the pressure at the power tool.
   B. lower than the pressure at the power tool.
   C. the same as the pressure at the power tool.
   D. the same as the pressure in the storage tank.

9. Rust must be removed from the trunk and rear panels of a vehicle.
   Refinisher I suggests using a grinder.
   Refinisher II suggests using a sandblaster.
   Who is right?
   A. I only B. II only C. Both I and II D. Neither I nor II

10. As a safety precaution, sanding and grinding should never be done without
    A. protective goggles.
    B. a hood and leather gloves.
    C. belt guards.
    D. a duster gun.

11. The tool at the right can be used
    A. with a standard-size file blade.
    B. with one hand.
    C. to remove rust.
    D. to cut away cured body filler.

(Courtesy of Indian River Community College)

12. The transformer-regulator
    I. boosts air pressure.
    II. filters out dirt and oil.
    A. I only B. II only C. Both I and II D. Neither I nor II

13. Which is the finest abrasive?
    A. 320 B. 80 C. 16 D. 240

14. A compressor's capacity is determined by the
    I. horsepower of its motor.
    II. number of cylinders it has.
    A. I only B. II only C. Both I and II D. Neither I nor II

15. An automobile's roof is being refinished. The tool at the right is pointed at the junction between the roof panel and the rear windshield molding. The tool is held on that one spot for 10 to 15 seconds. As a result,

    A. the whole windshield must be replaced.
    B. the roof panel must be resanded.
    C. a bluish mark indicates where the metal was burned.
    D. sanding dust is ejected.

16. When using a duster gun to clean the shop, the maximum safe air pressure is

    A. 15 psi. B. 35 psi. C. 60 psi. D. 90 psi.

17. An automotive jobber would regularly stock all of the following EXCEPT

    A. grinding discs graded 24D (open coat).
    B. sanding discs graded 120A (closed coat).
    C. sheets of sandpaper graded 320A.
    D. precut abrasive strips graded 600D.

18. Hand rubbing compound used with a polisher will

    I. produce a better shine.
    II. ruin the finish.

    A. I only B. II only C. Both I and II D. Neither I nor II

19. The abrasive at the right is designed for use with

    A. a grinder.
    B. a jitterbug sander.
    C. an orbital sander.
    D. an air file.

20. Which sanding disc is most likely to clog?

    A. 80D (open coat) used dry
    B. 80D (closed coat) used dry
    C. 80D (open coat) used wet
    D. 80A (closed coat) used wet

Score ________ Instructor's Signature ________________________________

unit 2

Refinishing Materials

A quality refinishing job requires more than just technical competence with the tools of the trade. The best sanding and spray gun techniques are wasted if a refinisher does not know the limitations of the materials with which he is working. The most carefully sanded surface will shrink and crack after it is painted if glazing putty has been used where plastic filler was required. The most skillfully applied lacquer will peel and flake if it has been applied directly over an enamel base coat. Any paint will run and sag if it has been thinned too much or used under conditions that prevent it from drying. Clearly, then, a refinisher must know how to match materials to work surfaces and shop conditions. Without this knowledge, he cannot produce professional-quality work.

As a starting point, therefore, this unit surveys a broad range of refinishing materials. It includes detailed coverage of base and top coat elements and briefer discussions of fillers, cleaning agents, and chemical paint removers. The emphasis is on developing an understanding of each material's composition, its compatibility with other materials, and its place in the overall refinishing process.

OBJECTIVE 2-A (written)

After doing the reading and shop exercises, you will be able to answer correctly without reference material a minimum of 14 out of 20 test questions on the following topics:

1. Paint composition
2. Lacquer and enamel characteristics
3. Paint mixing and matching
4. Primers and fillers
5. Cleaning agents
6. Chemical paint removers

Preparation:

1. Study pages 47 through 80.
2. Attend classroom discussions on Objective 2-A.
3. Read the Safety Checklist on pages 74 through 76.

FIG 2-1 A Enamel products. (E. I. du Pont de Nemours & Co., Inc.)

FIG 2-1 B Lacquer products. (E. I. du Pont de Nemours & Co., Inc.)

PAINT AND PAINT SOLVENTS

Paint is a mixture of three elements—pigment, solvent, and binder. The pigment is the color. It consists of solid particles of material that may be either natural or man-made. The purpose of the pigment is to cover the bare metal and thereby improve the appearance of the car's exterior. The solvent is the volatile portion of the paint, the part that evaporates. Its purpose is to keep the paint in liquid form during storage. The binder is the clear, sticky substance that keeps the pigment uniformly suspended in the solvent. It is the binder that changes the paint to a solid coating and allows that coating to adhere to the auto body surface. In this way, it serves to protect the car's exterior.

Paint Families

The paints used in auto refinishing are divided into two families—lacquers and enamels (Fig. 2-1). Each family includes not only different kinds of paints (synthetics and acrylics, for example) but related products like thinners, primers, and fillers. All of the products in one family are specifically designed for use with each other.

Ideally, in doing a repair, the refinisher matches the paint type to the original finish. Then, in preparing the surface, he limits himself to products of that particular family, be it lacquer or enamel. Again, that is ideally. In fact, restrictions on repair time, repair costs, and product availability frequently make it impossible to follow this procedure. When that happens, precautions must be taken to prevent the incompatibility of the products from ruining the new finish.

Lacquer Characteristics

The reasons for that incompatibility are found in the basic characteristics of lacquers and enamels. Lacquers, generally speaking, are fast drying. This quality is extremely important in refinishing, where multiple coats must be applied. Lacquers are also chemically very active. When wet, they can penetrate almost any finish and, if compatible, bond readily. This quality, combined with their fast drying time, makes them easier to use for spot repairs than enamels. On the negative side, however, lacquers have poor filling capabilities. Because they dry so quickly, there is less time for the paint to flow into deep sandscratches. For this reason, repair surfaces must be extremely well prepared. Final sanding with a 400- or 500-grit abrasive is always required.

Enamel Characteristics

Enamels, by contrast, have excellent filling capabilities. Therefore, surfaces do not have to be as finely sanded and fewer coats of paint can be used to cover them. Once applied, an enamel finish is extremely hard, durable, and (unlike a lacquer finish) rust resistant. It also requires no compounding or polishing, either during or after application (Fig. 2-2). Finally, and perhaps most important, enamels in general are less expensive than lacquers. Refinishing a panel or a whole vehicle with enamel substantially lowers the overall cost of a repair. The trade-off for all of these advantages is that enamels take much longer to dry.

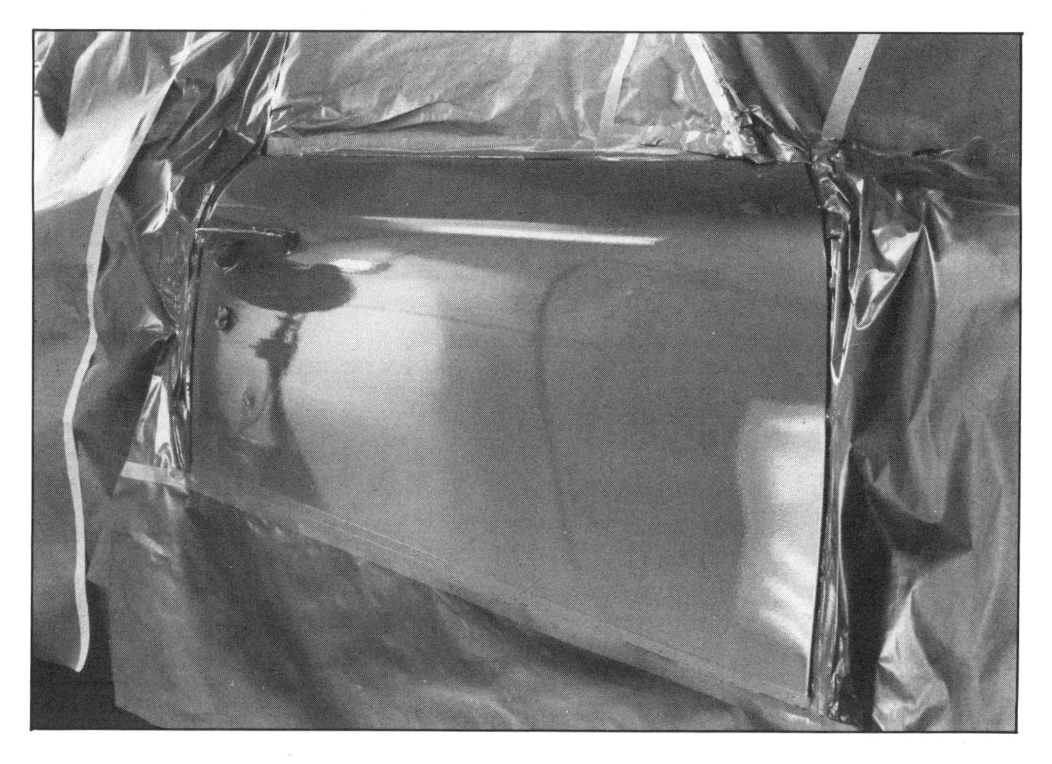

FIG 2-2
Fresh enamel.

Mixing Paint

All paint as it comes from the factory is too thick to apply. Before a paint can be used, therefore, it must be thoroughly mixed and the amount of solvent in it increased.

Thinners and Reducers

The process of thinning paint by adding solvents is called reduction. The nature of the solvent added depends on whether the paint being reduced is a lacquer or an enamel. Lacquer solvent is called thinner. Enamel solvent is called reducer. Keep in mind, however, that while the names of the products are different, their functions are exactly the same. Thinner or reducer (1) lowers the viscosity of the paint so that it can be sprayed and (2) keeps the paint wet long enough for it to flow (or level out) once it has been applied to a surface.

Both thinner and reducer are classified by how well they do these two things. Each, for example, is assigned a solvency factor. This designation is a measure of how well the product thins materials and penetrates surfaces. Thinner is an extremely strong solvent. It has a high solvency factor. Thinner is the component of lacquer paint that makes it chemically active, that enables it to penetrate and form a strong bond with the base coat or a compatible underlying finish. Reducer, on the other hand, is a weak solvent. It has a low solvency factor. Enamel paints thus have little penetrating power, a fact that in certain circumstances can create adhesion problems.

Thinners and reducers are also classified by evaporation rate. (This is, in fact, the more frequently used rating system.) The actual designations are fast, medium, and slow drying. Which category a particular solvent falls into determines how much flowing it will allow. This characteristic, in turn, determines the overall quality of the refinishing job. Insufficient time for flowing can produce a rough, grainy surface. Too much time can allow runs and sags to develop. The refinisher must therefore know what solvent to use and when. In hot, dry weather, for example, he might have to resort to a slower-drying solvent than he would normally use. In cool, wet weather, he might have to switch to a faster-drying product. In other words, the refinisher cannot simply select a favorite thinner or reducer and use it in all circumstances. He must daily choose the product that is designed to work at the temperature and humidity levels existing in his shop (Table 2-1).

Table 2-1 SHOP CONDITIONS AND SOLVENT USE

Temperature	Weather	Thinner	Reducer
Above 80° F. (warm shop)	Dry	Slow drying	Slow drying
70-80° F.	Dry	Medium drying	Medium drying
Below 70° F. (cold shop)	Dry	Fast drying	Fast drying
Above 80° F. (warm shop)	Wet	Slow drying (and retard last coat)	Medium drying
70-80° F.	Wet	Slow drying	Medium drying
Below 70° F. (cold shop)	Wet	Medium drying	Fast drying

FIG 2-3
Reducing paints. (E. I. du Pont de Nemours & Co., Inc.)

Reduction Formulas

Paint reduction must be done with care (Fig. 2-3). Overreduction disperses the pigment too thinly and breaks down the resins used in the binder. Both conditions can lead to early paint failure. Underreduction leaves the paint too thick to be sprayed properly. The spray gun cannot break the material into a fine mist of particles, a process called atomizing.

The reduction formulas for lacquers and enamels differ greatly. As a general rule, lacquer is reduced much more, usually somewhere in the area of 150 percent. In other words, 1 part lacquer is mixed with 1½ parts thinner to get a sprayable mixture. Enamel is reduced much less, generally between 25 and 35 percent. A frequently used formula is 4 parts enamel to 1 part reducer.

FIG 2-4
Using a viscosity cup. (E. I. du Pont de Nemours & Co., Inc.)

Viscosity

As noted, however, these formulas are generalizations. The products of different manufacturers vary greatly in their viscosity. For this reason, most refinishers test the final mix in some way. Probably the most widely used method of determining whether a paint is properly reduced is to immerse a wooden stirring stick in a filled spray can cup, remove it, and then time how long it takes the paint to run off. Five seconds is correct for any paint that is to be sprayed.

For a more exact measurement, there are devices called viscosity cups. These measure viscosity by how long it takes a set amount of the paint to flow through an opening in the bottom of a small container (Fig. 2-4). Pure thinner or reducer might take only 10 seconds to drain from the cup. Unreduced enamel, however, would require up to 100 seconds, unthinned lacquer more than 300. It is this gap that accounts for the very different reduction requirements of the two paint families. Lacquers simply start out as much thicker, heavier products.

Regardless of which method of measurement is used, it is always good practice to read the paint can label carefully and note the manufacturer's recommendations on reduction. Any adjustments for surface and shop conditions can then be made from there.

Matching Paint

Before any reduction can take place, however, the refinisher must make one other important decision besides paint family. He must decide what color to use. Making the choice is easy—vehicle manufacturers routinely identify their colors. Making the choice work, on the other hand, can be difficult, particularly when the vehicle is older. In such a case, the original top coat will have changed color with time. It will have faded, dulled, or taken on a different cast. To get a color match under these circumstances usually requires more than just careful reduction.

Factors in Aging

Four factors determine how quickly and to what extent a finish ages.

1. *Climate.* Vehicles used in tropical climates tend to deteriorate quickly. This statement is especially true of their finishes. Warm, moist air weathers paint prematurely and encourages the development of rust. Coastal regions are almost as hard on a finish. In this case, the salt air and not the moisture is the culprit. Salt in virtually any form, in fact, eats into an auto body, even through paint. For a similar reason, a cold climate can take a toll if the vehicle is exposed to salt used on snow- and ice-covered streets. The best conditions for preserving a vehicle's exterior, then, are found in inland areas that are high and dry.
2. *Environment.* Closely related to climate are environmental conditions. These can be natural and man-made. In many urban areas, for example, industrial fallout so severely damages vehicles that they must be refinished before they are a year old. A similar pattern of damage can occur naturally in certain rural areas, like those located near salt flats. In such areas, winds constantly expose vehicles to the corrosive effects of alkali.
3. *Upkeep.* A finish that is washed regularly and waxed or polished with moderation lasts longer than one not given such care. If, in addition, the vehicle is kept in a garage or carport, the life of the finish will be extended to its maximum. Care of this type not only keeps the finish away from harmful elements but reduces the length of exposure when it does occur.
4. *Color.* The owner's original choice of color also plays a significant role in the aging process. Some colors fade more quickly than others—the various shades of red and purple, for example. *Note:* Fading does not necessarily mean that a color gets lighter. It may get darker. Which type of change occurs depends on the top coat's component colors, the basic pigments from which it was originally mixed. To take a simple example, all greens are made from mixing blue and yellow. If the yellow fades, the green will get bluer—and the finish will get darker.

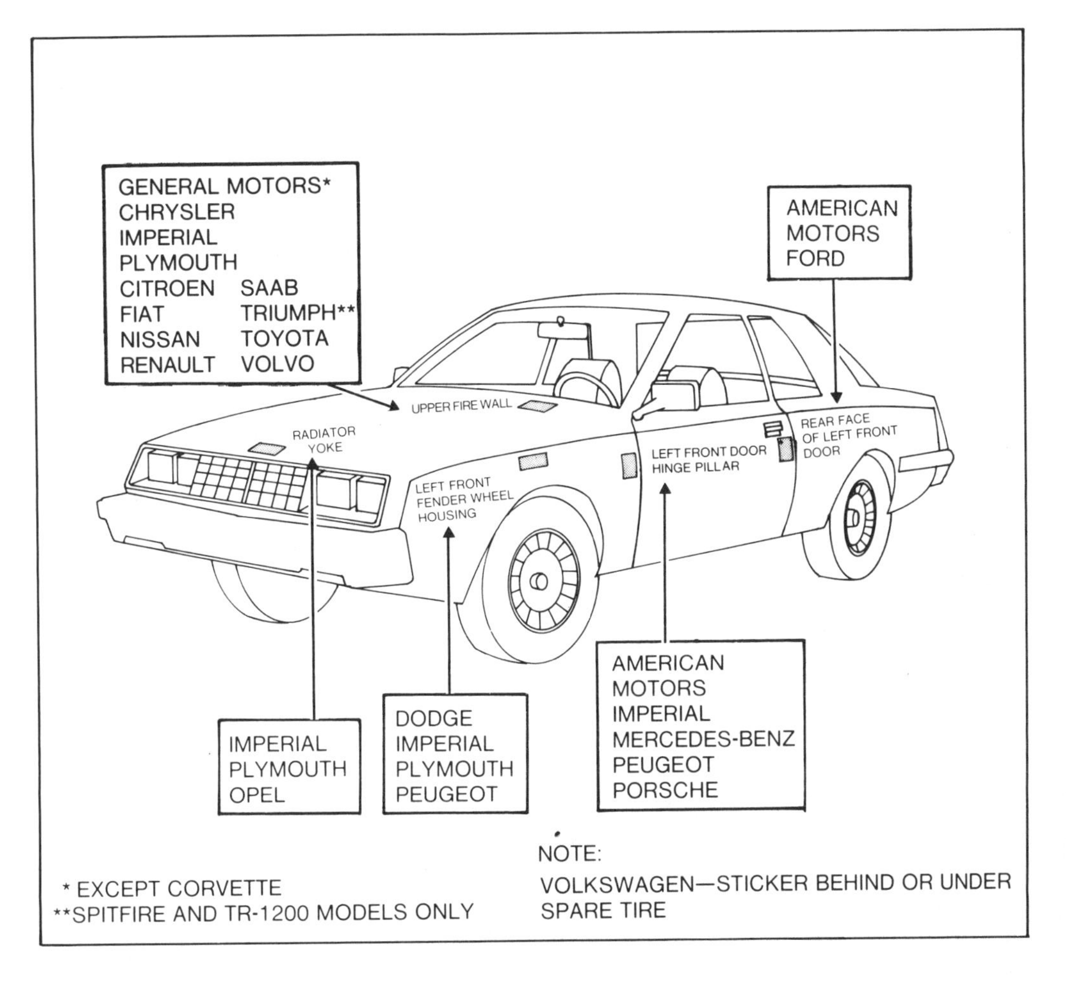

FIG 2-5
Color identification tag locations for some foreign and domestic cars.

Color Identification

Whether a finish is old or new, the color matching process begins with the vehicle's identification tag. This is a metal plate that carries information about the car's manufacture—the plant number, model year, style, and such. It also bears the color codes for both body and trim.

The identification tag is usually located on or around a vehicle's doors, radiator, or cowl assembly (Fig. 2-5). On the tag, the paint code is found somewhere below the model year, body, and style designations. Often clearly labeled, it consists of a letter, a number, or a combination of these (Fig. 2-6).

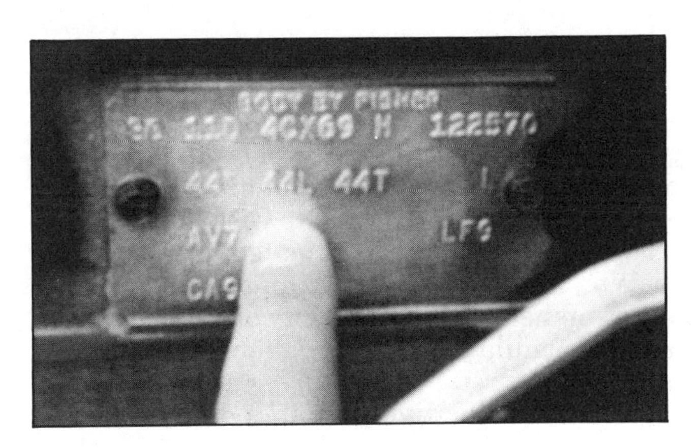

FIG 2-6
Color I.D. tag. (E. I. du Pont de Nemours & Co., Inc.)

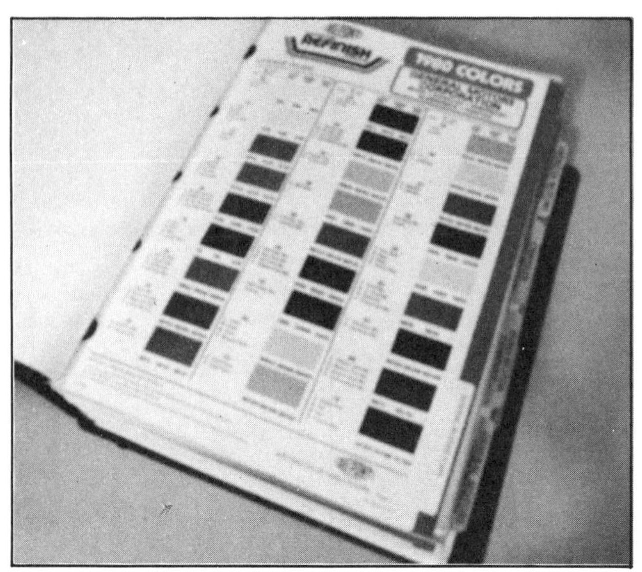

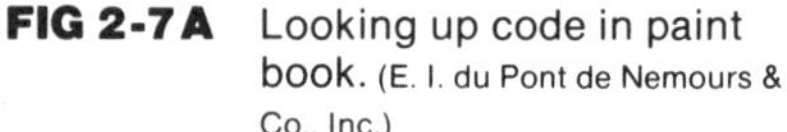

FIG 2-7A Looking up code in paint book. (E. I. du Pont de Nemours & Co., Inc.)

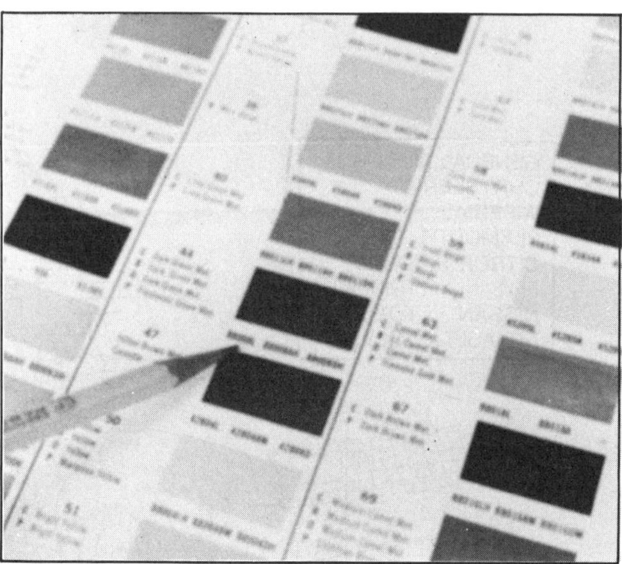

FIG 2-7B

The paint code is used to match the vehicle's original color with the paint system, or brand of products, used in the shop. The code corresponds to a color sample in a paint chip book. The book is the refinisher's most basic reference. It is divided into sections, one for each major auto manufacturer. The sections, in turn, are organized by make and model year.

Suppose a refinisher must match the top coat on a 1980 Buick. He checks the vehicle's identification tag and finds that the color code is 44. In the paint chip book, he turns to the General Motors section, locates the exterior colors for 1980 Buicks, and looks up 44 (Figs. 2-7A and B). Next to it he finds a color chip that in Buicks (B) is identified as "Dark Green Metallic." He notes that the color is indeed similar to the finish on the car. (Just to be sure that it is an exact match, however, he may compare the book and the vehicle side by side.)

Below each color sample in a chip book are the paint manufacturer's product codes. If there are three codes, it means that the color can be matched by using any of three different paints available from the manufacturer. The code itself identifies not only the specific color but the paint family and any special features as well. In the case of the Buick, if the refinisher must use a lacquer, he places an order for B8008LH. This product is a dark green (B8008), a lacquer (L), and a product with a high metallic content (H).

Ordering vs. Mixing

If the car is fairly new, the paint store will have the color on its shelves, premixed from the factory. If the vehicle is older, however, the color will probably have to be mixed to order in the required amount. Paint manufacturers provide the stores that handle their products with accurate formulas for this purpose. These formulas are adjusted and updated regularly as product composition and availability change.

It is also possible for the refinisher to mix his own colors. (The paint store will usually provide the formula.) Few refinishers do, however. Mixing for general refinishing work requires a fairly large variety of products. The number of basic colors is relatively small (perhaps eight or ten). These, however, must be stocked for lacquer and two or three forms of enamel. In addition, three different grinds of metallic must be kept on hand plus three to four reducing agents. Then there is special mixing, measuring, and storage equipment. Clearly, unless a refinisher does an extremely large volume of business or limits himself to only one kind of paint, mixing his colors in the shop is not practical.

Tinting

Mixing paint by formula, whether in the shop or in the paint store, has one very important limitation: the color is a match for the original factory finish, not one that has weathered or aged. The color, in other words, is not likely to match the existing top coat, at least not without some adjustment. This process is called tinting.

Tinting can be done using either a small selection of paints in basic colors (black, white, red, blue, yellow, brown, and green) or a specially manufactured tinting kit (Fig. 2-8). To take some of the guesswork out of the process, the refinisher should start with the paint formula. If the colors that went into the finish are known, it is easier to tell which have faded with time and which have become more prominent. Once this determination has been made, the fading process can be duplicated with small additions of paint. Consider once again the example of a green top coat that has taken on a bluish cast as its yellow faded. By comparison, the newly mixed color would be too green. To kill, or take down the yellow, the refinisher would have to add blue. If the top coat had become lighter (if its blue component had faded), just the opposite color correction would have been required (Table 2-2).

FIG 2-8
Tinting kit. (E. I. du Pont de Nemours & Co., Inc.)

Using Flattening Compound

Flattening compound is another material developed to age paint artificially. When added to a new top coat, it dulls the material's luster. This quality is especially valuable when the gloss on an older vehicle cannot be restored and a panel or spot repair must be made. By dulling the new finish, the contrast between the old and new surfaces is reduced. If this precaution were not taken, the high gloss of the new paint would from certain angles make it appear to be a different color. *Note:* Flattening compound is also used to finish instrument panels. These can reflect light into the driver's eyes, impairing his vision. Flattening compound reduces this hazard by dulling the panel's surface and eliminating glare.

Table 2-2 COLOR TINTING

Color	To tone down . . .	Add . . .
Beige	Green Red	Red Green
Blue	Green Red	Red Green
Bronze	Red Yellow	Yellow Red
Gold	Green Red	Red Green
Gray	Blue Yellow	Yellow Blue
Green	Blue Yellow	Yellow Blue
Maroon	Blue Yellow	Yellow Blue
Orange	Red Yellow	Yellow Red
Purple	Green Red	Red Green
Red	Blue Yellow	Yellow Blue
White	Blue Yellow	Yellow Blue
Yellow	Green Red	Red Green

OBJECTIVE 2-A1 (manipulative)

Working as a team with one other student and with the aid of Job Report Sheet 2-A1, you will mix a lacquer or an enamel paint. You will use a viscosity cup to measure the paint's thickness both before and after reduction.

Time Recommended:

30 minutes

Preparation:

1. Review pages 47 through 56.
2. Study pages 56 through 60.
3. Read the Safety Checklist on pages 74 through 76, items 1 through 6.

Tools and Materials:

1. Lacquer or enamel paint
2. Thinner or reducer
3. Mixing cup or spray gun container
4. Paint strainer and rack
5. Wooden stirring sticks
6. Clean shop cloths
7. Paint can opener or other prying tool
8. Viscosity cup
9. Stop watch or watch with a minute hand

Procedure:

1. On a table in the paint materials room, set up the rack and strainer. (If work space is not available in a storage area, use a part of the shop well away from any work that could contaminate the paint with dust.)
2. Read the paint can label for the recommended reduction.
3. Check the measuring cup or spray gun container for markings corresponding to the reduction formula. (Many 1-quart cups have indentations indicating paint levels for 1 to 1, 2 to 1, and 3 to 1 mixtures.) Then move the mixing cup into position under the strainer.
4. Place the paint can on the table and, using the opener, pry up the lid at several different points around the edge. At first, pry only enough to break the seal. This procedure will keep the lid from being bent and allow it to be replaced if all the paint is not used.
5. Using a wooden stirring stick, stir the paint 4 to 5 minutes. Use a circular motion in one direction only.
6. Place the stirring stick on a folded cloth. (This practice keeps the table clean and avoids contaminating the stick with dirt or traces of other pigments.)
7. Immerse the viscosity cup in the paint. Then lift the cup straight up and hold. Begin timing as soon as the top edge of the cup breaks the surface. Stop timing when the flow of paint from the cup changes from a solid stream to drips. Record the result on Job Report Sheet 2-A1.
8. Using both hands, lift the can of paint until the bottom is about 2 inches above the strainer. Tilt the top of the can and with one smooth motion pour the paint through the strainer. Fill the cup to the predetermined level.
9. Immediately replace the paint can lid.
10. Open the thinner or reducer in the same manner as the paint. Add the recommended amount, once again pouring the material through the strainer. Replace the container lid.
11. Using a wooden stirring stick and a circular motion, mix the paint and solvent. Be sure the stick is immersed to the bottom of the mixing cup. Periodically lift the stick to be sure that the material at the lower end is as thin as the material at the upper end.
12. When the paint is thoroughly mixed, measure its viscosity as in step 7 and record the result on Job Report Sheet 2-A1. *Note:* For all paints, lacquer or enamel, the proper viscosity reading for spraying is between 18 and 22 seconds.
13. If the viscosity reading is not within the acceptable range, correct the paint mix. If the reading is more than 22 seconds, add thinner or reducer. If it is less than 18 seconds, add paint. Stir and recheck using the viscosity cup.

MIXING PAINT

Student Name ______________________________ Date ______________

Time Started ____________ Time Finished ____________ Total Time ____________

Specifications

Type of paint: Lacquer ______ Enamel ______

Manufacturer ______________________________

Color ______________ Color code ______________

Reducing agent: Thinner ______ Reducer ______

Evaporation rate: Fast ______ Medium ______ Slow ______

Solvency factor: High ______ Low ______

Technique

Reduction formula: ______ part(s) paint, ______ part(s) thinner/reducer

Total amount of paint mixed ______________

Viscosity cup readings: Before reduction ______ seconds

After reduction ______ seconds

Paint mix correction: Yes ______ No ______

If yes, describe the nature of the correction. ______________________________

____

____

Checkup Questions

1. Describe the look and consistency of the paint when the can was first opened, before any stirring. ______________________________

____

____

____

How long was the paint stirred before a uniform consistency was achieved?

____

2. Give the reasons for selecting the particular thinner or reducer used. __________

____

____

Date Completed ______________ Instructor's Signature ______________________

PRIMERS

The finish on an automobile is only .002 (2/1000) inch thick. Of this, approximately half is top coat and half base coat. The top coat consists entirely of paint. The main component of the base coat is primer (Fig. 2-9).

Primer is the dull gray or reddish-brown material frequently seen on vehicles that have been only partially refinished. Its main purpose can be described in one word: adhesion. Primer is specially formulated to adhere to metal, fiberglass, and finished surfaces below and new applications of paint above.

There are several different types of primers. What makes each one different from the other is the secondary purpose it is designed to serve.

FIG 2-9
Cross section of finish with primer-surfacer.

Primer-Surfacer

Primer-surfacer, for example, is designed to fill the scratches left by sanding operations. It does this by tripling the solids content of the basic primer formula. This sharp increase in solid material allows the product to build up very quickly on a surface. Hence the "surfacer" element in the product name.

Reduction and Application

Because of its solids content, primer-surfacer, like paint, cannot be used directly from the can. It must first be reduced. The amount of reduction follows paint family lines, with the lacquer product being much more heavily reduced than the enamel. Always, however, consult the manufacturer's label for the proper reducing agent and the exact reduction formula.

Because it functions in part as a filler, primer-surfacer is applied in multiple coats. In the case of lacquer primer-surfacer, each of these coats is allowed to flash (or film over) before the next is applied. The total film of primer-surfacer is then allowed to dry through, or cure. This process usually takes about 30 minutes. In the case of enamel primer-surfacer, each coat must be allowed to dry fully, a process that could take up to 3 hours per coat. Once dry, both primer-surfacers must be sanded to reveal low spots. If any are found, more coats of the product are applied, and the whole procedure is repeated.

Lacquer vs. Enamel

Which primer-surfacer is used for a given job—lacquer or enamel—is largely determined by the top coat. Ideally, lacquer primer-surfacer should be used under lacquer paints and enamel primer-surfacer under enamels. If absolutely necessary, however, enamel can be applied over a lacquer base coat. This procedure works because the solvency rating of enamels is low. There is little chance that the enamel finish will penetrate the primer-surfacer and react with the original lacquer finish. The same cannot be said for the reverse use, however. Lacquer applied directly over an enamel primer-surfacer will penetrate and will react chemically with both the base coat and the old top coat. The result, if steps are not taken to prevent it, will be swelling of the old finish and eventual peeling and flaking of the new. Again, application of lacquer over an enamel primer-surfacer should be avoided.

Color Selection

Primer-surfacer comes in three colors: light gray, dark gray, and red oxide. The color used should closely match the vehicle's new finish. The light gray, for example, should be used under a beige or white top coat, the dark gray under a dark blue or black, the red oxide under a burgundy or maroon.

Zinc Chromate

Not all surfaces that require painting on a vehicle are sheet steel. Trucks and buses in particular have parts that are made from aluminum and zinc-coated metal. (The process of coating metal with zinc is called galvanizing. Galvanized steel is used for body elements that are likely to rust or corrode.)

Primers intended for use on sheet steel will not usually adhere to these nonferrous metals. Another material is therefore necessary to bind aluminum and zinc surfaces to base and top coats. That material is zinc chromate. (*Note:* While zinc chromate was developed specifically for nonferrous metals, it can be used with good results on iron and steel surfaces as well.)

Unlike primer-surfacer, zinc chromate does little or no filling. It is reduced and sprayed onto the work surface in a single coat. Then, if any filling is required, primer-surfacer is applied directly over it. So strong are its bonding properties that zinc chromate requires no preparation beforehand to promote adhesion. It is a nonsanding primer.

Sealer

Sometimes circumstances arise in which it is impossible to avoid mixing products that will react chemically. As already noted, this procedure, while not recommended, can be followed if certain precautions are taken. The most important of those precautions is selecting and using a good-quality sealer.

Sealer, like all products discussed in this section, provides adhesion. It also does some minimal filling. Its specialized purpose, however, is to

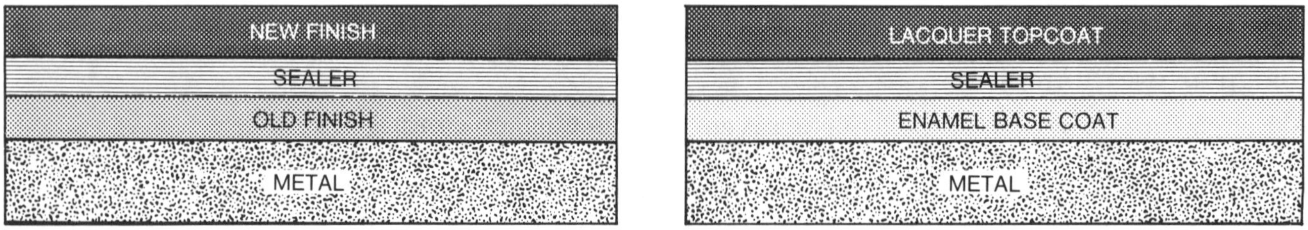

FIG 2-10 Cross section of finish with sealer.

keep primer-surfacer or an old finish from reacting with a new top coat (Fig. 2-10).

The element in sealer that enables it to do all these things is resin, the same sort of material used in wet-or-dry abrasives. The resin used in sealer, however, resists thinner and reducer as well as water. Thus, sprayed on in a single coat and allowed to dry, sealer effectively locks in whatever base coat elements it covers.

Sealing Problems

The chemical reactions that sealer prevents vary from mild to severe. Fresh paint, for example, can penetrate and mix with primer-surfacer, giving the new finish a dull appearance. This failure of the base coat, called lack of holdout, represents a mild chemical reaction. A more severe reaction occurs when the old finish actually bleeds through a new top coat applied directly over it. Reds refinished in white or a similar light color have a tendency to do this, blending almost instantly into pink. The worst consequences of incompatibility occur when lacquer is applied directly over any enamel product. Initially the new top coat looks fine. With time, however, the old finish swells, the new one flakes, and soon the whole paint job is ruined.

Types of Sealers

Individual sealers are made to block all of these chemical reactions. Bleeder seal, for example, makes it possible to apply a light top coat over any darker color, including a shade likely to bleed. Lacquer sealer can be used to prevent a fresh coat of lacquer paint from penetrating an enamel primer-surfacer. Enamel sealer can be used where the families of the paint products are reversed.

Sealer, then, protects the new top coat and preserves intact the carefully built up layers of the base coat. Its application is not an essential step in the refinishing process. It is, however, a wise one in any situation where the materials are potentially incompatible. It is certainly cheaper in terms of both time and money than redoing a whole paint job.

FILLERS

Sometimes the irregularities in a body panel are too great to be filled by repeated applications of primer-surfacer. A more substantial material must be used. Previously this material was lead. Its application required special cleaning agents (flux), special tools (an oxyacetylene torch), and special materials (solder). The application process was both time consuming and difficult to master. Today lead is used only for repairing surfaces that are subject to extreme stress, surfaces like panel edges and the areas adjoining hinges. What has replaced it are the various kinds of fillers.

Fillers are generally made from resins, the same clear, sticky material that is the basis of sealer and the glue used in abrasives. It is also the material from which plastics are made. Fillers, in fact, are sometimes called plastic solder or simply plastic.

Plastic Body Filler

Small dents, welds, holes, marks left by metalworking—these are the kinds of damage plastic filler is designed to cover. If such damage is present, filler is probably the first of three or more filling agents that will be used in the course of repairing and refinishing the surface. The filler is usually applied after the initial sanding of the panel. (The relatively coarse sandscratch left by 16- and 24-grit abrasives is necessary to provide a strong bond.) Under no circumstances can it be applied successfully to a painted or uncleaned surface.

Mixing

Plastic filler must be mixed before use. The product comes in two parts: the resin itself and a catalyst, or hardening agent. The resin is packed in cans that range in size from 1 quart to 5 gallons. (The latter size is frequently equipped with a pneumatic dispensing system.) The catalyst comes in tubes.

If applied right from the can, the resin portion of the filler would never set up, or harden. To start this reaction, the catalyst must be added. The proportions of the two products are usually expressed in approximate terms. One manufacturer, for example, suggests adding about ¼ teaspoon of hardener to a golf-ball-size lump of filler.

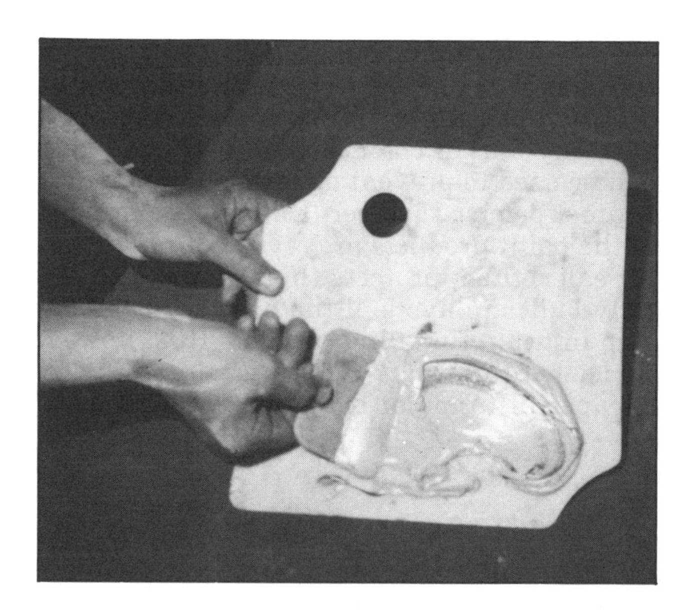

FIG 2-11
Mixing plastic filler. (David Keown)

The two materials are mixed on a piece of tile, glass, cardboard, or beaverboard (Fig. 2-11). To aid in the mixing process, hardener comes in colors—red, green, and blue. Since filler is usually light, a refinisher can tell when the product is properly mixed by the uniformity of its color. Red hardener and filler, for example, make a uniformly pink mixture.

Thorough mixing is essential if a repair made with filler is to last. An uneven mixture would contain areas of filler with too much hardener. These would crack or fail to bond. Areas with too little hardener would not set up properly.

Like thinner and reducer, hardener must be added in amounts that vary with shop conditions. In warm weather less is needed; in cold weather, more.

Application

In use, filler is applied with a rubber or plastic squeegee. This tool, if pulled firmly over the repair surface, will squeeze out any air bubbles that could interfere with bonding (Fig. 2-12).

Plastic filler should be applied to a whole damaged area rather than individual spots. The coats should be kept thin. Single applications that are more than ¼ inch thick lack the flexibility of metal and are likely to crack once the vehicle is put back in use. When cracking occurs, the only remedy is removal of the affected filler and a complete redoing of both the repair and the finish.

Properly applied, plastic filler takes between 10 and 15 minutes to dry. The initial shaping, however, is done when the product is just beginning to set up. A surform (or cheese-grater) file is used to contour the repair area by stripping away the outer layers of filler. Then, when the filled area is fully dry, a file board is used to smooth the surface in preparation for priming.

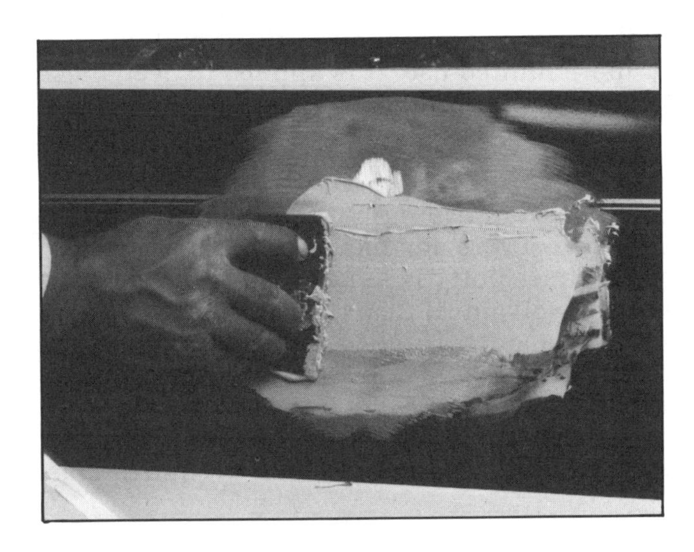

FIG 2-12
Applying filler. (3M Company)

Putty

Putty is a filler only in the general sense of the word. Chemically the product resembles primer-surfacer. It is, in fact, applied only over primer-surfacer and only when that product has failed to level or smooth a metal panel (Fig. 2-13).

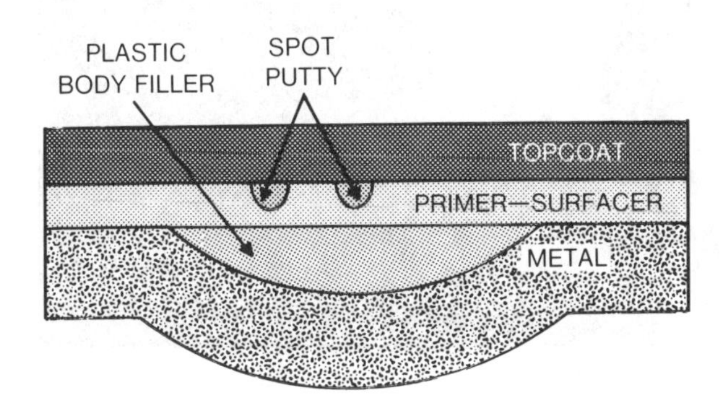

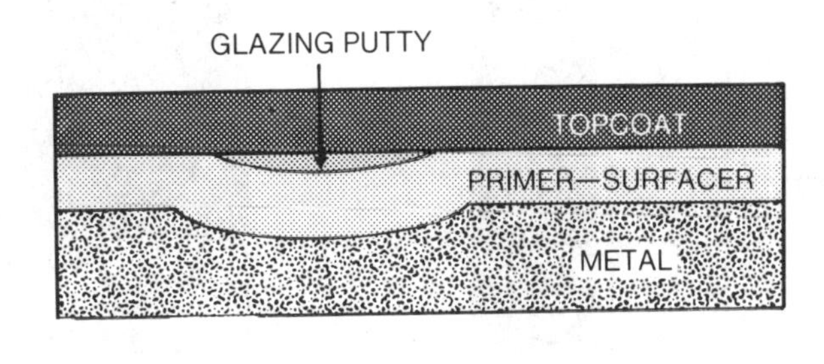

FIG 2-13 Filler applied to metal.

Putty applied to primer-surfacer.

Putty is a member of the lacquer paint family. There is no enamel equivalent of the product. This fact means that putty can be used only in situations where the base coat is lacquer. If it is used over enamel primer-surfacer, it will not adhere. Most vehicle repairs, however, are made with lacquer primer-surfacer. Only it dries fast enough to allow a shop to complete large numbers of repairs daily.

Putty, unlike filler, comes ready to use. It is squeezed from a tube and spread with a putty knife or rubber squeegee. This technique forces the putty into low spots.

Glazing vs. Spot Putty

There are two basic types of putty—glazing and spot. Glazing putty is the product intended for use on small scratches that cover a large area, scratches like those left by sanding. Its lower solids content (80 percent by volume compared to spot putty's 90 percent) makes glazing putty easier to spread (Fig. 2-14). It is applied in extremely thin, almost transparent coats that dry very quickly. This method of application not only fills rapidly but avoids the pitfalls of a one-time, thick buildup.

Spot putty is intended for more limited use. It is applied to deep nicks and scratches that even glazing putty cannot fill.

Misapplication

Putty is not intended for thick buildup. Using putty where filler might be more appropriate will result in severe shrinkage and cracking (Fig. 2-15). These conditions occur because putty is a highly absorptive material. It soaks up large amounts of solvent. It also releases them far more slowly than do other base coat elements. If putty is thickly applied (as it would have to be to fill a large dent), these two traits are compounded. The result is that the absorbed solvents do not fully evaporate until after the top coat is applied. Then they burst free, cracking the new finish. Again, never use putty to fill a repair that clearly requires plastic filler.

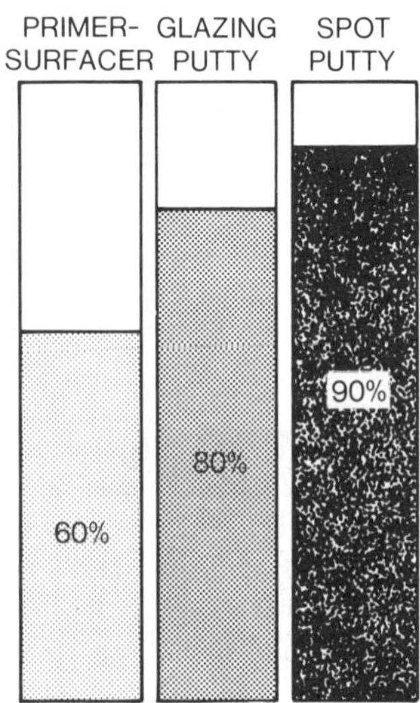

FIG 2-14 Solids content of primer-surfacer and putty compared.

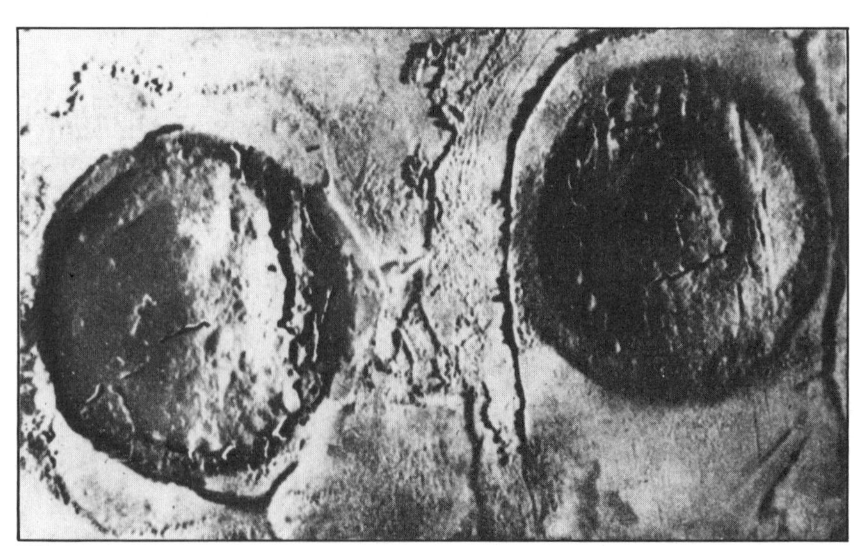

FIG 2-15 Cracking of putty applied too thickly.

OBJECTIVE 2-A2 (manipulative)

Working as a team with one other student and with the aid of Job Report Sheet 2-A2, you will use filler to cover metalworking marks or other minor panel damage, then prepare the cured surface for the application of primer-surfacer.

Time Recommended:

2 hours

Preparation:

1. Review pages 47 through 66.
2. Study pages 67 through 70.
3. Read the Safety Checklist on page 76, items 6 through 9.

Tools and Materials:

1. Squeegee
2. Cheese-grater file
3. Duster gun
4. File board
5. Bare panel—metalworked and ground or sandblasted
6. Plastic filler and catalyst
7. Selection of 17½-inch sandpaper strips (60D, 80D, 100D)
8. Respirator and safety goggles

Procedure:

1. Place a golf-ball-sized lump of filler on the mixing board. Squeeze approximately ¼ teaspoon of hardener from the tube onto the board beside it.
2. Use the squeegee to mix the two materials. Scoop and spread the filler repeatedly across the board. Continue in this manner until the filler is a single, uniform color.
3. Immediately apply the filler to the damaged portion of the panel. Press firmly to squeeze out any air bubbles that may have been trapped in the filler during mixing or application.
4. While it is still soft, wipe the filler from both the squeegee and the mixing board.
5. After the panel surface has dried 5 to 10 minutes, use a cheese-grater file to shape the filler to the contours of the panel.
6. Allow the filler to dry 5 to 10 minutes more.
7. Using a 17½-inch abrasive and a file board, sand the filler until it is smooth. Start with a 60D abrasive. Finish with an 80D.
8. Blow the sanding dust from the surface. If any low spots are visible, repeat steps 1 through 7.

USING PLASTIC FILLER

Student Name ______________________________ Date ______________

Time Started ______________ Time Finished ______________ Total Time ______________

Specifications

Type of panel ____

Condition (Describe damage.) ______________________________________

____

____

Technique

Plastic filler: Catalyst color ______________

Color when mixed ______________ Number of applications ______

Drying times:

Between application and contouring ______ minutes

Between contouring and sanding ______ minutes

Sanding: Abrasives used ______________________________________

Problems: Bubbles/air holes ______ Yes ______ No

Shrinking ______ Yes ______ No

Other (Explain.) ______________________________________

____

____

Describe any correction procedures used. ______________________

____

____

____

____

Checkup Questions

1. Was any more or less than 1/4 teaspoon of hardener needed for the filler mix? If yes, give the amount used. ______

   When might such adjustments be necessary? ______

2. Assume that, in step 8, low spots were found. Why couldn't they be filled with the plastic filler already mixed? ______

   Why couldn't they be filled with putty? ______

3. When in the course of the job were the respirator and safety goggles used? ______

Date Completed ______ Instructor's Signature ______

CLEANING AGENTS

Ironic as it may seem, the single most important technique in refinishing is probably not sanding or spray painting but cleaning. The cleaning of the work surface begins even before the repair does and continues throughout the whole refinishing process. Whether a panel is old and has had years of waxing and polishing or is straight from the factory, it needs to be cleaned. Whether it has already been sanded or is about to be, it needs to be cleaned. Whether it has been stripped to the bare metal or had several coats of primer-surfacer applied, it needs to be cleaned. The fact is, a refinisher spends nearly as much time cleaning surfaces as he does sanding and painting them. An understanding of when and how to use cleaning agents is therefore just as important to the success of a refinishing job as the ability to manipulate sanding discs or reducing agents.

Wax Remover

Every refinishing job begins with wax remover. Any auto body, but especially an older one, has accumulated residues of dirt, oil, wax, tar, and polish. All of these substances must be removed before any repair work is done. If not, they could be driven deep into the metal surface by sanding operations and eventually interfere with the adhesion and clarity of the new top coat.

Wax remover is a cleaning agent specifically formulated to remove these residues. The product is used by saturating a clean cloth and wiping the solvent onto the work surface. There it softens the layers of dirt and contaminants deposited on the finish. A second clean cloth is then used to dry the panel. Note that the panel must be wiped dry. If it should air dry, the residues would reharden and no cleaning would be accomplished. In such a circumstance, more wax remover would have to be applied and the panel properly wiped clean.

While ideal for pre-repair cleaning, wax remover should not be used for a final wipedown before spraying either paint or primer-surfacer. The solvent in the product is strong and has a relatively slow evaporation rate. (It takes time to dissolve wax, tar, and similar substances.) Together these two qualities could create the kind of adhesion problems wax remover itself was designed to prevent.

Metal Conditioner

In contrast to wax remover, metal conditioner is a cleaning agent that is nearly always used after the repair process has begun. Specifically, it is applied when (1) the old finish has been sandblasted or totally ground away, (2) a chemical stripper has been used, or (3) a factory-new replacement panel has been installed. What all of these circumstances have in common is that they involve bare metal. This is the only surface to which conditioner is applied. If it is used on any other, it causes problems. For example, plastic filler that absorbs metal conditioner does not allow primer-surfacer to adhere to it.

As a cleaning agent, metal conditioner is formulated to remove mainly grease and oil. These could come from chemical preparations, automotive products, or hand prints. Regardless of their source, however, all will interfere with the adhesion of any material applied over them. Like oil and water, oil and paint do not mix.

Anticorrosive Properties

Metal conditioner has functions that go beyond cleaning, however. It is, for example, one of several refinishing products with anticorrosive properties. These are important in any situation in which bare metal is exposed to air and moisture, as it frequently is in a paint shop. In such circumstances, rust begins to develop almost immediately. (On a freshly sandblasted surface, for example, it forms overnight.) If not prevented from the outset, this corrosion could eventually dislodge the new top coat from the inside out. The immediate application of conditioner to any metal exposed during the refinishing process is therefore more than accepted practice; it is a hard-and-fast rule.

Etching Function

Metal conditioner can also be used to provide adhesion. This function is especially important when a panel is new or has been chemically stripped. In both of these circumstances, there are no sandscratches to which a base coat can anchor itself. Rather than go through the long and dusty process of sanding an already bare surface, metal conditioner can be used to etch the panel instead. The component in the product that enables it to do this is acid. (Metal conditioner is sometimes called acid conditioner.) When rubbed onto the surface with a clean cloth, the product leaves the same kind of microscopic roughness as the finest sandpaper grits.

Tack Cloth

The use of tack cloth is the final step in all refinishing jobs immediately before the actual application of the paint. Basically, the product is cheesecloth soaked in varnish and partially dried. (It is sticky, not wet, to the touch.) Individually sealed packets keep the varnish moist enough to be effective as a cleaning agent.

Tack cloth is used to remove dust, lint, and other airborne contaminants from the work surface. It is wiped lightly over the repair area, never rubbed (Fig. 2-16). Heavy pressure could force some of the varnish to adhere to the base coat.

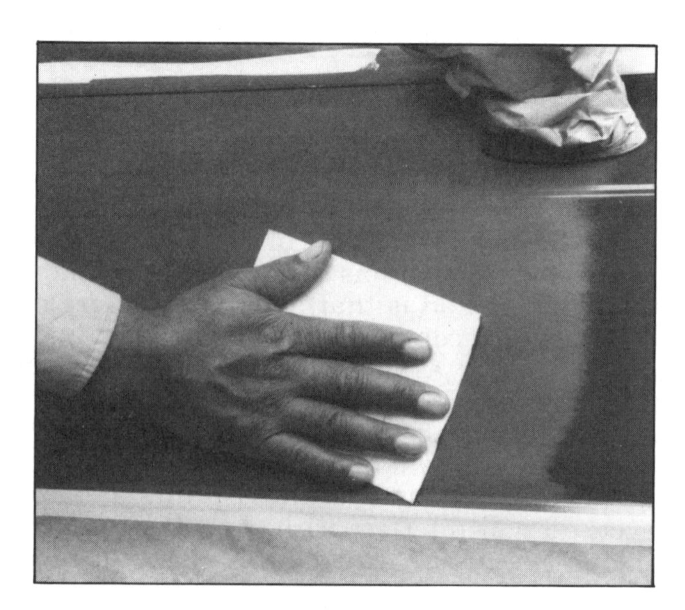

FIG 2-16
Tacking a surface before painting. (3M Company)

PAINT REMOVERS

Grinding and sandblasting are not the only ways to remove an old finish prior to repainting. Chemical paint removers are also available. While not particularly economical or efficient for refinishing whole vehicles or for large-scale production work, these products are useful for panel repairs. In such situations, they offer advantages that mechanical means of paint removal cannot match.

For one, they save time. If the paint film on a vehicle is thick, hours could be spent grinding off the finish and then smoothing the scratches left by this operation. Chemical paint removers do the same job in a fraction of the time, with a fraction of the effort, and with none of the surface damage. They are particularly helpful when a vehicle has already been refinished. Air-dried paint less than a year old does not sand as well as factory-baked paint. It clogs sanding and grinding discs after only a few strokes and thus consumes larger amounts of refinishing materials as well as larger amounts of time.

A second advantage that chemical paint removers offer is that they are cleaner. Of course, the surface must be wiped down carefully after they are used. (The smallest particle of a stripping agent can damage a new finish.) The paint removal process itself, however, generates no sanding dust to contaminate either the work area or the refinishing materials that must subsequently be used.

To achieve the same degree of control as mechanical sanders and grinders, chemical paint removers come in two basic types. The first removes only the color coat. The second removes the entire finish down to the bare metal. In addition, the performance of each product can be regulated by varying the amount of time it is left on the work surface or by repeated applications.

Stripper

Stripper is a chemical product that removes both base and top coats. It comes in liquid form. It is brushed onto the work surface in a thick coat and allowed to penetrate (Fig. 2-17). After an amount of time that varies with the given product, the old paint visibly lifts. It can then be removed with a paint scraper or a putty knife (Fig. 2-18). Afterward, the area is flushed clean with water.

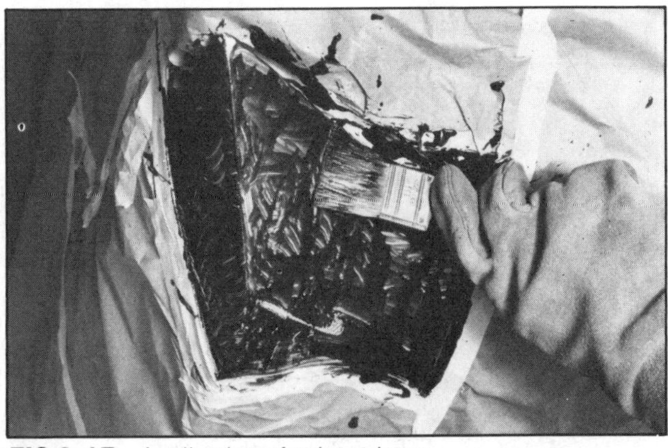

FIG 2-17 Application of paint stripper.

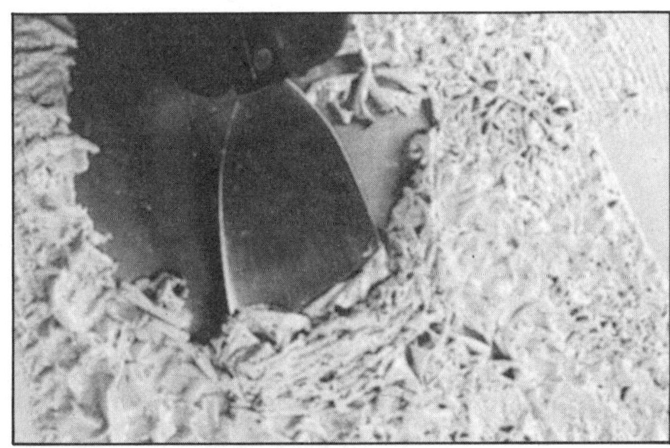

FIG 2-18 Scraping of lifted paint. (E. I. du Pont de Nemours & Co., Inc.)

Removing all traces of the stripper from the panel is essential. If the product can soften and lift an old finish, it can do the same to a new one. Flushing with water not only clears away the stripped paint but neutralizes any chemical that still remains on the repair surface.

Lacquer-Removing Solvent

Sometimes the problem with a new finish is only in the top coat. Drips, sags, wrinkles, and dirt in the finish are examples. To grind away these kinds of mistakes would leave marks in the base coat and require hours of costly sanding and rebuilding of the surface. To get around this problem, a product that removes the top coat without disturbing the primer-surfacer has been developed. It is called lacquer-removing solvent.

Although it was developed primarily for lacquer finishes, lacquer-removing solvent can be used on enamels as well, provided they are not factory baked. Applied to a lacquer finish, the product works by dissolving the paint film. Applied to an enamel top coat, it works by lifting. In both cases, when the material is wiped off, a portion of the softened pigment comes with it. This procedure may have to be repeated several times if the paint is especially thick.

SAFETY CHECKLIST

Paint and Paint Solvents:

1. The labels on all paints and paint products used in auto refinishing state that they contain strong, volatile, and sometimes even caustic chemicals. Such materials must be handled in a careful and informed way. Professionalism demands that a refinisher read product labels, observe manufacturer's recommendations, and take responsibility for protecting himself and others from the hazards associated with the products he uses.
2. All paints and paint products give off vapors that are extremely flammable—in fact, explosive. For this reason, such products should be stored well away from compressors, repair stations where electric tools are used, and smoking areas. The paint materials room must by law be posted with signs that warn employees and customers of the fire hazard. Inside, all materials (but particularly solvents like

FIG 2-19
Safety cabinets for paint storage. (E. I. du Pont de Nemours & Co., Inc.)

thinner and reducer) should be stored in metal safety cabinets (Fig. 2-19). A ban on smoking must be observed at all times.

3. Paint and paint product vapors are harmful if inhaled regularly over a long period of time. Such products should therefore be used only in open areas or in spaces equipped with approved filtering and ventilation systems.
4. Because of the hazard posed by storing large quantities of paint and other flammable materials in one spot, the refinishing shop should be equipped with several fire extinguishers. These should be inspected regularly and their use and operation understood by all shop personnel (Fig. 2-20).
5. As a precaution against fires started by spontaneous combustion, all used paint and cleaning rags should be placed in a lidded metal container until they can be either laundered or disposed of properly (Fig. 2-21).

FIG 2-20
Different types of fire extinguishers are used for different types of fires.

FIRES
A CLASS *A* FIRES ORDINARY COMBUSTIBLE MATERIALS SUCH AS WOOD, PAPER, TEXTILES AND SO FORTH. REQUIRES . . . COOLING-QUENCHING
B CLASS *B* FIRES FLAMMABLE LIQUIDS, GREASES, GASOLINE, OILS, PAINTS AND SO FORTH. REQUIRES. . .BLANKETING OR SMOTHERING
C CLASS *C* FIRES ELECTRICAL EQUIPMENT, SWITCHES AND SO FORTH. REQUIRES . . . A NONCONDUCTING AGENT

TYPE	USE	OPERATION
FOAM — SOLUTION OF ALUMINUM SULPHATE AND BICARBONATE OF SODA	OK FOR **A B**; NOT FOR **C**	*FOAM:* DON'T PLAY STREAM INTO THE BURNING LIQUID. ALLOW FOAM TO FALL LIGHTLY ON FIRE
CARBON DIOXIDE — CARBON DIOXIDE GAS UNDER PRESSURE	NOT FOR **A**; OK FOR **B C**	*CARBON DIOXIDE:* DIRECT DISCHARGE AS CLOSE TO FIRE AS POSSIBLE. FIRST AT EDGE OF FLAMES AND GRADUALLY FORWARD AND UPWARD
DRY CHEMICAL	MULTI-PURPOSE TYPE: OK FOR **A B C**; ORDINARY BC TYPE: NOT FOR **A**, OK FOR **B C**	*DRY CHEMICAL:* DIRECT STREAM AT BASE OF FLAMES. USE RAPID LEFT-TO-RIGHT MOTION TOWARD FLAMES
SODA-ACID — BICARBONATE OF SODA SOLUTION AND SULPHURIC ACID	OK FOR **A**; NOT FOR **B C**	*SODA-ACID:* DIRECT STREAM AT BASE OF FLAME

FIG 2-21
Safety storage container for oily rags.
(E. I. du Pont de Nemours & Co., Inc.)

Primers, Fillers, and Rubbing Compounds:

6. Among refinishing materials, zinc chromate has the most toxic fumes. These pose a hazard based on individual as well as repeated, long-term exposures. When spraying this product, therefore, the user must wear a respirator. Anyone who cannot leave the area during the spraying should do the same.
7. Sanding fully cured base coat elements like primer-surfacer and filler generates a large amount of dust, some of which is circulated in the air. These airborne particles pose a hazard to both vision and long-term respiratory health. Anyone engaged in such sanding should therefore wear safety goggles and a respirator.
8. Because of its method of application, filler is frequently considered less hazardous to use than other refinishing materials. This view, however, is not accurate. Most manufacturers caution users against breathing in the product's vapors and prolonged or repeated contact with the skin. Filler is not modeling clay. It should be worked with a squeegee or a putty knife, not with the hands. It should be mixed on a nonabsorptive surface. As soon as application is complete, the user should wash his hands to remove any traces of the product.

Paint Removers and Metal Conditioner:

9. Stripper and metal conditioner are both extremely caustic substances: conditioner can etch metal, and stripper can lift and blister layers of paint. Both products can burn the skin. Therefore, never touch bare hands to a surface on which either product has been applied. Always wear rubber gloves during application and, in the case of stripper, during removal. Special protective gear like vinyl-coated aprons and goggles is also recommended. Since the fumes from both products can cause irritation, wearing a respirator is another wise precaution. If either material contacts the skin by accident, it should be washed away immediately with cold water.

OBJECTIVE 2-A3 (manipulative)

Working as a team with one other student and with the aid of Job Report Sheet 2-A3, you will use stripper to remove the paint from a practice panel and then prepare the metal surface for application of primer-surfacer.

Time Recommended:

1 hour

Preparation:

1. Review pages 47 through 76.
2. Study pages 77 through 80.
3. Read the Safety Checklist on page 76, item 9.

Tools and Materials:

1. Squeegee
2. Putty knife
3. Painted practice panel
4. Stripper
5. Metal conditioner
6. Reducer
7. Safety goggles or face shield
8. Respirator
9. Rubber gloves
10. Canvas or vinyl-coated apron
11. Paintbrush
12. Hose
13. Clean shop cloths
14. Bucket, can, or other metal container

Procedure:

1. Place the panel on the floor or in a sturdy rack in the vehicle wash area.
2. Put on the apron, goggles, respirator, and rubber gloves.
3. Open the can of stripper and pour the required amount into the bucket. Replace the container cap.
4. Using the paintbrush, apply a thick coat of stripper to the painted panel.
5. Allow the material to remain on the surface until it visibly lifts the old paint.
6. Using the putty knife, scrape the paint from the panel.
7. When all the paint is removed, flush the panel with water and dry it. *Note:* This cleaning must be thorough. The smallest particle of stripper will eat through a new finish.
8. Wipe down the entire surface with enamel reducer.
9. Apply metal conditioner with a clean cloth and wipe dry with another. The panel is now ready for the application of primer-surfacer.

STRIPPING PAINT

Student Name ______________________ Date ______________

Time Started ____________ Time Finished ____________ Total Time ____________

Specifications

Panel size ____________

Panel finish (paint family and number of coats, if known) ______________

____

Stripper: Product name ______________________

Manufacturer ______________________

Metal conditioner: Product name ______________________

Manufacturer ______________________

Technique

Number of stripper applications ____

Time per application ______________________

Checkup Questions

1. How did the stripper affect the paint? (Describe the paint's appearance just before removal.) ______________________

____

____

2. Describe the appearance of the panel after the metal conditioner was applied.

____

____

____

3. What specific safety precautions do the manufacturers of the stripper and the conditioner recommend on their packaging? ____________________

____

____

Date Completed ____________ Instructor's Signature ____________________

Student Name ______________________ Date ______________

DIRECTIONS: Circle the best answer to each question.

1. Which color of paint is most likely to bleed?
   A. Black
   B. White
   C. Yellow
   D. Maroon

2. Lead is still used to repair
   A. rusted body panels.
   B. panel edges.
   C. deep nicks and sandscratches.
   D. small dents.

3. Zinc chromate is used to prime
   I. aluminum.
   II. steel.
   A. I only B. II only C. Both I and II D. Neither I nor II

4. The tool shown at the right is used to apply which of the following materials?
   A. Sealer
   B. Primer-surfacer
   C. Wax remover
   D. Glazing putty

5. To remove a defective finish without disturbing the base coat, use
   I. stripper.
   II. lacquer-removing solvent.
   A. I only B. II only C. Both I and II D. Neither I nor II

6. The fumes from which product are especially harmful if inhaled?
   A. Metal conditioner
   B. Zinc chromate
   C. Plastic filler
   D. Stripper

7. Which should be used to clean a surface immediately before painting?
   A. Tack cloth
   B. Wax remover
   C. Metal conditioner
   D. Lacquer-removing solvent

8. Thinner and reducer can be used
   I. to make paint sprayable.
   II. in the same paints.
   A. I only B. II only C. Both I and II D. Neither I nor II

9. The functions of primer-surfacer include
   I. filling sandscratches.
   II. adhesion of the top coat.
   A. I only B. II only C. Both I and II D. Neither I nor II

10. The reading obtained using the equipment pictured at the right is 16 seconds. The refinisher should therefore
   A. add paint.
   B. add solvent.
   C. stir the paint.
   D. strain the paint.

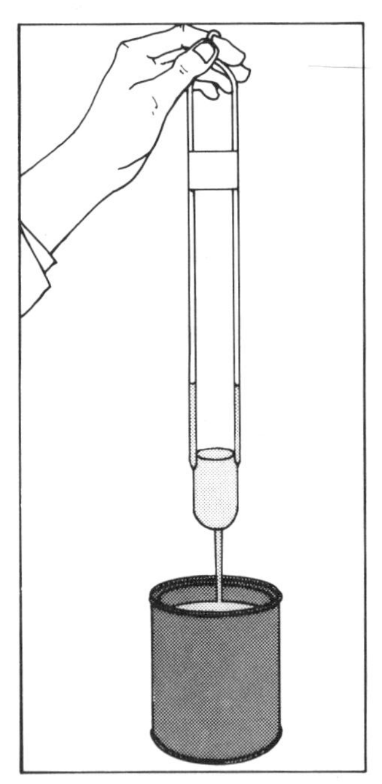

11. The best color of primer-surfacer to apply under a dark green top coat is
   A. green.
   B. light gray.
   C. dark gray.
   D. clear.

12. As a rule, enamel primer-surfacer
   I. is reduced more than lacquer.
   II. dries faster than lacquer.
   A. I only B. II only C. Both I and II D. Neither I nor II

13. All of the following contribute to rapid aging of paint EXCEPT
    A. a warm, moist climate.
    B. industrial pollution.
    C. regular washing and waxing.
    D. choice of color.

14. Which contains the greatest percentage of solids?
    A. Primer
    B. Primer-surfacer
    C. Glazing putty
    D. Spot putty

15. All of the following products are intended for use on bare metal EXCEPT
    A. stripper.
    B. plastic filler.
    C. metal conditioner.
    D. zinc chromate.

16. The product being applied at the right is most likely
    A. metal conditioner.
    B. stripper.
    C. reducer.
    D. zinc chromate.

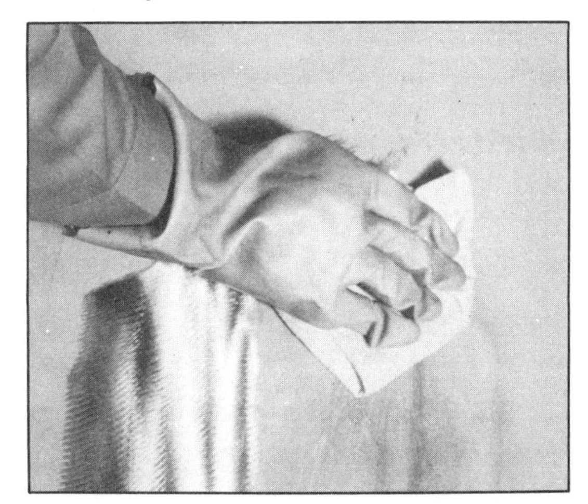

17. An older model vehicle has had three different color coats applied to it, one on top of the other. The owner wants this heavy paint film removed and a new finish applied.

    Refinisher I suggests grinding the old paint film away before anything else.

    Refinisher II suggests removing the old finish chemically, then following up with metal conditioner.

    Who is right?

    A. I only   B. II only   C. Both I and II   D. Neither I nor II

18. The correct order of application is
    A. sealer, primer-surfacer, lacquer.
    B. zinc chromate, primer-surfacer, enamel.
    C. primer, metal conditioner, enamel.
    D. stripper, lacquer-removing solvent, primer.

19. All of the following products come ready to use EXCEPT

A. wax remover.
B. plastic filler.
C. putty.
D. stripper.

20. The diagram at the right represents the factory-baked finish on a vehicle. If 1 is the metal surface, then 2 and 3 are

A. solvent and binder.
B. 4/1000 inch thick.
C. base and top coats.
D. enamel and lacquer.

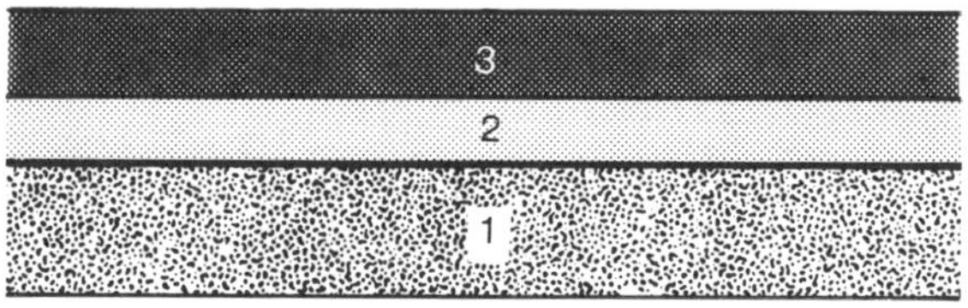

3
2
1

Score __________ Instructor's Signature ______________________________

unit 3

Spray Guns and Baking Equipment

The smallest spray gun is called an airbrush. As names go, this one is both descriptive and accurate. The tool is the refinisher's brush. Rather than bristles, however, it uses a stream of air to apply and spread the paint.

This arrangement offers several advantages. First, the refinisher has more control. The paint goes on in a mist that coats the surface far more thinly than any brush could. Such fine applications make possible translucent and specialized finishes not seen in areas other than refinishing. Second, the painter can work more quickly. The coverage of a spray gun is far greater than that of a brush—up to 12 inches. A brush of that width would be difficult to handle. It would also not lend itself to the careful, light applications of paint that auto refinishing requires. Third, the painter can achieve a smoother, cleaner finish. There are no brush marks and no hairs left embedded in the fresh paint. If the spray gun is properly handled, in fact, there are no surface irregularities of any kind (at least none that will not level themselves out and disappear as the paint dries).

Taken together, all these advantages make possible the smooth, seamless, mirrorlike finishes that are the mark of the professional refinisher. Such advantages have a price, however. The spray gun, being a far more complex tool than the paintbrush, cannot simply be picked up and used. To spray paint skillfully, a refinisher must first understand the construction and operation of the equipment he is using. He must know how to maintain it, and—most important—he must be willing to put in the time necessary to master its techniques and develop his own.

This unit provides introductions to all of these areas. It surveys the basic types of spray guns, details cleaning and maintenance procedures, and discusses the fine points of gun adjustment, movement, and triggering. In addition, throughout it emphasizes spray painting problems, describes symptoms, and explains solutions. The unit concludes with a brief overview of the various kinds of booths and lamps frequently used along with spray guns, either in the course of painting or afterward to bake the new finish.

OBJECTIVE 3-A (written)

After doing the reading and shop exercises, you will be able to answer correctly without reference material a minimum of 14 out of 20 test questions on the following topics:

1. Suction-feed vs. pressure-feed equipment
2. Spray gun design and operation
3. Spray gun maintenance and related problems
4. Spray painting technique and related problems
5. Paint spray booths
6. Heat lamps and baking equipment

Preparation:

1. Study pages 85 through 130.
2. Attend classroom discussions on Objective 3-A.
3. Read the Safety Checklist on pages 126 and 127.

SPRAY GUN CLASSIFICATIONS

The spray gun is a tool that combines compressed air and paint into a fine mist. It then disperses that mist evenly over a surface.

The air and paint enter the gun separately. They are metered by valves and only then mixed, either shortly before or shortly after they are expelled. Exactly where the mixing takes place and how both the air and the paint arrive at that point determine the equipment's classification.

Suction Feed vs. Pressure Feed

Spray painting systems are of two basic types—suction feed and pressure feed. What distinguishes the two systems is the way in which the paint is delivered. In suction-feed equipment, it is pulled from the paint container by a partial vacuum at the spray gun nozzle. In pressure-feed equipment, it is pushed from the paint container, which is pressurized separately from the spray gun itself (Fig. 3-1).

FIG 3-1
Using a pressure-feed spray gun to spray rustproofing compound. (The DeVilbiss Company)

Bleeder vs. Nonbleeder

Spray guns can also be categorized by their air delivery systems. A gun through which air flows continuously, independent of any triggering mechanism, is called a bleeder gun. Spray guns of this type lack valves to regulate their air flow. Disconnecting the air line is the only way to cut off their air supply, short of shutting down the compressor itself. (Protecting a compressor that is not equipped with an automatic cutoff switch is, in fact, the purpose of a bleeder gun.) Both of these procedures, however, are extremely inconvenient. For this reason, bleeder guns are seldom used in refinishing.

The spray guns found in paint shops are invariably of the nonbleeder type. These come with air as well as fluid valves. Both valve assemblies are adjustable at the gun, and both are controlled by the gun's triggering mechanism.

Internal Mix vs. External Mix

Spray guns can also be classified as internal or external mix. The terms refer, of course, to where the mixing of air and paint ultimately occurs—inside the gun or out.

Again the refinishing field favors one type of equipment over the other—in this case, the external mix. This preference is based on the fact that atomizing any liquid makes it dry more quickly. When the liquid is paint (especially a fast-drying paint like lacquer), the place where the drying process starts is crucial. If it begins outside the gun on the surface of a panel, the refinishing process is speeded. If it begins inside the gun in the narrow passageways leading to the nozzle, the refinishing process is brought to a halt. The spray gun cannot function if it is blocked by accumulations of dried paint. What is more, such blockages are extremely difficult to remove. For these reasons, internal-mix equipment is not recommended for use in auto refinishing.

To summarize, then, the spray painting equipment found in refinishing shops can be of either the suction-feed or pressure-feed type. Both systems employ spray guns that are entirely trigger activated. These atomize refinishing materials outside the nozzle, where their fast-drying properties cannot interfere with the gun's internal mechanism.

SUCTION-FEED EQUIPMENT

The nonbleeder, external-mix, suction-feed spray gun is the type most commonly found in paint shops. Such equipment can be recognized by its distinctive paint container, a cup-and-cap assembly attached directly to the gun (Fig. 3-2).

The cup's small capacity makes the suction-feed gun the ideal tool for panel and spot repairs. The limited amounts of color involved minimize paint waste. The ease with which the container can be cleaned also makes frequent color changes possible.

Design and Operation

Suction-feed equipment is designed around two basic principles. First, movement of air lowers the pressure in the area where it occurs. An airplane's flight is a good illustration of this concept. A plane gets its

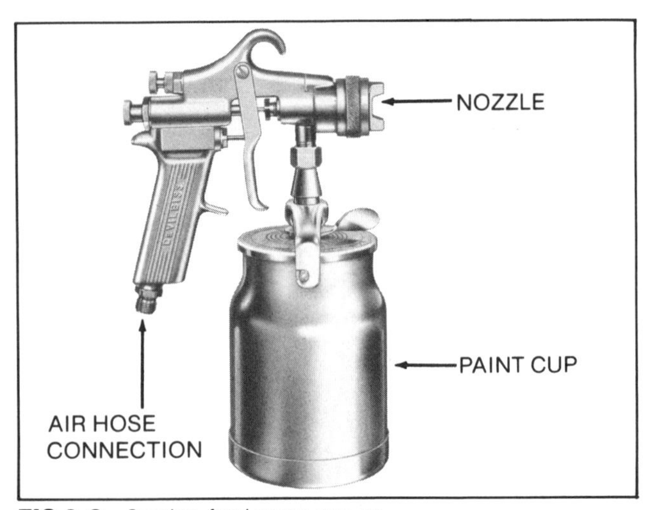

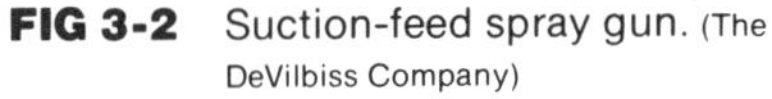
FIG 3-2 Suction-feed spray gun. (The DeVilbiss Company)

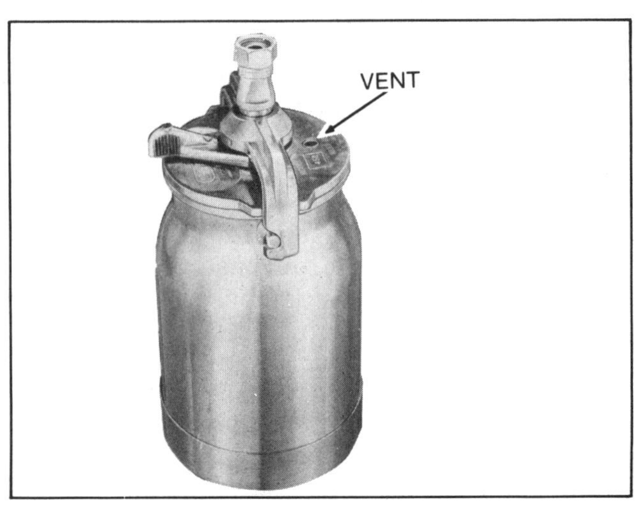

FIG 3-3 Suction spray gun cup and cap assembly. (Sharpe Manufacturing Company)

lift by creating more air movement, and hence lower pressures, above the wing than below it. Similarly, the suction-feed spray gun uses the movement of compressed air escaping from the gun to create an area of low pressure at the nozzle.

At that point, the second principle comes into play. It states that all substances move from areas of higher pressure to areas of lower pressure. As an example, consider an automobile tire. If the tire is at 30 pounds of pressure and the valve stem is suddenly removed, the tire will go flat as the air rushes to the outside, where the pressure is lower. In the case of the spray gun, the low pressure area is the partial vacuum at the nozzle tip. The paint, at atmospheric pressure, is attracted to this area. Indeed, so strong is the attraction that it overcomes gravity. It draws the paint up out of its container and through the gun. This siphoning action gives suction-feed equipment its name.

The spray gun itself, however, is more than just a pathway from paint cup to work surface. It is the device that controls both the amount of paint drawn from the cup and the degree to which that paint is atomized. The controls that regulate these two processes work together and can be best understood by considering the spray gun's structure as a whole.

Cup-and-Cap Assembly

The suction-feed cup-and-cap assembly consists of five basic parts: (1) the cup, (2) the cap, (3) the siphon tube, (4) the assembly nut, and (5) the release lever. All are made of aluminum. The cup has a capacity of 1 quart. It is attached to the spray gun by the cap assembly. The cap assembly consists of a lid penetrated by a long siphon tube. At the top of the tube is the nut that actually fastens the assembly to the spray gun. Below, resting on the lid itself, is the release lever used to break the seal between the paint cup and the cap. The lever speeds refills, color changes, and cleanups between jobs.

In use, the cap assembly is threaded onto the spray gun's fluid inlet and tightened with a gun wrench. Gun and cap are then slipped over the cup, pressed, and turned firmly. This action allows the cap assembly yoke to engage two studs on the cup's neck, thus locking the two units together.

The spray gun cap is lined with a rubber gasket. When the cap and cup are joined, the gasket forms a tight seal. It is not, however, an air-tight seal. There is an opening, or vent, in the cap (Fig. 3-3). The vent allows air to pass into the cup as the siphoning action empties it. The paint supply is thus kept at atmospheric pressure. Were this not the case, the pressure in the cup would gradually lower to match that at the nozzle, and the siphoning action would cease. (Should the vent become blocked while the gun is in use, this is, in fact, what would happen.)

The presence of the vent, while necessary, creates some obvious problems. Should the gun be tipped while in use, paint could drip from the opening onto the work surface. To avoid this problem, most schools and refinishing shops now use no-drip cups. These have a length of plastic or metal tubing leading either to the vent from the cup or from the vent to the outside (Fig. 3-4). The tubing may be internal or external. In either case, however, it makes at least a 180-degree turn. Thus, even if some paint drips from the vent, halfway up or around the tubing is as far as it can get.

Fluid and Air Inlets

Paint enters the spray gun through a fluid inlet located in front of the trigger. The inlet opens onto a passageway that leads directly to the nozzle. In the case of a suction-feed gun, the fluid inlet, once connected to the cup-and-cap assembly, becomes an extension of the siphon tube.

Air entering the spray gun follows a much longer route. The air inlet is located at the base of the spray gun handle. The air hose is threaded onto it. When the gun is triggered, compressed air passes through the entire length of the handle, along the air valve needle, and then out through the air cap.

It should be clear that in an external-mix gun at no time do the two systems of passageways meet. Paint and air enter separately and, if the gun is operating properly, leave the same way (Fig. 3-5).

Adjustment Valves

The fluid and air adjustment valves are responsible for metering all paint and air passing through the spray gun. Both are needle valves

FIG 3-4
Spray gun with no-drip cup.
(Binks Manufacturing Company)

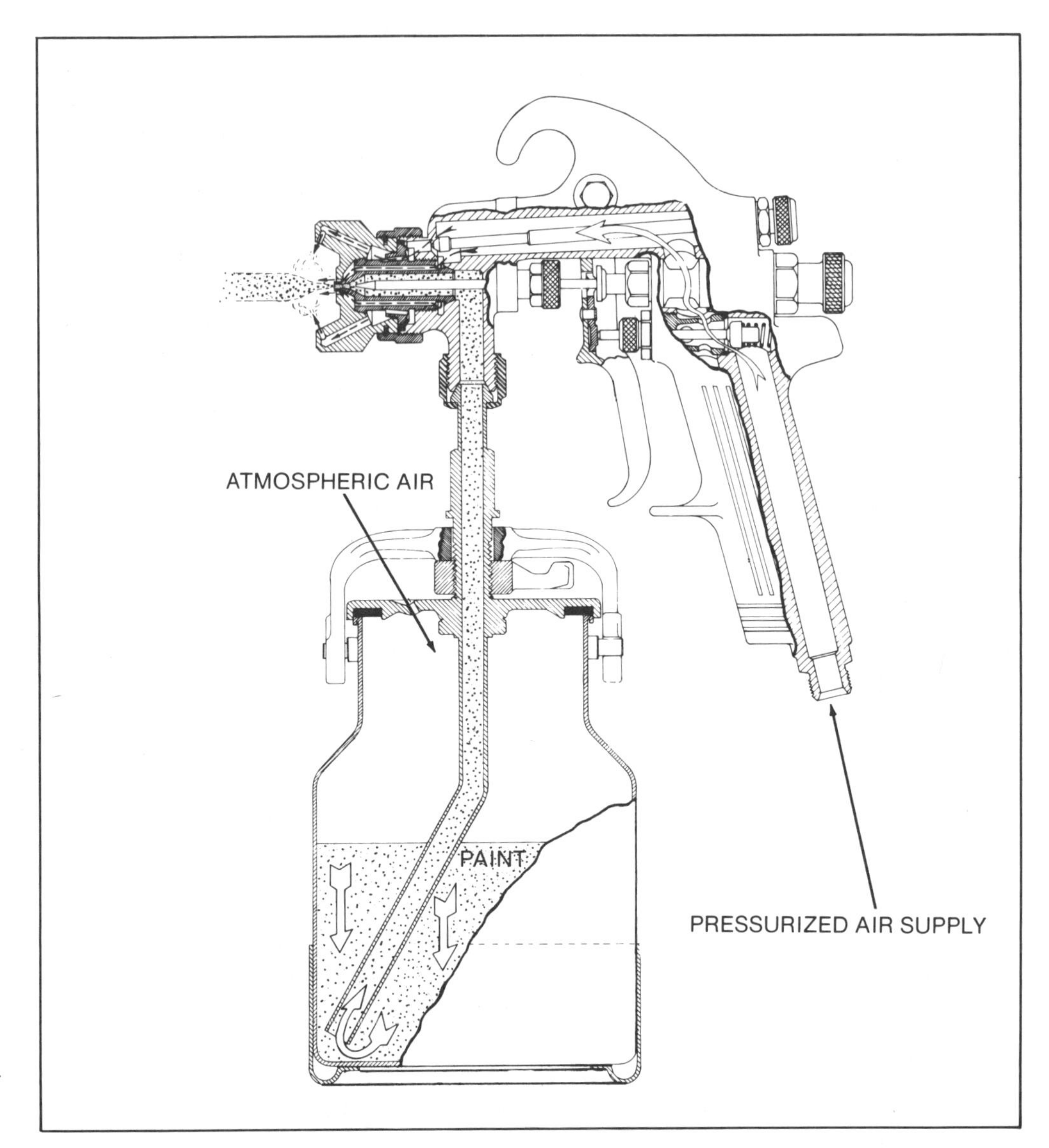

FIG 3-5
Air and paint flow in suction-feed gun. (Binks Manufacturing Company)

that extend from the back of the gun to the front. Their only truly visible portions, however, are their adjustment screws. These are located at the back of the gun above the handle.

The lower screw controls the fluid valve. This is the larger of the two valves, extending as it does from the handle through the trigger and all the way into the nozzle. Turning the adjustment screw changes the valve's contact point with the trigger. Counterclockwise turning, for example, lengthens the distance the trigger can travel. This added movement withdraws the needle farther from its seat in the nozzle tip and allows more paint to pass.

The air adjustment valve, also called the spreader valve, operates in a similar manner. It has, however, a shorter needle and a different, blunt tip. (The special tip is necessary because the air passageway that the valve controls is much wider than the needle.) The air adjustment valve regulates access to the air cap. Unlike the nozzle, the air cap has several openings. Turning the air adjustment screw thus does more than just pass a greater amount of air. As the valve is gradually opened, it passes that air through a greater number of openings.

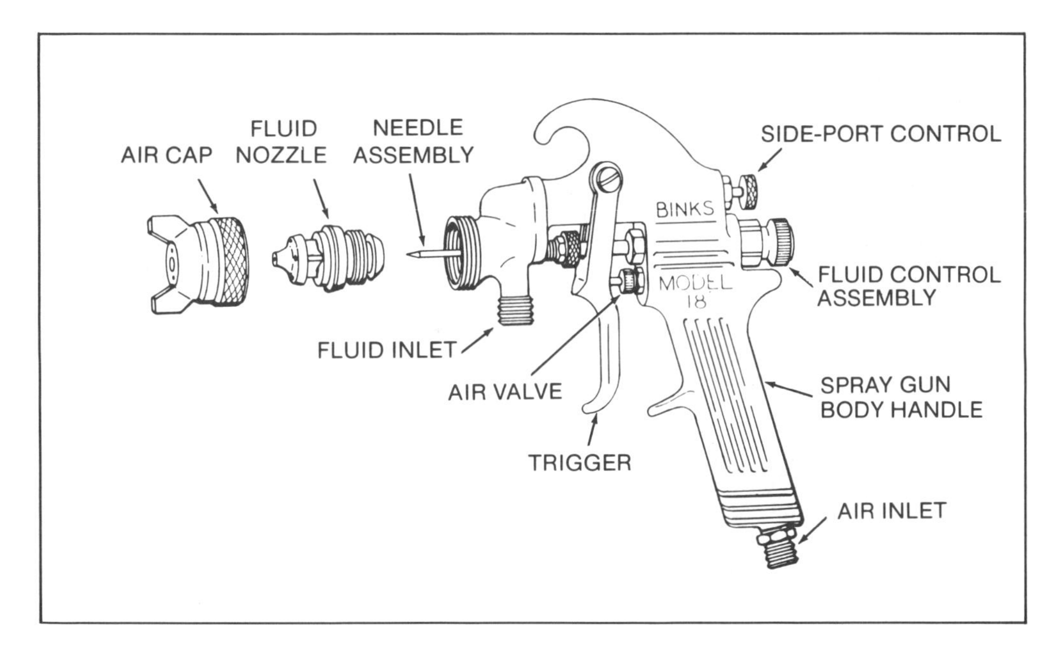

FIG 3-6
Spray gun. (Binks Manufacturing Company)

Nozzle

The purpose of the nozzle is to direct the paint flow into the jets of air emerging from the air cap. In order to do this, the nozzle wraps around the fluid needle's tip. The air cap is then fitted around the nozzle/needle assembly, virtually hiding it from view (Fig. 3-6).

In a suction-feed gun, however, the tip of the nozzle does extend beyond the air cap. This arrangement is what makes possible the siphoning action necessary to the gun's operation. It guarantees that the air flow (and thus the partial vacuum it creates) will lead the paint flow by at least a fraction of a second.

Nozzles come in various sizes and are matched to the fluid needles seated in them. The nozzles used in refinishing have diameters that range from .041 to .070 inch. The larger the diameter, the more paint the nozzle can pass. As a rule, suction-feed guns take larger nozzles. The extra width, like the extension of the nozzle tip beyond the air cap, helps to establish the siphoning action.

Air Cap

The air cap directs the spray gun's air flow so that it uniformly atomizes the paint and spreads it in a desirable pattern. The air caps used in refinishing are all of one type—external mix. These can be recognized by their multiple openings, or orifices, and their two air horns. Internal-mix caps do not have these features.

In use, the air cap is slipped over the spray gun nozzle and locked in place with its adjustment ring. (The ring is always tightened by hand, never with a wrench or other tool.) The normal position for the cap is with the horns set horizontally. This position produces the oval pattern, or vertical fan, characteristic of all spray guns. (*Note:* In diagrams, this horizontal arrangement can be misleading because one horn is hidden from view. For this reason, most of the spray gun illustrations in this text show the horns in the vertical position. Were this setting used, however, it would produce a horizontal spray pattern that is not practical for most refinishing work.)

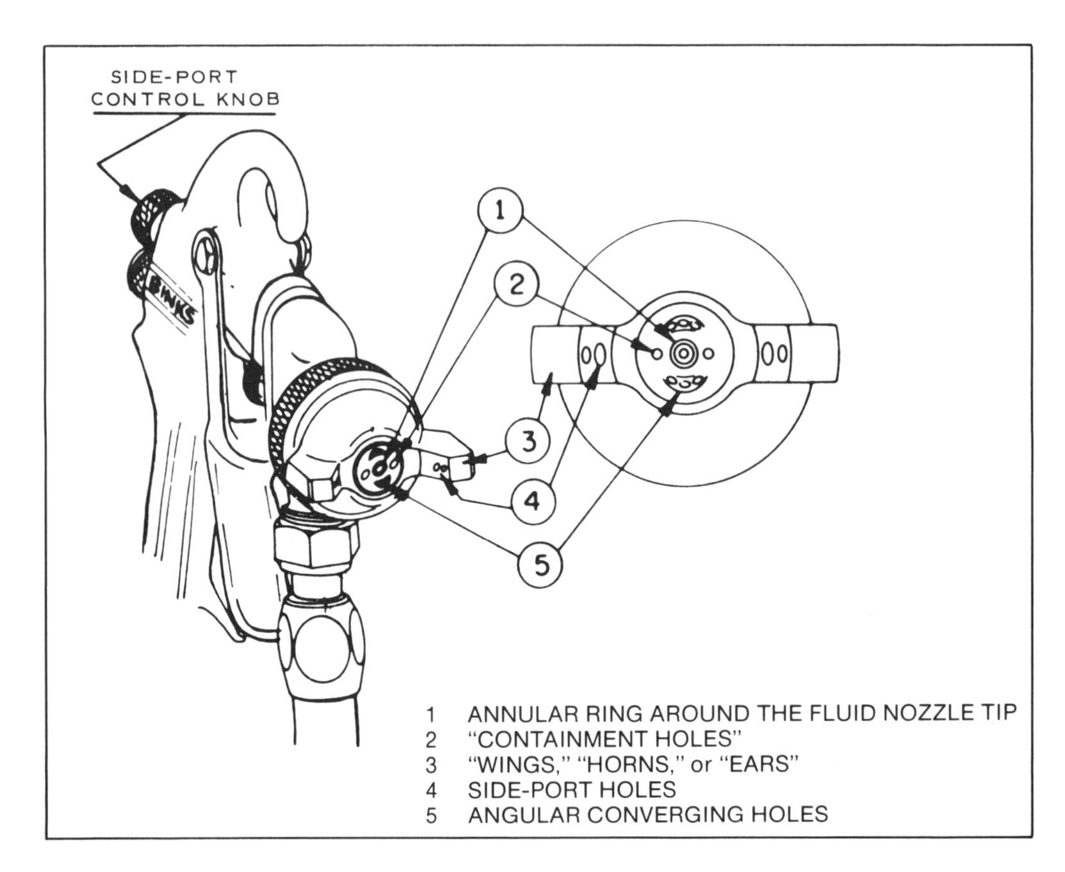

FIG 3-7
External mix spray gun cap.
(Binks Manufacturing Company)

The external-mix cap typically has at least five openings (Fig. 3-7). There is the central orifice, which fits around the fluid nozzle, and two or more auxiliary orifices surrounding it. When the air adjustment valve is closed, these are the only openings from which any air is emerging. The result is a concentrated circular spray pattern. As the adjustment screw is turned, however, and the valve opened, more air flows and enlarges the pattern. Finally, as the valve is opened to its farthest limits, air begins to flow from additional orifices in each of the horns. These disperse the paint into its fullest, oval pattern (Figs. 3-8A and B).

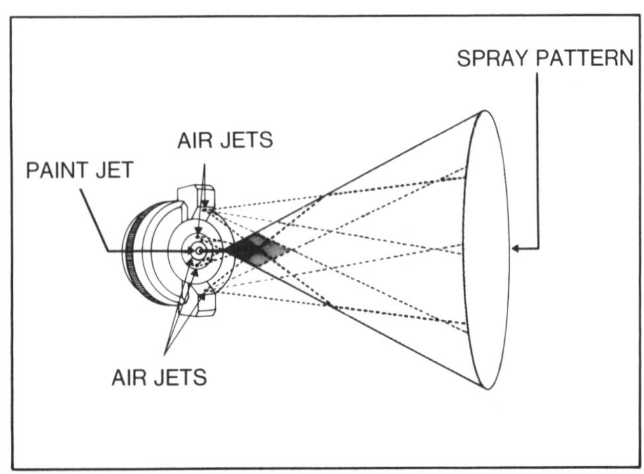

FIG 3-8A Spray gun nozzle and pattern.

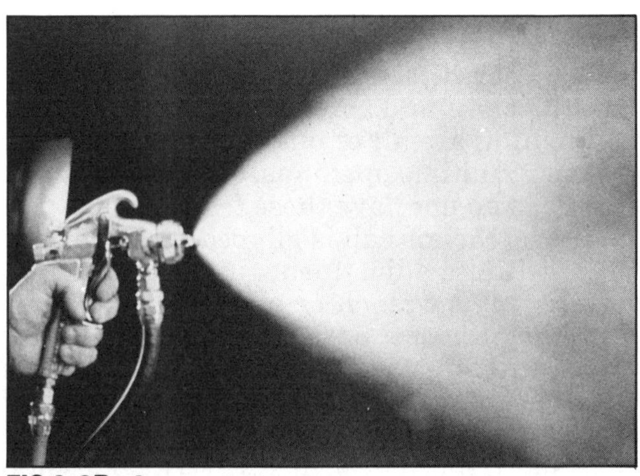

FIG 3-8B Spray pattern. (The DeVilbiss Company)

Trigger and Air Control Valve

The air control valve is not to be confused with the air adjustment valve. It is an entirely separate assembly with an entirely different purpose. The air adjustment valve meters the spray gun's air supply. The air control valve turns that supply on and off.

The air control valve is located below the spray gun's other two valve assemblies. Only about half as long, it extends from handle to trigger.

The trigger has internal contacts with both the fluid and the air control valves. These contacts are so positioned, however, that the air valve is always opened first. This arrangement prevents paint from dripping onto the work surface. Before any paint is released, the air flow is established. When the paint flow ceases, the air flow continues for a fraction of a second more. Thus paint never leaves the nozzle except when there is an air flow to atomize it.

Maintenance

More than any other piece of refinishing equipment, the spray gun is affected—and affected quickly—by lack of regular cleaning and maintenance. One of the most common symptoms of such neglect is a distorted spray pattern (Fig. 3-9). Even in suction-feed equipment, dried

SPRAY GUN TEST PATTERNS

CONDITION	CAUSE	CORRECTION
RIGHT	Correct Normal Pattern.	No Correction Necessary
 WRONG Heavy Top Or Bottom Pattern	1. Dirty or damaged air cap. 2. Dirty or damaged fluid tip.	1. Rotate air cap 180°. A. If pattern follows air cap, problem is in air cap. Clean and inspect. If pattern is not corrected, replacement is necessary. B. If pattern does not follow the air cap, the problem is in the fluid tip. Clean and inspect the tip for dried paint, dirt or damage. If the pattern is not corrected, replacement is necessary.
 WRONG Split Pattern	1. Air pressure too high for material viscosity being sprayed.	1. Reduce air pressure. 2. Increase material viscosity. 3. Pattern may also be corrected by narrowing fan size with spray width adjuster control knob.

SPRAY GUN TEST PATTERNS

CONDITION	CAUSE	CORRECTION
 WRONG	1. Dirty or distorted air horn holes. 2. Complete blockage of one air horn hole.	1. Rotate air cap 180°. A. If pattern follows air cap, clean and inspect the air horn holes. If horn holes are distorted replacement is necessary.
 WRONG Gun Spitting	1. Air getting into paint stream somewhere. *EXAMPLE:* Same symptoms as a siphon cup running out of paint.	1. Check and tighten fluid needle packing nut. 2. Tighten fluid tip. 3. Check fluid tip seat for damage. 4. Check siphon tube for crack. 5. Check for poor gun to cup seating.
Air Back Pressuring Into Cup	Excessive Air Blowing Back Into Cup.	1. Tighten fluid tip. 2. Check fluid tip seat. 3. Check for damaged fluid seat on tip or seat in gun head.

FIG 3-9 Distorted spray patterns.
(Sharpe Manufacturing Company)

paint can accumulate in or around nozzle and air cap openings. By restricting the passage of either air or paint, these accumulations can make it impossible for a spray gun to cover a surface evenly. Worse—dislodged unexpectedly by air or fluid pressure, they can make it necessary to sand an otherwise perfect finish. Spitting is another common sign of trouble. This condition occurs when air finds its way into the fluid passageways. A likely cause is a worn or loose fluid valve packing nut. Both these problems can waste a refinisher's time, effort, and materials—and both can be prevented.

Cleaning

The less time paint remains in or on a spray gun, the easier it is to remove. Fresh paint can simply be wiped from a gun's surface with a cloth moistened in thinner. Dried paint, on the other hand, may require soaking to dislodge or dissolve it. The best procedure, therefore, is to avoid dried paint by cleaning a spray gun immediately after use.

In some cases, however, even immediate cleaning may not be fast enough. The fast-drying materials used in refinishing virtually guarantee that blockages will occur, mostly in and around the air cap, nozzle, and fluid needle valve. To make matters worse, these parts are among the most sensitive in a spray gun. Precision made to fine tolerances, they can be easily damaged by careless cleaning. Three techniques in particular should be avoided.

1. *Never use metal cleaning implements or steel wool.* Nails, pieces of wire, welding tip cleaners, or drill bits are all the right size to remove paint from a blocked nozzle or air cap opening. Being metal themselves, however, they could also scratch or gouge the surfaces of these parts. This damage, in turn, could keep the parts from mating properly and cause spitting or other gun malfunctions. Steel wool used to clean paint from needle valves and flat surfaces could do similar damage.
2. *Avoid abrasive or corrosive cleaners.* These could eat into the spray gun body, ultimately doing the same kind of damage as steel wool or metal cleaning implements.
3. *Never soak a spray gun.* Soaking immerses parts of the gun that (a) are probably not dirty and (b) were never intended to be soaked in the first place. Prolonged exposure to solvent, for example, can swell gaskets and eat away packing nuts. The first could result in a leaking paint cup, the second in a trigger that seizes, or sticks.

FIG 3-10 Cleaning nozzle orifices. (The DeVilbiss Company)

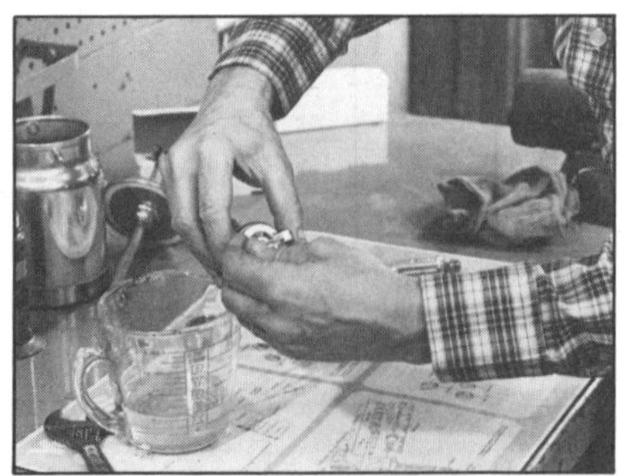

FIG 3-11 Soaking air cap in solvent. (The DeVilbiss Company)

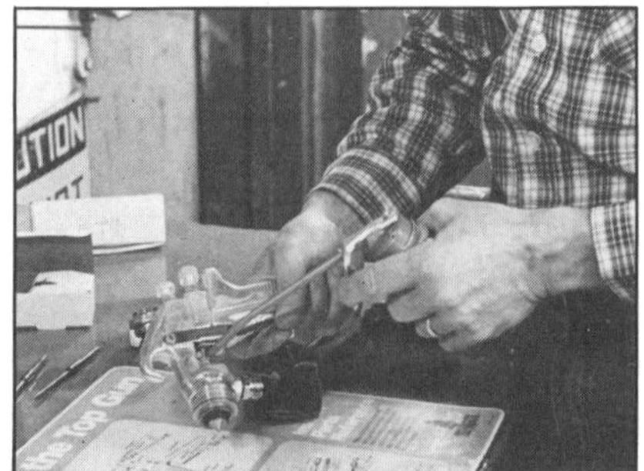

FIG 3-12 Lubing spray gun after cleaning. (The DeVilbiss Company)

The correct cleaning procedure makes only limited use of poking, soaking, and rubbing. It employs either thinner or a commercially produced gun cleaner. Both of these solvents are strong enough to remove paint. Neither damages underlying metal surfaces.

The actual cleaning process involves three basic steps: (1) forcing air back through the spray gun's fluid passageways, (2) running pure solvent through the system, and (3) wiping down the gun's exterior. Blocked orifices are cleared by scrubbing with a soft-bristle brush soaked in gun cleaner or thinner (Fig. 3-10). Stubborn blockages can be removed by soaking—only the part, however; not the gun. A clogged nozzle or air cap, for example, can be submerged for 10 to 15 minutes in a small amount of solvent and then blown dry with compressed air (Fig. 3-11).

Lubrication

For nonmoving parts of a spray gun, cleaning is the most important form of maintenance. For moving parts, lubrication is. How frequently this procedure is performed depends on how heavily a spray gun is used.

Failure to lubricate regularly can cause spray gun valves to stick. In addition, dried out packing nuts can allow air either to escape from places where it is needed (like behind the air control valve) or enter places where it is not (like the fluid inlet chamber). The former condition interferes with atomization of paint, the latter with its supply. Both can produce a spotted, uneven spray pattern.

Dismantling a gun for inspection and lubrication involves removing the trigger, all needle valves, the air cap, and the nozzle. All of these parts are then checked for wear, damage, and accumulations of dried paint. Lubrication is done with petroleum jelly or light machine oil. These are applied as the tool is reassembled or immediately after (Fig. 3-12). *Note:* Some parts, like the valve packing nuts, can be lubricated indirectly by applications of petroleum jelly to connecting parts.

Throughout this process, as with cleaning, there are precautions to be observed. Dismantling a spray gun for valve service exposes components at the back of the tool that are just as easily damaged as the nozzle and air cap at the front. Needle valves are especially sensitive to rough handling. Any action that might bend, nick, blunt, or abrade them should be avoided. Damage of this type to the fluid valve in particular could interfere with the fit between the valve tip and the nozzle. In that event, the needle valve would have to be replaced.

OBJECTIVE 3-A1 (manipulative)

Working as a team with one other student and with the aid of Job Report Sheet 3-A1, you will clean a suction-feed spray gun.

Time Recommended:

20 minutes

Preparation:

1. Review pages 85 through 95.
2. Study pages 95 through 97.
3. Read the Safety Checklist on page 126, items 1 through 4.

Tools and Materials:

1. Suction-feed spray gun that has been used for painting or a demonstration
2. Gun brush
3. Thinner or gun cleaner
4. Clean shop cloths
5. Respirator

Procedure:

1. Spread a clean shop cloth on a bench or other flat surface near a well-ventilated work station.
2. Place the spray gun on the cloth. Hold the cup firmly with one hand and, with the other, push the release lever counterclockwise until it feels loose. Let go of the release lever and grasp the cap assembly yoke. Turn it counterclockwise until the cap disconnects from the cup.
3. Slowly lift the gun until the cap is above the material level in the cup. Allow any paint that is in the siphon tube to drain back into the container.
4. Lay the gun and cap assembly on the cloth.
5. Pour the paint from the cup back into its can or into a similar storage container. Seal by pressing the lid into place.
6. Rinse the cup clean with thinner.
7. Using a cloth moistened with thinner, wipe all paint from the cap and siphon tube.
8. Pour ¼ to ½ cup of thinner into the spray gun container. Replace the cap assembly, making sure the yoke is securely fitted around the cup's connecting studs.
9. Loosen the spray gun's air cap approximately two turns. Be sure the fluid valve is fully open.
10. Put on the respirator.
11. Connect the spray gun to the transformer-regulator. Adjust the pressure to a setting of 45 psi (35 psi at the gun).
12. Hold the spray gun with outstretched arms. Be sure the cup vent is pointing away, toward the exhaust system paint arrestors or a ventilation source. Place a cloth over the gun's air cap and press hard. Trigger the spray gun and hold until air and thinner are forced out of the vent. Repeat this procedure four or five times.
13. Add ½ pint of thinner to the spray gun cup. Tighten the air cap. Point the spray gun toward the exhaust system and pull the trigger. Release when all of the thinner has been expelled.
14. Disconnect the gun from the transformer-regulator.
15. Moisten a cloth with thinner and wipe down the spray gun to remove any traces of paint. If necessary, use a gun brush and thinner to clean crevices, seams, and sharp angles.
16. Give the spray gun a final wipedown with a clean, dry cloth.
17. Place all paint-covered rags in a metal safety container until they can be disposed of properly.

SUCTION-FEED SPRAY GUN (CLEANING)

Student Name ______________________ Date ____________

Time Started ____________ Time Finished ____________ Total Time ____________

Specifications

Spray gun manufacturer ______________ Model ______________

Features: No-drip cup ______ Yes ______ No

Pressure gauge ______ Yes ______ No

Technique

Cleaning solvent: Thinner ______ Gun cleaner ______

Checkup Questions

1. Reducer is not used for cleaning spray guns. Why? ______________________________

____

____

2. In the space below, sketch:
   a. a front view of the spray gun's air cap. (Show the location of all orifices and indicate which ones pass paint and which ones pass air.)
   b. the no-drip feature of the spray gun's cup, if present. (Use arrows to show the flow of air into the cup.)

Date Completed ______________ Instructor's Signature ______________________

OBJECTIVE 3-A2 (manipulative)

Working as a team with one other student and with the aid of Job Report Sheet 3-A2, you will disassemble and lubricate a suction-feed spray gun.

Time Recommended:

45 minutes

Preparation:

1. Review pages 85 through 97.
2. Study pages 99 through 102.

Tools and Materials:

1. Suction-feed spray gun
2. Gun wrench
3. Screwdriver (optional)
4. Petroleum jelly and light machine oil
5. Clean shop cloths

Procedure:

1. Spread a clean shop cloth on a bench or other flat surface. As each part is removed from the spray gun, place it on the cloth in order. The sequence of parts can then serve as a guide for reassembly.
2. Place the spray gun on the bench. Use the gun wrench to loosen the nut above the cap assembly yoke. Disconnect the cup-and-cap assembly from the gun.
3. Loosen the spray gun's air cap by turning its retaining ring counterclockwise. Keep turning the ring until the part comes free. *Note:* When lifting the air cap from the gun, be careful not to bump or knock the nozzle. Its thin fluid tip extends through the air cap and is easily damaged.
4. Carefully place the gun wrench over the hex nut that holds the nozzle in position. Loosen the nut about one turn. Remove the wrench and complete separation of the nozzle by hand. Once again, be extremely careful not to bump, knock, or drop the part.
5. Remove the spreader valve from the back of the gun. Turn the adjustment screw counterclockwise until the valve needle can be withdrawn.
6. Using the gun wrench, loosen and remove the hex nut in which the spreader valve needle sits.
7. Remove the fluid adjustment screw. Turn the screw by hand until it comes free.
8. Carefully trigger the spray gun with one hand and catch the valve spring with the other as the part is forced from the valve opening at the back of the gun.
9. Using the gun wrench or a screwdriver, remove the trigger bearing screw (or nut) and the trigger. Note that the fluid and air control valve packing nuts located between the front of the gun and the handle are now fully exposed.

10. Using the gun wrench, loosen and remove the hex nut in which the fluid valve needle sits.
11. Working from the rear of the spray gun and using the gun wrench, loosen and remove the packing nut through which the fluid needle passes. Turn the nut counterclockwise until it is free. Then carefully push the fluid needle toward the back of the gun until the packing nut can be slipped off by hand.
12. Fully remove the fluid needle from the opening at the back.
13. Using the gun wrench, loosen the packing nut holding the air control valve in place. (This part is located at the front of the handle.) Remove both the packing nut and the valve needle.
14. Inspect all threaded openings in the spray gun body. Be sure that they are in good condition. Use Job Report Sheet 3-A2 to note damage, wear, or the presence of foreign material.
15. Inspect the fluid needle valve parts spread out on the cloth. Check the packing nut for cracks. Note if the valve needle is showing signs of wear or if it has been bent.
16. Reinsert the fluid valve needle in the gun body. Once the needle has penetrated the handle, slip the packing nut onto its point. Continue pushing the needle through to the front of the gun.
17. Push the nut into position over the fluid valve packing. Screw the nut in by hand and finish with the gun wrench. *Note:* Avoid excessive tightening with the wrench.
18. Inspect the fluid valve spring. Using one finger, apply a thin coat of petroleum jelly or light machine oil to the part. *Note:* Be sure that none of the grease contacts any other parts of the spray gun.
19. Working from the back of the gun, place the spring over the needle and push it into the valve housing. Press the adjustment screw into place and turn until all the threads are in the gun body.
20. Inspect the air control valve parts. Check the packing nut for cracks. Note if the valve needle is showing signs of wear or if it has been bent.
21. Reinsert the air control valve needle in the front of the handle. Slip the packing nut over the needle and push it into place. Screw the nut in by hand and tighten it with the gun wrench. Again, do not overtighten.
22. Reinstall the trigger. Tighten the bearing screw (or nut).
23. Inspect the spreader valve parts. Note if the valve needle is showing any signs of wear or if it has been bent.
24. Using the gun wrench, reinstall the spreader valve hex nut. Then reinsert the valve needle through it. Screw the needle in by hand.
25. Inspect the nozzle. Note any wear, cracks, or chips in the fluid tip.
26. Install the nozzle by hand. Use the gun wrench to finish tightening the hex nut that holds the part in place.
27. Inspect the air cap. Check all orifices for blockages.
28. Slip the air cap over the nozzle and tighten the retaining ring.
29. Using the thumb and forefinger of one hand, rub a small amount of petroleum jelly or oil onto the shaft of the air control valve needle. Trigger the gun and lubricate the fluid valve needle.
30. Place a drop of light machine oil on the trigger bearing. Be sure not to drip oil on other parts of the spray gun. Wipe away any excess with a clean shop cloth.

SUCTION-FEED SPRAY GUN (DISASSEMBLY AND LUBRICATION)

Student Name ______________________ Date ____________

Time Started ____________ Time Finished ____________ Total Time ____________

Specifications

Spray gun manufacturer ____________ Model ____________

Parts: Nozzle identification number ______

Air cap identification number ______

Technique

Inspection:	*Good*	*Worn*	*Damaged*	*Dirty*
Body threads	______	______	______	______
Fluid needle	______	______	______	______
Fluid packing nut	______	______	______	______
Air control valve needle	______	______	______	______
Air control valve packing nut	______	______	______	______
Spreader valve needle	______	______	______	______
Nozzle	______	______	______	______
Air cap	______	______	______	______
Trigger bearing	______	______	______	______

Lubrication:

Fluid valve spring	Yes ______	No ______
Fluid valve needle/packing nut	Yes ______	No ______
Air control valve needle/packing nut	Yes ______	No ______
Trigger	Yes ______	No ______

Checkup Questions

1. What is the only spray gun part that receives lubrication while the gun is disassembled? ____________________

2. How does the procedure described in step 29 lubricate the air and fluid valve packings and packing nuts? ____________________

____

____

Why couldn't this procedure be carried out before the valve needles were installed?

____

____

____

3. Where are the identification numbers found on the following parts?

   a. Air cap ____________________

   b. Nozzle ____________________

Date Completed ____________ Instructor's Signature ____________

PRESSURE-FEED EQUIPMENT

The pressure-feed spray gun is a type found less frequently in refinishing shops. It is used mainly in factories where either the sheer number of vehicles or their size creates a demand for large quantities of color. Pressure-feed equipment can meet this demand because its paint container ranges in size from 2 quarts up to 55 gallons. Such containers cannot, of course, be hand held. Paint is delivered to the gun the same way air is—through a hose. The presence of this second hose (as opposed to a cup-and-cap assembly) is what distinguishes a pressure-feed spray gun from a suction-feed spray gun (Fig. 3-13).

Design and Operation

Pressure-feed equipment is designed to succeed where suction-feed equipment fails in some major respect. These situations include three types of refinishing jobs.

1. *Whole vehicles.* The limited capacity of the suction-feed cup means that a whole vehicle cannot be refinished without the painter's stopping for frequent refills. This stop-and-go procedure increases the possibility of a color mismatch resulting from an altered spray gun technique or inadequately mixed paint.
2. *Production work.* The extra weight of the cup and its contents is usually not a problem with individual repairs. Where a suction-feed gun is used for production or assembly line work, however, that extra weight can become a major source of strain and fatigue.
3. *Sharply angled surfaces.* Because of its cup, a suction-feed gun has a limited range of operating positions. It cannot, for example, be inverted to paint the underside of a vehicle. In that position, the bottom of the siphon tube would be above the fluid level, and the paint flow would stop.

By removing the paint container from the refinisher's hand, pressure-feed equipment solves all of these problems. The spray gun can be moved easily and freely; the separate, or remote, tank can have virtually any capacity; and the paint supply can be pressure fed rather than siphoned. This last feature, of course, is the one that gives pressure-feed equipment its name.

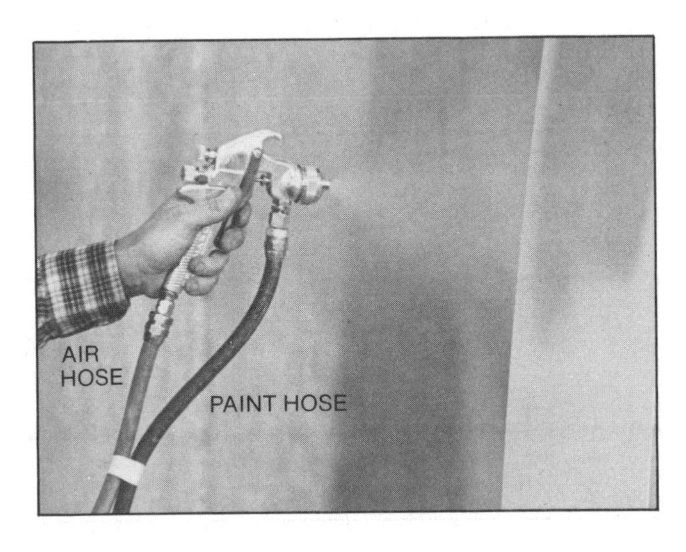

FIG 3-13
Pressure-feed spray gun.
(The DeVilbiss Company)

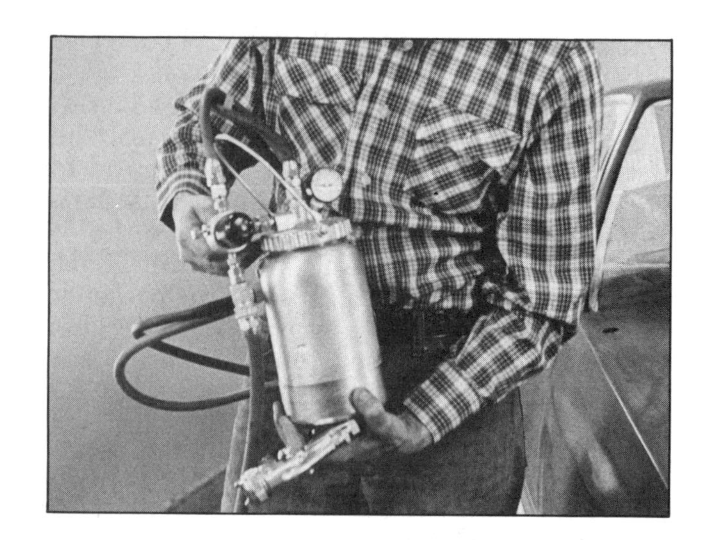

FIG 3-14
Portable pressure pot. (The DeVilbiss Company)

Pressure Pot

A remote tank is sometimes called a pressure pot. It is a much more complex assembly than the suction-feed gun's cup and cap. Use of a separate pot regulator means that instead of just a one-way tube for paint, there must be additional inlet and outlet connections for air. In the case of the larger pots, clamps to hold the cover firmly in place are also necessary. Despite all of this extra gear, some pots (the smaller ones) are still portable (Fig. 3-14). Usually they are equipped with hooks or handles so that they can be held, hung, or simply placed at a convenient location near the vehicle being painted. The larger tanks are, of course, stationary.

In use, the pot regulator divides the air flow coming from the transformer. Through one outlet it passes air to the spray gun at "line" pressure. This air is used to atomize the paint. Through another outlet it passes air at a lower psi to the paint pot. This air is used to pressurize the container and push the paint into the spray gun (Fig. 3-15). Thus, in pressure-feed equipment, the paint flows at a rate that is unaffected by the amount of air the spray gun is drawing. This fact, in turn, means that the amount of paint fed through the gun is closer to the minimum required for good coverage.

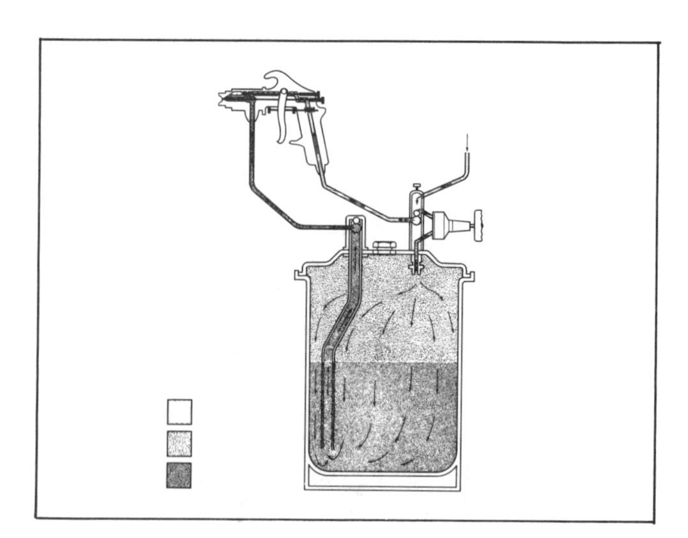

FIG 3-15
Paint and air flows in a pressure-feed system. (The DeVilbiss Company)

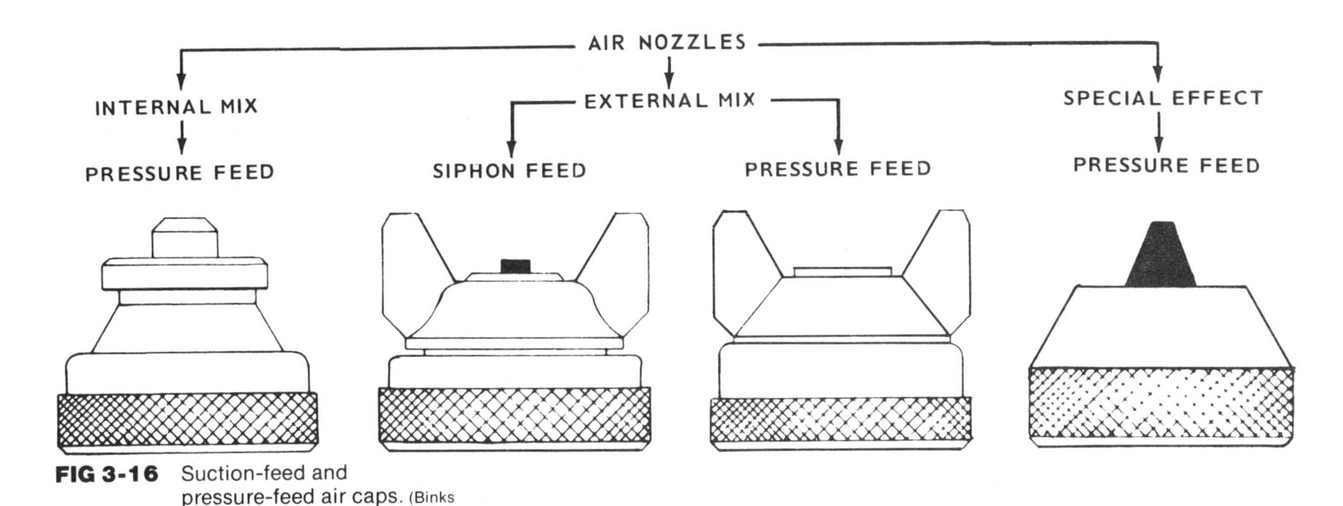

FIG 3-16 Suction-feed and pressure-feed air caps. (Binks Manufacturing Company)

Note that paint flow cannot be so accurately controlled with suction-feed equipment. With it, there is a direct relationship between the pressure set at the transformer-regulator and the paint flow. The higher the pressure, the faster the air emerges from the gun. The faster the air emerges, the greater the pressure drop at the nozzle. The greater the pressure drop at the nozzle, the more paint is siphoned from the paint cup.

Air Cap

Both pressure-feed and suction-feed systems use the same spray gun. Only the air cap is different. Since the paint in a remote tank is under pressure, there is no need to create or maintain a partial vacuum at the spray gun nozzle. The paint does not have to be drawn from the container, and the air supply does not have to lead it. Thus there is no reason for the nozzle tip to extend out into the path of the air jets. It can be, and in fact is, flush with the surrounding surface (Fig. 3-16). All other cap features are the same, including the number and location of air orifices and the presence and positioning of the air horns.

Maintenance

Service and maintenance procedures for pressure-feed equipment are essentially the same as for suction-feed equipment. The major difference is in their extent. Pressure-feed equipment, being larger, requires more cleaning. Paint pots are larger than paint cups. Fluid hoses are longer than siphon tubes. These facts mean that cleanups will take both more time and more solvent.

The fluid hose in particular complicates the cleaning process. Its presence means that air and solvent must be forced far greater distances back through the entire system. Thorough cleaning, therefore, depends on repeated flushings. The process, however, can be shortened by using a commercial hose cleaner (Fig. 3-17). This device, essentially a pressure pot with solvent, force-cleans hoses at higher psi's than hand cleaning allows. Whenever such equipment is available, it should be used. *Note:* A hose cleaner is intended for use on hoses only. Spray guns should be cleaned first, separately, and disconnected. The hose cleaner can then be used on the remainder of the system.

FIG 3-17
Commercial hose cleaner in use. (The DeVilbiss Company)

SPRAY PAINTING TECHNIQUE

The labels on many refinishing tools and materials warn that they are intended for use by professionals only. Nowhere is the truth behind that warning more apparent than with the spray gun. In the hands of a professional, the tool can look as easy to use as a paintbrush. That appearance, however, is misleading. Spray painting is not simply a matter of moving a spray gun back and forth, making one pass after another until, hit or miss, everything is covered with paint. It is a complicated technique involving careful attention to a half dozen different variables. The spray gun must first be adjusted, then positioned, then moved, and only then triggered. Its speed, distance, and angle must all be maintained. A special painting sequence must be followed. To cope with all of these factors at once takes practice. To start, it is best to approach them one by one.

Adjusting the Gun

Adjusting a spray gun is mainly a matter of regulating paint and air flows, both those to the gun and those within it. The process starts with the adjustment screw on the transformer-regulator. It must be turned in until the desired psi for the gun registers on its gauge. On the gun itself, the air cap horns must be positioned for a vertical pattern, the fluid adjustment valve at least partially opened, and the air adjustment screw turned till the correct degree of atomization is achieved.

Setting the Psi

Two factors determine the pressure set at the transformer-regulator: (1) the kind of equipment being used and (2) the nature of the material being sprayed. Generally, pressure-feed equipment takes a lower psi. The reason is that such equipment forces paint only a short distance through the narrow passageways of the gun. Suction-feed equipment, on the other hand, forces air all the way through the gun's interior to create a partial vacuum at the nozzle which in turn pulls the paint from its container. Clearly, the suction-feed system is much less direct. It therefore requires more pressure for its operation—usually at least 10 psi more.

The second factor affecting the transformer-regulator setting is the material being sprayed. The best advice here is to consult the container label for the manufacturer's recommendations. At least two rules, however, apply across the full range of products and manufacturers.

1. *Use lower psi's for spot repairs than for panel or overall refinishing* (Table 3-1). This technique reduces overspray in situations where it is most likely to cause problems. Overspray occurs when particles of atomized paint are dispersed in the air and fall back onto either the new finish or some portion of the vehicle not being painted. The result, in the case of the new finish, is a granular layer of color that will not flow or blend into the paint below it.
2. *Use lower pressures for lacquers than for enamels* (Table 3-1). In general, heavier, more viscous materials require higher psi's. Lacquers are thicker than enamels, but they are also reduced much more. Thus the material that is eventually sprayed has a somewhat thinner consistency and can take a lower psi. How much lower? For spot repairs, the difference is slight—about 5 psi. For panel repairs and overall refinishing, however, it can be as much as 20 psi.

Table 3-1 RECOMMENDED TRANSFORMER-REGULATOR PRESSURES*

	Type of Repair	
Type of Paint	Spot	Panel or Whole Vehicle
Acrylic lacquer	25–35 psi	35–45 psi
Enamel:		
Alkyd	30–40 psi	55–65 psi
Acrylic	30–40 psi	55–65 psi
Polyurethane	30–40 psi	50–65 psi

*With a 50-foot hose

Regulating Fluid and Air Flows

The flow of air and paint inside a spray gun is regulated by the adjustment screws above the handle. Turning these screws counterclockwise opens the paint and spreader valves. Specifically, it pulls the spring-loaded valve needles back from the passageways in which they are seated. The effect at the screws is one of tightening.

The two adjustment valves operate in tandem, but they do not start from the same point. The spreader valve, when fully closed, still passes air through its center orifices. The fluid valve, when fully closed, passes nothing. Therefore, the fluid valve must be opened first. With a minimal paint flow thus established, the ideal positions for both adjustment screws can be determined.

Proper adjustment is judged at the panel surface. Even paint applied with a spray gun shows a certain amount of roughness and irregularity, the pattern of thousands of atomized droplets hitting the metal. If a spray gun is properly adjusted, however, these irregularities will smooth themselves out, blending into one continuous liquid finish. This leveling process is called flowing.

Finding the adjustment screw positions at which the paint will flow is usually a matter of trial and error. If a test spraying produces drips and sags, for example, the refinisher knows that the fluid valve is probably open too far (Fig. 3-18). (There is too much material for the amount of air being passed.) The solution is either to decrease the paint

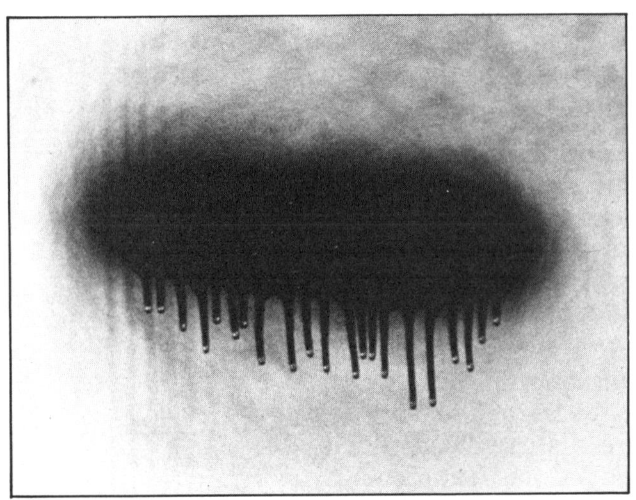

FIG 3-18 Drips in paint. (The DeVilbiss Company)

FIG 3-19 Close-up of dry spray. (Jay Storer)

supply or increase the air flow. If the test spraying produces a rough, granular surface that does not flow, the air valve is probably open too far. The result at the panel is a condition called dry spray (Fig. 3-19). (There is so much air that the paint dries before it hits the surface.) The solution is to increase the paint supply or decrease the air flow. *Note:* Dry spray, like virtually all painting problems, has many causes. A poorly adjusted spray gun is only one. Other possibilities include poor maintenance (a blocked vent in a suction-feed cap assembly, a partially blocked nozzle, a dirty fluid valve needle) and improper paint preparation (using an insufficiently reduced paint or a thinner that is too fast for shop conditions). What all of these conditions have in common is that they reduce paint flow while leaving the air supply unaffected.

The range within which paint and air flows can remain in balance without slipping over into dry spray or sagging is quite small. Once the two adjustment screws are set, their positions relative to each other must be maintained. A change in one adjustment, in other words, usually requires a change in the other.

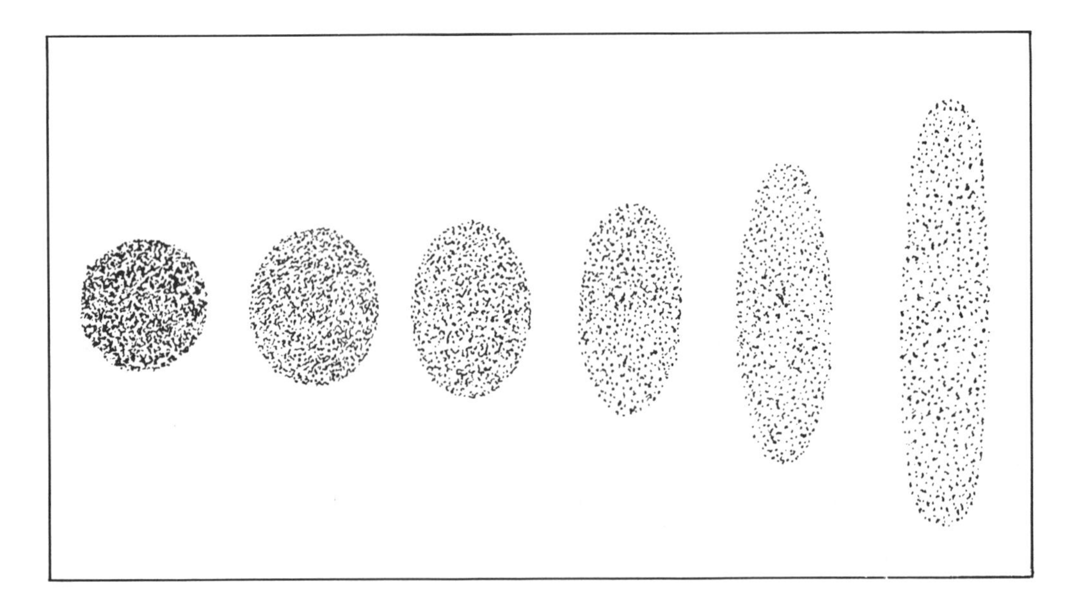

FIG 3-20
Spray patterns as affected by spreader valve. (Binks Manufacturing Company)

Selecting the Spray Pattern

The adjustment screws are also used in combination with the air cap to set the size and shape of the spray pattern. When both air and fluid valves are slightly open, the pattern produced is a circle approximately 3 inches in diameter. Advancing both screws by the same amount enlarges this circle to an oval. Advancing the screws still farther—to a point where both valves are more or less fully open—produces an extremely elongated oval some 12 inches high (Fig. 3-20).

Technically, of course, the oval could just as easily be 12 inches wide. The alignment of the spray pattern is determined by the air cap. If it is positioned with its horns in a vertical plane, the spray pattern will be just the opposite—horizontal (Fig. 3-21). If it is positioned with its horns in a horizontal plane, as it most often is in refinishing, the result will be a vertical pattern. Rotating the air cap 90 degrees in this manner in no way affects the atomization of the paint or its ability to flow once it reaches the surface.

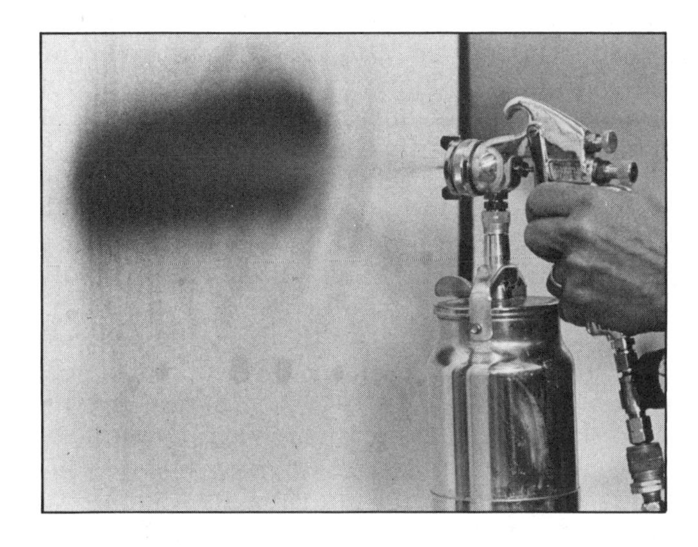

FIG 3-21
A vertical air cap gives a horizontal pattern. (The DeVilbiss Company)

Moving the Gun

Except for some preliminary strokes to band in panels, a spray gun has two basic moves—left to right and right to left. This limited range of movement guarantees that painting will progress in an orderly fashion. The refinisher can keep track of the number of paint applications at any point on the work surface. He can plan his painting sequence to avoid waste and foresee where overspray might be a problem. Mainly, however, with his basic moves reduced to so few, he can concentrate on the critical variables of positioning and speed. These are among the most difficult aspects of spray painting. Without mastering them, it is not possible to produce even minimally acceptable work.

Maintaining Distance

The ideal distance for applying automotive paint varies with the type of paint being used. For lacquers, a range of 6 to 8 inches is best; for enamels, 8 to 10 inches (Fig. 3-22). Any closer and the materials go on too thick or too wet. The result is dripping or sagging. Any farther and the opposite effect occurs. The paint, as it travels the extra distance to the surface, dries, producing the familiar gritty finish associated with

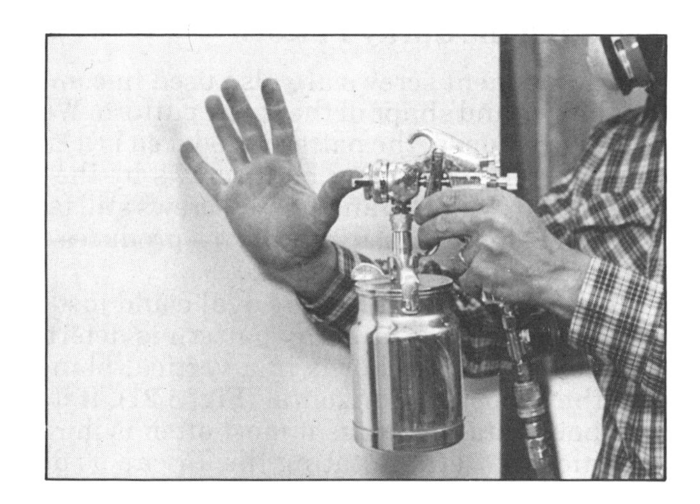

FIG 3-22
Judging distance from panel. A handspread is about 8 inches. (The DeVilbiss Company)

dry spray. When the paint does not dry in midair, the added distance often means that less material is actually deposited on the surface. The atomized particles are dispersed or otherwise fall short of the panel. The result is starved paint film. Unlike dry spray, this condition is not characterized by any roughness. The paint does flow. There is just not enough of it to cover the surface fully or evenly (Figs. 3-23A and B).

If a spray gun could be held in one spot, maintaining the correct distance would present no problem. Once the paint flow is established, however, the tool must be kept moving in order to avoid flooding any portion of the panel. That movement, in turn, can create as many problems as it solves, particularly if it is accomplished by mere wrist action.

Using the wrist to wave a spray gun from side to side is sometimes called fanning. Fanning has the effect of changing the gun's distance from the work surface. At the center of each stroke, the nozzle is relatively close to the panel. At either end, it is farther away. These positions follow the action of the wrist, which moves in an arc.

The technical name for this common spray painting mistake is, in fact, arcing. In a finish, it produces an easily recognized pattern—normal paint application at the center, dry spray at either end (Fig. 3-24). It is avoided by (1) using the whole arm rather than just the wrist to move the spray gun and (2) concentrating on distance through the full length of each stroke.

FIG 3-23A Spraying too near. (The DeVilbiss Company)

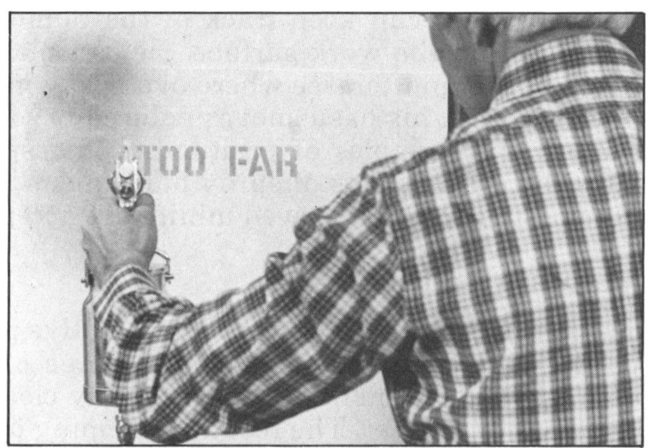

FIG 3-23B Spraying too far. (The DeVilbiss Company)

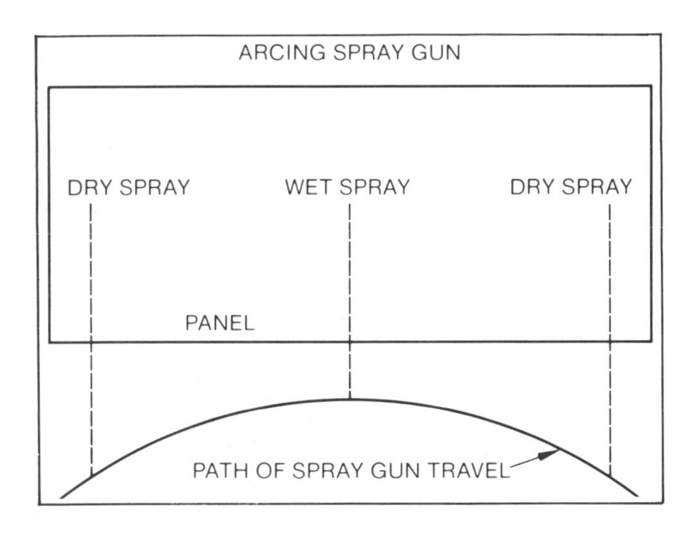

FIG 3-24
Results of severe arcing: overwetting at the center and dry spray at each end.

Maintaining Angle

There is only one proper angle between spray gun and work surface—a right, or 90-degree, angle (Fig. 3-25). This is the angle that exists when the tool is pointed directly at a vertical panel from an eye-level position. Unfortunately, a refinisher seldom works at eye level. Usually he approaches a panel from above and tilts the gun forward to compensate. If he misjudges and tilts the gun too far, the result at the surface is a band of color that is top heavy—wet and thick above, dry and thin below. A whole panel finished in this manner appears striped, a condition called zebra effect (Fig. 3-26).

Tilting thus produces horizontally the same result that arcing produces vertically. The reasons also are the same. Tilting, too, is wrist action. It, however, is action up or down rather than from side to side. When the spray gun is tilted forward opposite a vertical panel, the upper portion of the gun is closer to the work surface. The upper portion of the spray pattern thus receives more paint. The lower portion of the pattern, being farther from the gun, receives less. (If the gun is tilted back, of course, the heavy and light portions of the spray pattern are reversed.)

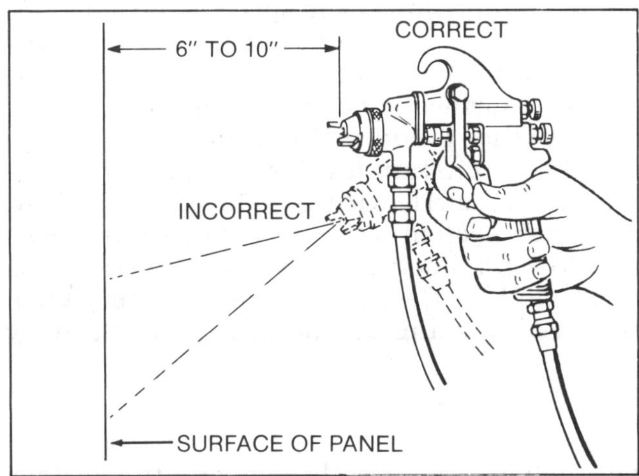

FIG 3-25 Hold the gun perpendicular to the surface being sprayed. (Binks Manufacturing Company)

FIG 3-26 Zebra effect. (David Keown)

FIG 3-27A Spraying too slow. (The DeVilbiss Company)

FIG 3-27B Spraying too fast. (The DeVilbiss Company)

The only way to avoid zebra effect is to hold the spray gun absolutely perpendicular to the surface being painted. This position is easy to judge for vertical and horizontal panels. Curved surfaces, however, are more difficult. They require a whole series of judgments on angle rather than just one. As panel contours change, the tilt of the gun must change with them. What would be an error when painting a vertical or horizontal panel—changing the angle between strokes—thus becomes an essential element of technique when painting a sloped or curved surface.

Maintaining Speed

The proper speed for a spray gun is the one that allows the paint to flow once it is applied to a surface. What that rate is depends largely on the fluid volume for which the gun is adjusted. The more material the fluid valve passes, the greater the speed necessary.

Varying this speed, once determined, causes many of the problems already discussed. If the speed is too fast, the extra turbulence dries or scatters the atomized paint before it reaches the surface. The result at the panel is dry spray or starved paint film. If the speed is too slow, too much paint is applied. The finish takes too long to dry, increasing the risk of drips and sags (Figs. 3-27A and B). Varying stroke speed from one pass to the next alternates these surface conditions. The result is an uneven or striped finish similar to that produced by tilting.

Maintaining spray gun speed at a constant level is primarily a matter of experience. To start, it is best to work with a reduced paint flow. Learning to control all the other system variables inevitably slows down the pace of painting. A low fluid setting can better tolerate this decrease in speed without any visible effect at the panel. Later, when the other techniques are mastered, picking up the pace is a relatively easy matter.

Triggering the Gun

A spray gun is triggered only when it is directly opposite the surface being painted. Thus, as he moves back and forth across a panel, a refinisher triggers his gun not once but many times.

The main virtue of this technique is that it reduces waste. A spray gun (especially a suction-feed model) consumes large amounts of paint. If the fluid valve is kept open continuously, a substantial amount of this material is deposited off panel. It lands on masking paper or is dispersed in the air as the gun's direction is reversed. In either case, it contributes nothing to the new finish. In fact, it can further damage the old one if the overspray extends beyond the masked portions of the vehicle. The result is a far more extensive refinishing job.

Basic Technique

The spray gun is positioned and the painting stroke begun about 6 inches off to one side of the panel. The trigger is pulled only when the panel edge is reached. Once depressed, the trigger is held in that position as the gun is drawn across the surface, then released at the far edge. The stroke is continued for 6 inches beyond the panel edge, reversed smoothly, and the whole sequence repeated going in the opposite direction (Fig. 3-28).

The most important point to remember is that each time the trigger is pulled it must be fully depressed. Failure to do so produces an area of dry spray at the panel edge, an area that gradually blends into normal coverage. This kind of flaw in a new finish is a sure sign that the paint flow was not fully established when the pass was begun.

Alternate Technique

It is possible to minimize the danger of making this mistake by slightly modifying the basic triggering technique. Instead of releasing the trigger fully at the far panel edge, the painter can ease back to the point where only the paint flow is cut off. (The air control valve remains open and continues to pass air through the gun.) This partial release shortens the gun's response time. Since the trigger is held closer to its contact point with the fluid valve, triggering at the panel edge becomes much more exact. *Note:* For the new spray painter, initially it will probably feel more natural to release the trigger fully.

STROKE SEQUENCE

The two basic strokes used by most automobile refinishers are simple and useful whether refinishing a single panel or an entire automobile body. They are banding and the 50-percent overlap.

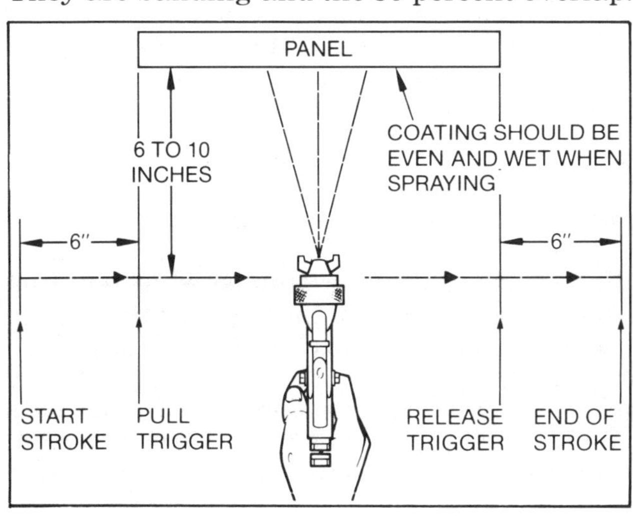

FIG 3-28
Triggering action.

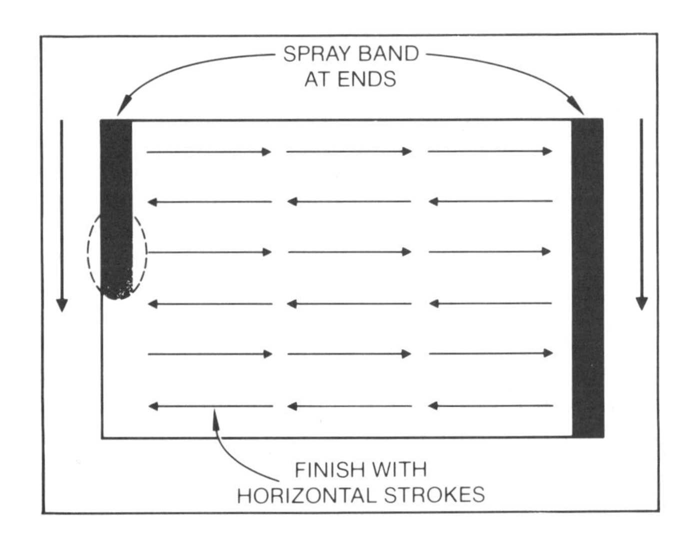

FIG 3-29
Banding a panel.

Banding

Banding is a technique sometimes used when refinishing a single panel. It simply means that the panel's edges are the first parts painted (Fig. 3-29). This places enough paint on the edge of the panel so that when the painter triggers his spray gun on and off at the beginning and end of each stroke, the edges of the panel receive sufficient paint even if the painter triggers on or off too early or too late.

When banding a panel, point the spray gun's air cap at the panel's edge. Make a single stroke approximately 3 inches wide along that edge, carefully following the contour of the panel with the spray gun so that a consistent distance is maintained between the gun and the panel surface. When banding is used, every edge of the panel being painted should be banded. When painting a panel that can be completely covered using horizontal strokes, however, some painters band only the ends of the panel.

In addition to insuring that the ends of the panel are well covered, banding also eliminates some panel overspray because it relieves the painter of the necessity of continuing his stroke all the way off the edge of the panel.

At one General Motors plant, car roofs, at their windshield and rear-window openings, are banded with a pressure-feed gun just before the car body is moved into line to be painted by the plant's automatic spray system, insuring that the edges of these roof openings get a good coat of paint.

The 50-Percent Overlap

When beginning to paint a panel, the direction of the first stroke doesn't matter. What does matter is that the return stroke, or back stroke, must lap halfway into the preceding stroke. This is accomplished by pointing the center of the gun's paint pattern at the edge of the pattern made by the preceding stroke and is called 50-percent overlap (Fig. 3-30). This is done to maintain a uniform coating thickness. A 50-percent overlap actually could be considered two coats in one, but is called a single coat because it is applied in one single spray application. Note that a coat with a very small overlap may be used for a first coat, or tack coat, when spraying alkyd enamel.

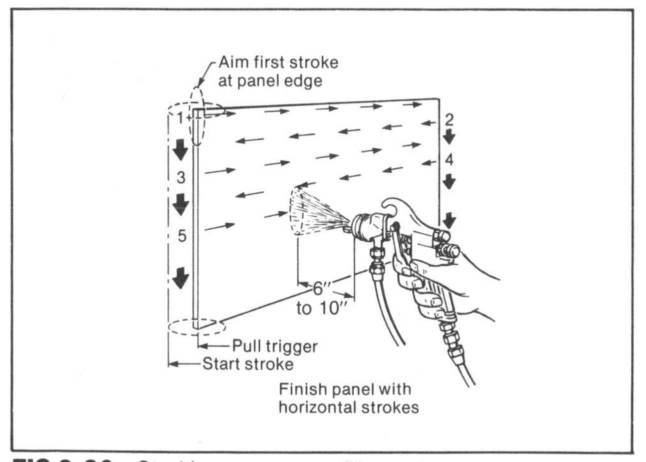

FIG 3-30 Stroking spray gun with 50-percent overlap. (Binks Manufacturing Company)

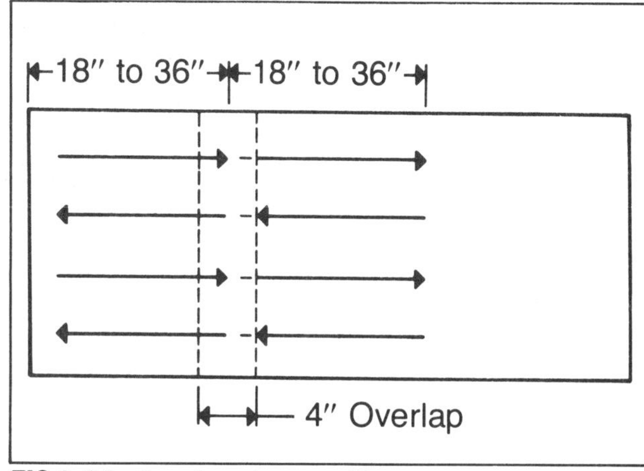

FIG 3-31 Spraying a long panel in separate sections. (Binks Manufacturing Company)

Most painters begin their strokes from the top of the panel they're working on. A right-handed painter would start at the top-right corner, a left-handed painter would start at the top-left. Each then would move the gun from his starting point to the opposite edge of the panel.

When dealing with long panels, the painter may choose to spray while walking from one end of the panel to the other, maintaining a uniform speed and distance between the spray gun and the panel. Or he may spray the panel in separate sections from 18 to 36 inches in length, lapping into the edge of each painted section approximately 4 inches when painting the next section (Fig. 3-31). Both methods work equally well, and painters usually choose the system which works most comfortably for them.

Creases, Corners and Curved Surfaces

An entire crease or corner should not be sprayed in one stroke (Fig. 3-32). Rather, each of the panels that meet to form the crease or corner should be sprayed separately as though the painter is banding that end of the panel (Fig. 3-33). Spraying a corner square-on will result in a buildup of material that is not uniform, with the areas of the corner closest to the spray getting more paint than the areas farther from the gun.

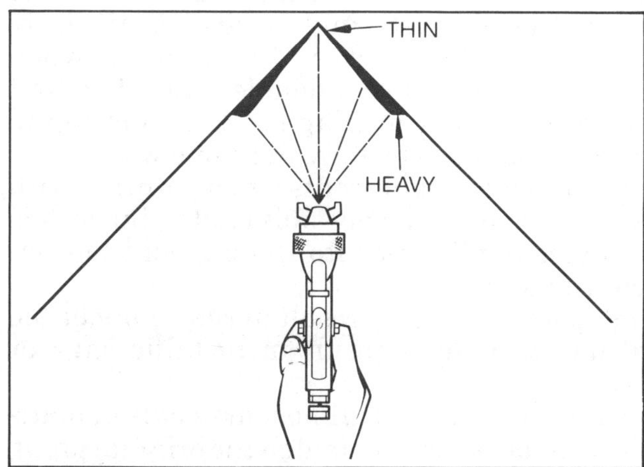

FIG 3-32 Spraying directly into a corner results in an uneven coating.

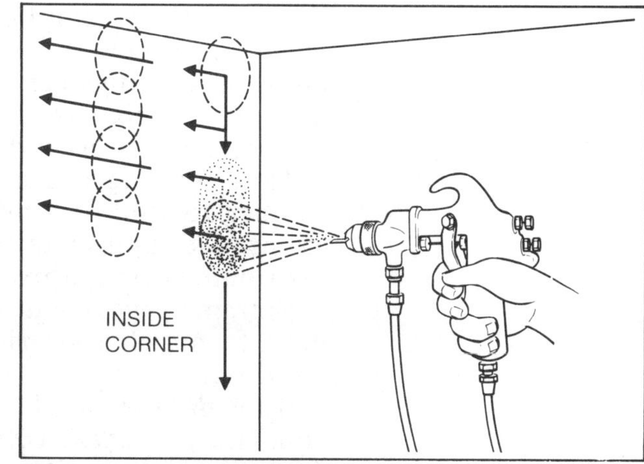

FIG 3-33 Spraying a corner to get an even coating, using a vertical spray pattern.

When spraying curved surfaces, the gun must be held at a constant distance from the panel as you paint and it must be tilted or tipped with the panel's contours so that it is kept square with the panel's surface.

CONTROL TECHNIQUES

The spray gun's speed of travel, its fluid adjustment, the air pressure, and the distance of the gun from the panel all determine the wetness of the coat. To choose the proper values from among these variables, the painter must paint a test panel and make adjustments as necessary.

Increasing the distance from the spray gun and the panel lightens the color, and decreasing that distance darkens the color. Increasing the speed of the stroke lightens the color, decreasing the speed of the stroke darkens the color. Increasing the air pressure lightens the color, and decreasing the air pressure darkens it.

Number of Coats Required

The number of coats of paint needed to adequately coat a panel is determined by the type of material being used. No matter what kind of material the painter is using, a minimum of two coats is required to produce enough depth to determine if the color will match the original coat. With lacquer, a minimum of five coats is required to make the same determination. Most acrylic enamels require at least three coats. Alkyd enamel may produce a long-lasting match with just two coats.

The properties of the binders used in the various kinds of paints are what account for the differences in the number of coats required for a match. Binders have a property called "hold-out" which is the binder's ability to suspend the pigment in the paint when it becomes solid, or dry, to produce a lasting finish. Binders shrink inwards as they dry and harden, thus the thinner the coat of paint, the more coats required to produce a lasting, matching finish.

Coats of Paint

A single coat of paint is one coat applied to a panel, overlapping each stroke by 50 percent. The speed of the stroke determines the wetness of the coat. Some painters use extremely wet single coats, particularly when painting with lacquer, by using slow strokes. Others, again, when painting with lacquer, prefer to use medium-wet double coats. The first medium-wet coat is sprayed in 50-percent overlap strokes from top to bottom, and the second is sprayed again in exactly the same way.

The advantages of using medium-wet double coats when painting with lacquer are that flowing time is increased, the possibility of paint runs is eliminated, and metallic particles don't sink into the pigment but are distributed evenly throughout the paint film.

Extremely wet coats, on the other hand, may result in runs, may be too dark to match the original paint, or may result in metallic sags or mottling.

Some painters apply lacquer with many fast, almost dry coats of material. This produces a color film that is too light to match the original paint. And if a metallic is involved, the outermost paint film will show an extreme amount of metallic and very little color. When sprayed this way, colors that do not have metallic will be lacking in binder depth. In either case, the hold-out of the color will be poor.

A full-wet coat of paint is achieved when the speed of the stroke is slowed down to obtain the greatest amount of depth of color and flowing. This is the type of coat used for the second coat when spraying an enamel job. As with a medium-wet coat, the 50-percent overlap is used. Only the speed of the stroke is changed. Application of a full-wet second coat of enamel usually is used to build color depth. This type of coat rarely is used in color matching except when color matching an enamel-finished car.

A full-wet coat of enamel usually is followed by a mist coat, or fog coat. The material is greatly reduced, and a retarder may be mixed into the material to increase the flowing of the material already on the panel. This coat is applied with a fast stroke. The width of the pattern is increased because the material is so much thinner. The gun is held at least 12 inches from the panel when painting this coat.

When spraying alkyd enamel, the normal procedure is to apply a mist coat, or tack coat, as a first coat. This is necessary because of the long flowing time of alkyd enamel. One quart of material, properly reduced, may cover the entire surface on some cars. Because it is so thin, there would be very little flowing of this coat of paint—to some extent it is thin enough to see through. But it also is wet enough to adhere well to a panel surface and form a bond. It dries enough in 20 to 30 minutes to allow application of a wet coat. The wet coat consists of approximately three quarts of reduced material applied with a stroke of standard speed.

Pattern Sizes

Lacquer should be sprayed with a pattern not more than 6 inches wide nor less than 5 inches wide with the gun held 6 inches from the panel. Enamel should be sprayed with a pattern no less than 8 inches wide at an 8-inch distance and no more than 10 inches wide at a 10-inch distance. When sprayed this way, neither paint will produce an unwanted spray mist at the edge of the stroke.

When spraying lacquer, it is desirable to have as little overspray as possible. To achieve this the fluid and pattern may be balanced at approximately two-thirds open. When painting with enamel, the two may be balanced at a quarter- to a half-turn from full open.

Not all materials can be sprayed in exactly the same manner. There are some factors in common, however. These are as follows:

1. All materials should be sprayed with a 50-percent overlap of the spray stroke.
2. Air pressure and fluid pressure (suction) must be balanced.
3. The fluid adjustment and pattern must be balanced.
4. The optimal spraying viscosity for all materials is in the same range.

There also are some unlike factors, and they are as follows:

1. Lacquers are sprayed at lower pressures with the gun 6 to 8 inches from the panel; enamels are sprayed at higher pressures with the gun 10 to 12 inches from the panel.
2. Lacquers require slower stroke travel; enamels require faster stroke travel.
3. Lacquers can be sprayed in double-wet coats; enamels must be allowed tack time between coats.

OBJECTIVE 3-A3 (manipulative)

Working with another student and with the aid of Job Report Sheet 3-A3, you will spray paint a test panel. You will select the proper pressure, and you will experiment with triggering the gun, with stroke sequence, and with 50-percent overlap.

Time Recommended:

1½ hours

Preparation:

1. Study pages 118 through 120.
2. Attend classroom discussion.
3. Read Safety Checklist on page 126, items 1 through 4.

Tools and Materials:

1. Test panel
2. Spray gun and air supply
3. Paint, reducer and clean-up materials

Procedure:

1. Set up the panel on an easel.
2. Mix the color you are using with the appropriate amount of reducer and fill the gun's paint cup.
3. Select an appropriate regulator-transformer pressure for the material you are spraying (see Table 3-1).
4. Position the gun's air cap horns for a vertical pattern.
5. Turn on the air compressor.
6. Open the fluid valve on the gun for minimal paint flow when the gun is triggered.
7. Open the spreader valve and trigger the gun. Experiment with positions of both valves until correct atomization is achieved.
8. Open the air and fluid adjustments equal amounts until the pattern is the size recommended for the material being sprayed, making sure the correct balance for proper atomization is maintained between the two adjustments.
9. Maintaining an appropriate distance (see Fig. 3-22), stroke the gun across the panel and trigger it to apply a band of paint. Maintain a 90-degree angle between the gun and the work surface.
10. Trigger the gun on as you begin your stroke and release the trigger as you end your stroke. Strive for a minimum of overspray.
11. Band the edges of your test panel.
12. With the edges banded, apply a coat of paint to the panel using the 50-percent overlap. Do this by spraying color onto the panel in uniform strokes, pointing the center of the spray pattern at the edge of the paint left by your previous stroke.
13. Experiment with the speed of your stroke to achieve a full-wet coat of paint, and a medium-wet coat.
14. Clean up your equipment and put it away.

JOB REPORT SHEET 3-A3

SPRAY PAINTING TECHNIQUE

Student Name ______________________________ Date ______________

Time Started ____________ Time Finished ____________ Total Time ____________

Specifications

Type of panel ____________________

Condition of original finish ____________________

Type of refinish coat ____________________

Technique

Transformer-regulator pressure setting ____________________

Result of test spray (mark one): Proper flow of material ____________________

Drips and sags ____________________ Dry spray ____________________

Spray pattern: Vertical ____________________ Horizontal ____________________

Distance of gun from panel ____________________

Angle between gun and work surface ____________________

Distance spray stroke continued after trigger is released ____________________

Edges banded (check one): Left and right ______

All four sides ______

Proper pattern sizes for:

Lacquer ____________________ Enamel ____________________

Checkup Questions

1. What are the likely results of not maintaining ideal spraying distances? ________

____

Of not maintaining the proper angle? ______________________________

2. Describe the 50-percent overlap, how it is obtained and where the painter should start on the panel to obtain it. ______________________________

____

____

3. Describe the proper method of spraying corners. ____________________

____

____

4. Describe the advantages of using double medium-wet coats. __________

____

____

Date Completed ____________ Instructor's Signature ____________________

SPRAY BOOTHS

There are two basic types of paint spray booths: the dry air booth and the air washer booth.

The Dry Air Booth

The dry air booth (Fig. 3-34) relies on the flow of air through a system of filters to remove spray dust and overspray from the air inside the booth. It is commonly used for spraying lacquers and other quick-drying materials. Exhaust filters at the end of the booth opposite the fan catch impurities. Intake and exhaust filters must be changed frequently to insure optimal performance.

Some dry booths have their intake filters in one end of the booth and their exhaust filters in the other end, but a simpler and less expensive form of dry booth has all its filters in one end of the booth only through which the exhaust fans draw air, in some cases from outside the shop. These should not be used when it is raining outside and the painter needs to spray lacquer, as lacquer will blush at the first hint of moisture, especially in warm climates.

The Air Washer Booth

The air washer booth typically is found only in very large operations. In this booth the air is drawn through a series of baffles and through curtains or over streams of flowing water. Airborne overspray and dust is caught by the water and held in suspension.

Of the several types of air washer booths, one is more commonly found in factory settings. This uses a stream of water which moves like a creek under the car as the car is being sprayed. Temperature-controlled dry air is admitted to the booth from above. Exhaust fans pull the dry air, which carries the overspray down into the running water. The running water removes the overspray.

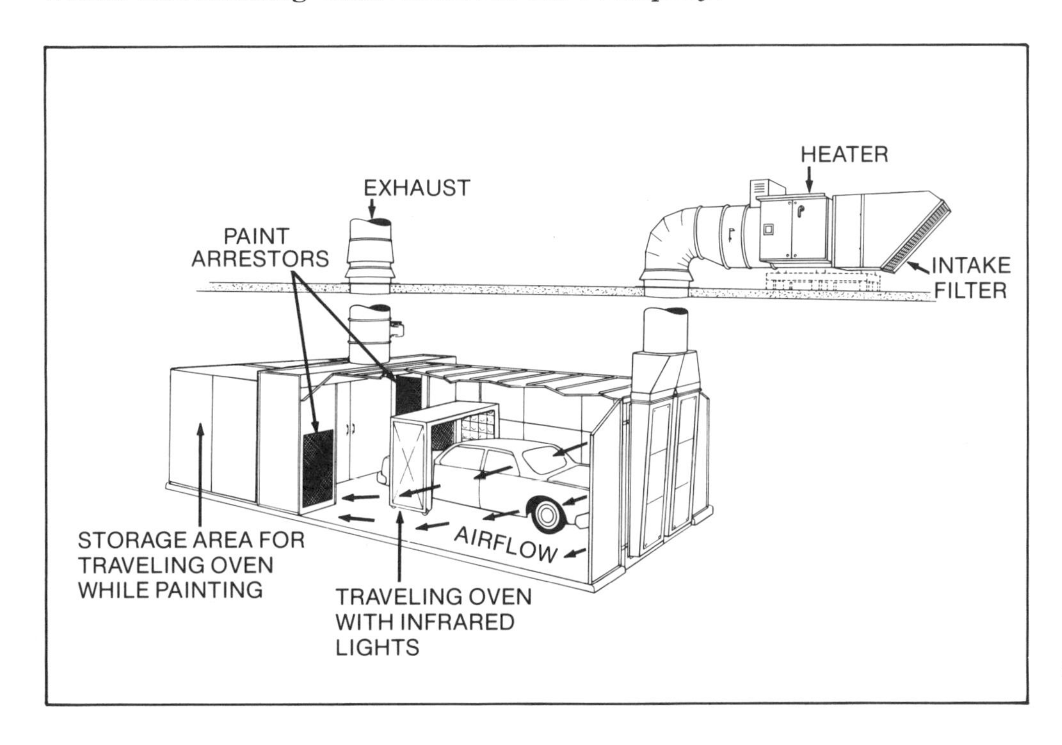

FIG 3-34

External cut away view of dry air spray booth. (The DeVilbiss Company)

FIG 3-35
Interior of spray booth.
(E. I. du Pont de Nemours & Co., Inc.)

Another type of air washer booth uses water which pours down one end of the booth. The air inside the booth is pulled by the exhaust fans into the flowing water, which captures the overspray and carries it away. These booths are available with temperature controls.

Almost all fully enclosed booths are constructed so they can be converted to drive-through booths (Fig. 3-35). This is done by removing the end panels and replacing them with doors and sealing strips.

Other Booth Types

Other types of booths include small bench-type booths used for the spraying of small articles; open floor-standing booths of various sizes for items ranging in size from very small to quite large; self-propelled booths which move along vehicles with the painter as the vehicle is being sprayed; and ceramic booths, especially useful for pieces requiring the use of porcelain enamel.

Booth Air Capacity

The amount of air a booth should move through during the filtration process is a variable controlled by local codes, and these can vary widely. Requirements could range from 9,000 to 12,000 cubic feet per minute. The amount of air circulated is important because if circulation is too slow, overspray will not be pulled from the booth. If it is too fast, drafts will form and excessive dirt and dust will be pulled into the booth. If the amount of air a booth's filtration system moves becomes an issue, local authorities and the booth's manufacturer should be consulted.

Intake Filters

Fiberglass is a commonly used filtration medium. Fiberglass filters usually are composed of two stages, the first of spun glass and the second of glass mat.

An alternative filter type is a sponge-like polyester material that is soft and pliable and contains a special adhesive that gives the material special dust-trapping capabilities.

Filters should be replaced as indicated by inspection. If the filter is clogged with paint, it should be replaced. A gauge called a manometer takes the guesswork out of filter replacement. This instrument measures the amount of draft, or air flow, in the booth. If the manometer reading drops below normal, a filter change likely is called for. Consult the booth manufacturer for the proper manometer reading.

If the draft is poor and the filters are in good condition, the exhaust fan may have an excessive amount of paint on its blades, reducing its efficiency. Or it could have a loose drive belt.

Exhaust Fans

Exhaust fans are belt-driven by a remote-mounted electric motor. This sort of drive arrangement is to keep overspray from coming into contact with the motor itself, reducing the likelihood of an explosion caused by the volatile overspray contacting a spark in the motor's armature. In addition to being safer, remote mounting of the fan drive motor keeps the motor cleaner than it might otherwise be, reducing maintenance. It also allows for easy pulley changes to alter the rotational speed of the fan.

A typical fan motor might develop three horsepower and require 200 to 230 volts of electrical current.

Some fans are built into the booth panels opposite the air entrance panels. They can also be built into the same panels the air enters through.

Booth Safety

Exhaust fans with remote motors are one element of safe, explosion-proof booths. Another element involves not driving the car to be painted into the booth, but rather, pushing it in. Pushing the car in eliminates exhaust fumes in the booth. But more importantly it allows the battery ground wire to be disconnected when the vehicle is still outside the booth, effectively rendering the vehicle's electrical system spark-free. In some areas, doing so is required by fire safety codes.

Spray Booth Maintenance

Keeping a spray booth clean is important for two reasons: to prevent freshly sprayed paint from becoming marred, and to minimize fire damage.

Cleaning the dry booth primarily consists of cleaning the booth's surfaces and changing the filters. To keep the booth surfaces clean they should be covered with booth coating. This is a waterborne latex material that can be brushed or sprayed on and then peeled off when replacement is necessary. Regular use of it not only keeps the booth clean, it protects the booth walls from rust. This coating usually is white, which gives the booth a nice reflective power, enabling the painter to better see the work. Paper should never be used as a surface cover as it is too flammable.

The booth should be cleaned regularly to keep up the efficiency of the filter system and minimize the fire hazard of an excessive buildup of overspray. Booths should be swept and hosed out after each use.

When cleaning booths, a nonferrous, non-spark-producing scraper always should be used for removing overspray and booth coating from booth surfaces and from the exhaust system. Sparks from the scraper could ignite combustible material in the booth.

In air washer booths, booth coating need be applied only on the booth's dry surfaces. Because the water removes the overspray from the air before it reaches the fan, the fan need not be coated.

When cleaning an air washer booth, the water in its washing chamber tank must be replaced with clean water. A substance called *water wash compound* must be added to this fresh water. The compound removes the stickiness from the overspray so that it won't stick to the surfaces of the wash chamber. Follow the recommendations of the compound manufacturer to determine the amount to be used.

No matter what the booth cleaning schedule is, the water surface inside the air washer booth should be skimmed at the end of each work day. Doing so will prevent overspray residue from sinking to the bottom of the water holding tank. Even when this routine is followed, the tank should be drained at regular intervals and any sludge on its bottom removed.

When the water chamber is being cleaned, its nozzles should be checked to make sure they are clean and open. If they are not they should be removed from the system and cleaned before the booth is used again.

The fans and exhaust systems in this type of booth will require very little maintenance unless the operator has neglected to clean the booth regularly, to add compound to the water, or to keep the water nozzles clean.

BAKING EQUIPMENT

The two basic types of baking equipment are radiant and convection. Radiant heat, supplied by quartz or infrared bulbs, penetrates the paint and heats the entire coating, causing the reduction materials to evaporate completely.

Convection ovens usually are not found in small shops because they are thick-walled rooms that actually are gas-fired ovens. They're expensive to build and operate and must conform to special building codes.

The most common baking booth is the drying room which uses infrared bulbs and which can be attached to one end of the spray booth so that the car can be rolled from the spray booth directly into the baking booth.

Though most of these rooms use infrared globes, some of them use quartz light tubes. These can be easily damaged. The bulbs in an infrared booth are special heavy-duty glass, and each screws into a special socket fixture designed to minimize the possibility of a spark.

No matter what sort of lights the baking booth has, it basically is the same sort of room as the spray booth. The difference is that it has no fan, no filters, no forced air. But it does have sealed doors to keep dirt and dust out.

Baking Booth Sizes

The baking unit does not have to be an entire room. For small jobs stand-mounted units containing as few as two bulbs (Fig. 3-36) can be

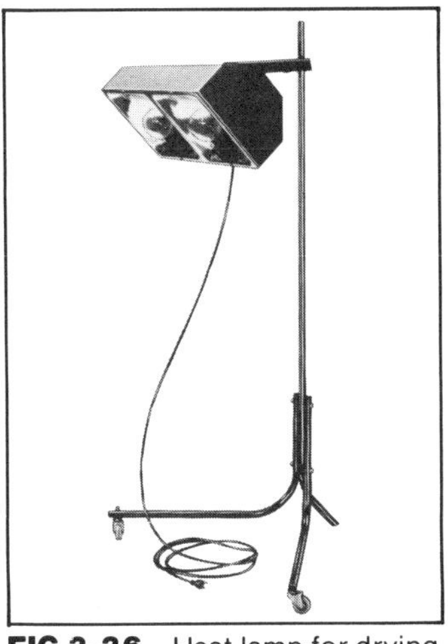

FIG 3-36 Heat lamp for drying paint. (The DeVilbiss Company)

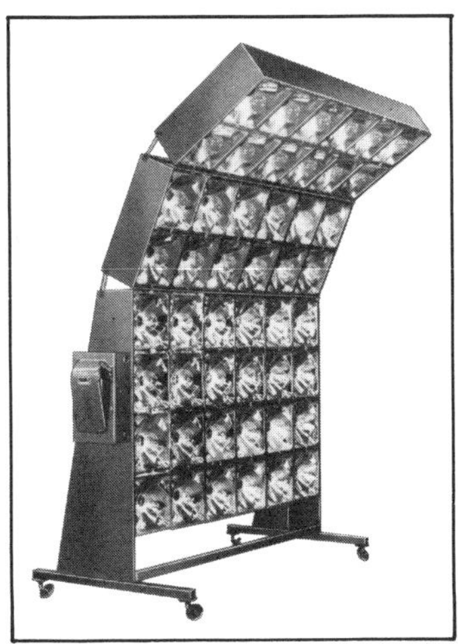

FIG 3-37 Portable bank of heat lamps. (The DeVilbiss Company)

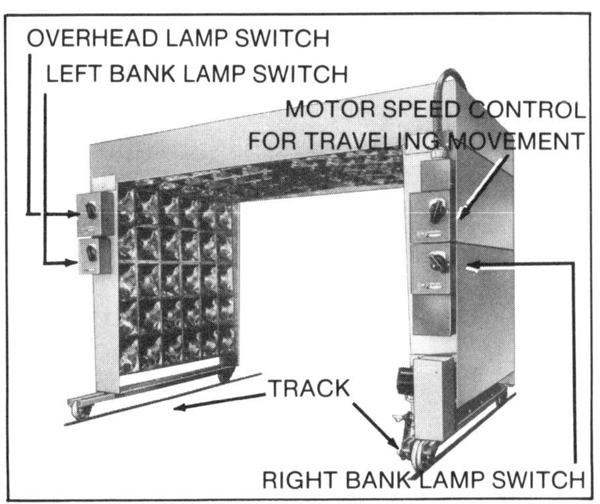

FIG 3-38 Traveling oven. (The DeVilbiss Company)

used. Units range from this small size to those of intermediate size (Fig. 3-37), and those shaped like an arch that roll back and forth along the entire vehicle (Fig. 3-38). The large and intermediate units can be used to dry small sections by switching on selected lamps.

Force Drying and Prewarming

When necessary these separate light panels can be used to force dry a panel or to bring the panel up to room temperature before it is painted. Care must be taken when force drying, however. Too much heat, obtained by moving the lights closer to the panel than 24 inches or so, can cause the paint to blister.

Prewarming a panel before spraying should only be used to bring the panel up to room temperature. Warming a panel too much can affect paint adhesion and flowing and thus can create many problems.

Operation and Maintenance

After the vehicle or panel has been sprayed, it is moved from the spray booth into the baking booth. The amount of initial evaporation time that should elapse between completion of the spray job and moving the vehicle or panel into the baking booth will depend on the recommendation of the paint manufacturer.

Actual drying time of the paint under the lights will depend on the paint type. This drying time should be obtained from the paint manufacturer. Variations in drying time depend on how much the paint has been thinned and how thick the coating is. This information will be found on paint can labels.

There are situations when the spray coating can be force dried. This is particularly true with lacquer finishes that need to be compounded without excessive time loss. The temperature used for baking lacquer ranges from 120 degrees to approximately 140 degrees. Enamel can be baked at temperatures of up to 185 degrees. Remember that lacquer dries from the bottom up but enamel dries from the top down. So even after the top coat of an enamel job seems dry, the paint job remains soft, or "green," for several days and must be considered very fragile.

Though many shops use fast-drying paint that requires no baking,

baking generally cures most paints better and gives them improved adhesion. It has no effect on the color.

The most common mistake made with baking equipment is to overheat the panel surface by placing the lights too close to the panel. The proper distance can be as much as 40 inches. The lights can be as close as 18 inches from the panel, but only if they are moving constantly. Otherwise blisters will form in the finish.

When the paint is dry and the vehicle removed, let the booth and its bulbs cool completely. Hose down the booth with water. The bulbs and fixtures should not get wet. Any dead bulbs in the lamp units should be replaced and the tracks on any rolling units should be greased.

SAFETY CHECKLIST

Spray Guns:

1. Applying either base or top coat elements with a spray gun disperses a fine mist of these products in the air. To protect himself from years of exposure to potentially harmful vapors, chemicals, and pigment metals, the refinisher should always wear a respirator when spray painting.
2. The hoses that supply air (and, in the case of pressure-feed equipment, paint) to a spray gun are designed to withstand extremes of pressure. The special linings that give them strength, however, cannot be stressed without limit. When hoses are under pressure, therefore, care should be taken that no vehicles or jacks are rolled or driven over them. The additional external load could cause a blowout.
3. When cleaning a spray gun, always be sure that the air cap has been well loosened and the transformer pressure lowered to no more than 35 psi before trying to force air back through the system. The cleaning rag used to block the nozzle is not heavy enough to protect the hand from penetration if extreme pressures are used.
4. Running pure solvent through spray painting equipment is another cleaning procedure that requires special precautions. Setting the fluid valve for maximum flow, as the procedure requires, guarantees that a large quantity of solvent will be dispersed in the immediate vicinity of the painter. This constitutes both a health and a fire hazard. The refinisher should therefore always carry out the procedure in an area well ventilated by windows, bays, or specially installed exhaust fans.

Spray Booths:

1. Thinners, thinned paints, and overspray are extremely volatile and their explosive potential is considerable, so observe the ban on smoking when in an area where spray painting is being done and avoid the use of a tool whose motor or operation could produce sparks.
2. When painting a car disconnect its battery ground cable *before* rolling it into the spray booth.
3. Accumulations of overspray on booth walls can be highly flam-

mable. Make sure all booth surfaces are cleaned and properly recoated as necessary. When cleaning them use a spark-free scraper. For the same reason always make sure the booth's filters are clean and free of overspray.

4. Never use a spray booth for storing or mixing paint. The fire hazard already is substantial just from spray painting. Stored paints and refinishing materials would only add more fuel in the event of an accident that led to a fire. This excess could make the difference between the booth's holding up in an explosion or fire and its being demolished, thus allowing the damage to spread.

OBJECTIVE 3-A4 (manipulative)

Working as a team of four students, with the aid of Job Report Sheet 3-A4, you will clean and inspect the paint spray booth, replace filters, and replace paint arrestors.

Time Recommended:

1½ hours

Preparation:

1. Review pages 85 through 127.
2. Study pages 127 through 130.
3. Attend classroom discussion.

Tools and Materials:

1. Four shop brooms
2. Water hose
3. New filters
4. New arrestors
5. Stepladder
6. Air hose with dust gun

Procedure:

1. Sweep the floor of the booth completely before wetting it.
2. Turn off all electric current to the booth by shutting the switch off at the power box.
3. Remove all filters and arrestors. Hose down and wash the entire booth with water. Place the stepladder as needed to wash the higher parts of the booth.
4. Spray the water on each part of the booth until the water is clear running off of it.
5. Sweep all of the water out of the booth into a drain, or outside of the shop.
6. Use the air hose and dust gun to blow the water from the area where filters and arrestors are installed.
7. Install filters and arrestors, making sure they are placed with their proper faces outward and are held securely in place.
8. Where necessary, remove and replace booth coating.
9. If the booth you're cleaning is an air washer booth, skim the water supply and check the water nozzles for plugging.

10. Check the fans and exhaust system and clean as necessary.
11. Remove all tools and materials used for cleaning from the booth and close all doors. Check the seals on all doors for cracks and air leaks.
12. Turn on the booth's power supply at the main switch box.
13. Turn on the booth exhaust system and allow it to run for 30 minutes to assist the evaporation of water from the overhead parts of the booth.

JOB REPORT SHEET 3-A4

CLEAN, INSPECT SPRAY BOOTH

Student Name ______________________ Date ____________

Time Started ____________ Time Finished ____________ Total Time ____________

Specifications

Type of booth ______________________

Use of booth: Spraying only ______ Spraying and baking ______

Types of filters ______________________

Type of booth coating ______________________

Type of paint sprayed in booth ______________________

Technique

1. Has the floor of the spray booth been swept clean while it is dry? ______
2. Has the booth's electric power been shut off at its master switch? ______
3. Have all filters and arrestors been removed from the booth? ______
4. Have all the booth's panels been washed clean with water? ______
5. Has all water been swept from the booth floor? ______
6. Has booth coating been removed and replaced as necessary? ______
7. Have all filter openings been blown free of water? ______
8. Have all filters and arrestors been securely replaced? ______
9. Has the water wash been skimmed or cleaned and refilled as necessary? ______
10. Have the nozzles been checked and cleaned? ______
11. Has the booth power supply been turned back on? ______
12. Has the exhaust system been run for 30 minutes to help dry the booth? ______
13. Has the exhaust system been shut off and all items used returned to their storage places? ______

14. Have the door seals been inspected? ______

15. Was the manometer checked? ______

Checkup Questions

1. Does the exhaust draft seem normal and does it move air properly? ______ If not, why? ______________________________

2. What are the problems associated with too little and too much air flow through the booth? ______________________________

   ____

3. Why is the elimination of overspray buildup important to spray booth safety?

   ____

   ____

Date Completed ______________ Instructor's Signature ______________

Student Name ______________________ Date ______________

DIRECTIONS: Circle the best answer to each question.

1. The spray gun nozzle passes
   I. paint.
   II. air.
   A. I only   B. II only   C. Both I and II   D. Neither I nor II

2. A spray gun is fully triggered
   A. only once, at the start of painting.
   B. before the painting stroke is begun.
   C. 6 inches off to one side of the panel.
   D. at the panel edge.

3. When using a spray gun, to go from Pattern I to Pattern II,
   A. close down the fluid adjustment valve.
   B. close down the spreader valve.
   C. rotate the air cap 90 degrees.
   D. loosen the air cap.

PATTERN I   PATTERN II

4. A spray gun nozzle is blocked with dried paint.
   Refinisher I suggests using a short length of soft copper wire to clear the passageway.
   Refinisher II suggests submerging the spray gun in a bucket of solvent for 5 minutes.
   Who is right?
   A. I only   B. II only   C. Both I and II   D. Neither I nor II

5. The spray gun type most commonly found in paint shops is
   I. external mix.
   II. nonbleeder.
   A. I only   B. II only   C. Both I and II   D. Neither I nor II

6. Pressure-feed equipment is characterized by all EXCEPT
   A. a remote tank.
   B. an internal-mix cap.
   C. a fluid hose.
   D. use in assembly line painting.

7. Arcing a spray gun causes
   I. zebra effect.
   II. atomization of paint.
   A. I only B. II only C. Both I and II D. Neither I nor II

8. Which procedure takes the lowest psi?
   A. A spot repair with lacquer
   B. A spot repair with enamel
   C. A panel repair with lacquer
   D. Refinishing a whole vehicle with enamel

9. To change a spray gun's pattern from circle to vertical fan,
   A. turn the fluid adjustment screw clockwise.
   B. turn the air adjustment screw counterclockwise.
   C. raise the psi at the transformer-regulator.
   D. hold the gun farther from the work surface.

10. The spray gun component at the right is the
   A. fluid valve needle.
   B. air valve needle.
   C. trigger mechanism.
   D. siphon tube.

(Davenport Photography)

11. The roof of a car is the only panel that needs painting.
   Refinisher I suggests using suction-feed equipment because the cup will hold just the right amount of paint.
   Refinisher II suggests using pressure-feed equipment because it holds more paint and is easier to set up and clean.
   Who is right?
   A. I only B. II only C. Both I and II D. Neither I nor II

12. All of the following spray gun components fit together EXCEPT
   A. nozzle and fluid needle.
   B. nozzle and air cap.
   C. trigger and air adjustment valve.
   D. siphon tube and fluid inlet.

13. Both the fluid and air adjustment valves on a spray gun are closed. If the gun is held still and the air valve opened, what will be the effect at the panel?
   A. A circular spray pattern 3 inches in diameter
   B. A circular spray pattern first, then drips and sags
   C. A circular spray pattern expanding to an oval
   D. Nothing

14. All of the following are causes of dry spray EXCEPT
    A. spreader valve open too far.
    B. fluid valve open too far.
    C. spray gun held 12 inches from the work surface.
    D. spray gun moved too fast for the paint flow.

15. The paint flow in a suction-feed spray gun is reduced. All of the following are possible causes EXCEPT
    A. dried paint on the fluid needle.
    B. vent in the cup's cap assembly blocked.
    C. nozzle partially clogged.
    D. auxiliary orifice in the air cap clogged.

16. A properly adjusted spray gun produces a pattern in which the paint is
    I. wet and thick enough to flow.
    II. dry and heavy enough to avoid overspray.
    A. I only   B. II only   C. Both I and II   D. Neither I nor II

17. In the spray gun at the right, all of the indicated points require regular lubrication EXCEPT
    A.   B.   C.   D.

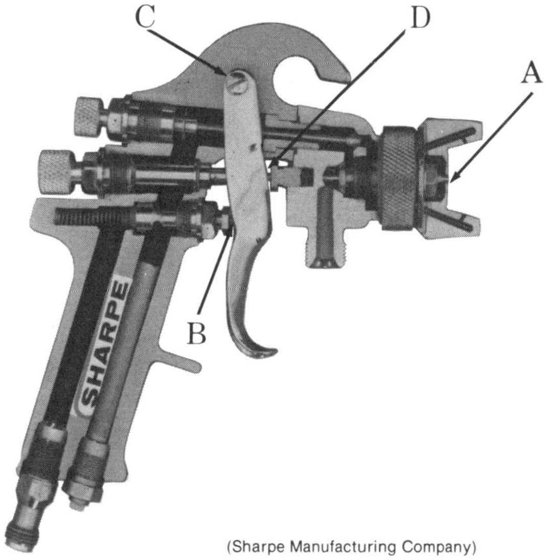

(Sharpe Manufacturing Company)

18. Which of the following darkens the color being sprayed?

Decreasing distance between gun and panel ______

Increasing distance between gun and panel ______

Increasing speed of stroke ______

Decreasing speed of stroke ______

Decreasing air pressure ______

Increasing air pressure ______

19. Explain the proper procedure for spraying a corner.

____

____

____

____

20. Describe the two main types of spray booths and their differences and outline cleaning procedures for both. ______________________________

____

____

____

____

____

unit 4

Surface Preparation

No automotive finish can be more smooth or durable than the surface over which it is applied. If that surface is rough or irregular, then at the very least the new finish will lack depth and shine; at the very most, it will allow sandscratches to show through the new top coat. If the surface is covered with lint from cleaning cloths or dust from sanding, new paint will magnify it. Finally, if rust is beginning to swell or blister the surface, paint will neither hide nor halt the deterioration. There are, in other words, limits to what a new coat of paint can do, and many of those limits are defined by conditions at the panel surface.

To control these conditions, preparation for refinishing proceeds in a series of well-defined steps. These include sanding, priming, filling, and (where necessary) sealing—all sandwiched between and interspersed with rounds of cleaning and even more sanding. It is a time-consuming process, first tearing down, then building up a panel's surface. Short of using faster-drying materials or force-drying techniques, however, there are no shortcuts. The steps remain basically the same whether the old finish is in fairly good condition or so heavily damaged that it must be removed down to the bare metal.

This unit describes the details involved in each step of the preparation process. In so doing, it begins to tie together all of the information about tools and materials presented in the first three units. It also introduces a large body of new information on the purposes and basic techniques of masking.

OBJECTIVE 4-A (written)

After doing the reading and shop exercises, you will be able to answer correctly without reference material a minimum of 14 out of 20 test questions on the following topics:

1. Surface analysis
2. Featheredging and wet vs. dry sanding
3. Masking materials and techniques
4. Primer-surfacer characteristics and application
5. Sealer use and application
6. Cleaning and final wipedown procedures

Preparation:

1. Study pages 135 through 178.
2. Attend classroom discussions on Objective 4-A.
3. Read the Safety Checklist on pages 174 and 175.

SURFACE ANALYSIS

The first step in any refinishing job is a thorough analysis of the work surface. The refinisher must evaluate the condition of the old paint film, its thickness, and its composition. Together these three things determine how much preparation the job will require. In particular they determine how much sanding must be done and how many base coat elements must be applied prior to painting.

Film Condition

The analysis begins with a close visual inspection of the surface. If the current finish is in good condition, smooth and blemish-free, it may actually have to be roughed up to give the new paint something onto which it can hold (Fig. 4-1). In such cases, a light sanding is normally used to increase adhesion.

If, on the other hand, chips, cracks, or small dents are present, the finish will have to be sanded more extensively (Fig. 4-2). This process produces deep sandscratches and requires follow-up applications of primer-surfacer and putty.

The most serious sort of damage extends beyond the top coat. Blisters, pits, and holes fall into this category (Fig. 4-3). All indicate that no part of the old finish can be trusted as a base for the new. Such defects demand complete removal of the paint film in order to expose the underlying problem (rust, for example). This procedure, in turn, usually requires grinding and application of plastic filler in addition to sanding and resurfacing.

To summarize, then—as the amount of damage to a surface increases, so does the amount of work necessary to prepare it for refinishing.

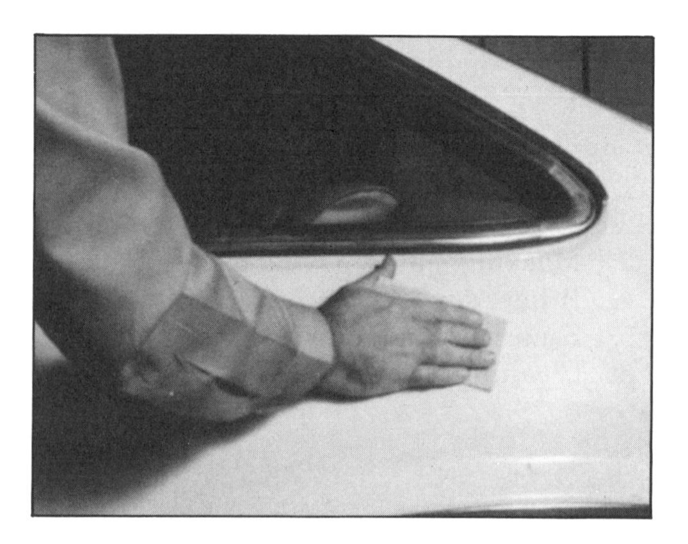

FIG 4-1
Light hand sanding to prepare old finish that is not damaged. (E. I. du Pont de Nemours & Co., Inc.)

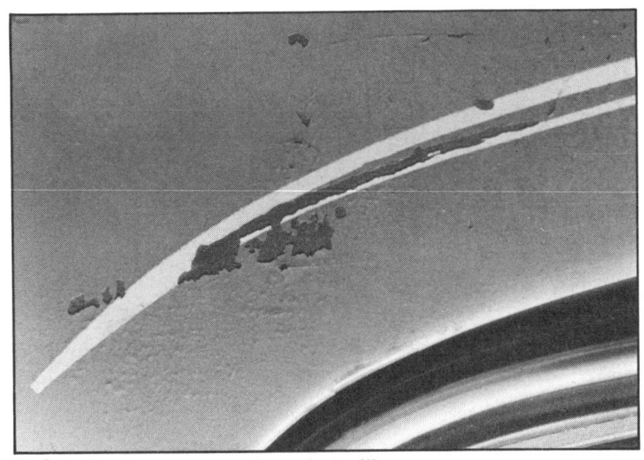

FIG 4-2 Damaged surface that will require heavy sanding, priming, and filling. (Jay Storer)

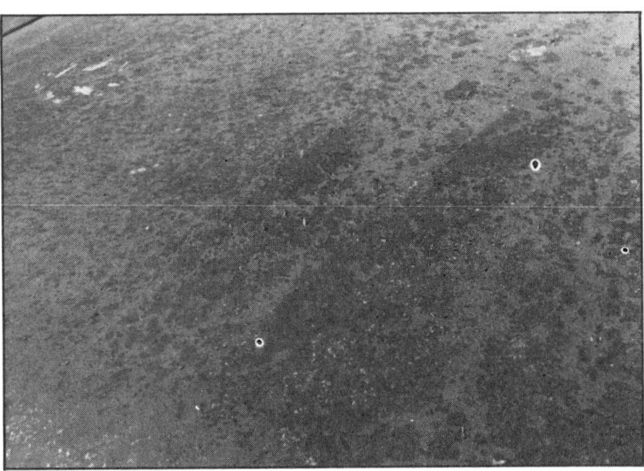

FIG 4-3 Blisters, pits, and holes that will require complete removal of old paint. (Jay Storer)

Film Thickness

When the old finish is in very good condition, there is always the possibility of painting directly over it. The main limitation on this procedure is the thickness of the total paint film. When this figure equals or exceeds .006 (6/1000) inch, the risk of paint failure increases dramatically.

Failure, in this case, means cracking. The solvents in fresh paint can penetrate a built-up film to such a degree that it becomes impossible for them to escape before the outer surface dries. Their evaporation later when the vehicle is exposed to sunlight (and its body panels start to store heat) causes the damage.

Using a Dry Film Gauge

The easiest way to determine whether a finish is near the .006 limit is to measure the paint buildup with a dry film gauge (Fig. 4-4). This tool consists of a magnetic contact point and a dial (the so-called gauge) that reads out in mils, or thousandths of an inch. The device operates by measuring the attraction between the magnetic tip and the metal surface of the body panel located somewhere below the paint. (*Note:* The tool does not work on fiberglass or plastic surfaces.)

FIG 4-4 Using a dry film gauge to measure paint thickness. (Courtesy of Indian River Community College)

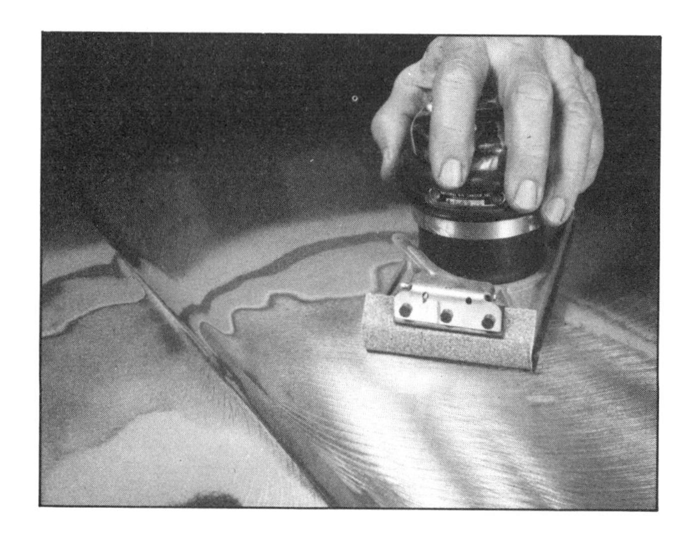

FIG 4-5
Featheredge from sanding, exposing five layers of paint and primer.

To use the film gauge, the operator first turns the device's film thickness dial to its maximum setting—usually 25 mils. He then applies the tool to the panel so that the gauge and magnetic contact rest on its surface. With the tool in this position, the operator begins moving the dial to progressively lower settings. He continues until the magnetic button at the tip pops up. The reading at this point is the thickness of the paint at that particular spot on the panel.

A paint film of average thickness produces a reading of 2 mils (.002 inch) on a dry film gauge. The .006-inch cutoff point converts to 6 mils. In practice, however, a lower reading—usually 4 mils—is considered grounds for complete or partial removal of an old finish.

Test Featheredging

A film gauge is a very expensive tool. Many paint shops are therefore not equipped with the device. Instead, refinishers use an alternate technique. They estimate film thickness by test featheredging.

Essentially, test featheredging involves sanding a small portion of the finish down to the bare metal and counting the layers of paint and primer-surfacer that are exposed (Fig. 4-5). Combining this information with what he knows to be the depth of the average paint film, a refinisher can then make an educated guess as to how close the surface is to the .006 limit.

For a finish that has undergone two color changes since the original paint was applied, for example, a refinisher might reason along these lines:

1. The average thickness of a finish (including both base and top coats) is .002 inch. This is the thickness of the original finish.
2. There have been two color changes without resurfacing (essentially two top coats). At .001 inch each, this is another .002 inch, for a total of .004.
3. To be on the safe side, each of the previous refinishers probably applied a sealer. This additional element amounts to perhaps another .001 inch. The total is now .005 inch.
4. A new top coat with sealer would add between .001 and .002 inch. This would bring the total film depth to between .006 and .007. This figure is at or above the cut-off point. Therefore, some or all of the old paint should be removed before refinishing.

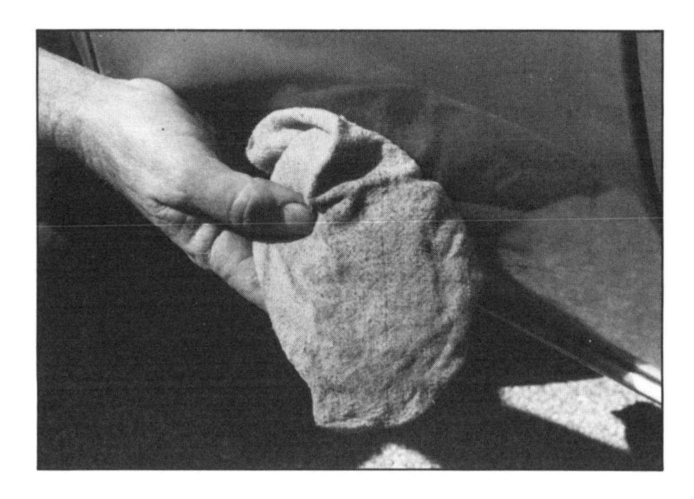

FIG 4-6
Testing for lacquer or enamel finish with a rag moistened with thinner.

Film Composition

The final determination that a refinisher must make about a surface is its composition. Is it lacquer, or is it enamel? The answer to this question is important if the new finish is to last. It tells the painter what kinds of products he must use if he is to avoid compatibility problems—lacquers over a lacquer finish, enamels over enamel, and a sealer between if he decides to mix the two.

Identifying the old finish when a vehicle has never been repainted is a relatively simple matter. The refinisher consults the vehicle identification plate and cross-checks with the paint manufacturer's color chip book. If a vehicle has been repainted in whole or in part, however, there may be doubt about the nature of the finish. In such situations, it is advisable to test the top coat with lacquer thinner.

To conduct this test, select a relatively inconspicuous spot on or near the surface to be refinished. Apply a small amount of thinner to a clean rag and rub it lightly on the selected spot. If the finish is lacquer, some color will rub off onto the rag (Fig. 4-6). If the finish is enamel that has been air or heat dried at the 165-degree temperature commonly used in refinishing shops, it will soften and sometimes lift. If, however, the finish is factory-baked enamel, even hard rubbing with the cloth will not affect it.

OBJECTIVE 4-A1 (manipulative)

Working as a team with two other students and with the aid of Job Report Sheet 4-A1, you will first identify and measure the finish on a panel. Then, by test featheredging, you will determine how often the panel has been painted.

Time Recommended:

30 minutes

Preparation:

1. Review pages 135 through 139.
2. Study pages 139 through 142.
3. Read the Safety Checklist on pages 174 and 175, items 1 through 3.

Tools and Materials:

1. Dry film gauge
2. Orbital or vibrator sander
3. Sandpapers (80D and 280A)
4. Thinner
5. Clean shop cloths
6. Respirator and safety goggles

Procedure:

1. Moisten a clean shop cloth with thinner. Select a small spot on the panel's surface and rub the cloth across it. Use no more than three or four light strokes.
2. Check the cloth for any traces of color. If none are found, check the surface for any signs of softening or lifting. Enter your conclusions about the nature of the finish on Job Report Sheet 4-A1.
3. Remove the dry film gauge from its case. Grasp the gauge by its handle and place it on the panel. The dial and rubber stop at the tool's tip should be contacting the surface.
4. Still holding the gauge, turn the dial until the number 25 is opposite the red mark on the tool's housing.
5. Slowly lower the dial's reading to 24, then 23, and so on. Continue in this manner until the tool clicks and the red indicator button above its tip pops up.
6. Note the reading on the dial. Enter this figure on Job Report Sheet 4-A1.
7. Return the dial to the 25-mil position. Repeat steps 3 through 6 at least three more times, selecting a different area of the panel for each reading.
8. Once four readings have been taken, estimate how many times the panel has been painted. (Allow 2 mils for each paint job.) Enter your estimate on Job Report Sheet 4-A1.
9. To determine how many coats of paint are in fact on the panel, do a test featheredge. Using an orbital or a vibrator sander and an 80D abrasive, cut through the paint all the way down to the bare metal. Then use a 280-grit abrasive and by hand taper back the edge of the paint so that each coat of material can be seen clearly.
10. Starting from the metal and moving outward, count the number of coats of paint and primer-surfacer. Enter this figure on Job Report Sheet 4-A1.

JOB REPORT SHEET 4-A1

SURFACE ANALYSIS

Student Name ______________________________ Date ______________

Time Started ____________ Time Finished ____________ Total Time ____________

Specifications

Type of panel ______________________________

Finish (Give color and describe any damage.) ______________________________

____

____

Technique

Thinner test results: Check the entries that apply and answer the related questions.

Paint removed _____ How much color was removed? (Was there any visible effect at the panel?) ______________________________

____

____

Paint softened _____ Describe the symptoms of softening. ______________

____

____

Paint lifted _____ Describe the symptoms of lifting. ______________

____

____

Panel finish: Lacquer _____ Factory-baked enamel _____ Air-dried enamel _____

Film gauge results: On a separate sheet of paper, draw an outline of the panel and indicate by numbers where each reading was taken. Attach your sketch to this job report sheet.

Reading 1 _____ mils Reading 3 _____ mils

Reading 2 _____ mils Reading 4 _____ mils

Estimated number of paint coats _____

Test featheredging results:

Number of paint coats ______ Number of primer-surfacer coats ______

If the two figures are different, explain why. ______

______

______

Checkup Questions

1. Why was it necessary to take four different readings with the dry film gauge?

   ______

   ______

   ______

   What factors might create large differences between readings? ______

   ______

   ______

2. Did the estimated number of paint coats and the actual number match? If not, why? ______

   ______

   ______

3. When in the course of the job were the respirator and goggles used? ______

   ______

   ______

Date Completed ______ Instructor's Signature ______

INITIAL CLEANING

The first step in the actual preparation process is cleaning. At this early stage, only the repair area and adjacent panels need be included.

At least two separate procedures are involved. The first is a cleaning in the ordinary sense of the word. Water and detergent are used to wash away any dust, dirt, or road film that may be on the vehicle's exterior. The second procedure is a chemical cleaning. It is designed to remove not only stubborn forms of dirt that soap and water cannot dislodge (things like road tar) but substances deliberately applied to the auto body to protect it. Chief among the latter are wax and polish.

Polish in particular is a problem because it contains tiny abrasive particles of silicone. If these are not removed from a surface, they can react with new paint to produce a condition called fisheye. As the name suggests, fisheye is characterized by hollows, or eyes, in the new paint film (Fig. 4-7). These, however, are not related to any dents in the panel surface. Rather they are the result of a chemical reaction. Thus, if he fails to clean a surface properly, a refinisher risks spending hours rebuilding and smoothing only to have the new finish ruined by what amounts to little more than dirt.

Fisheye can be avoided in two ways—before the fact and after. Before the fact involves using wax remover to wipe down the repair area in advance of any systematic sanding. (For a review of this product's characteristics and use, see Unit 2, page 71.) After the fact involves adding a product called fisheye eliminator to subsequent coats of paint once the condition has appeared. Clearly, the careful refinisher will opt for prevention. He will take the time to clean a surface properly and fall back on eliminator only when this procedure fails.

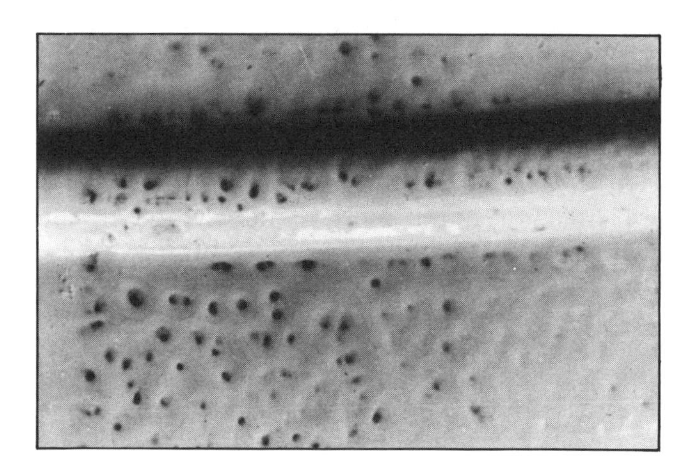

FIG 4-7
Fisheyes in paint. (E. I. du Pont de Nemours & Co., Inc.)

SANDING

After all wax, polish, grease, and dirt have been removed from a vehicle's surface, it is ready for sanding. Just how much sanding is required depends on whether the existing finish is in good condition, merely chipped and scratched, or severely damaged. The last situation would require removal of the old paint down to the bare metal. Since the basic procedures for doing this (grinding, sandblasting, and chemical stripping) were fully discussed in Unit 1, this section will concentrate on the first two situations.

FIG 4-8
Wet sanding.

Good Finishes

A refinisher is most likely to encounter a good finish only when a vehicle's color is being changed simply as a matter of the owner's personal preference. In such cases, the surface is by definition smooth and free from irregularities like sandscratches. Its major problem, in fact, is that it is too smooth.

Wet Sanding

To provide adhesion, therefore, a perfect surface must be roughened in some fashion. The method usually employed is wet sanding. This technique is slower than dry sanding but produces a finer finish (adhesion, in other words, without visible sandscratch). It also saves on sandpaper. Dry sanding a whole vehicle, for example, normally consumes six to eight abrasive sheets, 9 by 11 inches each. The same job done wet takes only four sheets. The saving is a direct result of the wet sanding technique, which reduces clogging.

When wet sanding, the refinisher usually works with the folded sandpaper in one hand and a hose adjusted to a trickle of water in the other (Fig. 4-8). He sands with a back-and-forth scrubbing action. As he moves across a panel, he directs the stream of water so that it clears both the surface and the abrasive of sanding dust. *Note:* Some refinishers prefer to work with a sponge instead of a hose. This technique, however, requires that both sponge and sandpaper be rinsed periodically in a container of water. These extra moves, particularly when large areas must be covered, make unnecessary demands on the refinisher's time and energies.

Choice of Abrasive

The choice of abrasive used on a good finish is determined by the nature of the new top coat. A surface over which enamel is to be applied should be sanded with either a 320- or 400-grit paper, depending on the kind of enamel to be used. Among abrasives, these two fall in the lower range of the very finest grits. They are adequate in this situation because enamels have good filling capacities and can therefore tolerate more sandscratch. (In fact, they require it. Remember that the solvents in enamel have less penetrating power. Enamel paints therefore require additional adhesion, and this is what more sandscratch provides.)

Lacquers, on the other hand, do not have enamel's ability to fill. Thinned to the great extent that they are, they require a more finely prepared surface. Sanding with at least a 500-grit abrasive is recommended.

Damaged Finishes

Chipping, cracking, and minor body work all qualify a finish as slightly damaged. A surface of this type requires much more extensive sanding than a good one. The extra sanding, in turn, makes it necessary to fill and, where bare metal is exposed, apply rust inhibitor.

Dry Sanding

To speed sanding of a damaged finish, much of the initial work is done dry (Fig. 4-9). While this technique has the advantage of removing more material more quickly, it also contributes to faster clogging of the abrasive. Refinishers use various methods to relieve this problem. When the sanding is being done mechanically, the sanding pad can be rapped either with a hand tool or against a solid surface to dislodge the sanding dust. When the work is being done by hand, simply slapping the sandpaper across the palm achieves the same result. Should either technique fail to produce an increase in cutting action, however, the abrasive should be discarded. Using glazed or worn sandpaper, particularly with a mechanical sander (and particularly dry), can scratch or burn a metal surface.

Protective Techniques

Certain body features (panel edges, for example) demand special care when being dry sanded. The backing pads of power tools are the problem here. Their fixed shapes and sizes make it almost inevitable that when a refinisher is sanding a repair area near one panel edge he will damage the panel edge opposite. A strip of masking tape applied along the full length of the adjoining panel before any sanding is begun will prevent such damage from occurring (Fig. 4-10).

When a panel edge itself must be sanded, only the lightest pressure should be used. During the sanding, the surface should be checked frequently to avoid removing too much material. Remember, panel edges

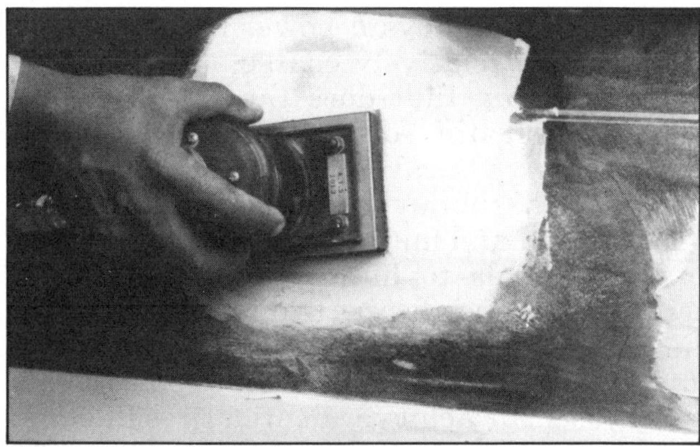

FIG 4-9 Dry machine sanding. (E. I. du Pont de Nemours & Co., Inc.)

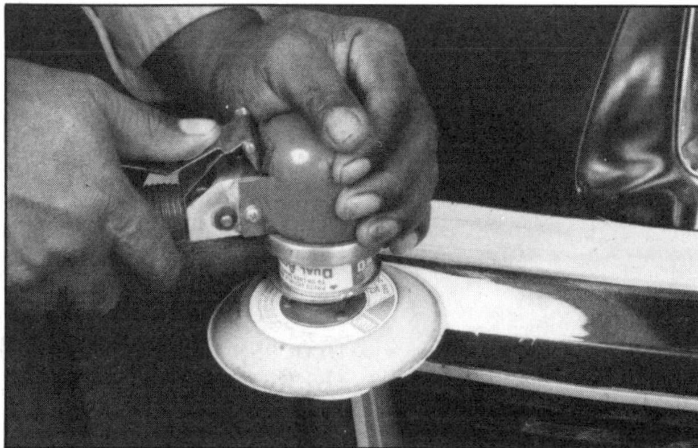

FIG 4-10 Masking tape used to protect a panel from scratching. (3M Company)

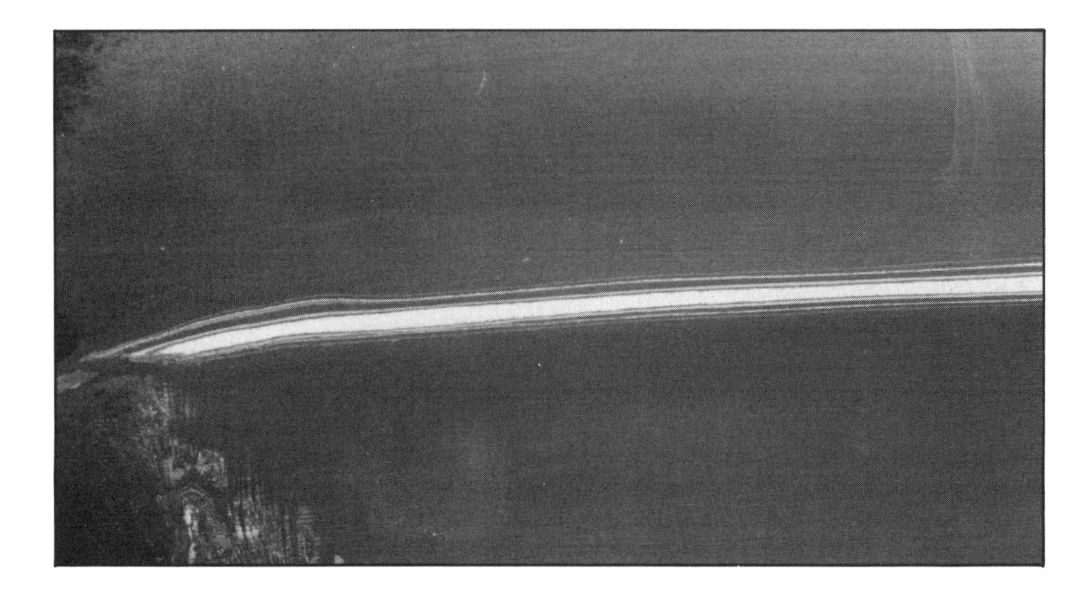

FIG 4-11
A crease sanded through several layers of paint to bare metal. (Jay Storer)

are among those areas that cannot be repaired with plastic filler. They must instead be soldered, a much more involved and time-consuming procedure.

Creases are also sensitive repair areas. Sanding a crease by applying pressure directly on its center will quickly cut right through to the metal (Fig. 4-11). The better procedure is to sand up to the crease, first on one side, then on the other. By this indirect means the refinisher applies just enough pressure to sand out the crease itself. (*Note:* This procedure is identical to that recommended for compounding creases—understandable, since compounding is basically just sanding with a much finer abrasive.)

Featheredging

Preparing any chipped or filled surface for painting begins with featheredging, one of the refinisher's most important skills. The term describes the process by which the abrupt break between old paint and a chipped area (or old paint and new filler) is graded into one continuous surface. A fully tapered, or feathered, edge is smooth to the touch and virtually undetectable once the surface is painted.

In practice, there are two forms of featheredging—rough and fine. Rough featheredging is done first. It employs a power tool (usually a vibrator or dual-action sander) and a relatively coarse abrasive (80D, for example). It is rough featheredging that does the actual cutting down of the paint or filler edge. Fine featheredging, on the other hand, is the follow-up. It uses a finer abrasive to cover the scratch left by the coarser one. The technique is thus similar to cross-grinding. Fine featheredging is usually done by hand and may even be done wet.

Beyond proceeding from power tools to hand sanding and from coarse abrasives to fine, there is no one correct way to featheredge. The process is quite flexible. The choice of sander, for example, depends on the individual refinisher's taste, technique, and selection of power tools. Different tools can, in fact, be used to achieve identical results. The same is true of sandpaper grits. For fine featheredging, recommendations can vary, depending on the source, from 180 all the way up to 320 (Table 4-1).

As for actual sanding technique, only two general rules apply.

1. *Sand out from each featheredge approximately 3 to 5 inches.* This border gives the featheredge a more gradual taper. It also guarantees that during priming none of the material will fall on unsanded paint. If primer is applied to such a surface, it will eventually peel, taking the new finish with it.
2. *Where a panel has a number of small repair areas, these should be featheredged as a whole rather than individually.* This technique is really just a logical extension of the previous rule. If the repairs are, in fact, relatively near each other, 5-inch borders sanded around them are likely to overlap and merge into one large repair anyway (Fig. 4-12).

Table 4-1 PAINT PREPARATION METHODS

	Rough Featheredging		Fine Featheredging		Hand Sanding Primer-Surfacer	
	Tool	Abrasive	Tool	Abrasive	Lacquer	Enamel
Method 1	Air file	80D	Sanding block	320A	360A, then 500A	360A-400A
Method 2	Orbital or vibrator sander	80D	Sanding block	180A-220A	360A, then 500A	320A-400A
Method 3	Polisher	80D	Sanding block	240A	360A, then 500A	320A-400A

Special Finishes

Automobiles today are being built of lighter materials. Many, particularly those with sculptured lines, have fiberglass or plastic body components. Because these are more fragile than metal, special care must be taken when sanding them in preparation for refinishing.

Fiberglass

Fiberglass is exactly what its name says it is—fiberlike strands of glass woven into cloth. The cloth is chopped into small pieces and then pressed into mats. Auto body panels are molded from these. A major difficulty in sanding such material is the exposure of glass threads.

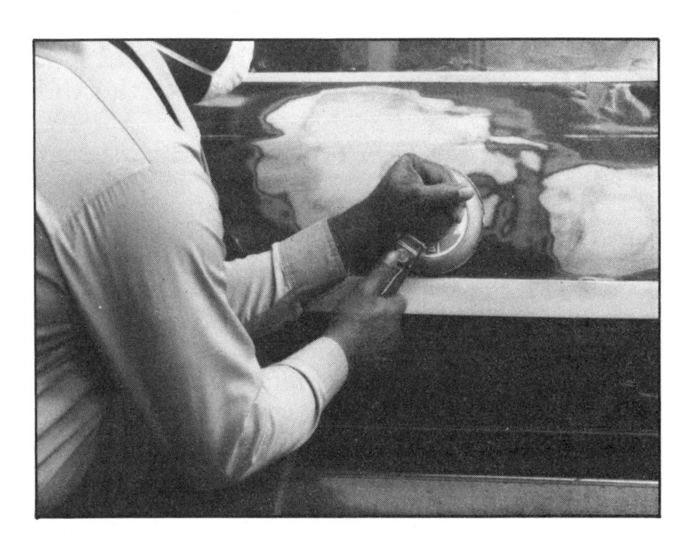

FIG 4-12
Small repair areas that become one big area when featheredged. (3M Company)

When these are bent back or raised above a panel's surface, they must be sealed down with glass resin before primer-surfacer can be applied. (Fig. 4-13).

To start, the exposed threads are first trimmed. A single-edged razor blade is the ideal tool for this job. Then the resin is mixed with its catalyst, methyl-ethyl-ketone. M.E.K., as it is known among refinishers, looks like water but is, in fact, 60 percent active oxygen. When M.E.K. combines with glass resin, it generates the heat required for drying. *Note:* Eight drops of M.E.K. will cure 1 ounce of resin at a temperature of 70 degrees Fahrenheit. More is required in cool, moist weather. The activated resin is brushed onto the thread-damaged area. Once dry, it is sanded and cleaned before primer-surfacer is applied over it.

Vinyl

Parts of late model cars are also made from soft plastic and vinyl. Gravel shields, header panels, and headlamp doors are examples. When these surfaces need refinishing, they, too, must be sanded to increase adhesion. The trick, as always, is to do the job without doing any visible damage. Sanding on these so-called soft fascia therefore requires a very light touch and at least a 320-grit abrasive.

Flexible Panels

An increasing number of panels on modern automobiles are made of flexible materials. In order to insure that new paint applied to such parts does not crack as the parts flex, special attention is required from the refinisher, as follows:

Since the part is flexible, the paint must be flexible. Any paint can be made to flex. In order to do this a paint flex additive available from your local paint jobber must be added to both the primer and the color coat. The amount to be added will be noted on the can the additive comes in. The mixture usually is one-to-one with lacquer, but varies from two-to-one to four-to-one with enamels.

First, hand sand the part using 320 to 400 sandpaper. To avoid damage to the part do *not* use a machine sander.

Using a lacquer-based primer to which the flex additive has been added, prime the part. Light sand the primer and spray the part with a color coat containing the flex additive. Apply as many parts as you would to an ordinary panel, making sure always to use the flex additive.

Allow to dry in the normal manner, being careful to avoid excessive heat.

MASKING

Once cleaned and sanded, the vehicle surface is ready to be filled. The filling agent of first resort, however, is primer-surfacer—a product that requires a spray gun for application. Use of this tool means that nearby panels will almost certainly be exposed to overspray. Therefore, before a refinisher can proceed any further in preparing the surface, he must protect these adjacent areas. He does so by masking.

Masking involves applying paper and/or tape to panels, glass, and trim. How extensive the coverage depends on the type of repair being done. If the whole vehicle is being refinished, masking is minimal. Only those surfaces that are never painted—wheels, windows, bumpers, and chrome trim—receive protection. If only a portion of the vehicle is being painted, however, masking is much more extensive. In addition to glass and trim, panel surfaces must be covered as well.

Materials and Equipment

The paper used in masking is a special type—sturdy and nonabsorbent yet easy to manipulate and fold. It comes in a variety of widths ranging from 3 to 36 inches. The 12-, 18-, 24-, and 36-inch widths are the ones most frequently used in refinishing.

Masking paper is held in place by masking tape. It, too, comes in a number of widths—⅛ inch being the narrowest, 3 inches being the widest. In refinishing, the ¾-inch width is the most commonly used. Masking tape adheres well to smooth surfaces. It also stands up to moisture, whether in the form of water or paint. Its most important quality, however, is its ability to pull free from a surface without doing damage or leaving behind any adhesive.

In the shop, both masking materials are dispensed together from a device called an apron taper. In its simplest form, an apron taper consists of a mount for a roll of paper, a mount for a roll of tape, and a cutting bar (Fig. 4-13). As paper is pulled from the machine, tape is automatically attached to one edge. When the sheet reaches the proper length, it is pulled upward against the cutting bar and torn from the dispenser. The portion of the tape that overlaps the paper's edge is then used to attach the sheet to the vehicle. *Note:* Some apron tapers can hold up to four different widths of paper and as many rolls of tape.

Preparation

While masking tape has excellent adhesive qualities, there is one important limit on its use. It must be applied to a clean, dry surface. Masking therefore begins the same as virtually every other step in the refinishing process—with cleaning.

FIG 4-13
Apron taper. (3M Company)

FIG 4-14
Removing insignia. (Badger Air-Brush Co., *Air-Brushing Techniques for Custom Painting, Volume II*)

Avoiding Underspray

Dirt, oil, and water—all of the things that cause paint to peel—have the same effect on masking tape. A molding on a panel that has been wet sanded, for example, must be thoroughly rinsed, wiped dry, blown out with a duster gun, and wiped dry again before masking with tape. If not, traces of sanding dust or water could coat the tape's adhesive and create pockets into which paint could seep. The result would be a condition called underspray in which paint reaches a supposedly protected surface. Once begun, underspray can only get worse. The seeping paint weakens the surrounding adhesive. This situation leads to even bigger pockets that allow even more paint to collect under the tape. The cycle continues until the tape curls and finally pulls away entirely.

Removing Bumpers and Trim

Another key procedure that must be carried out in advance of masking is the removal of bumpers and trim. These items are not, however, removed in every case. There are three determining factors.

1. *Interference with painting.* In most late-model vehicles, there are finished body panels located directly behind the front and rear bumpers. Because of the limited amount of clearance, it is almost impossible to reach these panels by working around the bumpers. Most refinishers remove the bumpers and their mounts whenever they get in the way.
2. *Masking time.* In general, the smaller and more irregular a piece of trim, the more time it will take to mask. In some cases, however, the part is so irregular that masking would take more time than the volume of work allows. Lettering used to spell out vehicle make and model names is a prime example. For this type of trim, many refinishers prefer removal to masking (Fig. 4-14). (It should be noted, however, that in some cases the reverse is true. Removal takes more time than masking. Oldsmobiles and Cadillacs are examples. Their model names are bolted onto fenders from the inside. Reaching the fasteners is so difficult that masking is preferable.)
3. *Breakage.* Removal is also not without its risks. Where the piece of trim is delicate or its fasteners corroded, for example, breakage is always a possibility. Indeed, with older cars, it should be considered

a likelihood. Remember, if the part is broken, any time saved by removing it may eventually be lost in the search for a replacement.

Technique

There is no set procedure for masking a vehicle. (Too many body styles exist for such a rigid approach.) Instead, the refinisher handles each job differently. He considers the type of car, the extent of painting to be done, and the kinds of masking materials available. He then adjusts his technique to these conditions.

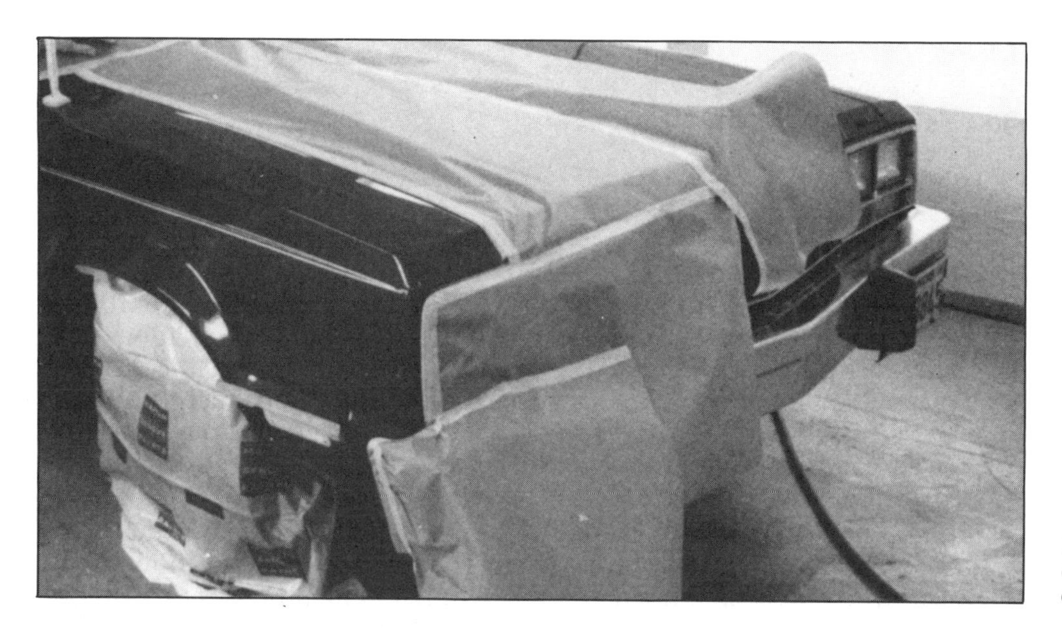

FIG 4-15
Masking front fender for enamel. (The Martin-Senour Company)

General Application Procedures

If there is no single masking procedure, however, there are at least some general rules.

1. *Extend masking only as far as the material being sprayed requires.* If a fender is being painted, the refinisher does not cover the rest of the vehicle with masking paper. Such a procedure would be a waste of time and materials. Rather, he masks only that portion of the body nearest to the repair area. Just how far he extends the masking depends on what material he is spraying. For lacquer primer-surfacer, 12 inches is enough. For lacquer paints, on the other hand, up to 24 inches is needed. All enamel products, being thicker and heavier, require at least 36 inches (Fig. 4-15).
2. *Apply pretaped paper to the longest edge of a panel or surface.* From there, it can easily be folded to fit the area's narrower contours. Application to a shorter edge would cause two kinds of difficulty. If the paper were cut to the shorter length, additional masking would be required to cover the panel's wider portions. Such a procedure would involve more cutting and taping (meaning more work) and more seams (meaning a higher risk of underspray). If the paper were cut to the longer length but applied to a shorter edge, it would have to be folded under. This procedure would be a waste of pretaping and could lead to tearing if the adhesive catches the underside of the paper at the wrong point.

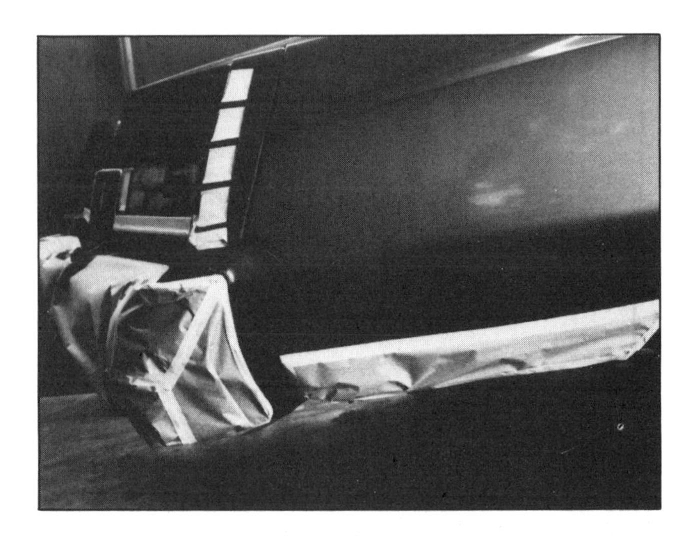

FIG 4-16
Taped folds on rear bumper. (3M Company)

3. *Do not stretch masking materials during application.* Both masking paper and masking tape have a certain amount of flexibility. This quality allows them to be applied to curved surfaces and drawn snugly against straight ones. What is called for in both instances, however, is firm pressure—pulling the paper tight, not stretching it. Stretching weakens masking paper and puckers tape. These conditions, in turn, could lead to seepage, bleedthrough, or tearing.
4. *Tape down all seams and folds.* This procedure serves a dual purpose. First, obviously, it reduces the possibility of underspray. Second, it smooths out the masking paper. The smoothing is necessary to control overspray. A deep fold, for example, can deflect atomized paint, sending it off in some unexpected direction. There it might land on an unprotected surface. Taping the fold shut makes the flow of air over the masking more predictable and thus increases the refinisher's control of the painting process (Fig. 4-16).

Masking Special Parts

Beyond these general procedures, certain vehicle surfaces require special masking techniques. Most of these parts are smaller than panels. Most have irregular or curved contours. Finally, despite the fact that they are never painted, most are located on or near surfaces that are frequently painted.

1. *Windshields.* Because of their slope and location, the front and rear windshields receive large amounts of overspray. This fact requires special masking procedures. To start, windshields must be covered in two steps—the moldings first and then the glass. Doing the moldings separately allows the refinisher to mask without having to pull along 2 to 3 feet of masking paper. He can thus work with a great deal of control and accuracy. This ability is very important when the refinisher is covering a molding's outer edge, the one that may butt against surfaces being painted. A molding's inner edge is not so critical. There the tape can (and usually does) overlap onto the windshield itself. Once the molding is masked, paper from the apron taper can be placed quickly. It is simply lapped halfway into the molding tape. Exact placement is not necessary.

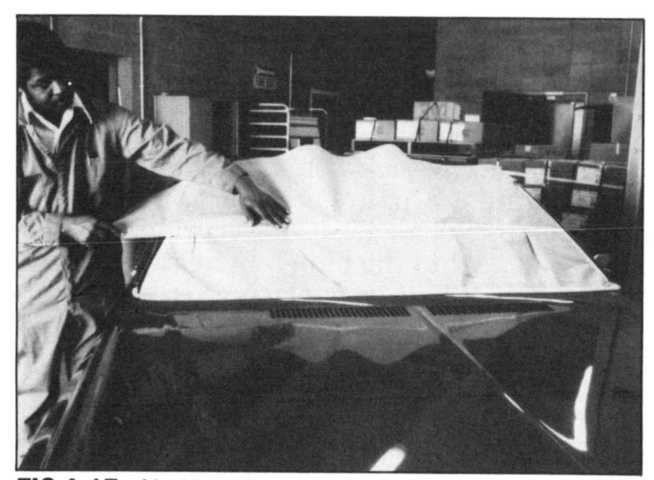

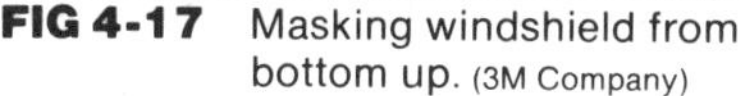

FIG 4-17 Masking windshield from bottom up. (3M Company)

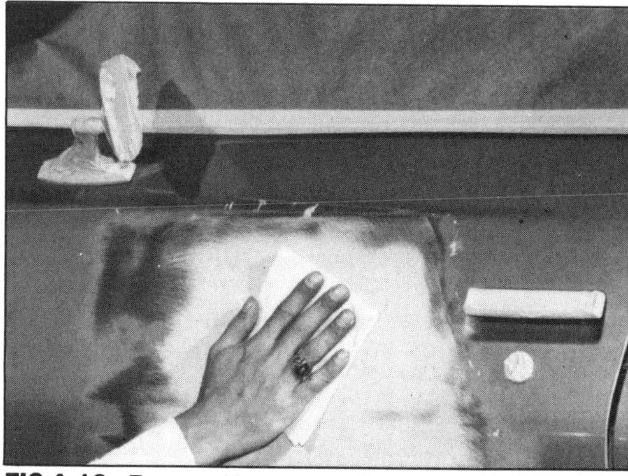

FIG 4-18 Tape masking on moulding and mirror. (3M Company)

A second procedure that windshields require is masking from the bottom up (Fig. 4-17). This sequence is more than just an example of starting with the longest edge. It is a precaution against underspray. In most instances, it takes more than one sheet of masking paper to cover a windshield. When the topmost portion of glass is masked last, the pocket formed by the overlap of the second sheet opens downward. Thus, if any paint gets under the tape, it runs off harmlessly onto the bottom layer of paper. If the top sheet of paper were placed first, however, the pocket would open upward. Any paint getting under the tape would have a clear path to the glass below.

2. *Moldings and trim.* If they are not removed, moldings and flat trim are usually masked with tape only. Tape may be used on door handles and mirrors, also (Fig. 4-18). The refinisher simply chooses a width that matches the molding (or comes close to it). The tape is then applied in one continuous piece along the molding's full length. Special care, however, must be taken to seal edges and to avoid overlaps that could keep paint from reaching the panel surface. Quickly running a fingernail along the molding's edges is a good precaution to take against both problems. *Note:* If only a limited number of tape widths is available, it may be necessary to mask some moldings in two stages—once again, bottom first and then top. This procedure duplicates on a smaller scale the one used in masking windshields. The reason is the same as well—avoiding underspray in an area subjected to large amounts of overspray.
3. *Mirrors and ornaments.* Side-view mirrors and hood ornaments are also considered trim. Their irregular surfaces plus the fact that they are freestanding, however, combine to make them more time-consuming to mask. For this reason, some refinishers use a shortcut. They cover such fixtures with paper or plastic bags. While this procedure may be adequate when such parts are far from the area being painted, it is not adequate when they are in the direct path of the spray gun. In such situations, paper bags will usually bleed through and plastic bags will disintegrate. (Thinner, in particular, eats through the thin plastic bags very quickly.) It is therefore best to cover such surfaces with paper and/or multiple layers of mask-

ing tape. Which technique a refinisher uses will depend on the size and shape of the mirror or ornament.

4. *Lamps.* Headlamps are among the few surfaces on a vehicle for which masking paper is cut to both size and shape. First, the retaining ring around the lamp is covered with masking tape. Since this metal ring often butts against a painted surface, it is treated much like a windshield molding. The tape is accurately placed along the outside edge (the one next to the panel) but extended onto the glass along the inside edge. Masking paper is then applied to the lamp face, overlapping the tape. If the lamp is circular, the refinisher usually cuts the paper into a roughly circular shape before applying it. If the lamp is rectangular, he generally tapes one edge in place and then uses a knife or razor to cut the remaining edges to fit. *Note:* Taillights present an easier case. Being smaller, they can be masked using tape alone (Fig. 4-19).
5. *Wheels.* Wheels are fairly large, awkward areas to mask. The task is made easier, however, by the fact that such masking does not have to be done with any great degree of accuracy. The job need only be thorough and fairly neat.

   There are two basic wheel masking techniques. The first involves covering a wheel with a reusable shroud, or wheel mask. This cover is usually made of plastic or nylon that is specially coated to repel paint. It is secured at the back of the wheel with an elastic or cord tie. The second technique involves covering the wheel with a sheet of 36-inch masking paper. The paper is pulled around to the back of the wheel and fastened with tape. Of the two techniques, wrapping the wheel with masking paper is probably the most effective. After three or four jobs, the reusable covers often become sources of paint contamination.
6. *Lettering.* When lettering either is not or cannot be removed, it is usually masked with ¼-inch tape (Fig. 4-20). This procedure must be done with extreme care to insure that all of the lettering but none of the panel behind it is covered. For this reason, it is usually a good idea to begin with the bottom edge of the trim. This surface is the

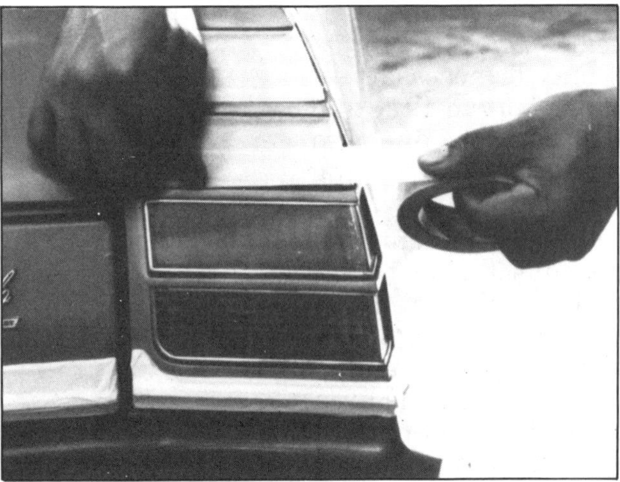

FIG 4-19 Masking taillights with tape. (3M Company)

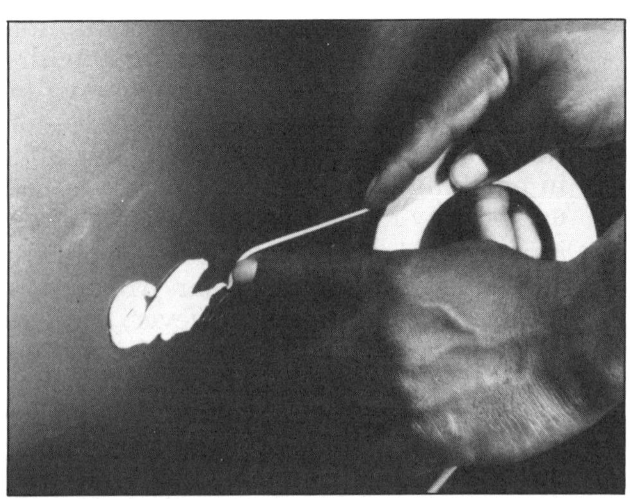

FIG 4-20 Masking lettering with ¼-inch tape. (3M Company)

most difficult to see. From there the tape can be wrapped more easily over the lettering's upper surfaces, interior curves, ridges, and hollows.

As an alternative, lettering can be covered with petroleum jelly. Because the risk of contamination is so great with this technique, however, the material must be applied with even more care than the ¼-inch tape. A thin film is spread over the lettering as a final step before painting. It is wiped off only after the finish is fully dry. At that point, the paint covering the lubricant film cracks easily and flakes away with only light pressure.

Removing Masking

There is more to unmasking a vehicle than simply pulling off the paper. The removal procedure must be carried out carefully, systematically, and—most important—at just the right time.

There is such a thing as leaving masking in place too long. Where tape butts directly against fresh paint, a bridge of material can sometimes form. If the masking is removed while the paint is still relatively wet, this layer of material separates easily. If it is allowed to dry, however, it clings so that part of the new finish is pulled away with the tape. The result is a jagged or even chipped edge that is obvious enough to ruin the finish.

To avoid this problem, masking should be removed from lacquer within 30 minutes of application for a spot or panel repair, within 4 hours for a whole-vehicle repair. Some kinds of enamel, on the other hand, can wait as long as 18 to 24 hours. Regardless of which kind of finish is applied or how much drying time is allowed, the refinisher should always check all tape before removal. If he spots any bridges, he can then use a razor to slash the paint close to the masking's edge. If done carefully, this procedure leaves no telltale marks and eliminates entirely the risk of removing any portion of the new finish with the tape.

As for actual removal technique, masking paper should be stripped away one edge at a time. It is always pulled directly outward at a 90-degree angle. To protect the new finish, removal proceeds inch by inch. Paper is never yanked along its full length or torn into small pieces from all directions. Rather, the action is continuous in one direction, slow and steady. Remember, at this stage, the paint is still quite fresh. It can easily be scratched, gouged, or cut by the sharp edges of paint-stiffened paper.

OBJECTIVE 4-A2 (manipulative)

Working as a team with three other students and with the aid of Job Report Sheet 4-A2, you will mask a vehicle for application of lacquer to its hood, right (or left) front fender, and right (or left) door.

Time Recommended:

1 hour

Preparation:

1. Review pages 148 through 155.

2. Study pages 156 through 160.
3. Read the Safety Checklist on page 175, items 2 and 6.

Tools and Materials:

1. Masking paper (12- and 36-inch widths)
2. Masking tape (¾ inch)
3. Screwdriver and/or socket wrench for removing trim (optional)
4. Fast-drying reducer
5. Clean shop cloths

Procedure:

1. Determine which (if any) trim elements can be more easily removed than masked. Use the screwdriver and/or socket wrench to detach these from the vehicle.
2. Saturate a clean shop cloth with fast-drying reducer and wipe down all surfaces to be masked. Give special attention to the moldings and panel edges that will be in direct contact with the masking tape.
3. Mask the windshield. First, thoroughly mask all windshield moldings, sealing down tape edges with a thumbnail. If the hood butts directly against the glass, raise the hood panel and attach the paper to the front of the cowl assembly. To guarantee that a full 12 inches of the windshield is covered, extend the masking with a second sheet of paper. Close the hood. If there is a separate grilled panel between the hood and the glass, begin masking with this panel. Do not open the hood. Working from the bottom up, simply extend the paper back from the panel's far edge up onto the windshield. *Note:* In both cases, extend the paper beyond the windshield's side moldings at least far enough to cover the vehicle's front parts.
4. Mask the window in the door that is to be primed. Again, mask the molding separately. Secure the papers to the molding at the bottom of the glass. Then extend the paper upward, overlapping the windshield masking. Tape the top edge in place. *Note:* On a truck or other vehicle where the door fully frames the glass, the center window will have to be masked, moldings first and then glass.
5. Mask the panel next to the door. Use a single sheet of masking paper applied vertically. (In most instances, this sheet will overlay the door's window masking at the top.)
6. Mask the fender that is not being primed. Apply the taped edge of the paper to the fender edge adjoining the hood. Extend the paper onto the *header panel* and/or headlamp at the front of the vehicle. Extend it onto the windshield masking and at the rear door. Make any folds or pleats necessary and tape them in place.
7. Mask the front header panel and/or grill, deflector/gravel shield, front scoop, and related elements. *Note:* A header bar is a separate panel extending the full width of the hood. When present, it usually supports the grill. If portions of the fender to be primed extend into this area, some front end elements may have to be individually masked—the headlamps or bumper, for example. In these cases, cover all adjoining edges carefully. Tape down any fold or

portions of paper that could keep primer-surfaces from reaching the fender area.

8. Use the 36-inch paper to cover the wheel under the fender being primed. Lap the paper over the top of the wheel and *secure from behind.* Fold the remaining edges back around the sides of the wheel and tape in place.
9. Mask all trim that has not been removed from the panels being primed, using care to seal all edges and overlaps by running a fingernail over them. Use long, continuous pieces of tape. Use paper and/or tape to cover any side-view mirrors or free-standing hood ornaments. Cover moldings with one or two lengths of masking tape (which will depend on the size of the moldings present and the available widths of the tape). Use the same technique to mask door handles, locks, and other flat, regular trim.
10. If vehicle headlamps are so located that they have not been covered in any previous segment, mask them now separately. Start by masking the lamp molding (retaining rings). Carefully cover any remaining openings or moldings with tape. Then cut masking paper to the approximate size and shape of the lampface and tape in place over the glass. Also, at this point mask any fender side lamps. They can be covered with a length or two of masking tape, much like moldings or other flat trim.
11. Use ⅛- or ¼-inch tape to mask any lettering.
12. After painting, remove the masking, making sure you do so within 4 hours if spraying lacquer or 18 to 24 hours if spraying enamel. Where paint bridges are found between panel and masking tape, cut through with a single-edged razor. To remove the paper, pull it away from the car at a 90-degree angle, proceeding inch by inch in a smooth, slow fashion. Remove the masking tape in the same way.

MASKING A VEHICLE HOOD, FENDER, AND DOOR

Student Name ______________________ Date ____________

Time Started ____________ Time Finished ____________ Total Time ____________

Specifications

Panels being masked ____________ Make, model car ____________

What size masking paper used? ____________

Technique

Are all moldings and other surfaces where masking tape is to be applied completely dried and cleaned? ______

Have bumpers, trim, and molding been removed where possible? ______

Was trim not easily removable thoroughly masked? ______

How far beyond the area being sprayed was masking extended? ____________

Why? ______________________

Was masking paper applied with all seams and folds taped down? ______

Why? ______________________

Was the windshield glass and its surrounding molding masked separately? ______

Why? ______________________

Describe masking treatment used for headlamps and associated moldings. ________

____

Describe method of masking wheels. ______________________

Why was this method chosen? ______________________

____

How much time should elapse after painting before masking is removed? ________

Why? ______________________

Describe method of removing masking tape where paint bridges are present. ________

____

Checkup Questions

1. How is an apron taper used? ____

   ____

2. What is underspray and how can it be avoided? ____

   ____

3. Describe the technique for masking lettering. ____

   ____

4. How should masking paper be removed? ____

   ____

Date Completed ____________________ Instructor's Signature ________________________________

PRIMING

With nearby surfaces safely masked, the repair area can be primed. In automobile refinishing, the material most frequently used for this purpose is primer-surfacer. Its dual function, as its name implies, is to prime the surface for the new paint (to provide adhesion, in other words) and to resurface those areas marked by filling and sanding operations.

Primer-Surfacer Selection

Which primer-surfacer is used—lacquer or enamel—depends largely on top-coat/base-coat compatibilities and on how much time is available for the overall repair job. Both lacquer and enamel primer-surfacers compare favorably with each other in terms of adhesion, corrosion resistance, holdout, and flow characteristics. Where they differ markedly is in drying time. Lacquer primer-surfacer, like all lacquer products, is fast drying. It requires at most 30 minutes to cure fully enough to sand. Enamel, on the other hand, needs 3 to 4 hours, depending on shop conditions, to reach that same point. Lacquer primer-surfacer is therefore the more frequently used product, particularly for spot repairs. (For a more complete review of primer-surfacer characteristics, see Unit 2, pages 61 and 62.)

A minor factor that enters into the selection of a primer-surfacer is whether it is to be applied to plastic or vinyl. For this specialized use there are primer-surfacers containing elastomer, a resinous material that allows the finish to flex and stretch with the surface it covers. Elastomer is also available as an additive that can be mixed with ordinary primer-surfacers as well as paints.

Application Techniques

Primer-surfacer is applied with a spray gun (Fig. 4-21). The transformer-regulator setting is low—about 45 psi (35 psi at the gun). The material is sprayed on in multiple coats—at least four for most repairs. The determining factor is how many coats of paint are already on the panel. The more coats of paint there are, the more coats of primer-surfacer will be necessary to build up the repair to the proper level (Fig. 4-22). Each

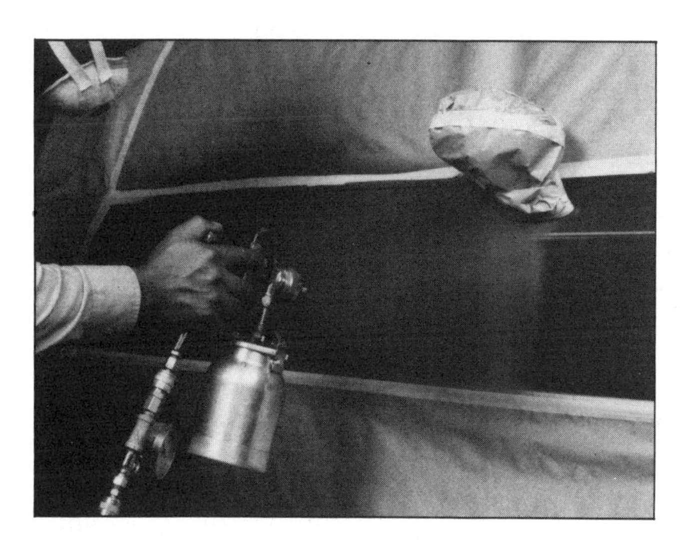

FIG 4-21
Applying primer-surfacer.
(3M Company)

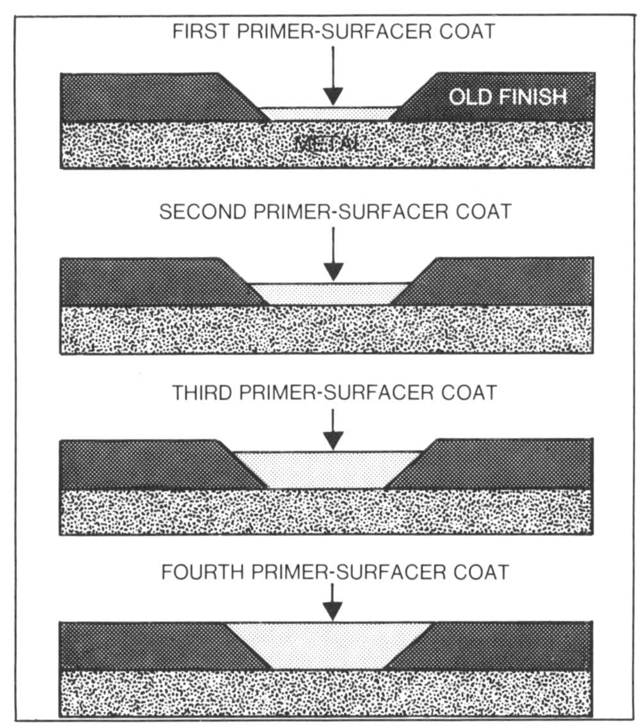

FIG 4-22 Building up a repair area with primer-surfacer.

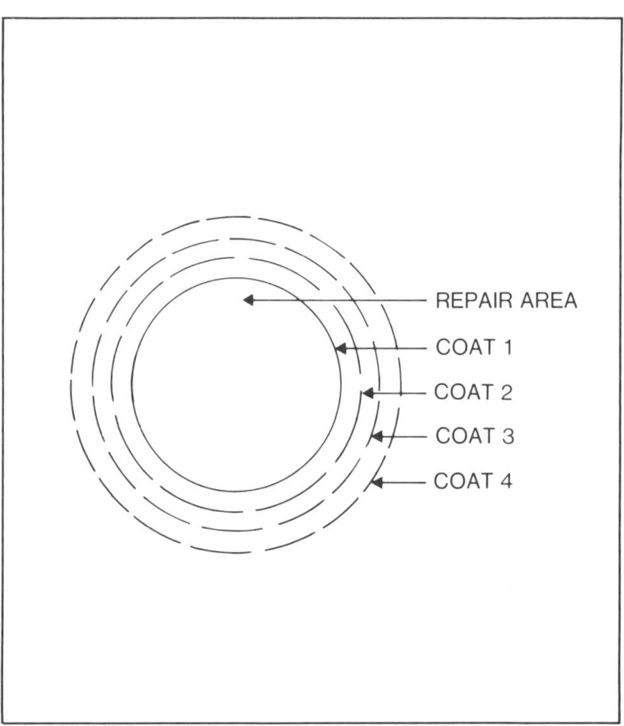

FIG 4-23 Overlapping method of applying primer-surfacer on a spot repair.

coat of primer-surfacer is allowed to flash, or look dry, before the next is applied over it. Flash time for lacquer primer-surfacer is about 5 minutes.

When the surface is thoroughly dry, it is sanded. This procedure reveals any low spots, which can then be filled with putty. A fifth (and in some rare cases a sixth) coat of primer-surfacer is applied to complete the required filling. The surface is finish sanded with an extremely fine abrasive.

Care should be taken to apply primer-surfacer only where it is needed. Small areas should be primed by adjusting the spray gun's pattern to its smallest dimensions. This technique keeps the repair from growing and thus makes the most economical use of expensive refinishing materials.

For spot repairs, there is a special application technique. It is used for paint as well as primer-surfacer. Basically it involves lapping each coat slightly beyond the last one (Fig. 4-23). The effect is a kind of reverse featheredge. The spray gun simply follows the taper of the repair. It applies more material where more has been sanded away (at the center) and less material where less has been removed (at the edge). The result is a surface that is already roughly contoured before any sandpaper has even touched it.

Application Problems

Primer-surfacer is an extremely thick, heavy material (remember its 60-percent solids content). This fact can lead the uninformed refinisher to make unnecessary adjustments in his spray painting technique, adjustments that in themselves create problems. For example, in an attempt to compensate for the viscosity of primer-surfacer, a refinisher might increase the pressure at the transformer-regulator. Pressure that is too high, however, creates overspray. Pressure that is too high for the amount of material being passed by the spray gun creates dry spray. Both are problems that would not exist if the ideal setting of 45 psi were used.

Dry Spray

Dry spray in particular is a very common problem with primer-surfacer and, in fact, one of the principal causes of holdout problems. The reason is simple. Primer-surfacer is a naturally porous material. This quality is aggravated when primer-surfacer goes on dry. It becomes so porous that it actually absorbs the color sprayed over it. This absorption process is what causes the dull finish associated with lack of holdout.

Primer-surfacer applied dry also presents more fundamental problems. It neither adheres well nor flows sufficiently to fill sandscratches. It fails, in other words, in both of its primary functions. It is therefore best when spraying primer-surfacer to resist the temptation to raise the regulated pressure. Properly reduced, the material can be sprayed at 45 psi to the same standard as paint—wet enough to flow, but dry enough to avoid drips and sags.

Overwetting

At the other extreme are refinishers who try to get around primer-surfacer's tendency to dry spray by overwetting a surface. They apply either too much material at once or too many coats too quickly. The result is a surface that takes an excessive amount of time to dry. This mistake could, for example, eat up most of the time gained by using a lacquer primer-surfacer instead of an enamel-based product.

Once a surface has been overwet, the refinisher's options are limited. He must either wait the extended time for it to dry or apply heat. Under no circumstances should he use a partially triggered spray gun to fan the work surface. Blowing air directly on freshly applied primer-surfacer dries the outermost coat but does nothing for the material underneath. In fact, the dry outer film traps the solvents in the earlier coats and preserves the primer-surfacer in a semi-cured, or gummy, state. Gummy primer-surfacer cannot be dry sanded and wet sands poorly.

To avoid overwetting surfaces, allow adequate flash time between primer-surfacer coats. When faster drying is required, use a heat lamp (Fig. 4-25). The lamp warms the material through and, unlike fanning, gradually affects inner as well as outer film layers.

Sanding and Filling

Sanding of primer-surfacer, like featheredging a repair area, proceeds in two stages. In the first stage, the new base coat is dry sanded by hand to eliminate the high spots and to isolate the low. This procedure may be repeated any number of times, depending on how deep the low spots are and how the refinisher chooses to fill them—all at once with putty or gradually with more applications of primer-surfacer. The abrasives used for this kind of sanding are usually in the 280- to 360-grit range. (The coarser grits are used for enamel finishes, the finer ones for lacquer.)

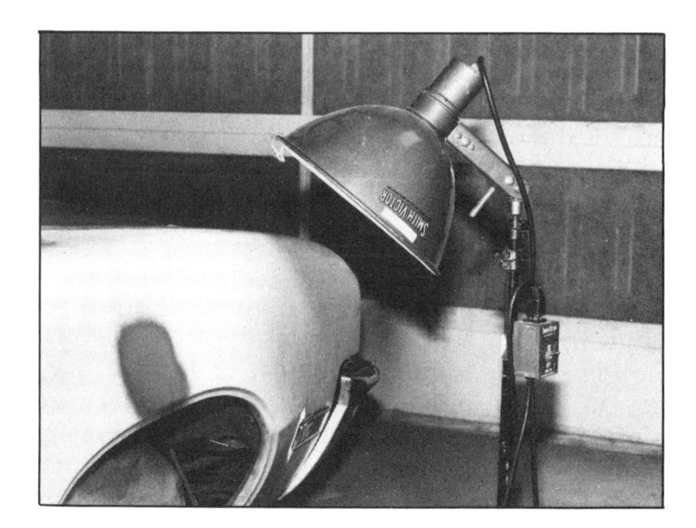

FIG 4-24
Force-drying paint spray with heat lamp.
(Davenport Photography)

Once the proper degree of filling has been achieved, the surface is ready for the second stage of sanding. Because this is likely to be the final sanding of the whole preparation process, it is done wet for maximum smoothness. The abrasives used are extremely fine—at least 400 grit for enamel top coats and 500 grit for lacquers.

Problem Areas

The most critical problem in sanding primer-surfacer is not, however, how often or with what to sand but when to sand. As it dries, primer-surfacer shrinks—in some cases, as much as 50 percent. As the solvents evaporate out, the material sinks down into sandscratches and other irregularities. The result is a new surface that, while not so deeply flawed, still follows the uneven contours of the original (Fig. 4-25). To bring it to a uniform level, the refinisher sands down the high spots to match the low. Should this sanding be started too early, however, the primer-surfacer will continue to shrink after the surface has been leveled (Fig. 4-26). As a result, sandscratches and other markings will gradually reappear, making necessary more sanding or filling. The only sure way to avoid this kind of wasted effort is to apply the initial two or three coats of primer-surfacer at the correct intervals and allow them to dry thoroughly before any sanding is begun.

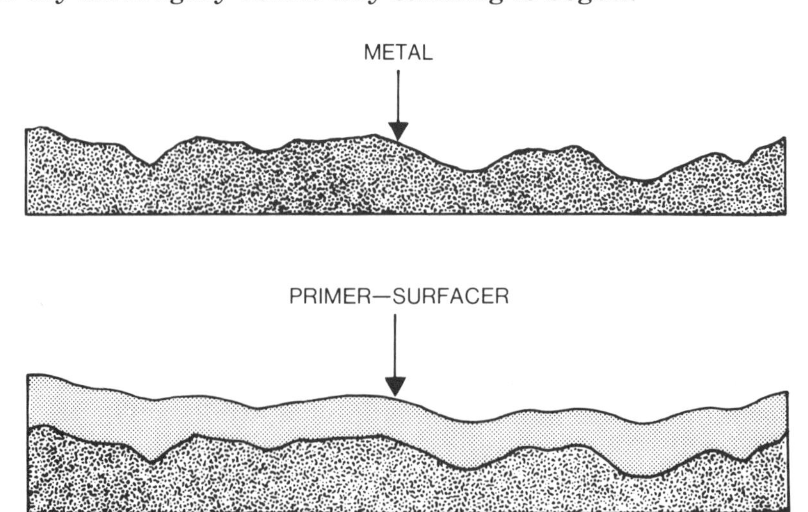

FIG 4-25
Primer-surfacer follows the contours of the panel to which it is applied.

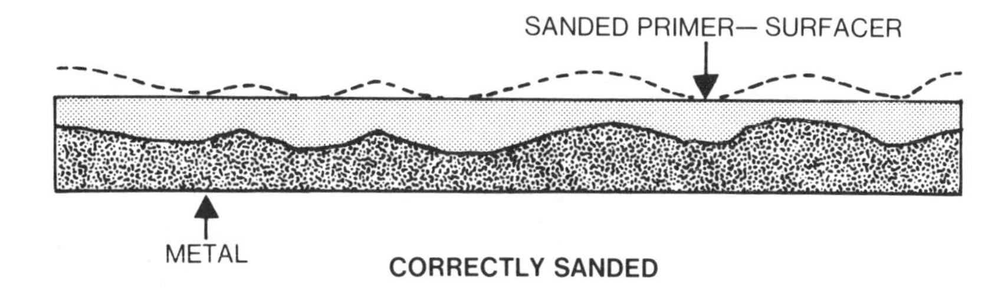

FIG 4-26 Correct and incorrect sanding of primer-surfacer.

Oxidation is another primer-surfacer problem, one that occurs with less frequency, perhaps, but has potentially more damaging effects. It is a direct consequence of wet sanding (and the porous nature of primer-surfacer). If water remains on primer-surfacer for a long period of time, it soaks through to the metal. Soon tiny rust-colored spots appear on the base coat. These indicate that oxidation, or rusting, is taking place somewhere below. If the rust is not removed, it will eventually eat through the finish. All of the new primer-surfacer must therefore be sanded away and the bare metal treated with conditioner. This remedy means, of course, that the whole area will have to be resurfaced. This duplication of effort can be avoided by (1) confining wet sanding to the very last stages of primer-surfacer application, (2) doing all wet sanding on primer-surfacer as briskly as possible, and (3) blowing the surface dry immediately afterward.

Checkup Technique

After a number of coats of primer-surfacer and putty have been applied, the imperfections left on a surface are generally quite small and difficult to see. Nonetheless, if a refinisher is to turn out quality work, he must be able to find such flaws and eliminate them. A special checkup technique can help.

The technique takes advantage of the fact that primer-surfacer comes in different colors. The refinisher uses a small aerosol can of the product to mist the repair area with primer-surfacer of a contrasting shade. (If, for example, red oxide is used to prime, then light gray can be used to check.) When the mist coat is dry, the refinisher resands. Any gray that remains on the surface after the sanding is complete indicates a low spot. Such spots are then filled before the last coat of primer-surfacer is applied, thus producing the smoothest possible surface.

FINAL CLEANING

It should now be obvious that the preparation process itself exposes a body panel to numerous contaminants that, if left on the surface,

FIG 4-27
Masking tape loosening and curling from moisture.
(Jay Storer)

could ruin a new finish. The list includes sanding dust, water, slow-drying solvents, body oils, and lint—and these are the result of using correct procedures. Careless technique can expand the number of potential troublemakers to include residues of wax, polish, gasoline, and strong solvents.

To remove these substances requires more than just flushing the repair area with water, as in wet sanding. The final cleaning of a vehicle before painting must be much more thorough and physically more extensive. The proper procedure, in fact, has six separate steps.

1. *Remove all masking.* If the masking has done its job, it is now full of primer-surfacer, sanding dust, and water. These residues could be displaced by spray painting. What is more, if water has worked its way under any of the tape, the masking could be ready to loosen and curl (Fig. 4-27). Should this failure occur in the booth, panels not being refinished could be exposed to underspray.
2. *Compound the area surrounding the repair.* (When a whole panel is being refinished, the nearest 8 to 10 inches of any adjacent panel will do). This step is necessary for lacquers and optional for enamels. Its purpose is to expose the true color of the old finish so that the new one can be properly matched and blended. Afterward, rinse the area, dry it, and reblow any nearby crevices or moldings. *Note:* Since compound does contain some oil, it is a wise precaution to go over the area with wax remover.
3. *Wash the whole vehicle.* To eliminate the possibility of taking any loose dust or dirt into the spray booth, the whole vehicle (and not just the repair area) should be washed. Any soap or detergent used should be thoroughly rinsed from the surface. At this point in the preparation process, residues of either could contaminate the new finish.
4. *Dry the vehicle using a combination of compressed air and hand wiping.* A duster gun operating at 35 psi should be used to chase water from the vehicle's surface. When most of the moisture is cleared, the pressure should be reset to 70 psi and the tool used to blow out the areas under moldings and between panels (Fig. 4-28). The logic of using such high pressure is to exceed any setting that might be required for spraying paint. Thus, if the water around panels and moldings is not dislodged by the duster gun, a refinisher

FIG 4-28
Blowing water from beneath moldings after washing the car. (David Keown)

can be sure that it will not be dislodged by a spray gun. After the vehicle's crevices have been blown out, the surface should be visually checked and any remaining moisture wiped away with a clean, dry cloth. Remask.

5. *Use fast-drying reducer to wipe down the entire repair area.* This material is strong enough to cut through wax remover, fingerprints, and any other oily residues. It dries fast enough, however, not to damage existing finishes or to interfere with top coat bonding. (The latter is true even when the top coat is a potentially incompatible material like lacquer.)
6. *Tack all surfaces to be painted.* Tacking is the final step in the whole preparation process. Technically, the procedure should be left till the vehicle is actually in the spray booth (Fig. 4-29). That way, with the door closed and the ventilation system turned on, no new lint, dust, or other airborne particles can settle on the surface. Tack cloth is used folded as it comes from the packet. As each face loses its adhesive effect, the cloth is refolded to expose a new surface. In this manner, the refinisher can keep track of which faces are still fresh and thus make maximum use of each cloth. Once the whole area to be refinished is tacked, the vehicle is ready for painting or sealing, as the case may be.

FIG 4-29
Using a tack rag in the spray booth. (E. I. du Pont de Nemours & Co., Inc.)

OBJECTIVE 4-A3 (manipulative)

Working as a team with two other students and with the aid of Job Report Sheet 4-A3, you will prepare a chipped or slightly damaged body panel (factory-baked lacquer) for refinishing with lacquer.

Time Recommended:

4 hours

Preparation:

1. Review pages 135 through 167.
2. Study pages 168 through 172.
3. Read the Safety Checklist on pages 174 and 175, items 1 through 6.

Tools and Materials:

1. Vibrator or orbital sander
2. Suction-feed spray gun
3. Duster gun
4. Sanding blocks (hard and sponge rubber)
5. Squeegee
6. Socket wrench (for battery ground cable)
7. Masking paper and tape
8. Clean shop cloths
9. Respirator and safety goggles
10. Rubber gloves
11. Wooden stirring sticks
12. Hose (or sponge and bucket)
13. Wax remover
14. Metal conditioner
15. Lacquer primer-surfacer
16. Aerosol can of lacquer primer-surfacer (contrasting color)
17. Thinner
18. Fast-drying reducer
19. Putty
20. Selection of sandpapers (80D, 280A, 320A, 500A)
21. Hand rubbing compound
22. Tack cloth

Procedure:

1. Saturate a clean cloth with wax remover. Apply to the panel and wipe dry with another clean cloth.
2. Using a vibrator or an orbital sander equipped with an 80D abrasive, featheredge the chipped or damaged areas of the panel. *Note:* For all mechanical sanding, spraying, or cleaning operations, wear a respirator. For sanding and cleaning, use safety goggles as well.
3. Tear a piece of sandpaper (280A or 320A) in half. Fold into three

equal pieces and, sanding by hand, sand out from the feather-edged repair a distance of 3 to 5 inches in all directions.

4. Use a duster gun to blow the sanding dust from the panel.
5. Where bare metal has been exposed, apply metal conditioner. *Note:* For this procedure, wear rubber gloves as well as a respirator and goggles.
6. Use 12-inch masking paper to mask all adjacent panels and/or glass. Cover all moldings and trim on the repair panel itself with masking tape.
7. Mix 1 part lacquer primer-surfacer with 1½ parts thinner. Stir thoroughly.
8. Set the transformer-regulator at 40 psi (30 psi at the gun). Test the spray gun on a piece of masking paper. When properly adjusted, the gun should produce a 6-inch pattern that flows well when applied from a distance of 6 to 8 inches.
9. Apply four coats of primer-surfacer to the repair area. Allow each coat to flash before applying the next one. After the last coat, allow the panel to dry 30 minutes. *Note:* The first coat should cover only the bare metal exposed by sanding (or, if the feather-edging does not extend that far, only the old primer-surfacer). The remaining coats should then be overlapped an equal distance out into the 3- to 5-inch border sanded around the repair. Under no circumstances should the primer-surfacer be allowed to contact any painted surface that has not been sanded beforehand.
10. Using a 320A abrasive and a hard rubber sanding block, dry or wet sand the primer-surfacer to expose any imperfections or low spots.
11. With a squeegee, apply putty sparingly to any scratches or spots not filled by the primer-surfacer. Allow these areas to dry for 30 minutes.
12. Sand the puttied surface with the same abrasive used on the primer-surfacer. Blow the area clean with the duster gun.
13. Check for imperfections. Use the primer-surfacer in the aerosol can to apply a contrasting color of the product to the panel and sand with a hard rubber sanding block. If any low spots are found, fill with more putty, allow to dry, and resand.
14. Wet sand the panel using a 500A abrasive and a sponge sanding block. Rinse all sanding debris from the panel and wipe it dry with a clean cloth.
15. Remove all masking.
16. By hand, compound 8 to 10 inches into one adjacent panel to expose its true color. Blow any compounding dust from the work area.
17. Take the vehicle to the wash rack and rinse all surfaces thoroughly.
18. After air drying the vehicle with a duster gun operating at 35 psi, reset the transformer-regulator to 70 psi and blow all moisture from between crevices and under moldings near the repair panel. With a clean, dry cloth, wipe up any water that is dislodged.
19. Disconnect the battery ground cable. Push the vehicle into the spray booth.
20. Close the booth doors and turn on the exhaust system.

21. Remask any moldings or trim on the repair panel. Remask all adjacent panels and glass. Do last the panel that has been compounded so that it can be uncovered during spray painting without affecting other masking. (*Note:* For lacquer refinishing, 18- or 24-inch paper is an adequate masking material.)
22. Wipe down the entire panel with fast-drying reducer.
23. Tack the panel to be painted.

APPLYING PRIMER-SURFACER

Student Name ______________________ Date ______________

Time Started ____________ Time Finished ____________ Total Time ____________

Specifications

Type of panel ______________________________

Condition of finish (Describe the nature and extent of damage.) ______________

____

____

Technique

Rough featheredging method:

Type of sander ______________ Abrasive ______________

Fine featheredging method:

Type of sander ______________ Abrasive ______________

Metal conditioner: Yes ______ No ______

Surfaces masked ______________ ______________

______________ ______________

______________ ______________

Primer-surfacer: Type ______________ Color ______________

Psi at the transformer-regulator ______ Psi at the gun ______

Number of putty applications ______

Two-color checkup sanding: Yes ______ No ______

Wet sanding method: Hose ______ Sponge and bucket ______

Type of sanding block ______________ Abrasive ______________

Checkup Questions

1. When the wax remover was wiped from the panel, what visible residue was picked up on the cloth? ______________________________

____

____

2. Describe the difference between a freshly applied coat of primer-surfacer and one that has flashed. ______________________________

____

____

3. Why must a 3- to 5-inch border be sanded around a repair area before primer-surfacer is applied? ______________________________

____

____

Date Completed ______________ Instructor's Signature ______________________

SEALING

In the refinishing process, sealer is the first material used that requires the protection of the spray booth for application. The reason is that most sealers are nonsanding. Thus there is no opportunity for removing dust, dirt, or other foreign particles once they have settled on or become embedded in the sealer coat.

When to Seal

Technically, sealing is an optional step. On closer consideration, however, it is probably not that optional. Certainly sealing is necessary when applying paint over a potentially incompatible base. Enamel refinished with lacquer, for example, will lift and swell if not protected by sealer.

Most other problems that require sealing, however, involve compatible surfaces. They might, in fact, be considered examples of compatibility carried to the extreme, since all involve deep penetration of top coat solvents into the finish layers below. (Not surprisingly, lacquer solvents are the worst offenders in this respect.)

Lack of Holdout

When the base coat is a porous material like primer-surfacer, for example, the penetration can be so great that it actually takes some of the color with it. The result is a finish so dull that it cannot even be compounded to a shine. This is the classic case of lack of holdout. Rather than just bonding, the base and top coats actually combine. Once this reaction has occurred, the only solution is to remove both and start again.

Bleeding

Where the new finish is applied directly over the old one, the comparable condition is called bleeding. In these circumstances, however, the solvent penetration is far more likely to free color from the old top coat. This material then floats to the surface and blends with the fresh paint, changing its color or giving it an unwanted cast. Fortunately, few colors bleed—mainly reds and maroons. When one of these is being refinished, bleeder seal is used to prevent the reaction. *Note:* All sealers serve very narrowly defined purposes. Bleeder seal, for example, protects against bleeding only. It will not prevent an old enamel finish from being damaged by fresh lacquer or vice versa.

Sandscratch Swelling

Strong solvents can cause physical as well as chemical reactions. Freshly cut surfaces, for example, are especially sensitive to thinner. This sensitivity is important in refinishing because, with all of the sanding, a repair surface is nothing but fresh cuts—sandscratches, in other words. Sandscratches absorb large amounts of top coat solvent, which causes them to swell. The swelling, in turn, prevents the paint from filling as completely as it should. The result is that as the swelling goes down, impressions of the scratches are left in the new finish (Fig. 4-30). They are themselves too fine to be seen, but their effect is quite noticeable. The new top coat, being rougher than is ideal, scatters

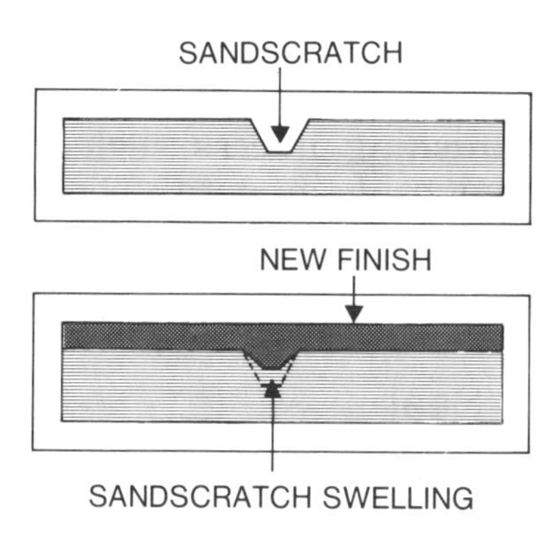

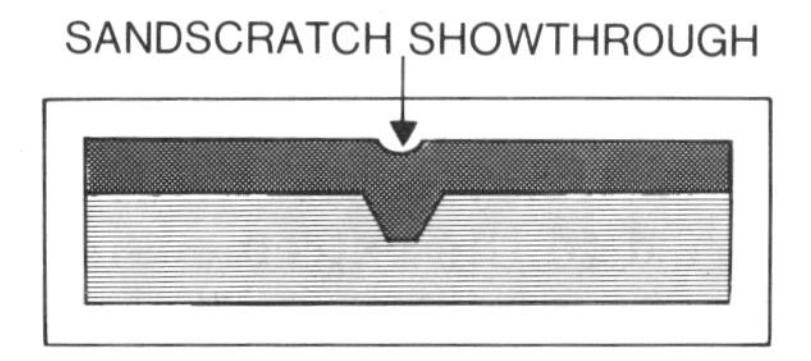

FIG 4-30 Sandscratch swelling and its effect.

light and thus appears dull. It will likely require compounding as an extra step to bring out its shine.

The best use of sealer, given all of these potential problems, can be summarized in three rules.

1. *Use sealer when applying lacquer over any base or color coat.* The only exception is factory-baked lacquer.
2. *Sealer is optional with an enamel top coat.* Nonetheless, to be on the safe side, use the product when applying enamel over any potentially incompatible surface.
3. *Use sealer even between compatible color coats if bleeding is a possibility.*

Pigmented vs. Clear Sealers

There are two main types of sealers—pigmented and clear. Pigmented sealers are thick and must be reduced. They are sprayed at higher psi's and may even require sanding. Clear sealers, on the other hand, are merely strained before use. They are sprayed at lower psi's and are never sanded. Both products are usually applied in a single wet coat.

Pigmented sealers are probably the more widely used of the two products. They come in the same basic shades as primer-surfacer—red oxide and dark and light gray. They have, however, a slightly different, less intense cast that makes them more suitable as a base coat for many light or more translucent colors.

SAFETY CHECKLIST

Preparation Process:

1. Because surface preparation involves so many detailed steps, there may be a tendency to regard safety precautions as needless complications of an already complex process. The major long-term safeguard, however, can be stated and observed simply: when dry sanding, using a duster gun, or spray painting, always wear a respirator.

2. The fact that so much preparation is done outside the spray booth does not mean that the process is hazard-free compared to painting. In both cases, the major volatile materials are the same. Reducing agents are used in both primer-surfacer and paint, and in about the same proportions. Thus the explosive potential of the products is similar. Therefore, when working with primer-surfacer, thinner, or reducer, observe the smoking ban and avoid the use of any tool whose motor or operation produces sparks.
3. The preparation process generates a large number of soiled cloths and rags, some of them filled with flammable material. Those coated with primer-surfacer should be placed in a safety container (one with a lid) until they can be picked up for disposal. All others can be laundered for reuse.

Fiberglass Surfaces:

4. When sanding on fiberglass, use rubber gloves as well as a respirator and goggles. Remember, the material is, in fact, glass. Its dust presents the same hazards as glass shards or slivers.
5. Virtually all materials associated with fiberglass spot repairs are extremely hazardous, especially M.E.K. and acetone. (The latter is used to clean up after a repair.) M.E.K.'s potential for danger is obvious from its composition (60 percent active oxygen). As for acetone, when it is exposed to heat, it can evaporate with explosive force. So dangerous are these two materials that some insurance companies will not cover buildings where the products are used or stored. Therefore, except when actually in use, both materials should be kept in tightly closed containers. They should never be mixed with substances or in proportions other than those specified on their container labels.

Masking:

6. Paper and paint by themselves are flammable. Together, however, they present an extreme fire hazard. Used masking material must therefore be disgarded immediately. It should be folded or compacted as much as possible and then placed in a lidded safety container. It should never be strewn around the shop or allowed to collect out in the open where sparks, matches, or a stray cigarette could ignite it.

OBJECTIVE 4-A4 (manipulative)

Working as a team with two other students and with the aid of Job Report Sheet 4-A4, you will prepare a body panel with a good enamel finish for repainting with lacquer.

Time Recommended:

1 hour

Preparation:

1. Review pages 135 through 175.
2. Study pages 175 through 178.
3. Read the Safety Checklist on pages 174 and 175, items 1 through 6.

Tools and Materials:

1. Suction-feed spray gun
2. Duster gun
3. Sanding block (sponge rubber)
4. Socket wrench (for battery ground cable)
5. Masking paper and tape
6. Clean shop cloths
7. Respirator and safety goggles
8. Hose (or sponge and bucket)
9. Paint rack and strainer
10. Wooden stirring stick
11. Wax remover
12. Fast-drying reducer
13. Sealer for lacquer (pigmented or clear)
14. Sandpaper (500A)
15. Tack cloth

Procedure:

1. Saturate a clean cloth with wax remover. Apply the material to the panel and wipe up with a second clean cloth.
2. Using a 500A abrasive and a sponge rubber block, wet sand the panel and wipe dry with a clean cloth.
3. By hand, compound 8 to 10 inches into adjacent panel to expose its true color. Blow away compound dust from one repair area.
4. Take one vehicle to the wash rack and rinse all surfaces thoroughly.
5. After air drying the vehicle with a duster gun operating at 35 psi, reset the spray booth reducing regulator to 70 psi and blow all moisture from between crevices and under moldings near the repair panel. With a clean, dry cloth, wipe up any water that is dislodged.
6. Disconnect the battery ground cable, and push the vehicle into the spray booth.
7. Mask any moldings or trim on the repair panel. Use 18- or 24-inch paper to mask all adjacent panels and glass.
8. Give the repair panel a final wipe down with fast-drying reducer.
9. Open the sealer and stir well. Reduce and/or strain the sealer into the spray gun cup, as the manufacturer requires. Test the material on a piece of masking paper.
10. Reset the reducing-regulator to 45 psi (35 psi at the gun). When properly adjusted, the spray gun should form a 6-inch pattern that flows well when applied from a distance of 6 to 8 inches.
11. Tack the panels to be painted.
12. Apply the sealer in a single coat.
13. Allow the panel to dry 20 minutes (longer if the temperature is below 70°F).
14. Tack the panel. Its surface is now ready for the application of the new lacquer top coat.

JOB REPORT SHEET 4-A4

APPLYING SEALER

Student Name ______________________ Date ____________

Time Started ____________ Time Finished ____________ Total Time ____________

Specifications

Type of Panel ______________________

Finish: Type ____________ Condition ____________

Color ____________

Technique

Wet Sanding Method: Hose ______ Sponge and Bucket ______

Type of Sanding Block ______ Abrasive ______

Surfaces Washed ______________________

____

____

Sealer: Type ______________________

Pigmented ______ Clear ______

Reduced ______ Ready To Use ______

Sanding ______ Non-Sanding ______

Total Number of Coats ______

Checkup Questions

1. Why was the use of sealer required for this procedure and not for the one detailed in Objective 4-A3? ______________________

   ____

2. Why was no primer-sealer applied as part of the procedure? ______________________

   ____

3. How does lacquer sealer compare with lacquer primer-sealer in terms of:

a) viscosity? ____________________

b) color? ____________________

c) reduction? ____________________

Date Completed ____________ Instructor's Signature ____________________

Student Name ______________________ Date ______________

DIRECTIONS: Circle the best answer to each question.

1. Flash time for lacquer primer-surfacer is
   A. 5 minutes.
   B. 30 minutes.
   C. 3 to 4 hours.
   D. overnight.

2. In the course of repainting a vehicle, all of the following require sanding EXCEPT
   A. a top coat in "mint" condition.
   B. clear sealer.
   C. primer-surfacer.
   D. glazing putty.

3. The tool at the right is resting on the hood of a car. The button has popped up at the point indicated on the dial. This result means that the refinisher will have to
   A. do a test featheredge.
   B. use a sealer to prevent an adverse chemical reaction.
   C. remove at least some of the existing finish.
   D. move the dial to a lower setting.

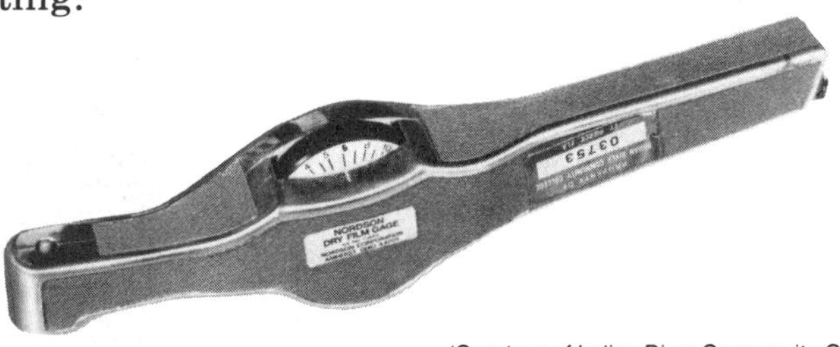

(Courtesy of Indian River Community College)

4. Which cleaning procedure comes last?
   A. Washing
   B. Compounding
   C. Final wipedown
   D. Tacking

5. Rough featheredging is usually done
   A. wet.
   B. by hand.
   C. with an 80D abrasive.
   D. after fine featheredging.

6. The first coat of primer-surfacer must be
   I. allowed to flash before sanding.
   II. applied with a pressure of 35 psi at the gun.

   A. I only   B. II only   C. Both I and II   D. Neither I nor II

7. Gummy primer-surfacer can be caused by all of the following EXCEPT
   A. applying a second coat of primer-surfacer before the first has flashed.
   B. applying too much primer-surfacer per coat.
   C. fanning freshly applied primer-surfacer to speed drying.
   D. using a heat lamp to speed drying.

8. Compared to wet sanding, dry sanding
   I. produces a smoother finish.
   II. makes more economical use of sandpaper.

   A. I only   B. II only   C. Both I and II   D. Neither I nor II

9. Which pair of procedures is in the wrong order?
   A. Rough featheredging, fine featheredging
   B. Rough featheredging, test featheredging
   C. Application of primer-surfacer, application of putty
   D. Wet sanding of primer-surfacer, sealing of primer-surfacer

10. The surface at the right has been misted with a lighter shade of primer-surfacer, then sanded. The light areas represent
    A. sanding that remains to be done.
    B. areas that must be filled.
    C. fisheye.
    D. places where the primer-surfacer has flaked off.

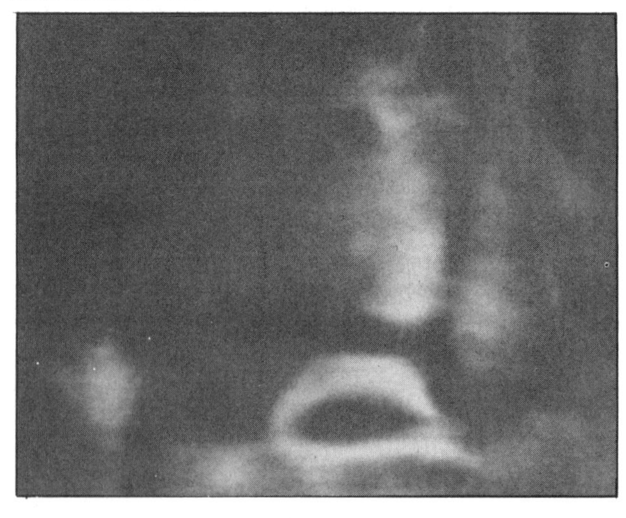

11. After four coats of primer-surfacer, sandscratches are still visible on a surface. Possible reasons include
    I. scratches too deep for primer-surfacer to fill.
    II. surface sanded before primer-surfacer was dry.

    A. I only   B. II only   C. Both I and II   D. Neither I nor II

12. A well-feathered edge
    A. is tapered over a distance of at least 3 inches.
    B. exposes all paint film layers down to the bare metal.
    C. creates a microscopic dent in the finish.
    D. is impossible to achieve between new filler and old paint.

13. A vehicle with a factory-baked lacquer finish is being repainted with lacquer.
    Refinisher I suggests finish sanding with a 600-grit abrasive, followed by a thorough cleaning and application of a clear sealer.
    Refinisher II suggests wet sanding with a 320-grit abrasive, followed by a thorough cleaning and application of the new lacquer top coat.
    Who is right?
    A. I only B. II only C. Both I and II D. Neither I nor II

14. Primer-surfacer that goes on dry can cause problems with all of the following EXCEPT
    A. adhesion.
    B. sanding.
    C. filling.
    D. holdout.

15. A small amount of lacquer thinner rubbed on a vehicle softens the finish. The surface could be
    I. enamel applied in a paint shop.
    II. factory-baked lacquer.
    A. I only B. II only C. Both I and II D. Neither I nor II

16. On the windshield shown, the two vertical strips of masking tape (arrows) were probably applied to
    A. hold the vehicle's windshield wipers in place.
    B. repair tears.
    C. seal shut folds or pleats.
    D. cover seams where smaller pieces of paper were added.

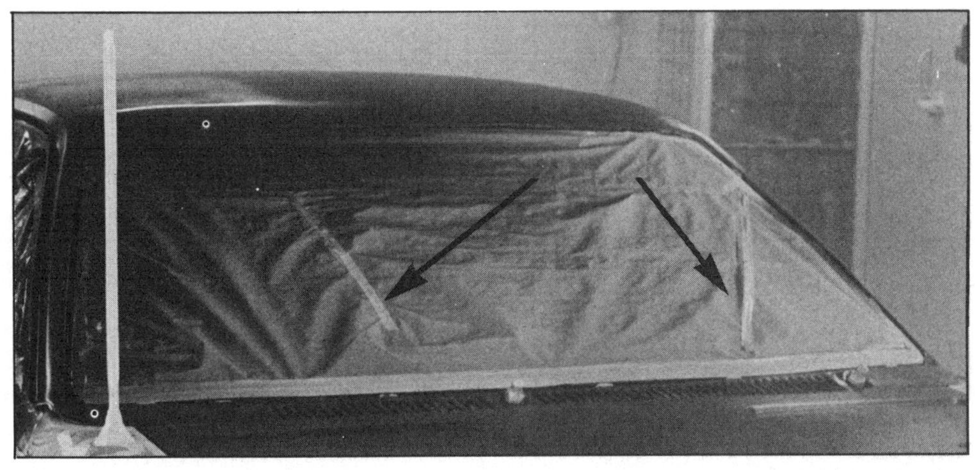

(The DeVilbiss Company)

17. Which combination is common in refinishing shops?

  I. ¾-inch tape mounted on an apron taper

  II. 12- and 24-inch masking papers

  A. I only B. II only C. Both I and II D. Neither I nor II

18. All of the following could cause underspray EXCEPT

  A. masking a ¾-inch molding with 1-inch tape.

  B. masking the top half of a windshield before the bottom half.

  C. failing to clean a surface thoroughly before masking it.

  D. painting over curled masking tape.

19. The front end of an Oldsmobile Ninety-Eight must be repainted.

  Refinisher I suggests saving some time on the job by removing the model name plates from both fenders rather than masking them.

  Refinisher II suggests saving some time on the job by covering the two side-view mirrors and the hood ornament with plastic bags.

  Who is right?

  A. I only B. II only C. Both I and II D. Neither I nor II

20. To remove masking properly, the paper must be pulled

  I. all at once along its full length.

  II. straight out from the surface covered.

  A. I only B. II only C. Both I and II D. Neither I nor II

Score ________ Instructor's Signature ________________________________

unit 5

Lacquer Refinishing

The first automobile finish was a combination of lampblack and varnish. It was brushed on laboriously by hand in multiple coats. Once dry, each application had to be rubbed with pumice and water to smooth out the brush marks. The whole process took nearly a month and made the paint shop a major bottleneck in automobile manufacturing. Vehicles could be mass-produced, but only as quickly as the one available finish would allow.

This form of refinishing was used until 1924, when nitrocellulose lacquer was invented. Made from the action of nitric acid on natural fibers, the new finish was the first to be sprayed onto a vehicle. Its most important characteristic, however, was its fast drying time. From application of the first coat to drying of the last, the whole finishing process was reduced to a matter of hours. The paint shop could finally keep pace with the assembly line (Fig. 5-1).

Unfortunately, nitrocellulose lacquer did have one major drawback: it was no more durable than the lampblack-and-varnish finishes it replaced. Those tended to crack within a year. Nitrocellulose lacquer tended to chip within the same period of time. This factor led to its gradual replacement with a new product starting in the mid-1950s. That product was acrylic lacquer.

Today acrylic is virtually the only lacquer paint in use. Though it is still a relatively delicate finish, it continues to be popular for two reasons. First, lacquer is the factory finish applied to most General Motors passenger cars. The need to refinish these vehicles with compatible materials keeps the demand for lacquer products high. Second, the fast-drying characteristics of lacquer plus the ease with which it can be blended make it the ideal material for spot repairs.

FIG 5-1
Hand paint spraying on car assembly line. (General Motors Corporation)

To work successfully in refinishing, however, a painter must master more than just spot repair techniques. There are three basic types of repairs—spot, panel, and whole vehicle—and the refinisher must be able to determine which a given job requires. What is more, he must understand the problems each kind of repair presents in terms of masking, equipment adjustment and handling, and the actual application of paint. This unit explores these basic differences. It also reviews and expands previous discussions of lacquer characteristics. Finally, it introduces some of the fine color adjustment and repair techniques to which lacquer paints in particular lend themselves.

OBJECTIVE 5-A (written)

After doing the reading and shop exercises, you will be able to answer correctly without reference material a minimum of 14 out of 20 test questions on the following topics:

1. Acrylic lacquer characteristics
2. One- and two-gun methods of spot repair
3. Trimming out and finishing new panels
4. Interior and exterior painting in whole-vehicle repairs
5. Color coating
6. Heat repairs of minor film damage

Preparation:

1. Study pages 183 through 227.
2. Attend classroom discussions of Objective 5-A.
3. Read the Safety Checklist on page 227.

ACRYLIC LACQUER CHARACTERISTICS

Acrylic lacquer paints are made from the same kind of clear, resinous material that goes into safety goggles. They are, in other words, plastic based. As such, they resist breakdown and corrosion of the outer paint film. The plastic elements also toughen acrylic lacquer finishes, making them harder and more chip-resistant than the old nitrocellulous top coats.

Drying Time

Lacquer paints, like other lacquer products, are fast drying. The standard typically used to measure this quality is the amount of time it takes a material to become dust-free. The term *dust-free* is used to describe the point at which a finish is sufficiently dry that dust will no longer adhere to it. Lacquers are generally dust-free in a few minutes. Some enamels, on the other hand, take more than an hour to reach this point.

FIG 5-2 Blushing on a panel sprayed with lacquer in humid weather. (E. I. du Pont de Nemours & Co., Inc.)

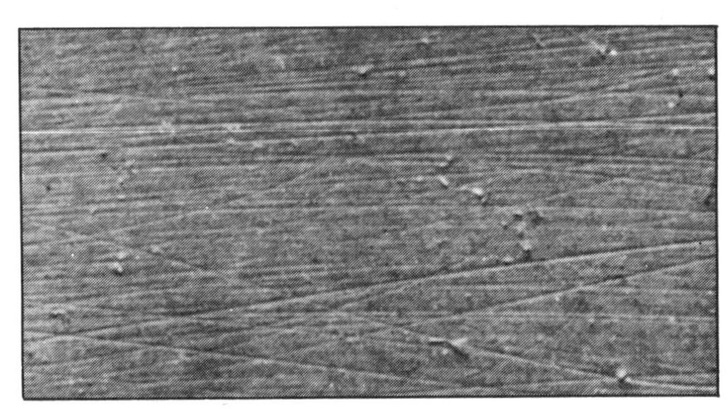

FIG 5-3 Sandscratch showthrough on a lacquer finish. (The Martin-Senour Company)

The obvious advantage of a lacquer repair, then, is that a vehicle can be refinished and delivered to its owner in a short period of time. The car does not remain in the spray booth very long and seldom ties up a drying room. (When baking lamps are used, for example, a small lacquer repair can take as little as 20 minutes to dry.)

Blushing

There is, however, such a thing as a finish's drying too quickly, particularly in humid weather. Lacquer top coats drying in such conditions tend to trap and hold moisture in their lower layers. When this happens, the finish takes on a milky appearance, a condition called blushing (Fig. 5-2).

Blushing can be prevented in two ways.

1. *Use a high-grade thinner.* This type of thinner is intended for use in a warm shop. Even at temperatures above 80 degrees Fahrenheit, it evaporates slowly. Thus any paint with which it is mixed takes longer to dry. This effect, in turn, gives absorbed moisture the extra time it needs to evaporate before the paint films over.
2. *Add retarder to the final coat.* Retarder is a special paint additive. It is a kind of insurance policy, a guarantee that in the most extreme shop conditions even a high-grade thinner will not fail. Retarder is measured by the capful. An extremely strong solvent, it can rewet an entire surface, thus allowing trapped moisture to escape.

Sandscratch Showthrough

The speed with which acrylic lacquer dries is also one of the reasons surfaces must be so finely sanded before a lacquer top coat can be applied. When drying time is cut, so is the amount of time the paint has to flow. This fact means that sandscratches can be bridged rather than filled. Later, when the paint sinks into them, the scratches reappear (Fig. 5-3). Therefore, no surface finish sanded with a relatively coarse abrasive can be successfully painted with lacquer. The sandscratch always shows through.

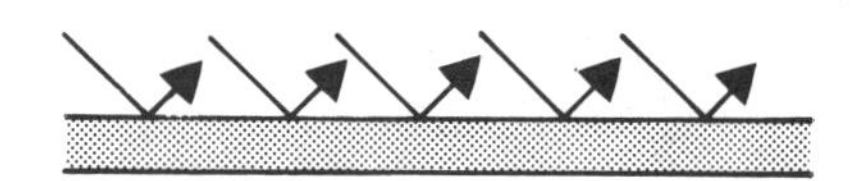

ENAMEL FINISH

LACQUER FINISH

FIG 5-4 Uneven surface of a lacquer finish makes it appear dull. Enamel shines because its surface is smooth and level.

Compounding

When a new finish needs sanding or compounding, it is usually a sign that something has gone wrong in the refinishing process. Dirt has embedded itself in the new paint, overspray attached itself, or sand-scratch swelling left tracks in the new top coat. The fact is, however, that one form of sanding—compounding—is the required final step for every new lacquer top coat.

A freshly applied lacquer finish has a characteristic dull shine. This appearance contrasts with freshly applied enamel, which is almost mirrorlike. The absence of shine in a lacquer top coat is a direct result of extremely small irregularities that tend to disperse light (Fig. 5-4). These irregularities exist because lacquer does not flow long enough to level itself out fully. This extra degree of smoothness must be achieved by machine compounding instead.

The choice of when to begin compounding, however, is critical. It is possible to start too soon. Remember that primer-surfacer is a porous material. Just as it can absorb water, it can—and does—absorb thinner, including thinner from paint. This process makes the primer-surfacer swell. What is more, the swelling is greatest where the buildup of primer-surfacer is greatest—over deep sandscratches. If compounding is begun before the swelling goes down (in other words, before the thinner has fully evaporated), the original scratch pattern will reappear (Fig. 5-5). This situation is similar to the reappearance of sandscratches when the primer-surfacer itself is sanded before it is fully dry.

A new lacquer finish must therefore be allowed to dry thoroughly before compounding. In the case of air drying, up to 18 hours is needed (24 if retarder has been used). The comparable time for force drying is 1 hour.

Chemical Activity

Lacquers are by far the most chemically active paints. It is this trait that, for example, allows a refinisher to identify a lacquer top coat by rubbing it with a thinner-moistened cloth. It is this trait also that allows a new lacquer finish to form a superior bond with an old one.

The key to understanding both of these reactions is the means by which lacquers dry—evaporation. In evaporation, the solvent (in this case, thinner) vaporizes. This process leaves behind the hardened paint

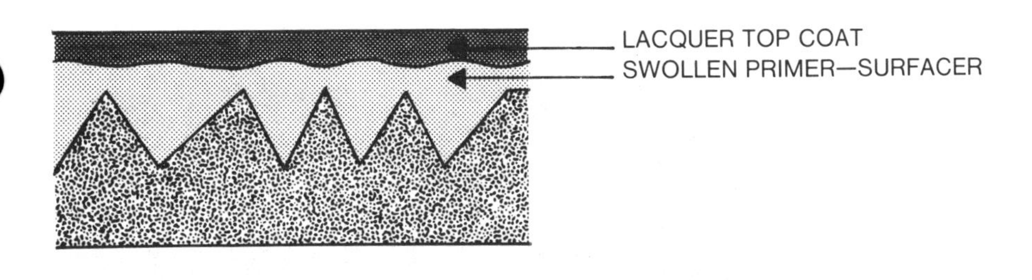

FIG 5-5
Lacquer surface that is compounded too soon after spraying looks good.

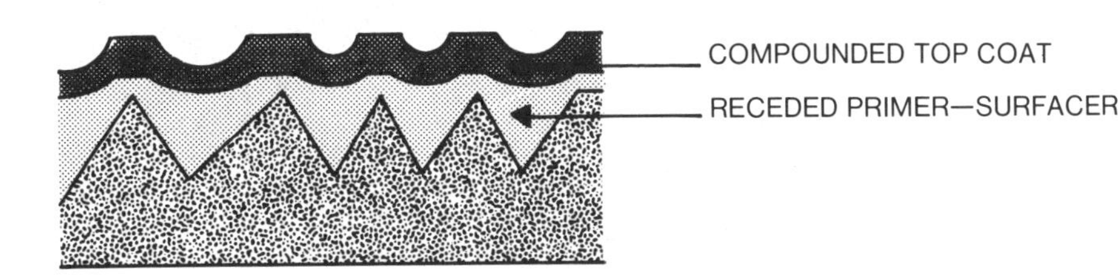

The next day the sandscratch pattern reappears because the surface was compounded too soon.

film. With lacquers, however, this change is not permanent. If any amount of lacquer solvent contacts the finish thereafter, it will again soften.

Solubility

This ability of lacquers to be affected by thinner long after—indeed, years after—they have dried is called solubility. (Lacquers are said to be soluble in thinner, enamels insoluble.) The exact extent to which a lacquer finish is affected depends on the concentration of the thinner to which it is exposed. In the case of the lacquer test, for example, the surface is exposed to a small amount of pure thinner. At this strength, the thinner actually dissolves some of the paint, which rubs off onto the rag. When a new top coat is applied over an old one, the thinner is not pure. It is mixed with binder and pigment, and thus merely softens the old finish. This reaction, however, gives the new finish far more to hold onto than sandscratch tooth. The two surfaces actually merge rather than simply adhere to each other. This is a superior form of bonding that enamels cannot match.

Such extreme reactivity, however, has disadvantages, too. Any finish as sensitive to thinner as lacquer is can also be affected by many thinnerlike substances. Transmission fluid, for example, can easily spot a lacquer finish. The same is true of battery acid, brake fluid, and even tree sap and bird droppings. The fact that lacquer is sensitive to all of these substances gives it a reputation for being a delicate, or touchy, finish (Fig. 5-6).

Reflowing

Thinner, however, is not the only thing that will soften lacquer. In the case of a factory-baked finish, heat will soften it also. In fact, if high enough temperatures are used, heat can even reflow a vehicle's original lacquer top coat. This effect is possible because manufacturers mix a special thermoplastic agent with their paints. (*Thermo-* is a prefix meaning *heat,* as in *thermometer.*)

The thermoplastic quality of factory-baked lacquer is important to the refinisher on two counts. First, if heat is applied to an original lacquer top coat, scratches and other imperfections can be filled with

FIG 5-6
Stain spotting on a lacquer finish.

freshly flowed paint. Indeed, this fact is the basis of a technique frequently used by dealers to repair minor film damage in new cars. Second, if temperatures can be raised high enough (to the range of 240 to 260 degrees Fahrenheit, for example), the slight irregularities that result in fresh lacquer's dull appearance can be eliminated. In other words, at such temperatures the finish can be flowed smooth rather than having to be compounded to that state. It is this technique that auto manufacturers use to eliminate compounding in assembly line painting. *Note:* The latter technique is confined to manufacturers because the baking equipment found in paint shops cannot produce the required temperatures. Even if it could, however, shops would not use it in this fashion. Temperatures that high would damage or destroy a vehicle's glass, upholstery, and plastic fittings. When assembly line painting is done, these items have not yet been installed (Fig. 5-1).

SPOT REPAIRS

The smallest type of repair a refinisher must be able to handle is a spot repair (Fig. 5-7). Despite its size, such a repair probably takes more skill and concentration than panel and whole-vehicle repairs combined. The reason is simple. A spot repair is usually located in some open area of a

FIG 5-7
Damage that can be fixed with spot repairs. (Jay Storer)

panel where it can be hidden only by very skillful blending of the old and new finishes. Such blending is easy to do with brush-applied color. It is much more difficult with a spray gun and automotive paint. One note of encouragement, however—it is easier to do with lacquers than with any other top coat material.

Refinishers have developed two basic techniques for coping with the problems involved in blending old and new paint films. The more flexible method uses two spray guns, the other (which is more difficult to master) uses only one.

Two-Gun Method

As already noted, factory-baked lacquer finishes are thermally flowed rather than compounded. This process creates a high gloss that no spot repair done in a paint shop is likely to match (at least, not without compounding). The two-gun method of spray painting, however, is a technique designed to minimize this difference. It is based on alternate applications of paint and thinner.

Preparation and Technique

The first of the two spray guns used is prepared as it would be for any lacquer top coat: 1 part of paint is mixed with 1½ parts of acrylic lacquer thinner. The second gun, however, is prepared very differently. Its contents are 95 percent thinner and only 5 percent color. Clearly, this mixture is not a coat of paint in the ordinary sense of the word. It is what refinishers call a mist coat.

The guns are usually marked with tape to distinguish them. The gun with the color coat is marked #1; the gun with the mist coat is marked #2 (Fig. 5-8). The first gun is used to spray paint onto the repair area, usually in a somewhat dry form. The second gun is used to mist thinner over the paint. This application sequence has the effect of reflowing the dry spray. In the case of chemically active lacquer, it also merges the old and new paint films at the repair edges. It thus prevents the formation of any dividing line that might make the repair visible once the job is complete. The color in the #1 gun is applied at least five times, and each application is followed by a mist coat. The pressure set at the transformer-regulator is 35 psi (25 psi at the gun).

FIG 5-8
Preparation for two-gun repair.

Advantages

The two-gun method has three major advantages.

1. *By allowing color to be sprayed on somewhat dry, it avoids drips and sags.* In this respect, the technique is of special help to the inexperienced spray painter. By rewetting the repair surface, it easily compensates for those spray painting mistakes that result in dry spray of one form or another.
2. *The two-gun method allows for the maximum amount of flowing that can be achieved without resorting to special additives and factory baking.* The finish that results is thus not as glossy as one that is thermally flowed. It is, however, better than the surface produced by a one-gun repair in which there is no mist coating.
3. *Compared to a one-gun repair, the two-gun method reduces the amount of compounding needed to equalize the luster of the old and new paint films.* This point is an outgrowth of the last one. If a surface flows more, it is smoother, shinier, and hence requires less compounding. Mist coating increases the amount of flowing and thus accounts for the two-gun method's superior results.

One-Gun Method

The one-gun method of spot repair sounds as if it would be the easier technique to master. The refinisher employs a single spray gun to apply repeated, overlapping coats of paint. The technique is similar to that used for applying primer-surfacer to a spot repair. Primer-surfacer, however, is a base coat. It will not be seen after the vehicle is painted and thus does not have to be blended into the surrounding finish. Color, on the other hand, is a top coat. It will be seen and must therefore be carefully blended into the old paint film.

Blending color without benefit of a mist coat, however, takes genuine skill—and a great deal of practice. There is no margin for error. The first coat must be sprayed on wet enough to flow. It must remain wet long enough to soften the old paint film. Each successive coat must be applied at just the right moment and at just the right overlap to keep the repair edges flowing together. Flow and pattern, spray gun adjustment and spray painting technique—all must come together at once in repeated bursts of paint application.

Three reminders can help.

1. *Use a low pressure setting—not more than 45 psi at the transformer-regulator (35 psi at the gun).* This precaution offers a double benefit. First, it reduces the likelihood of dry spray, which, with this repair technique, would be very difficult to eliminate. Second, it keeps down overspray, thus maintaining good visibility in the spray booth. Visibility is especially important in the one-gun method because the refinisher must be able to aim his spray gun accurately and respond quickly to any changes in the repair surface.
2. *Select the right thinner for shop conditions and combine it with the paint in the recommended amount.* Remember, a medium-grade thinner is intended for use when temperatures are 70 to 80 degrees Fahrenheit and humidity is normal. Extremely warm, moist conditions require a slower-drying product; cool, damp ones a faster product.

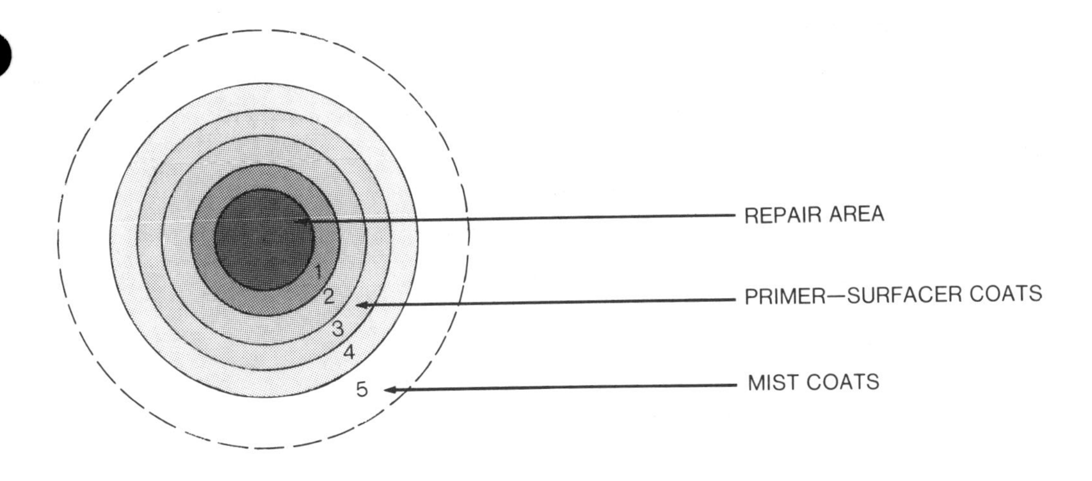

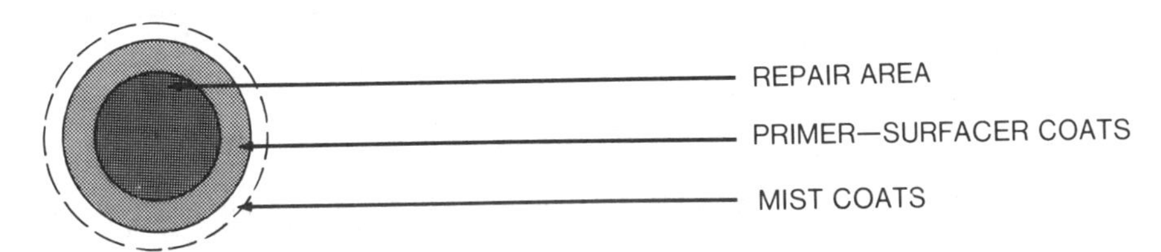

FIG 5-9 One- and two-gun methods of spot repair compared.

3. *Extend each paint application at least ½ inch beyond the preceding one.* This overlapping technique is a major difference between the one- and two-gun methods. Overall, it enlarges the repair area, usually by at least 2 to 3 inches. This practice is necessary, however, to keep the repair edges flowing and to promote the blending of the old and new paint films. In other words, overlapping is the one-gun method's substitute for mist coating (Fig. 5-9).

OBJECTIVE 5-A1 (manipulative)

Working as a team with one other student and with the aid of Job Report Sheet 5-A1, you will do a lacquer spot repair using the two-gun method.

Time Recommended:

1½ hours

Preparation:

1. Review pages 183 through 191.
2. Study pages 191 through 196.
3. Read the Safety Checklist on page 227, items 1 through 6.

Tools and Materials:

1. Vibrator or orbital sander
2. Suction-feed spray guns (three—two for paint, one for primer-surfacer)
3. Duster gun
4. Polisher with compounding pad
5. Sanding blocks (hard and sponge rubber)
6. Socket wrench (for battery ground cable)
7. Squeegee
8. Paint rack and strainer
9. Wooden stirring sticks
10. Respirator and safety goggles
11. Rubber gloves
12. Hose (or sponge and bucket)
13. Masking paper and tape
14. Clean shop cloths
15. Selection of sandpapers (80D, 280A, 320A, 400A, 500A)
16. Tack cloth
17. Wax remover
18. Metal conditioner
19. Lacquer primer-surfacer
20. Aerosol can of lacquer primer-surfacer (contrasting color)
21. Thinner
22. Fast-drying reducer
23. Glazing putty
24. Machine rubbing compound
25. Acrylic lacquer paint

Procedure:

1. Clean the entire panel. Apply wax remover with one cloth. Wipe the panel dry with another.
2. Featheredge the damaged area. Start with a vibrator or an orbital sander equipped with an 80D abrasive. Finish by hand, using a 280A or 320A paper to sand a 3- to 5-inch border around the repair area. Blow all sanding dust from the panel.
3. If any bare metal has been exposed by the sanding, apply conditioner. *Note:* Avoid getting this material on adjacent paint or exposed primer-surfacer.
4. Using 12-inch paper, mask adjoining panels and/or glass. On the repair panel itself, use masking tape to cover all moldings and trim.
5. Mix 1 part lacquer primer-surfacer with 1½ parts thinner.
6. Test spray the primer-surfacer on a piece of masking paper. Set the transformer-regulator at 40 psi (30 psi at the gun). When properly adjusted, the spray gun should form a pattern approximately the size of the repair area at a distance of 6 to 8 inches.
7. Apply four coats of primer-surfacer to the repair area, overlapping each slightly and allowing flash time between. After the last coat, allow the panel to dry 30 minutes.

8. Using a hard rubber block and a 320A abrasive, sand the primed area.
9. Use putty to fill any low spots exposed by the sanding. Apply the product sparingly with a small rubber squeegee and allow an additional 30 minutes of drying time. Resand as in step 8.
10. Make a final check for imperfections. Give the repair a fifth coat of primer-surfacer, this time using a contrasting color. Allow 20 minutes of drying time. Then resand using a hard rubber block and a 320A or 400A abrasive.
11. Wet sand the repair area. For this final sanding, use a 500A abrasive and a sponge rubber sanding block.
12. Wipe the panel with a moistened cloth to remove all sanding dust. Blow dry.
13. Machine compound the repair and the area immediately surrounding it. Avoid working more than 2 square feet of the surface at a time. When finished, blow all compounding residue from the panel.
14. Remove all masking and wash down the panel with a wet cloth. Wipe dry and blow with a duster gun to remove any traces of moisture or lint.
15. Move the panel or vehicle into the spray booth. *Note:* In the case of a vehicle, disconnect the battery ground cable first.
16. Remask adjacent panels, glass, or trim and give the panel a final wipedown with fast-drying reducer.
17. Open the paint and, using a wooden stirring stick, stir it by hand for 4 to 5 minutes.
18. Transfer the paint to another container and rinse out the can. Pour in ½ inch of thinner, press the lid back in place, and shake so that the thinner is forced against both the bottom and top of the can. Continue shaking until the can's interior is clean and bright.
19. Add the thinner from the can to the paint and stir at least 2 minutes more.
20. Strain 1 inch of color into one of the remaining two spray gun cups. Add 1½ inches of thinner through the same strainer. Stir this mixture 2 minutes. Then attach the gun to the cup and label it #1 (or *P* for *paint*).
21. Strain ½ inch of color into the last spray gun cup. Fill this cup with thinner to the 1-quart mark. Stir 2 minutes and attach the gun. Label this combination #2 (or *T* for *thinner*).
22. Set the transformer-regulator at 35 psi (25 psi at the gun) and test both spray guns. The #1 gun should be positioned 6 to 8 inches from a sheet of masking paper and adjusted to produce a pattern approximately the size of the repair area. (*Note:* At the given distance and pressure, the paint should go on somewhat dry. Do not adjust the spray gun to compensate for this condition.) The #2 gun should be aimed toward the exhaust system paint arrestors and triggered. Its pattern should be approximately 6 inches wide at a distance of 6 inches when observed at eye level. (*Note:* Because of the extreme thinness of the material in the #2 gun, proper adjustment will most likely be achieved when the spreader and fluid valves are more closed than open.)
23. Tack the panel.

24. To begin the actual application of paint, use the #2 gun to mist the repair area. The primed spot should have what refinishers call a thinner shine. In other words, it should look barely wet, not soaked.
25. Immediately disconnect the air hose and switch to the #1 gun. Apply a dry film of color to the primed spot. Just aim the gun and trigger it once briefly. Do not attempt to wet the area thoroughly. *Note:* For larger spot repairs, some stroking action may be necessary.
26. Immediately switch back to the #2 gun and apply a second mist coat, this time slightly overlapping the fresh paint.
27. Continue in this fashion, alternating spray guns, until five applications of paint and six applications of thinner have been made. *Note:* The paint should always be applied in the same spot. The thinner should always just overlap it.
28. Allow the panel to air dry at least 4 hours or overnight before unmasking. To force dry, allow 10 minutes of flowing time and bake for 1 hour at a temperature of 165 degrees Fahrenheit.
29. Compound the repair area lightly or as required to bring its shine up to that of the old finish.

JOB REPORT SHEET 5-A1

ACRYLIC LACQUER SPOT REPAIR (TWO-GUN METHOD)

Student Name ______________________ Date ______________

Time Started ______________ Time Finished ______________ Total Time ______________

Specifications

Type of panel ______________________________

Condition of finish (Describe the nature and extent of any damage.) ______________

____

____

Technique

Rough featheredging method:

Type of sander ______________ Abrasive ______________

Fine featheredging method:

Type of sander ______________ Abrasive ______________

Metal conditioner: Yes _____ No _____

Surfaces masked ______________ ______________

______________ ______________

______________ ______________

Primer-surfacer: Type ______________ Color ______________

Psi at the transformer-regulator _____ Psi at the gun _____

Total number of coats _____

Number of putty applications _____

Two-color checkup sanding: Yes _____ No _____

Wet sanding method: Hose _____ Sponge and bucket _____

Type of sanding block ______________ Abrasive ______________

Compounding method:

Type of polisher ____________________ Rpm/psi ______

Type of compound ____

Paint reduction: Type of thinner ____________________________________

Formula ______ part(s) paint, ______ part(s) thinner

Additives used ____________________________________

Drying process:

Air ______ Force drying ______ Total drying time ____________________

Checkup Questions

1. Why was it important to rinse out the paint can (step 18)? ____________________

____

____

2. Describe how the paint applications looked both before and after mist coating.

____

____

____

3. By how much does the finished repair differ in size from the original primed spot?

____

____

____

Date Completed ____________________ Instructor's Signature ______________________________

Working as a team with one other student and with the aid of Job Report Sheet 5-A2, you will do a lacquer spot repair using the one-gun method.

OBJECTIVE 5-A2 (manipulative)

Time Recommended:

1½ hours

Preparation:

1. Review pages 183 through 196.
2. Study pages 197 through 200.
3. Read the Safety Checklist on page 227, items 1 through 6.

Tools and Materials:

1. Vibrator or orbital sander
2. Suction-feed spray guns (two—one for paint, one for primer-surfacer)
3. Duster gun
4. Polisher with both compounding and polishing pads
5. Sanding blocks (hard and sponge rubber)
6. Socket wrench (for battery ground cable)
7. Squeegee
8. Paint rack and strainer
9. Wooden stirring sticks
10. Respirator and safety goggles
11. Rubber gloves
12. Hose (or sponge and bucket)
13. Masking paper and tape
14. Clean shop cloths
15. Selection of sandpapers (80D, 280A, 320A, 400A, 500A)
16. Tack cloth
17. Wax remover
18. Metal conditioner
19. Lacquer primer-surfacer
20. Aerosol can of lacquer primer-surfacer (contrasting color)
21. Thinner
22. Fast-drying reducer
23. Glazing putty
24. Machine rubbing compound
25. Acrylic lacquer paint
26. Acrylic lacquer retarder
27. Liquid polish

Procedure:

1. Prepare paint and panel as in Objective 5-A1, steps 1 through 19.
2. Strain 1 inch of color into the remaining spray gun cup. Then add

1½ inches of thinner through the same strainer. Stir this mixture 2 minutes and attach the spray gun to the cup.

3. Test the spray gun on a piece of masking paper. Set the transformer-regulator at 45 psi (35 psi at the gun). When properly adjusted, the spray gun should form a pattern approximately the size of the repair area at a distance of 6 to 8 inches.
4. Tack the panel.
5. Apply the first coat of paint in a short burst so that it covers the primer only. *Note:* For larger spot repairs, some stroking action may be necessary.
6. Allow the first coat to flash and then apply the second. This coat should overlap the first by at least ½ inch in order to keep the repair edges flowing together.
7. Continue in this manner, extending the repair area ½ inch with each paint application, until a total of five coats have been applied. *Note:* If the color does not appear to have good depth at this point, an extra coat or two may be used.
8. Pour all but ½ inch of color from the spray gun cup. Add thinner to the ½-quart mark, then two caps full of retarder. Stir well.
9. Test and readjust the spray gun to compensate for the thinness of the new mixture. Aim the gun toward the exhaust system paint arrestors and trigger. At a distance of 6 inches, the tool should form a pattern 6 inches wide when viewed at eye level.
10. Mist the repair area with the retarder mix. Be sure to overlap the repair by at least 1 inch along all edges.
11. After 10 minutes of drying time, carefully inspect the repair. In particular, observe the blend area between the old and new paint films. If more flowing is needed (in other words, if a dividing line is still visible), apply a second mist coat.
12. Allow the repair to dry overnight or force dry for at least 1 hour at a temperature of 165 degrees Fahrenheit.
13. Machine compound, then polish the repair area to bring its shine up to that of the old finish.

ACRYLIC LACQUER SPOT REPAIR (ONE-GUN METHOD)

Student Name ______________________________ Date ______________

Time Started ______________ Time Finished ______________ Total Time ______________

Specifications

Type of panel ____

Condition of finish (Describe the nature and extent of any damage.) ______________

____

____

Technique

Rough featheredging method:

Type of sander ______________ Abrasive ______________

Fine featheredging method:

Type of sander ______________ Abrasive ______________

Metal conditioner: Yes ______ No ______

Surfaces masked ______________ ______________

______________ ______________

______________ ______________

Primer-surfacer: Type ______________ Color ______________

Psi at the transformer-regulator ______ Psi at the gun ______

Total number of coats ______

Number of putty applications ______

Two-color checkup sanding: Yes ______ No ______

Wet sanding method: Hose ______ Sponge and bucket ______

Type of sanding block ______________ Abrasive ______________

Compounding method:

Type of polisher ____________ Rpm/psi ______

Type of compound ____________

Paint Reduction: Type of thinner ____________

Formula ______ part(s) paint, ______ part(s) thinner

Additives used ____________

Drying process:

Air ______ Force drying ______ Total drying time ____________

Checkup Questions

1. Why does the one-gun method need a higher psi than the two-gun method?

____

____

____

2. What changes were made in either spray gun adjustment or technique to overlap each application of paint ½ inch beyond the last? ____________

____

____

3. By how much does the finished repair differ in size from the original primed spot? How does this result compare with the two-gun method? ____________

____

____

4. Now that you have done both one- and two-gun spot repairs, which technique do you prefer? Why? ____________

____

____

Date Completed ____________ Instructor's Signature ____________

FIG 5-10
Panel repair.

PANEL REPAIRS

As spot repairs grow in size, there comes a point at which it is no longer reasonable to consider them spots at all. As they increase in number, there also comes a point at which it is no longer efficient to refinish them individually. In both these circumstances, the experienced refinisher does a panel repair (Fig. 5-10).

This procedure is a simpler, easier one for two reasons. First, panel edges are natural boundaries across which blending is not necessary. Second, the size of the repair area allows the refinisher to use standard spray painting techniques, including left-to-right movement and triggering at the panel edge.

There are two basic kinds of panel repairs. The first involves refinishing a panel that has been previously painted. The second involves finishing a replacement panel that has never been painted before. Finishing and refinishing are thus two distinctly different processes. The two terms should not be used interchangeably.

Refinishing

The preparation required for panel refinishing is extensive but at this point familiar. It includes sanding, priming, and possibly some spot use of metal conditioner. It also involves thorough cleaning and compounding of adjacent surfaces.

Checking Color Match

Prerepair compounding is necessary in this case to expose a vehicle's true color. While blending may not be a problem in a panel repair, color matching still is. In fact, a mismatch is even more apparent when it coincides with a body part like a door or a fender. Such panels are already well defined by body seams, moldings, and adjoining panel edges. A color difference, no matter how slight, just adds to these factors and is in turn emphasized by them (Fig. 5-11).

If properly cleaned and compounded, however, adjoining panels can serve as color guides during the painting process. The refinisher simply lifts the masking from a small portion of an adjoining panel, checks the color match, and presses the masking back in place. If the color is not

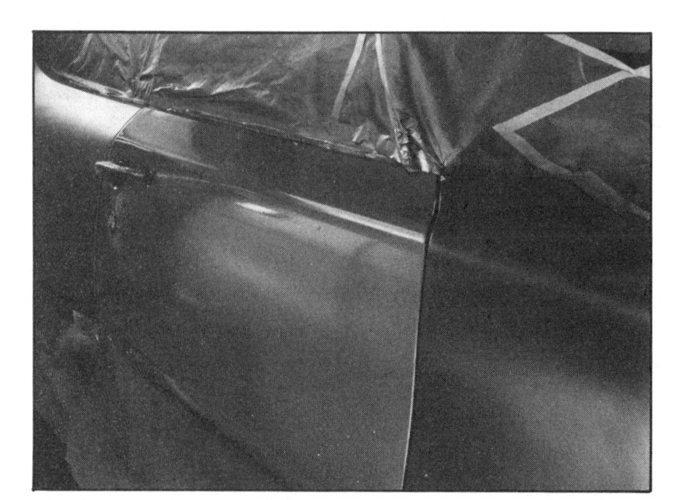

FIG 5-11
Mismatch between door and fender.

quite right, he adjusts his spray gun technique to lighten or darken the shade. *Note:* In those rare cases where color mixing and adjustments in spray gun technique fail to produce a match, some paint manufacturers suggest blending into the adjacent panels. The major problem with this solution is that it is temporary. With time, the color mismatch becomes more apparent. This result occurs because paint gets lighter as it dries. After six months, the customer has no difficulty recognizing the blend area or the fact that it is on previously undamaged panels.

Number of Color Coats

Panels are painted using a different application technique from that employed with spot repairs. Paint is applied in double coats. The refinisher starts at the top or bottom edge of the panel and works his way to the opposite edge, using the standard 50-percent overlap. Then, without waiting for the paint to flash, he returns to his starting point and paints the whole panel again in exactly the same manner. In other words, he applies two single coats, one on top of the other without any drying time between. The transformer-regulator setting is about 45 psi (35 psi at the gun). Note that this pressure is slightly higher than that used for spot repairs (two-gun method).

Most refinishers apply four double coats of lacquer, or a total of eight single coats. This kind of coverage results in good color depth and durability. With more coats, the refinisher risks the kind of excessive paint buildup that invites shrinking and cracking. With fewer coats, he could produce a paint film so thin that it weathers prematurely.

Finishing

The finishing of a new panel involves some basic changes in preparation and painting procedures. For one, if the panel is not factory primed, extensive metal conditioning is required. (Usually hoods and fenders come primed. Doors are shipped bare.) For another, the edges and undersides of the panel must be painted before it is installed (Fig. 5-12).

The latter process is called trimming out. It is usually done with a spray gun adjusted to a narrow (3-inch) pattern. The number of coats of paint a given edge receives depends on whether it will be exposed to the elements once the panel is installed. The interior edges of a new door,

FIG 5-12
Trimming out a new panel.

for example, might be given only three single coats; the inner edges of a fender, a full eight.

Once the trimmed-out portions have dried (a process that usually takes about 30 minutes), the panel is installed. From this point on, it is treated the same as a panel being refinished.

OBJECTIVE 5-A3 (manipulative)

Working as a team with two other students and with the aid of Job Report Sheet 5-A3, you will take a new body panel (door, hood, or fender) through the entire lacquer finishing process from trimming out to installation, painting, and compounding.

Time Recommended:

2½ hours

Preparation:

1. Review pages 183 through 203.
2. Study pages 203 through 208.
3. Read the Safety Checklist on page 227, items 1 through 6.

Tools and Materials:

1. Suction-feed spray guns (two—one for paint, one for primer-surfacer)
2. Duster gun
3. Polisher with both compounding and polishing pads
4. Rack or stand
5. Paint rack and strainer
6. Wooden stirring sticks
7. Respirator and safety goggles
8. Rubber gloves (optional)
9. Hose (or sponge and bucket)
10. Masking paper and tape
11. Clean shop cloths
12. Selection of sandpapers (280A, 320A, 500A, 600A)

13. Tack cloth
14. Socket wrench
15. Metal conditioner (optional)
16. Lacquer primer-surfacer
17. Thinner
18. Fast-drying reducer
19. Hand and machine rubbing compounds
20. Acrylic lacquer paint
21. Liquid polish

Procedure:

1. Place the panel, interior side up, on a sturdy rack. Wipe down the interior surfaces and edges with fast-drying reducer.
2. If the panel is factory primed, scuff sand it using a 280A abrasive. Then blow it clean with a duster gun. If the panel is not primed, apply metal conditioner.
3. Mix 1 part primer-surfacer with 1½ parts thinner.
4. Set the transformer-regulator at 40 psi (30 psi at the gun). Test the spray gun on a piece of masking paper. When properly adjusted, the tool should form a 6-inch pattern that flows well when applied from a distance of 6 to 8 inches.
5. Apply two single coats of primer-surfacer to the panel interior and edges. Allow flash time between the coats and 20 minutes of drying time after them.
6. Using a 320A abrasive, scuff sand all primed surfaces and blow them clean. Apply an extra coat of primer-surfacer to any low spots or areas that are sanded through. Allow 10 minutes of drying time.
7. When the spots primed last are dry, wet sand them with a 500A abrasive. Use a moistened cloth to wipe any sanding residue from the panel and blow dry.
8. Turn the panel over and repeat steps 1 through 7. *Note:* Since this surface is the panel's exterior, the final wet sanding with the 500A abrasive should be done overall rather than confined to spots.
9. Move the panel to a rack in the spray booth.
10. Give the panel a final wipedown with fast-drying reducer.
11. Open the paint and stir it by hand for 4 to 5 minutes. Transfer the paint to another container and use a small amount of thinner to rinse out the can. Add this material to the paint and stir 2 minutes more.
12. Strain 1 part paint and 1½ parts thinner into a spray gun cup and mix thoroughly.
13. Set the transformer-regulator at 45 psi (35 psi at the gun). Test the spray gun on a piece of masking paper. Proper adjustment at a distance of 6 to 8 inches will be determined by the type of panel being painted. A deck lid, for example, will require a pattern 6 inches wide because its whole interior must be painted. A door, on the other hand, will require a much narrower pattern because only its edges must be covered.
14. Tack the panel interior.

15. Apply the paint in three single coats (very wet). Cover the edges and all other portions of the interior that will be exposed once the panel is installed. Allow 30 minutes of drying time.
16. Outside the spray booth, compound a portion of the vehicle surface to expose its true color. Select a panel that will be adjacent to the new one once it is installed. By hand, compound into this panel a distance of 8 to 10 inches. Then wipe any compounding residue away with a moistened cloth and blow with a duster gun.
17. When the new panel is dry, remove it from the booth and check its exterior for overspray. Look along or near the panel edges. If any overspray is found, use a 500A abrasive to wet sand it away. Wipe the panel clean.
18. Install the panel. Start the bolts in their holes. Once the panel is aligned, with uniform spacing on all sides, tighten the bolts.
19. Push the vehicle into the spray booth. Be sure to disconnect the battery ground cable beforehand.
20. Use 18- or 24-inch paper to mask adjacent panels and glass. Mask the compounded panel last so that its paper can be pulled up for color checks during painting.
21. Give the new panel a final wipedown with fast-drying reducer and tack.
22. Apply a single wet coat of paint to the panel exterior. When the bottom edge is reached, begin again at the top and immediately apply a second wet coat. Then allow flash time. *Note:* This sequence equals a double wet coat and is the standard application technique for most lacquer top coats.
23. Repeat this double coating process two more times for a total of six single coats. Then allow the panel to dry for 30 minutes.
24. Check the newly painted surface for nibs. If any are found, wet sand the affected area with a 600A abrasive. Then wipe the panel clean and blow dry.
25. Replace the paint in the spray gun with a new mixture consisting of 1 inch of paint and 2 inches of thinner. Retest the gun and make any adjustments necessary to produce a 6-inch pattern that flows well when applied from a distance of 6 to 8 inches.
26. Tack the panel.
27. Apply a final double coat of paint to the panel surface.
28. Allow the panel to air dry overnight or at least 4 hours before unmasking. To force dry, allow 10 minutes of flowing time and bake for 1 hour at a temperature of 165 degrees Fahrenheit.
29. Check the panel for signs of roughness. If any are found, wet sand as in step 24.
30. Machine compound the panel, working no more than 2 square feet of surface at a time. Use a duster gun and a moistened cloth to clean away any compounding residue.
31. Switch to the polishing pad. Apply liquid polish to the panel and buff until the shine equals that of the surrounding surfaces.

ACRYLIC LACQUER PANEL REPAIR

Student Name ______________________________ Date ______________

Time Started ____________ Time Finished ____________ Total Time ____________

Specifications

Type of panel ______________________________

Condition of panel: Factory primed ______ Bare ______

Make of car ____________ Model ____________ Year ____________

Type of finish ____________ Manufacturer's paint code ____________

Name of color ______________________________

Technique

Metal conditioner: Yes ______ No ______

Primer-surfacer: Type ____________ Color ____________

Total number of coats (panel interior) ______

Total number of coats (panel exterior) ______

Wet sanding method: Hose ______ Sponge and bucket ______

When used/purpose ______________________________

____

____

Compounding method: Mechanical ______ Hand ______

When used/purpose ______________________________

____

____

Paint reduction: Type of thinner ______________________________

Formulas ______________________________

____

Surfaces masked: ______________________ ______________________

______________________ ______________________

______________________ ______________________

Drying process:

Air ______ Force drying ______ Total drying time ______________________

Checkup Questions

1. Why was it important to rinse out the paint can (step 11)? ______________________

____

____

2. Describe how paint sprayed on interior portions of a panel can end up as overspray on exterior portions. ____

____

____

3. How does a coat of paint in a spot repair differ from a coat of paint in a panel repair? ____

____

____

Describe the difference between a single wet coat and a double wet coat. Give a use for each. ____

____

____

Date Completed ______________ Instructor's Signature ______________________

WHOLE-VEHICLE REPAIRS

The most extensive form of refinishing possible is a whole-vehicle repair. Because of the sheer size of the job, the refinisher faces an entirely new set of problems. For the first time he must consider how to move himself and his equipment around the vehicle. He must determine in advance the best order in which to paint various body panels. In some cases, he must even refinish the inside of the car before he can begin painting the outside. With no other kind of repair is the detailed, step-by-step nature of the refinisher's work quite so apparent.

There is a compensating factor, however. While the refinisher must do more work with a whole-vehicle repair, in some critical respects he does not have to be so exacting about it. With panel and spot repairs, for example, he must take pains to match the old top coat. After a whole-vehicle repair, however, there is no old top coat to match. Thus one of the most difficult aspects of refinishing is eliminated by the repair process itself.

Interior Work

Painting a whole vehicle, then, makes it possible to change the top coat color entirely. If such a repair is not to look like the refinishing job it is, however, the painter must do his initial work on the car's interior. He must, in effect, trim out panels that are already installed. These include doors and hoods.

Masking Techniques

In both cases, spray painting, no matter how well controlled, will expose interior compartments to overspray. To protect these areas, the refinisher must install masking. He uses two basic techniques. First, he runs a strip of masking paper around each compartment opening. This masking is designed to shield adjoining surfaces. Second, he protects the compartment's contents with drop cloths or larger sheets of paper. This more extensive masking catches particles of paint deflected deep into the car's interior (Fig. 5-13).

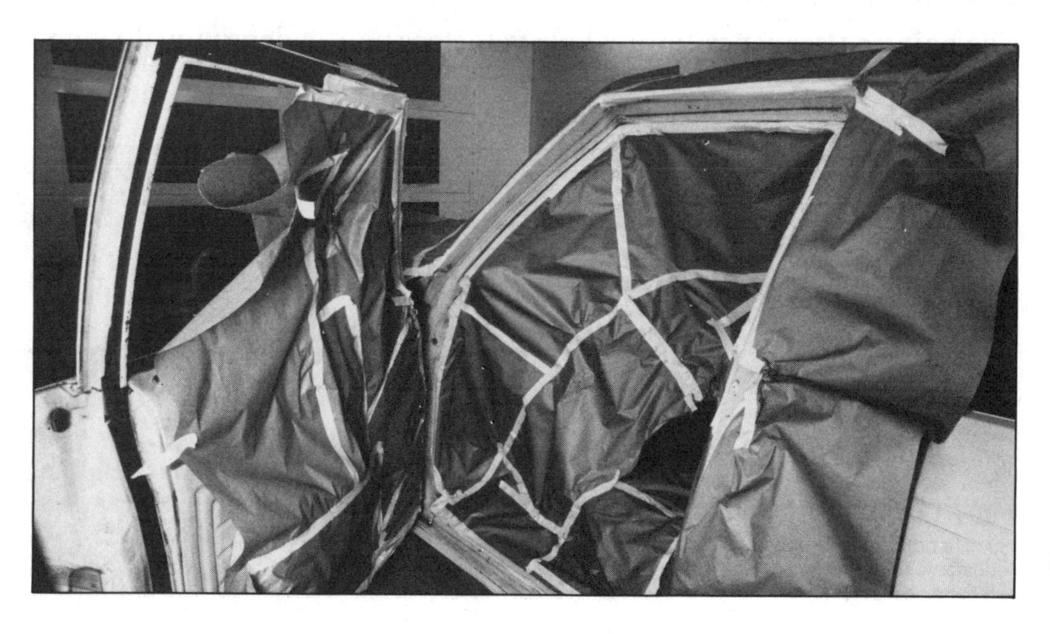

FIG 5-13
Interior masking.

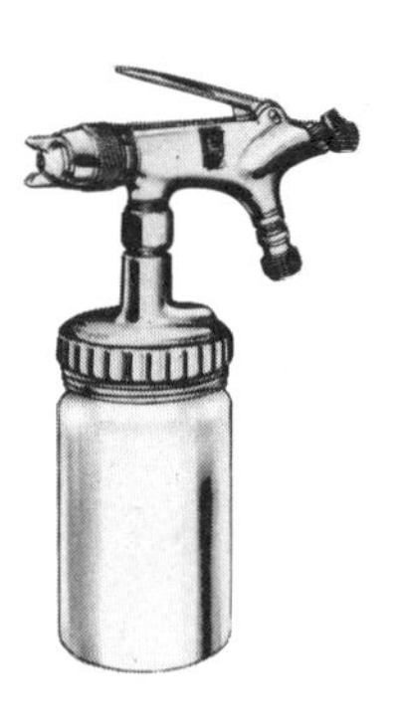

FIG 5-14
Touch-up spray gun. (The DeVilbiss Company)

Using a Touch-up Gun

Because of the confined space in which he must work when painting panel interiors, the refinisher needs a special spray gun. Called a touch-up gun, the tool falls in size midway between regular suction-feed equipment and an airbrush (Fig. 5-14). A touch-up gun operates at low pressures—normally 35 psi at the transformer-regulator and 25 psi at the gun. For interior work, it is used to apply a minimal three coats of paint. Once again, this kind of coverage is sufficient for surfaces that are not continuously exposed to the weather.

Exterior Work

For exterior work, the refinisher switches back to a regular suction-feed gun. To give himself the freedom of movement he needs to work his way around a car, he equips the gun with a 50-foot air hose. With a hose of this length, a pressure at the regulator of 45 psi should produce the required 35 psi at the gun. (Note that these settings are the same as those used for panel painting.)

Hose Handling

While necessary to reach all parts of a vehicle, a 50-foot hose can itself pose problems for the refinisher. There is always the risk that, in moving from one side of the car to the other, he will pull the hose into some freshly painted panel. To avoid such damaging contacts, the refinisher must know at all times exactly where the hose is.

One way for him to gain a margin of safety is to feed the hose over his opposite shoulder (Fig. 5-15). (A right-handed painter, for example, would pull the hose over his left shoulder and feed slack as needed with his left hand.) This technique allows the painter to control the hose without really paying attention to it. By placing his body between the vehicle and the hose, the refinisher is forced to maintain more slack. That slack, in turn, is kept where it can do no harm—behind the painter and away from the car.

Painting Sequence

The painting sequence for a whole-vehicle repair is determined by one key factor—overspray. Since no exhaust system is 100-percent effective,

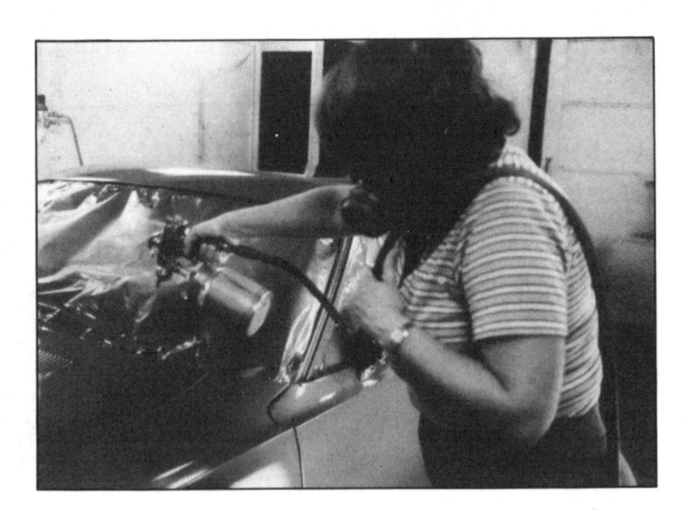

FIG 5-15
Hose handling technique of feeding hose to gun with left hand. (David Keown)

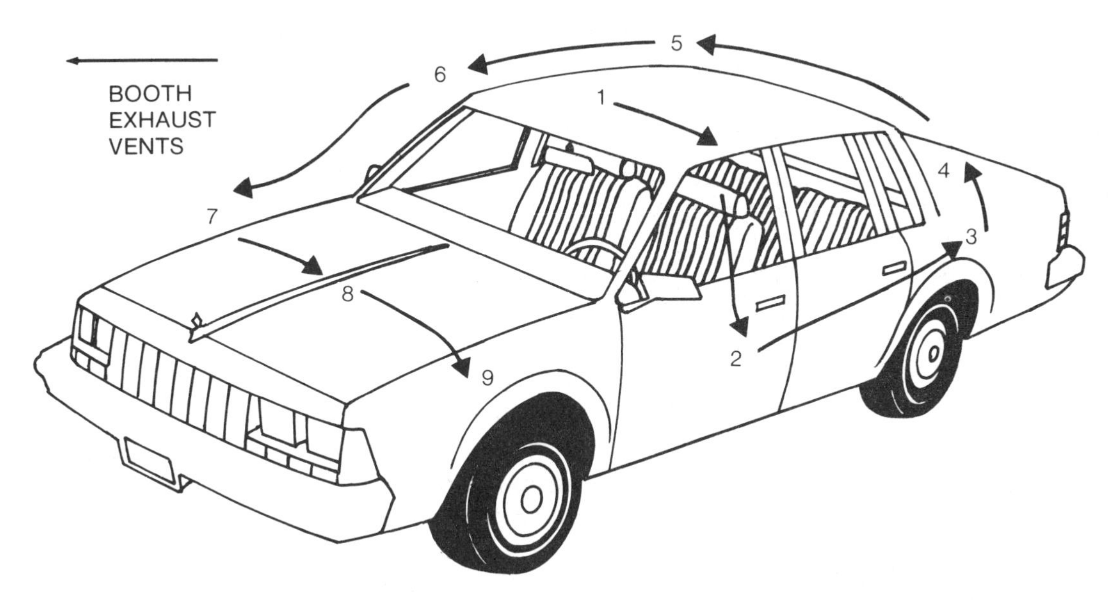

FIG 5-16 Painting sequence to avoid overspray damage.

a certain amount of overspray remains in the booth. Being heavier than air, eventually it falls—and at least some of it ends up on the vehicle.

While it is not possible to eliminate this damaging fallout, it is possible to minimize its effects by observing two simple precautions.

1. *Paint the highest body panel first.* Usually this is the roof. Overspray from this initial painting will fall onto lower body panels. There it will be reflowed when these panels are themselves painted a little later in the refinishing process.
2. *Paint the end of the vehicle nearest the exhaust fan last.* The flow of air in a booth tends to pull overspray from the back to the front. The object of working with the exhaust system airflow is to draw most of the overspray across panels that have not yet been painted. In this way, any excess pigment that attaches itself to the vehicle can be reflowed later by applications of paint. If the vehicle is positioned with its front end nearest the exhaust vents, for example, the refinisher might move from the roof to the left front door, back around the trunk, up the right side of the car, and finally across the fenders and hood (Fig. 5-16).

A more complete, systematic sequence of painting all the panels on an automobile is as follows:

1. Spraying starts at the beltline (lower edge of the side windows) and continues until the side of the roof nearest you is sprayed so the last stroke laps the center of the vehicle's roof.
2. Move to the opposite side of the vehicle and continue spraying from the center of the roof to its outside edge and on down to the beltline.
3. Spray the upper deck panel, deck lid and rear-end panel.
4. Spray one rear quarter panel.
5. Spray the other rear quarter panel.
6. Spray the rear door and the rocker panel below it.

7. Spray the front door and the rocker panel below it.
8. Move to the other side of the car and spray the rear door and rocker panel.
9. Spray the front door and rocker panel.
10. Spray the fender adjacent to the door just painted, starting at the bottom and working upward until the last stroke laps the center line of the hood.
11. Moving around the front of the car, spray from the center of the hood on that side continuing downward on the fender until you reach its bottom edge.
12. Move to the front of the car and spray any front edges of hood, fenders, gravel shields, or lower panels.

When this procedure is used to apply each coat of any automotive refinishing material and the recommended number of coats are applied, the finish thickness will be consistent over the entire vehicle.

OBJECTIVE 5-A4 (manipulative)

Working as a team with three other students and with the aid of Job Report Sheet 5-A4, you will refinish a whole vehicle in a contrasting color of acrylic lacquer.

Time Recommended:

20 hours

Preparation:

1. Review pages 183 through 212.
2. Study pages 212 through 218.
3. Read the Safety Checklist on page 227, items 1 through 6.

Tools and Materials:

1. Vibrator or orbital sander
2. Suction-feed spray guns (two—one for paint, one for primer-surfacer)
3. Touch-up gun
4. Duster gun
5. Polisher with both compounding and polishing pads
6. Sanding blocks (hard and sponge rubber)
7. Socket wrench (for battery ground cable)
8. Squeegee
9. Paint rack and strainer
10. Wooden stirring sticks
11. Respirator and safety goggles
12. Rubber gloves
13. Hose (or sponge and bucket)
14. Masking paper and tape
15. Clean shop cloths
16. Selection of sandpapers (80D, 280A, 320A, 500A, 600A)

17. Tack cloth
18. Wax remover
19. Metal conditioner
20. Lacquer primer-surfacer
21. Thinner
22. Fast-drying reducer
23. Glazing putty
24. Hand and machine rubbing compounds
25. Acrylic lacquer paint
26. Liquid polish

Procedure:

1. Clean the vehicle with wax remover. Proceed one panel at a time, applying the remover with one cloth and wiping it dry with another.
2. Featheredge any chips or scratches in the old finish. To taper broken edges, use a vibrator or an orbital sander equipped with an 80D abrasive. To finish, use a 280A or 320A abrasive to hand sand a 3- to 5-inch border around each featheredged area. Blow the sanding dust from all panel surfaces.
3. Apply conditioner to any bare metal exposed during the featheredging process.
4. Mask any windows, bumpers, moldings, or trim that might be exposed to overspray during the application of primer-surfacer to the featheredged areas. For lacquer primer-surfacer, 12-inch paper is an adequate masking material.
5. Mix 1 part lacquer primer-surfacer with 1½ parts thinner.
6. Test spray the primer-surfacer on a piece of masking paper. Set the transformer-regulator at 40 psi (30 psi at the gun). When properly adjusted, the spray gun should form a 6-inch pattern that flows well when applied from a distance of 6 to 8 inches.
7. Apply four coats of primer-surfacer to the featheredged areas, allowing flash time between. After the last coat, allow the primer to dry 30 minutes.
8. Using a hard rubber block and a 320A abrasive, sand the primed areas.
9. Use glazing putty to fill any low spots exposed by the sanding. Apply the product sparingly with a rubber squeegee and allow an additional 30 minutes of drying time.
10. Sand the puttied areas with the same abrasive used in step 8. Blow all sanding dust from panel surfaces.
11. Apply a fifth coat of primer-surfacer to all repair areas and allow it to dry 20 minutes.
12. Open the doors, hood, and deck lid. Remove the rubber weather strips and metal step plates from the door areas.
13. Wet sand the whole vehicle, including the interior surfaces that will have to be painted. Use a 500A abrasive and a sponge rubber sanding block.
14. Remove all masking.

15. Rinse the vehicle thoroughly to remove all sanding dust. Using a duster gun, chase all water from panel surfaces and dry completely with clean cloths.
16. Disconnect the battery ground cable and push the car into the spray booth.
17. Close the spray booth doors and turn on the exhaust system.
18. Set the transformer-regulator pressure at 70 psi and use the duster gun to force any water from around moldings, doors, hood and trunk openings, glass, and trim. Wipe any water from panel surfaces with a clean, dry cloth.
19. Mask windows, bumpers, front and rear lights, grill, moldings, door handles, mirrors, and trim. Tape down any folds in the masking paper.
20. Using long sheets of 12-inch paper, mask interior door and post trim, floor mats, and instrument panel. Lay sheets of 36-inch paper (or drop cloths) over the seats, the engine, and the trunk compartment.
21. Give the interior areas to be painted a final wipedown with fast-drying reducer.
22. Mix 1 part acrylic lacquer paint with 1½ parts thinner. Strain the mixture into both a regular suction-feed spray gun and a touch-up gun.
23. Set the transformer-regulator at 35 psi (25 psi at the gun) and test both tools. Initially the two guns should be adjusted to produce patterns approximately 3 inches wide at a distance of 6 to 8 inches. Readjustments, however, will be necessary during painting to cover larger areas (like the interior deck lid).
24. Tack all interior surfaces to be painted.
25. Apply three single coats to these areas. Angle the gun as needed to assure complete coverage. Use the touch-up gun for hard-to-reach places like the front door posts or hood hinges. *Note:* Proceed around the vehicle from one compartment opening to another in sequence. In this way, by the time the last area is painted, the first should be ready to receive its next coat. After all three coats have been applied, allow 30 minutes of drying time.
26. Close doors, hood, and deck lid on the safety catch only. Inspect the exteriors of these panels. If any overspray is found, wet sand it away with a 500A abrasive. Immediately wipe up any sanding residue with a moist cloth.
27. Go over the vehicle's exterior one last time with fast-drying reducer.
28. Refill the full-size spray gun. Set the transformer-regulator at 45 psi (35 psi at the gun). Test and readjust the gun as necessary to produce a 6-inch pattern that flows well when applied from a distance of 6 to 8 inches.
29. Tack the vehicle one panel at a time. Be sure to refold the tack cloth as residue builds up on the portion being used.
30. Apply one double wet coat of lacquer to each vehicle panel. Start at the passenger side of the roof and work toward the center. Then change sides and work from the center to the driver's side. Next paint the door (or doors) on the driver's side. From there, work toward the back or front of the vehicle, depending on the direction of the air flow in the spray booth.

31. Immediately apply two more double coats in the same fashion for a total of six single coats. Then allow the vehicle to dry for 30 minutes.
32. Carefully check each panel for nibs. If any are found, wet sand them away using a 600A abrasive. Wipe the affected surface (or surfaces) clean and blow dry.
33. Replace the paint in the spray gun with a new mixture consisting of 1 part paint and 2 parts thinner. Retest the gun and make any adjustments necessary to produce a 6-inch pattern that flows well when applied from a distance of 6 to 8 inches.
34. Tack the whole vehicle a second time.
35. Apply a final double coat of paint, proceeding around the vehicle as in step 30.
36. Air dry the new finish at least 12 hours before unmasking. For force drying, follow the recommendations on the paint can label.
37. Machine compound the new finish. Work on an area no larger than 2 square feet at any given time. Compound hard-to-reach places by hand. When the compounding is complete, blow any residue from the vehicle, rinse, and wipe dry.
38. Apply liquid polish to the vehicle, one panel at a time. Allow a haze to form. Then buff with a polishing pad until a high gloss is achieved.

ACRYLIC LACQUER WHOLE-VEHICLE REPAIR

Student Name ______________________________

Date Started ____________ Date Finished ____________ Total Time ____________

Specifications

Make of car ____________ Model ____________ Year ____________

Type of finish ____________ Manufacturer's paint code ____________

Name of color ______________________________

Condition of finish (Describe the nature and extent of any damage.) ____________

____

____

Technique

Rough featheredging method:

Type of sander ____________ Abrasive ____________

Fine featheredging method:

Type of sander ____________ Abrasive ____________

Metal conditioner: Yes ______ No ______

Primer-surfacer: Type ____________ Color ____________

Psi at the transformer-regulator ______ Psi at the gun ______

Total number of coats ______

Number of putty applications ______

Wet sanding method: Hose ______ Sponge and bucket ______

Type of sanding block ____________ Abrasive ____________

Surfaces masked ____________ ____________

____________ ____________

____________ ____________

Paint reduction: Type of thinner ____________________

Formulas ____________________

____

Drying process:

Air ______ Force drying ______ Total drying time ____________

Compounding method:

Type of polisher ____________ Rpm/psi ______

Type of compound ____________________

Checkup Questions

1. How was the 50-percent overlap necessary for a single coat achieved when painting interior panel edges? ____________________

____

____

2. List the interior surfaces painted with the touch-up gun.

____________ ____________ ____________

____________ ____________ ____________

3. Why was no drying time necessary between steps 30 and 31? ____________

____

____

4. What adjustments did you make to the spray gun in step 33? Why were they necessary? ____________________

____

____

Date Completed ____________ Instructor's Signature ____________

COLOR COATING

Color coating is used to correct slight differences in color. When a panel has been refinished, for example, and does not quite match adjacent surfaces, color coating is employed to restore uniformity to the finish.

The procedure is basically a simplified form of refinishing. It does not involve extensive sanding, filling, or resurfacing of any kind. The problem is confined to the top coat, and the correction is made entirely at that level. Since there is no question of compatibility (the existing and new finishes are the same except for the slight difference in color), sealing is not necessary. One lacquer top coat is simply applied over another with, hopefully, more satisfactory results.

Working as a team with one other student and with the aid of Job Report Sheet 5-A5, you will color coat a finished body panel with acrylic lacquer.

OBJECTIVE 5-A5 (manipulative)

Time Recommended:

1 hour

Preparation:

1. Review pages 183 through 218.
2. Study pages 219 through 222.
3. Read the Safety Checklist on page 227, items 1 through 6.

Tools and Materials:

1. Suction-feed spray gun
2. Duster gun
3. Polisher with compounding and polishing pads
4. Paint rack and strainer
5. Wooden stirring stick
6. Socket wrench (for battery ground cable)
7. Clean shop cloths
8. Masking paper and tape
9. Acrylic lacquer paint
10. Thinner
11. Acrylic lacquer retarder
12. Wax remover
13. Fast-drying reducer
14. Sandpaper (600A)
15. Machine compound
16. Polish
17. Tack cloth

Procedure:

1. Clean the panel with wax remover.
2. If there are any imperfections (like stains or minor scratches) in the

repair area, sand these out by hand. Use a 600A abrasive. Then blow the panel clean with a duster gun.

3. Machine compound both the panel to be repaired and a portion of one adjacent panel.
4. Disconnect the battery ground cable and push the car into the spray booth.
5. Using 18- or 24-inch paper, mask adjoining panels and/or glass. On the repair panel itself, use masking tape to cover all moldings and trim.
6. Give the panel a final wipedown with fast-drying reducer.
7. Mix 1 part acrylic lacquer paint with 1½ parts thinner. Stir well and strain into the spray gun cup.
8. Set the transformer-regulator at 45 psi (35 psi at the gun). Test the spray gun on masking paper. When properly adjusted, it should form a pattern 6 inches wide at a distance of 6 inches.
9. Tack the repair panel.
10. Apply one medium wet coat of color followed within 2 minutes by a second coat. Then allow the paint to flash. Apply two more coats in the same manner.
11. Remove all but ½ inch of color from the spray gun cup. Add two caps full of retarder and refill the cup with thinner to the ½-quart mark. Stir.
12. Retest the gun and make any necessary adjustments.
13. Apply one mist coat of the retarder mix to the panel.
14. Air dry the repair at least 4 hours. To force dry, allow an initial evaporation time of 20 minutes. Then bake a maximum of 30 minutes at a temperature of 165 degrees Fahrenheit.
15. Machine compound and then polish the panel to restore its shine.

ACRYLIC LACQUER COLOR COATING

Student Name ______________________ Date ____________

Time Started ____________ Time Finished ____________ Total Time ____________

Specifications

Make of car ____________ Model ____________ Year ____________

Type of finish ____________ Manufacturer's paint code ____________

Name of color ______________________

Repair panel ______________________

Condition of finish (Describe the nature of the color correction required.) ____________

____

____

Technique

Sanding: Yes ______ No ______ (If yes, describe any imperfections removed.)

____

____

____

Surfaces masked ____________ ____________

____________ ____________

____________ ____________

Drying process:

Air ______ Force drying ______ Total drying time ____________

Checkup Questions

1. What was the purpose of the compounding in step 3? ______

______

______

2. Was an exact color match achieved? If not, suggest why. ______

______

______

3. How does color coating differ from an ordinary panel repair? ______

______

______

Date Completed ______ Instructor's Signature ______

HEAT REPAIRS

The lacquer finishes currently being applied to new cars have been mixed at the factory with a special thermoplastic additive. This material makes it possible to reflow an original lacquer finish by applying heat.

The original reason for using a thermoplastic agent was to eliminate final compounding from assembly line painting. (See pages 187 and 188.) Outside the factory, however, it had an additional, unforeseen benefit. The additive made it possible for refinishers to repair some forms of minor film damage without using refinishing materials at all.

A scratch that does not extend deep into the paint film is the kind of damage that can be repaired in this fashion. Ordinarily a refinisher would sand down and resurface the entire scratch area, then repaint it. Now, with a new finish, he can use a tool called a heat gun to do a one-step repair.

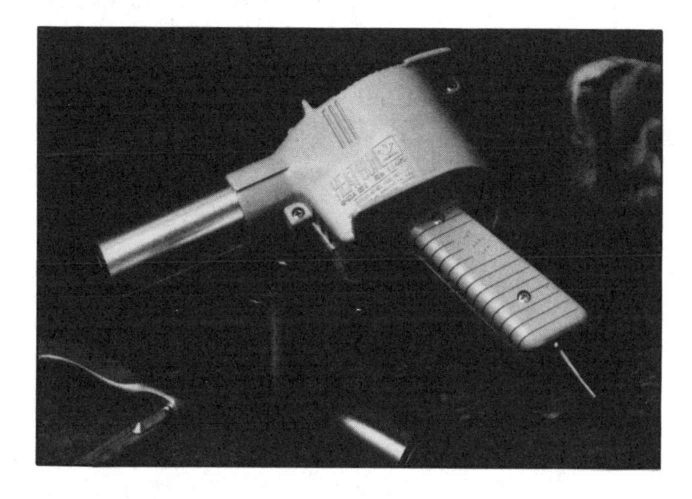

FIG 5-17
Heat gun. (Ideal Industries, Inc.)

A heat gun looks and operates very much like a hand-held hair dryer. It has an electric heating element and can be adjusted to blow either warm or cool air. If held in one spot while set on warm, it can produce enough heat to soften and then reflow the lacquer finish in a limited area. Thus, by applying the gun to a scratch, for example, a refinisher can simply fill it with reflowed paint (Fig. 5-17).

OBJECTIVE 5-A6 (manipulative)

Working as a team with one other student and with the aid of Job Report Sheet 5-A6, you will do a heat repair of minor film damage to a factory-baked lacquer top coat.

Time Recommended:

30 minutes

Preparation:

1. Review pages 183 through 223.
2. Study pages 223 through 226.
3. Read the Safety Checklist on page 227, items 1 through 6.

Tools and Materials:

1. Heat gun
2. Clean shop cloths
3. Tack cloth
4. Wax remover
5. Liquid polish

Procedure:

1. Clean the damaged area with wax remover and then tack.
2. Switch on the heat gun and adjust it to supply warm air. Apply heat to the damaged paint film by pointing the gun at it from a distance of about 4 to 5 inches. *Note:* If the damage extends beyond the gun's heat spot, move the tool slowly back and forth over the whole area.
3. When the damaged area takes on a shiny, wet look and the scratches flow together, readjust the gun to supply air only and cool the panel.
4. When the reflowed area is completely cooled, apply polish and buff by hand to a uniform gloss.

JOB REPORT SHEET 5-A6

ACRYLIC LACQUER HEAT REPAIR

Student Name ______________________ Date ____________

Time Started ____________ Time Finished ____________ Total Time ____________

Specifications

Make of car ____________ Model ____________ Year ____________

Type of finish ____________ Manufacturer's paint code ____________

Name of color ______________________

Location of paint film damage ______________________

Nature and extent of damage ______________________

____

____

Technique

Gun movement required: Yes ______ No ______

Length of time heat applied ______ minutes

Checkup Questions

1. Why must any wax be removed for this repair (step 1)? ____________

____

____

2. Describe how the paint looked as the reflowing took place. ____________

____

____

3. Was the color of the damaged area affected by reflowing? ______________________

____

____

Date Completed ______________ Instructor's Signature ________________________

SAFETY CHECKLIST

1. As with other kinds of paints, the overspray of lacquer is extremely flammable and volatile. For this reason remember to obey the ban on smoking when in or around an area where lacquer is being sprayed.
2. Of equal importance is that you always wear a respirator when you're in or around an area where lacquer is being sprayed. Paints and their reduction materials are caustic and should never be inhaled.
3. When using lacquer thinner on a rag to check a car's finish, be aware that it is highly flammable. Use it carefully in an open area where there is adequate ventilation. Put out all smoking materials to conduct this test.
4. Adjust the air pressure on your spray equipment so it yields the least overspray possible. Minimizing the possibility of overspray buildup will by extension minimize the fire danger of this buildup.
5. Disconnect the battery ground cable of the car being sprayed before rolling the car into the spray booth. Doing so eliminates the possibility of exhaust pollutants contaminating the booth's interior, but more importantly it renders the car's electrical system incapable of producing a dangerous spark.
6. Read the directions on the cans of all materials you will be using for the job. Take the time and care necessary to do the job properly the first time so as to minimize the possibility of having to reexpose yourself to sanding dust, paint overspray, etc. when having to redo a job.

TEST 5-A

Student Name ______________________ Date ____________

DIRECTIONS: Circle the best answer to each question.

1. All lacquer paints in use today are made from
   A. lampblack and varnish.
   B. nitric acid and natural fibers.
   C. acrylics.
   D. thermoplastic compounds.

2. All of the following claims for lacquers are true EXCEPT
   A. dust free in minutes.
   B. eliminates compounding.
   C. chemically active for years.
   D. harder than nitrocellulose top coats.

3. The two-gun method is used for
   A. spot repairs.
   B. panel repairs.
   C. whole-vehicle repairs.
   D. color coating.

4. A heat gun is used to
   I. reflow minor scratches.
   II. speed the drying of paint.

   A. I only B. II only C. Both I and II D. Neither I nor II

5. The vehicle pictured is in a spray booth. The shaded areas have already received one double wet coat of acrylic lacquer. The exhaust fan is located at X. If the whole vehicle is being refinished, which panel should be painted next?

   A. B. C. D.

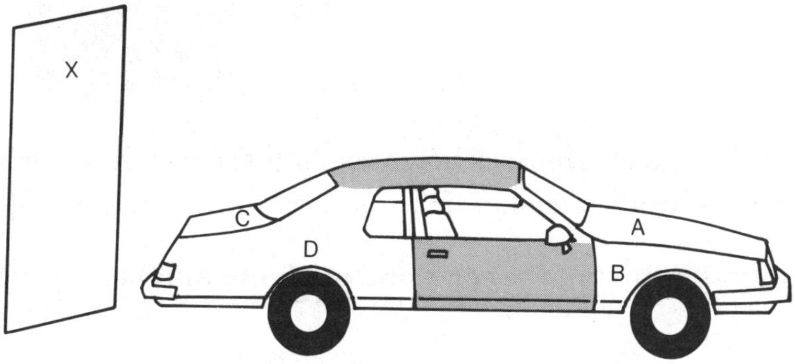

6. A car is being repainted a different color. Compared to the vehicle's exterior, the doorjambs receive
   A. more coats of paint.
   B. fewer coats of paint.
   C. the same number of paint coats.
   D. no coats of paint.

7. A lacquer mist coat consists of
   A. 1 part paint, $1\frac{1}{2}$ parts thinner.
   B. $1\frac{1}{2}$ parts paint, 1 part thinner.
   C. 5 percent paint, 95 percent thinner.
   D. 95 percent paint, 5 percent thinner.

8. Which procedure takes the lowest psi?
   A. Spot repair, one-gun method
   B. Spot repair, two-gun method
   C. Panel repair
   D. Whole-vehicle repair

9. A new body panel is refinished
   I. before installation.
   II. after installation.
   A. I only   B. II only   C. Both I and II   D. Neither I nor II

10. The purpose of the second gun in the two-gun method is to
    I. eliminate dry spray.
    II. blend the new repair into the old paint.
    A. I only   B. II only   C. Both I and II   D. Neither I nor II

11. The product at the right is
    A. a fast-drying solvent.
    B. a medium-drying solvent.
    C. a slow-drying solvent.
    D. an extremely slow-drying solvent.

(E. I. du Pont de Nemours & Company)

12. The refinished fender of a sportscar is brighter than the rest of the vehicle.
    Refinisher I suggests that compounding the adjoining panels will solve the problem.
    Refinisher II suggests remixing the color and applying another top coat directly over the existing one.
    Who is right?
    A. I only   B. II only   C. Both I and II   D. Neither I nor II

13. A whole-vehicle repair usually requires all of the following EXCEPT
   A. a 50-foot air hose.
   B. color blending of the old and new top coats.
   C. use of a touch-up gun.
   D. a transformer-regulator setting of 45 psi.

14. Which procedure produces the best shine?
   A. One-gun method
   B. Two-gun method
   C. Mist coating
   D. Thermal flowing

15. Lacquer is considered a touchy finish because it
   I. will rub off if touched with thinner.
   II. can be spotted by tree sap and bird droppings.

   A. I only B. II only C. Both I and II D. Neither I nor II

16. All of the following are possible causes of blushing EXCEPT
   A. using a poor-quality thinner.
   B. using the wrong thinner for shop conditions.
   C. adding too much retarder to the paint.
   D. rainy weather.

17. Color coating differs from normal lacquer repair of a damaged surface in all of the following ways EXCEPT
   A. sanding is minimal.
   B. the old finish is never removed.
   C. only half as much paint is applied.
   D. retarder is not necessary.

18. The doors and fenders of a GM car are chipped and scratched from parking lot damage. The owner wants a more durable finish applied to these panels.

   Refinisher I suggests that six coats of acrylic lacquer will give good coverage and at the same time save the owner some money.

   Refinisher II suggests fifteen coats of acrylic lacquer for extra strength and durability.

   Who is right?

   A. I only B. II only C. Both I and II D. Neither I nor II

19. The diagram at the right shows a one-gun lacquer repair to a vehicle panel. Which letter is correctly identified below?
   A. Original repair area
   B. Sealer coat
   C. Original repair area
   D. Mist coat with retarder

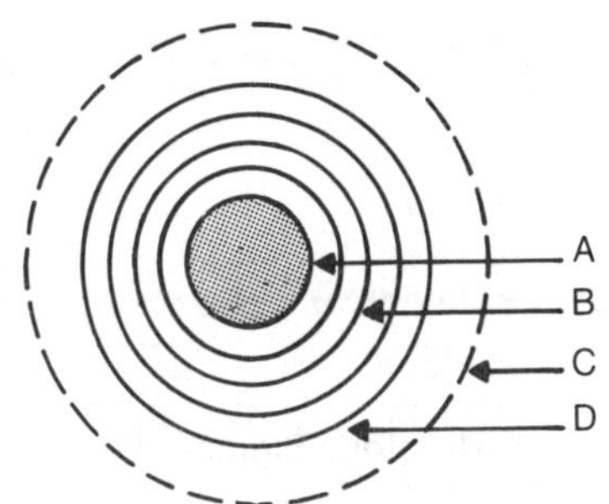

20. A summary of spray gun techniques for applying lacquer to panel-sized or larger surfaces would include all of the following EXCEPT

A. spraying distance: 8 to 12 inches.

B. pressure at the gun: 25 to 35 psi.

C. fan width: 6 inches.

D. application: double wet coats.

Score __________ Instructor's Signature ______________________________

unit 6

Enamel Refinishing

Enamels were invented in the early 1930s. At that time, the only automotive finish in widespread use was nitrocellulose lacquer. Enamels were developed to remedy the shortcomings of this product.

Recall that lacquer's main advantage was its speed. A thin, fine-textured paint once reduced, lacquer dried quickly. It also dried hard—so hard, in fact, that it was brittle and would chip at the slightest impact. This fact led to demands for a tougher, more resilient finish.

The first product to meet these demands was alkyd enamel. A thicker, more full-bodied paint even when reduced, alkyd enamel had good resistance to damage. To achieve this durability, however, its manufacturers had to sacrifice some speed. Alkyd enamel did not dry brittle, but then it did not dry very fast either. Its chemical makeup also made spot repairs difficult if not impossible.

As a result, enamels were forced into a process of refinement similar to that of lacquers. Ten years after acrylic lacquer came onto the market, acrylic enamel appeared. Like lacquer, it was faster drying. Unlike alkyd enamel, it could easily be used for spot repairs.

The newest development in enamel finishes is polyurethane-based paint. Brought out in the early 1970s, it is the most durable top coat currently available. This fact has made it a favorite finish for trucks, boats, and heavy equipment. Now, however, polyurethane enamel is coming into use in automotive work. This trend is rooted in a hard economic reality. Today people are keeping their cars longer, and they want a finish that will last longer, too.

Enamel is the factory finish of all Ford, Chrysler, American Motors, and most foreign cars. It is also the original finish applied to all trucks, including those manufactured by General Motors. This huge potential market makes enamel the most frequently used refinishing material. Lacquer has its place (particularly with GM passenger cars and spot repairs of all kinds); but unless a refinisher works for a GM dealer, he is far more likely to find himself using enamel products.

This unit therefore discusses enamel characteristics in detail. It then distinguishes alkyd, acrylic, and polyurethane enamels from each other on the basis of individual characteristics, special problems, and application procedures. In the shop exercises, it concentrates on the type of repair for which each product is particularly well suited—alkyd enamel, being cheapest, for whole-vehicle repairs; acrylic enamel, being both faster drying and easily reflowed, for spot repairs; and polyurethane enamel, being most durable, for exterior panel repairs. To complete coverage of the enamel paint family, special-use enamels are introduced and briefly discussed. These are mostly metallic finishes designed for use on bumpers, truck interiors, and similar surfaces.

OBJECTIVE 6-A (written test)

After doing the reading and shop exercises, you will be able to answer correctly without reference material a minimum of 14 out of 20 test questions on the following topics:

1. Enamel characteristics
2. Spot repairs with acrylic enamel
3. Panel repairs with polyurethane enamel
4. Whole-vehicle repairs with alkyd enamel
5. Enamel additives
6. Special-use enamels

Preparation:

1. Study pages 233 through 260.
2. Attend classroom discussions of Objective 6-A.
3. Read the Safety Checklist on page 260.

ENAMEL CHARACTERISTICS

Enamels, unlike lacquers, are a true family of paints. There are three different types of enamels currently in use in the automotive field—alkyd, acrylic, and polyurethane—compared to only acrylic on the lacquer side. Each type of enamel differs from the others in minor respects like exact drying time, cost, reduction, coverage, and details of application. However, all share key characteristics that distinguish them as a group from acrylic lacquers.

Chemical Activity

Compared to lacquers, enamels are not just chemically inactive. They are practically inert. The main reason for this difference is the two-step mechanism by which enamels dry. The first step is evaporation. This process is frequently termed drying from the inside out. (In other words, solvent vaporizes, passing from the paint film into the air.) The second step involves movement in the opposite direction, from the outside in. The paint film absorbs oxygen from the air, a process called oxidation (Fig. 6-1).

It is oxidation that makes enamel insoluble. It causes a permanent change in the paint binder. After oxidation has occurred, no amount of reducer applied will penetrate an enamel finish, and no amount of heat will soften it. The change can be likened to that which takes place in an egg when it is cooked. Heat causes the egg to solidify in such a way that it cannot be returned to its original state by either the addition of liquid or the application of more heat.

Such irreversible change has benefits and drawbacks. On the positive side, it makes for an extremely hard, durable, and corrosion-resistant finish. On the negative side, it adds to the refinisher's already burdensome and lengthy list of repair procedures. Consider two examples.

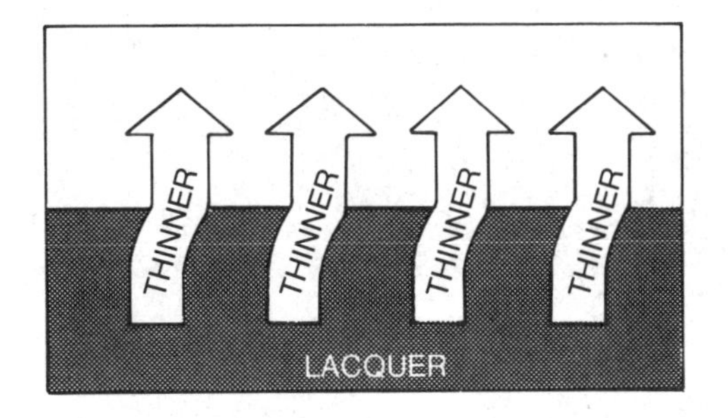

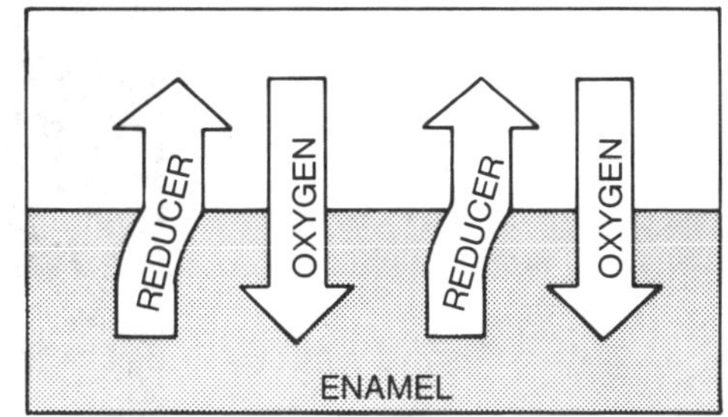

FIG 6-1 Comparison of how lacquers and enamels dry.

1. *Spot repairs with enamel are extremely difficult and, in some cases, impossible to perform.* Because of its insolubility, an enamel finish does not allow proper blending of the old paint with the new. Thus a dividing line frequently remains at the repair edges. It can be eliminated with additives and mist coats, but most refinishers simply prefer to avoid the extra steps and do a panel repair instead. This procedure, in turn, consumes more time and adds to the amount charged the customer.
2. *For even the simplest refinishing jobs, enamel may require sealing.* Since enamel is not reflowed or softened by the reducer in fresh paint, bonding can be a problem even with an identical top coat. Lacquers require sealing to prevent bonding from going too far (to the point of sandscratch swelling or lifting, for example). Enamels may require sealing just to adhere. For them, sanding is frequently not enough.

Drying Time

Enamels of all kinds are slower drying than lacquers. This trait is not as unfortunate as it might at first sound. While it does lengthen the time that individual repairs take, it also eliminates the problems that speed can cause. Blushing, for example, is virtually unheard of in a new enamel top coat. Enamel's slower drying time allows moisture to escape. Sandscratch showthrough is another problem that is virtually eliminated. Any finish that remains wet longer flows more and has a better chance to fill. This fact is one reason enamel can tolerate a more roughly finished surface than lacquer.

Avoiding Nibs

What freshly applied enamel cannot tolerate is the smallest particle of dust or dirt. Because enamels take so long to become dust-free, nibs are a special problem. Nibs are tiny airborne impurities that escape the booth exhaust system and settle out onto a new coat of paint. They look like (and are) the kind of dirt that tacking is designed to eliminate, but they reach the vehicle surface long after tacking has taken place (Fig. 6-2).

In a lacquer top coat, nibs can be compounded out. New enamel, however, cannot be compounded until it is fully dry, a state it does not reach until oxidation is complete. For some kinds of enam 's, this fact means waiting 30 days to compound. To avoid such delays, therefore, special precautions must be taken to eliminate nibs in the first place. Three steps are especially important.

FIG 6-2
Nibs in paint.

1. *Clean the vehicle thoroughly before taking it into the spray booth.* This procedure guarantees that the auto body itself does not become a source of contamination. In particular, openings that are not covered or stuffed with masking paper should be blown clear of dirt. Examples include fender skirts and spaces created by the removal of headlamps or grills (Fig. 6-3).
2. *Clean the spray booth.* Walls and floors should be washed down and dried thoroughly. (See Unit 3, pages 123 and 124.) In hot, desert climates, however, water can be sprinkled or misted onto the floor to keep down any dust or dirt tracked into the booth by the vehicle.
3. *Check the booth's draft gauge* (Fig. 6-4). If the air flow is not at maximum, inspect and, where necessary, replace booth filters and arrestors. If air flow is still below what it should be, clean the fan and/or service the fan belt. Where the booth does not have a draft gauge, a simple test can serve as a substitute. With the exhaust system running, hold open the door to the paint mixing area. Then let the door go. The exhaust system should pull it shut. Any system that cannot exert this kind of pull is not functioning well enough to remove enamel overspray.

FIG 6-3
Washing down fender skirts before painting. (Badger Air-Brush Co., *Air-Brushing Techniques for Custom Painting, Volume II*)

FIG 6-4
Spray booth draft gauge.
(David Keown)

Using Additives

One way to shorten the time it takes for an enamel repair is to accelerate the drying process. This objective can be accomplished by applying heat, using additives, or both.

If the repair is to be force dried, for example, baking resin is added to the original paint mix. Baking resin does for enamels what retarder does for lacquers—it keeps the outermost coat of paint from drying before all the solvent in the interior layers has had a chance to evaporate. Sealing in solvent is good for no paint, but with enamels the effects are particularly devastating. Lacquers may blush or later, if too much paint is applied, crack. With enamels, however, the solvent vapors are unable to break through the tougher paint film. Instead they swell it into tiny ridges. Eventually the vapors do manage to evaporate through the paint, but the film remains stretched and puckered, a condition described as wrinkling (Fig. 6-5). For this reason, baking resin is sometimes called antiwrinkle.

Baking lamps are not the only heat source that will cause an enamel finish to wrinkle. If the new paint is exposed to intense sunlight, the same thing will happen. In either case, it is essential to (1) use the right reducing agent for shop conditions, (2) avoid applying coats of paint that are either too thick or too numerous, and (3) add baking resin according to directions on the container label.

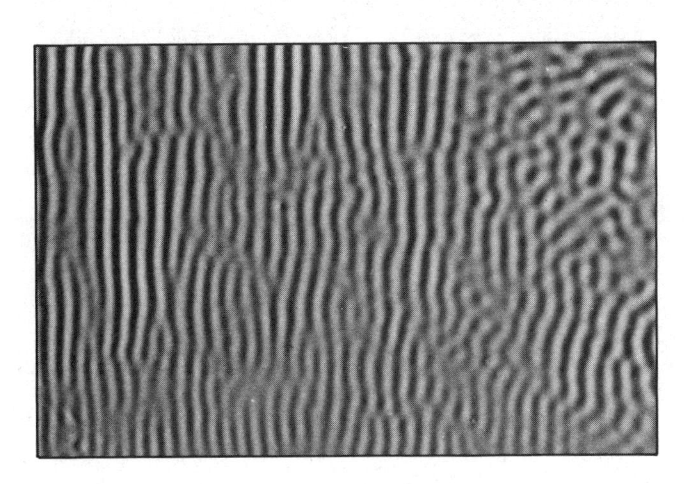

FIG 6-5
Wrinkling in enamel finish.
(E. I. du Pont de Nemours & Co., Inc.)

Other additives are available to speed air drying. These are variously called oxidizers, accelerators, or hardeners. As the first name suggests, they work by advancing the rate at which the new paint film absorbs oxygen. In other words, they speed the second step in the enamel drying process.

Viscosity

The enamel mixture that goes into a spray gun cup is thicker than its lacquer equivalent, and so is the enamel paint film that results. This greater viscosity, more than anything else, accounts for enamel's superior filling capacities and its tolerance for coarsely finished surfaces. It also means that a can of enamel stretches further than a can of lacquer. Recall that for good coverage acrylic lacquer needs an average of four double coats. Enamel at most requires three *single* coats, and many refinishers use only two. Clearly, the thicker paint covers better.

Nothing, however, is gained in refinishing without some cost. If enamel's viscosity eliminates lacquer's filling and coverage problems, it also creates a few new problems of its own.

Removing Drips and Sags

Any paint that goes on thick has a greater tendency to drip and sag. This tendency can be the result of flooding the surface with more material than the paint film itself can support or applying the material under conditions that prevent it from drying within its normal time span.

Fortunately, most enamels lend themselves to a simple correction technique. Isolated drips can be removed with masking tape. The refinisher just waits until the last coat of paint applied is tacky. (Depending on the kind of enamel being used, the time can vary from 10 to 20 minutes.) To be sure that the paint is ready, the refinisher touches some of the overspray on the masking (Fig. 6-6). When it feels sticky but does not come off on his finger, he proceeds. Using a piece of ¾-inch masking tape, he presses gently on the run, then pulls the tape away. The excess paint usually comes away with it (Fig. 6-7). Any roughness left behind on the surface is then reflowed with a mist coat.

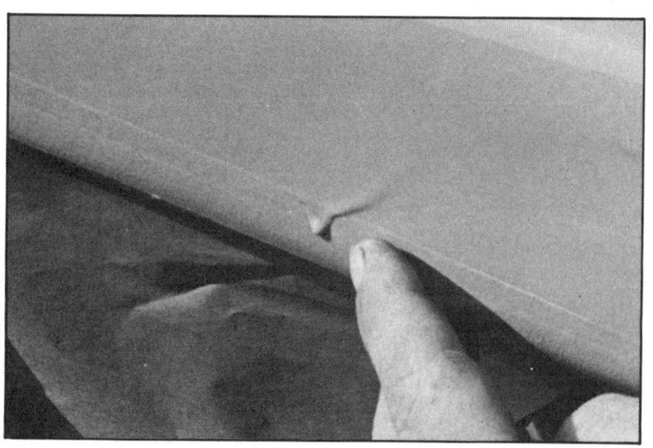

FIG 6-6 Testing overspray with finger. (Jay Storer)

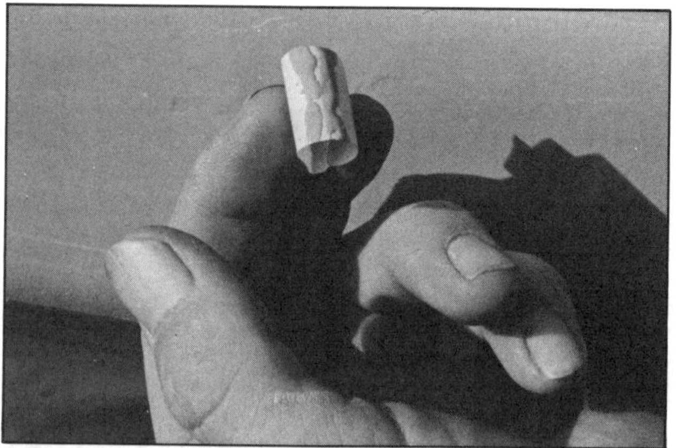

FIG 6-7 Removing slow-drying enamel drip with masking tape. (Jay Storer)

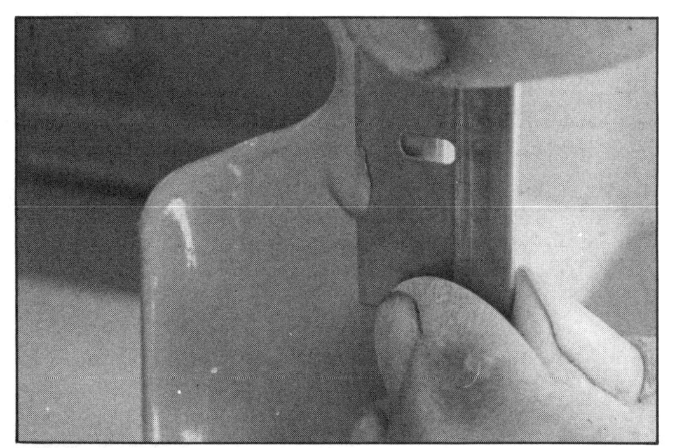

FIG 6-8 Removing fast-drying enamel drip with razor blade. (Jay Storer)

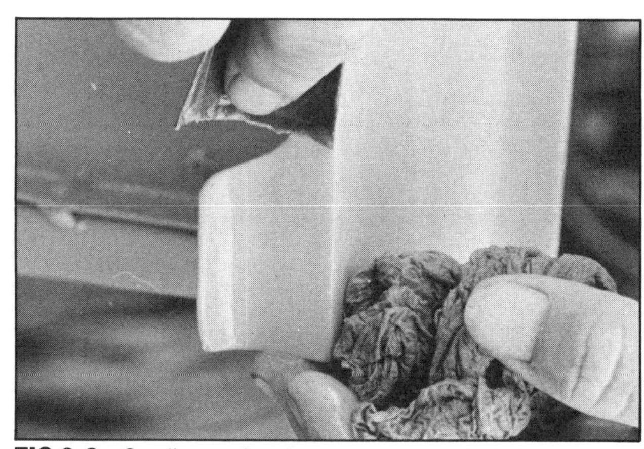

FIG 6-9 Sanding surface to remove last trace of drip in fast-drying enamel. (Jay Storer)

The technique works because enamel dries at such a slow rate. A drip also takes longer to dry, mainly because it is an area of excessive paint buildup. With lacquer, longer might be only a matter of seconds. With enamel, however, it is usually several minutes. During this time, the drip remains wet while the surrounding paint dries beyond the point where mere touching will damage it.

Sags, unfortunately, are a different story. There the damage is too extensive for masking tape to effect a repair. In such cases, the refinisher has no choice but to wash down the entire panel with reducer and repaint.

Enamels with hardener additives, sometimes called two-part enamels, dry so fast that the tape method will not work. Within two days to two weeks after painting, these hardened drips can be sliced off with a razor blade (Fig. 6-8). Any remaining traces of the drip may be wet sanded and compounded to level and smooth the surface (Fig. 6-9). When done with care, the drip will completely disappear.

Controlling Overspray

Overspray is a problem in all spray painting procedures, but because of enamel's viscosity, it is especially troublesome in enamel refinishing. Unlike lacquer overspray, which is light and tends to float in the air, enamel overspray is heavy and tends to fall. It requires a strong air flow through the booth to remove it. An exhaust system functioning at anything less than peak efficiency will allow such overspray to attach itself to panels not being painted. If missed while it is still wet, such damage is difficult to remove. Enamel cannot be compounded until it is thoroughly dry, and even then does not compound easily or well. If the vehicle is to be returned with a perfect finish, therefore, these panels also must be repainted.

Checking the booth's exhaust system is the refinisher's best defense against enamel overspray. The precautions and procedures discussed in connection with nibs (pages 235 and 236) are equally valid here.

Avoiding Orange Peel

Using a thicker paint also means changes in spray gun adjustment. Pressure at the transformer-regulator must be raised to force the thicker

FIG 6-10
Orange peel in enamel.
(Davenport Photography)

material through the gun, and the spreader valve must be opened farther to disperse the heavier droplets of paint. If either of these settings is too extreme, however, the paint's ability to flow may be reduced. The effect this situation produces at the panel is called orange peel (Fig. 6-10).

Orange peel is the enamel equivalent of dry spray in lacquer. If lacquer is subjected to excessive air pressures, its solvent evaporates in midair. The paint is deposited on the panel gritty and too dry to flow—the classic case of dry spray. Enamel, however, is too thick to dry out so completely. In similar circumstances, its solvent content is merely reduced. This reduction, in turn, leaves the paint wet enough to do some flowing but too dry to level itself out entirely. In the end, the finish retains a rough, dimpled appearance that looks exactly like the skin of an orange.

To correct orange peel usually requires removing the paint and refinishing the whole panel. When the paint is still fresh, it can be washed away with reducer. Once the paint has dried, it must be sanded away. Complete removal, however, is a drastic remedy. Clearly, it is better to avoid the condition in the first place. Always reduce paint carefully according to the manufacturer's directions and test the spray gun—repeatedly, if necessary—until it is in perfect adjustment.

ALKYD ENAMEL

Alkyd enamel is known as synthetic enamel or sometimes just plain enamel. It is the slowest of the slow-drying paints. Under normal shop conditions, it requires about 30 minutes between applications and must stand overnight before any masking can be safely removed.

Because it takes so long to dry, however, alkyd enamel carries the lowest price tag of any automotive paint, including lacquer. It also has a good rate of coverage. It takes only 1 gallon reduced 25 to 50 percent to paint a medium-sized car. These two factors combine to make alkyd enamel a popular choice for whole-vehicle repairs.

Working as a team with three other students and with the aid of Job Report 6-A1, you will refinish a whole vehicle in a shade of alkyd enamel that closely matches its existing top coat.

OBJECTIVE 6-A1 (manipulative)

Time Recommended:

40 hours

Preparation:

1. Review pages 233 through 240.
2. Study pages 241 through 243.
3. Read the Safety Checklist on page 260, items 1 through 7.

Tools and Materials:

1. Vibrator or orbital sander
2. Suction-feed spray guns (two—one for paint and sealer, one for primer-surfacer)
3. Duster gun
4. Sanding blocks (hard and sponge rubber)
5. Socket wrench (for battery ground cable)
6. Squeegee
7. Paint rack and strainers
8. Wooden stirring sticks
9. Respirator and safety goggles
10. Rubber gloves
11. Hose (or sponge and bucket)
12. Masking paper and tape
13. Clean shop cloths
14. Selection of sandpapers (80D, 280A, 320A, 400A)
15. Tack cloth
16. Wax remover
17. Metal conditioner
18. Lacquer primer-surfacer
19. Thinner
20. Alkyd enamel reducer (both fast-drying and grade required by shop conditions)
21. Glazing putty
22. Enamel sealer
23. Alkyd enamel paint

Procedure:

1. Clean the vehicle with wax remover. Proceed one panel at a time, applying the remover with one cloth and wiping it dry with another.
2. Featheredge any chips or scratches in the old finish. To taper broken edges, use a vibrator or an orbital sander equipped with an 80D abrasive. Then hand sand a 3- to 5-inch border around each

featheredged area. Use a 280A or 320A abrasive. Blow the sanding dust from all panel surfaces.

3. Apply conditioner to any bare metal exposed during the featheredging process.
4. Mask any windows, bumpers, moldings, or trim that might be exposed to overspray during the application of primer-surfacer to the featheredged areas. For lacquer primer-surfacer, 12-inch paper is an adequate masking material.
5. Mix 1 part lacquer with 1½ parts thinner.
6. Test spray the primer-surfacer on a piece of masking paper. Set the transformer-regulator at 40 psi (30 psi at the gun). When properly adjusted, the spray gun should form a 6-inch pattern that flows well when applied from a distance of 6 to 8 inches.
7. Apply four coats of primer-surfacer to the featheredged areas, allowing each coat to flash before applying the next. After the last coat, allow 30 minutes of drying time.
8. Using a hard rubber block and a 280A or 320A abrasive, sand the primed areas.
9. Fill any low spots with glazing putty. Apply the product sparingly with a small rubber squeegee and allow an additional 30 minutes of drying time.
10. Sand the puttied areas with the same abrasive used in step 8. Blow all sanding dust from panel surfaces.
11. Apply a fifth coat of primer-surfacer to all repair areas and allow it to dry 20 minutes.
12. Using a sponge rubber sanding block and a 400A abrasive, wet sand the whole vehicle.
13. Remove all masking.
14. Rinse the vehicle thoroughly to remove all sanding dust. Using a duster gun, chase all water from panel surfaces and dry completely with clean cloths.
15. Disconnect the battery ground cable and push the car into the spray booth.
16. Close the spray booth doors and turn on the exhaust system.
17. Set the transformer-regulator pressure at 70 psi and use the duster gun to force any water from around moldings, doors, hood and trunk openings, glass, and trim. Wipe any water from panel surfaces with a clean, dry cloth.
18. Mask windows, bumpers, front and rear lights, grill, moldings, door handles, mirrors, and trim. Tape down any folds in the masking paper.
19. Wipe down all exposed vehicle surfaces with fast-drying reducer.
20. Mix 2 parts enamel sealer with 1 part reducer. Strain the mixture into the spray gun cup.
21. Adjust the transformer-regulator to a setting of 45 psi (35 psi at the gun). Test spray the sealer on a piece of masking paper. When properly adjusted, the spray gun should produce an 8-inch pattern that flows well when applied from a distance of 8 to 10 inches.
22. Tack all exposed vehicle surfaces.
23. Apply the sealer to the whole vehicle in a single coat. (*Note:* This coat is literally single. Overlap strokes only slightly, not the 50

percent typically used for spray painting.) Allow 20 minutes of drying time.

24. While the sealer coat is drying, clean the spray gun used to apply it. Then reduce approximately 1 gallon of alkyd enamel paint according to the directions on the can label. (As a rule, reduction will be somewhere in the area of 25 to 50 percent. In other words, it will range from 4 parts paint and 1 part reducer to 2 parts paint and 1 part reducer.) Refill the spray gun.
25. Test spray the paint on a piece of masking paper. Set the transformer-regulator at 55 psi (45 psi at the gun). When properly adjusted, the gun should produce an 8-inch pattern that flows well when applied from a distance of 8 to 10 inches.
26. Tack the sealer coat.
27. Apply a single wet coat of enamel, starting at the passenger side of the roof and working toward the center. Then change sides and work from the center to the driver's side. Next paint the door (or doors) on the driver's side. Then work toward the back or front of the vehicle, depending on the direction of the air flow in the spray booth.
28. Allow the first coat of enamel to dry 20 to 30 minutes. Then test the overspray on the masking. When the overspray is tacky, the vehicle is ready for the next coat of paint.
29. Apply two more single wet coats of paint. Allow each to dry 20 minutes.
30. Inspect the new finish for any imperfections, particularly any areas that have not flowed out properly. If any are found, apply a mist coat. Place 1 inch of paint in the spray gun cup and fill to the 1-quart mark with reducer. Apply to the affected panels at a distance of 10 to 12 inches. *Note:* Do not attempt to wet the panel thoroughly. Just cover the surface with a light mist of reducer. After a few moments, the mixture will penetrate the paint, restoring its bright color.
31. Allow the vehicle to dry overnight before unmasking. To force dry alkyd enamel, allow 15 minutes flowing time after the last coat. Then bake at a temperature of 165 degrees Fahrenheit for 1½ hours.

JOB REPORT SHEET 6-A1

ALKYD ENAMEL WHOLE-VEHICLE REPAIR

Student Name ____________________

Date Started ____________ Date Finished ____________ Total Time ____________

Specifications

Make of car ____________ Model ____________ Year ____________

Type of finish ____________ Manufacturer's paint code ____________

Name of color ____________________

Condition of finish (Describe the nature and extent of any damage.) ____________

____

____

Technique

Rough featheredging method:

Type of sander ____________ Abrasive ____________

Fine featheredging method:

Type of sander ____________ Abrasive ____________

Metal conditioner: Yes ______ No ______

Primer-surfacer: Type ____________ Color ____________

Psi at the transformer-regulator ______ Psi at the gun ______

Total number of coats ______

Number of putty applications ______

Wet sanding method: Hose ______ Sponge and bucket ______

Type of sanding block ____________ Abrasive ____________

Surfaces masked ____________ ____________

____________ ____________

____________ ____________

Sealer: Pigmented ______ Clear ______

Sanding ______ Nonsanding ______

Number of applications ______

Paint reduction: Type of reducer ______

Formula ______

Additives used ______

Mist coat: Yes ______ No ______ If yes, give reasons for use. ______

______

______

Drying process:

Air ______ Force drying ______ Total drying time ______

Checkup Questions

1. Why was lacquer primer-surfacer used under an enamel top coat? ______

   ______

   ______

   What special precautions, if any, did this procedure require? ______

   ______

   ______

2. Why was no polishing recommended as part of this repair? ______

   ______

   ______

3. Having now refinished whole vehicles with both lacquer and enamel, which job did you find easier? Why? ______

   ______

   ______

Date Completed ______ Instructor's Signature ______

ACRYLIC ENAMEL

Just as alkyd enamel was developed in response to lacquer's shortcomings, so acrylic enamel was developed in response to alkyd's. While cheap and damage resistant, alkyd enamel was difficult to use for spot repairs. Slow to dry, it was very slow if not impossible to reflow. Where the edges of a spot repair met the old top coat, a dulled or misty-looking area remained. The borders of the repair could be seen even after the new finish was applied.

The first method that refinishers used to get around this problem was to refinish the whole panel. This solution, however, was wasteful of both time and materials. The second solution was to apply a special uniforming finish to the repair. This procedure was basically a form of mist coating. Unfortunately, by the time the technique was introduced, alkyd enamel had developed such a bad reputation where spot repairs were concerned that few refinishers gave the new method a chance. The third solution was acrylic enamel.

Acrylic enamel is said to dry like lacquer and flow like enamel. It is, in fact, the fastest drying enamel paint. Some forms are dust-free in less than 10 minutes and, with the use of oxidizer, can be unmasked in 2 hours. Same-day repairs are thus possible.

Acrylic is also the only enamel paint that blends easily. This fact, taken with its fast-drying capabilities, has made acrylic enamel a genuine alternative to lacquer for spot repairs. In fact, many refinishers feel that it is a superior alternative because it requires no compounding. It should be noted, however, that what is meant in this case is that enamel requires no compounding to create gloss. It may, in fact, require the procedure to eliminate it. With older vehicles in particular, freshly applied enamel often outshines the existing top coat. This difference creates a dividing line that must be eliminated. Compounding accomplishes this result by roughing up the new paint without leaving any visible scratches.

Acrylic enamel's major shortcoming is that it does not cover as well as other enamels. Thus a whole-vehicle repair can take as much as 1½ gallons of paint compared, for example, to only 1 gallon for alkyd enamel. Since acrylic is also slightly more expensive, its use for larger repairs depends on which the individual customer values more—speed or low cost.

OBJECTIVE 6-A2 (manipulative)

Working as a team with one other student and with the aid of Job Report Sheet 6-A2, you will do a spot repair using acrylic enamel.

Time Recommended:

3 hours

Preparation:

1. Review pages 233 through 247.
2. Study pages 248 through 252.
3. Read the Safety Checklist on page 260, items 1 through 7.

Tools and Materials:

1. Vibrator or orbital sander
2. Suction-feed spray guns (two—one for paint, one for primer-surfacer)
3. Duster gun
4. Sanding blocks (hard and sponge rubber)
5. Socket wrench (for battery ground cable)
6. Squeegee
7. Paint rack and strainer
8. Wooden stirring sticks
9. Respirator and safety goggles
10. Rubber gloves
11. Hose (or sponge and bucket)
12. Clean shop cloths
13. Masking paper and tape
14. Selection of sandpapers (80D, 280A, 320A, 400A)
15. Tack cloth
16. Wax remover
17. Metal conditioner
18. Lacquer primer-surfacer
19. Thinner
20. Aerosol can of lacquer primer-surfacer (contrasting color)
21. Glazing putty
22. Fast-drying reducer (alkyd enamel)
23. Acrylic enamel paint
24. Acrylic enamel reducer
25. Hand rubbing compound
26. Retarder

Procedure:

1. Clean the repair panel with wax remover. Apply the product with one cloth and wipe the panel dry with another.
2. Featheredge the damaged area. Start with a vibrator or an orbital sander equipped with an 80D abrasive. Finish by hand using a 280A abrasive to sand a 3- to 5-inch border around the repair area. Blow all sanding dust from the panel.
3. If any bare metal has been exposed by the sanding, apply conditioner.
4. Using 12-inch paper, mask adjoining panels and/or glass. On the repair panel itself, use masking tape to cover all moldings and trim.
5. Mix 1 part lacquer primer-surfacer with 1½ parts thinner.
6. Test spray the primer-surfacer on a piece of masking paper. Set the transformer-regulator at 40 psi (30 psi at the gun). When properly adjusted, the spray gun should form a pattern that is approximately the size of the repair and flows well when applied from a distance of 6 to 8 inches.
7. Apply four coats of primer-surfacer to the repair area, overlapping each slightly and allowing flash time between. After the last coat,

allow the panel to dry 30 minutes.

8. Using a hard rubber block and a 320A abrasive, sand the primed area.
9. Use putty to fill any low spots exposed by the sanding. Allow an additional 30 minutes of drying time and resand as in step 8.
10. Make a final check for imperfections. Give the repair a fifth coat of primer-surfacer, this time using a contrasting color. Allow 20 minutes of drying time and resand as in step 8.
11. Wet sand the repair area. For this final sanding, use a 400A abrasive and a sponge rubber sanding block.
12. Wipe the panel with a moistened cloth to remove all sanding residue and blow dry.
13. By hand, compound the area around the repair or the whole panel, as necessary, to judge its true color. Blow all compounding residue from the panel surface.
14. Remove all masking and wash down the panel with a wet cloth. Wipe dry and blow with a duster gun to remove any traces of moisture or lint.
15. Move the panel or vehicle into the spray booth. *Note:* If a vehicle, disconnect the battery ground cable first.
16. Remask adjacent panels, glass, or trim, this time using 36-inch paper. Then give the panel a final wipedown with fast-drying reducer.
17. Open the paint and, using a wooden stirring stick, stir it by hand for 4 to 5 minutes.
18. Transfer the paint to another container and rinse out the can. Pour in ½ inch of acrylic enamel reducer, press the lid back in place, and shake so that the reducer is forced against both the bottom and top of the can. Continue shaking until the can's interior is clean and bright.
19. Add the reducer from the can to the paint and stir at least 2 minutes more.
20. Reduce the paint according to the directions on the can label. For 25-percent reduction, use 2 inches of paint and ½ inch of reducer. For 50-percent reduction, use 1 inch of paint and ½ inch of reducer.
21. Test spray the paint on a piece of masking paper. Set the transformer-regulator at 55 psi (45 psi at the gun). When properly adjusted, the gun should produce a pattern that is approximately the size of the repair and flows well when applied from a distance of 8 to 10 inches.
22. Tack the panel.
23. Apply the first coat of paint in a short burst so that it covers the primer only. The paint should go on wet and flow well. Allow the repair to dry a minimum of 10 minutes.
24. Apply the second coat in the same manner but allow it to lap the first by at least 1 inch on all sides. Give the panel another 10 minutes of drying time.
25. Apply the third coat so that it laps the second by 2 inches. Again allow 10 minutes of drying time.
26. Remove all but 1 inch of paint from the spray gun cup. Add 1½ inches of acrylic enamel reducer and 1 capful of retarder and stir.

27. Apply one mist coat of this new mixture to the repair, lapping it generously on all sides. *Note:* Do not readjust the spray gun. The previous settings should combine with the thin material to produce a mist coat that laps the repair by up to 5 inches.
28. Air or force dry the repair according to the recommendations on the paint can label and unmask.
29. Check the repair carefully for proper texture and blending. If the spot looks brighter or glossier than the surrounding finish, compound by hand to take down the shine.

ACRYLIC ENAMEL SPOT REPAIR

Student Name ________________________ Date ______________

Time Started ______________ Time Finished ______________ Total Time ______________

Specifications

Type of panel ________________________________

Condition of finish (Describe the nature and extent of any damage.)

____

____

____

Technique

Rough featheredging method:

Type of sander ______________ Abrasive ______________

Fine featheredging method:

Type of sander ______________ Abrasive ______________

Metal conditioner: Yes ______ No ______

Surfaces masked ______________ ______________

______________ ______________

______________ ______________

______________ ______________

Primer-surfacer: Type ______________ Color ______________

Psi at the transformer-regulator ______ Psi at the gun ______

Number of putty applications ______

Two-color checkup sanding: Yes ______ No ______

Wet sanding method: Hose ______ Sponge and bucket ______

Type of sanding block ______________ Abrasive ______________

Paint reduction: Type of reducer ________________

Formula ________________

Additives used ________________

Mist coat: Yes ______ No ______

If yes, give reasons for use. ________________

____

____

Drying process:

Air ______ Force drying ______ Total drying time ________________

Checkup Questions

1. Why were two different widths of masking paper used in steps 4 and 16?

____

____

____

2. You have now had a chance to do spot repairs using both lacquer and enamel. Which repair procedure works best for you? Why? ________________

____

____

3. Why was no sealer used as part of this repair? ________________

____

____

Date Completed ________________ Instructor's Signature ________________

POLYURETHANE ENAMEL

Polyurethane is the most durable of the enamels. It gets both its name and its toughness from the main ingredient in its binder—clear, liquid polyurethane. This material makes the paint resistant to all solvents and all solventlike substances. From reducer and gasoline to tree sap and bird droppings—polyurethane enamel is sensitive to none of the things that sooner or later can affect lacquer and other forms of enamel. It is also less sensitive to weathering, dulling, chipping, scratching, and other minor film damage. As a measure of its durability, consider the fact that polyurethane enamel was used to finish storage tanks in chemical factories before it made its way into the automotive field.

What is a benefit in terms of maintaining a finish, however, can be a burden when trying to replace it. Polyurethane enamel is so hard that it is actually difficult to sand by hand. Not surprisingly, it also does not lend itself to spot repairs. Being the most durable member of the enamel family apparently goes hand in hand with being the most insoluble.

Reduction

When mixing or applying polyurethane, it is important to remember that the material is unlike virtually any finish or base coat over which it might be applied. This fact has two consequences. First, polyurethane enamel must be mixed with only those products that are polyurethane based as well. (These include reducer and additives like fisheye eliminator.) Second, polyurethane must be applied over an enamel sealer, never directly onto a lacquer or other enamel finish.

Polyurethane comes in two parts—the color and the activator (Fig. 6-11). The activator is not a reducing agent. (As noted above, there is a polyurethane reducer.) Rather the activator is a combination of binder and catalyst: It serves much the same purpose as the catalyst in filler and has much the same effect. It hardens the material to which it is added. Thus, once the color and activator have been combined, the mixture must be sprayed. If allowed to sit, whether in a can or a spray gun cup, it will solidify within 1½ hours.

While this figure sounds impressive, the fact is that polyurethane ranks behind acrylic enamel in drying time. The use of activator does

FIG 6-11
Two additives for polyurethane enamel (center) are 192S Activator (right), the second product in a two-package system, and 189S Fast Accelerator to hasten dry time. (E. I. du Pont de Nemours & Co., Inc.)

not eliminate the need for an additive to speed the drying process. That additive is called accelerator. Its addition can cut the drying time for a polyurethane finish by as much as one half. The accelerator, then, is to polyurethane-based paints what oxidizer is to alkyd and acrylic enamels. That the name of the product is different is a further reminder that polyurethane is an isolated member of the enamel paint family; it can be combined only with specially made polyurethane-based products and no others.

Application

Polyurethane is applied at about the same pressures and in much the same manner as other enamels with one exception—the number of coats. Where other enamels require three single coats, polyurethane requires only two. The product thus has the best rate of coverage in the enamel paint family. This fact is especially fortunate since it also has the highest price. (It costs more even than acrylic lacquer.) Polyurethane's use therefore depends on the value that the refinisher and the customer place on competing factors—cost and durability (Table 6-1).

Table 6-1 ENAMEL CHARACTERISTICS

	Alkyd	Acrylic	Polyurethane
Lowest cost	1	2	3
Fastest drying	3	1	2
Best coverage	2	3	1

OBJECTIVE 6-A3 (manipulative)

Working as a team with one other student and with the aid of Job Report Sheet 6-A3, you will refinish an installed replacement panel (alkyd or acrylic enamel in good condition) with polyurethane.

Time Recommended:

2 hours

Preparation:

1. Review pages 233 through 254.
2. Study pages 254 through 258.
3. Read the Safety Checklist on page 260, items 1 through 7.

Tools and Materials:

1. Suction-feed spray gun
2. Duster gun
3. Socket wrench (for battery ground cable)
4. Paint rack and strainers
5. Wooden stirring sticks
6. Respirator and goggles

7. Hose (or sponge and bucket)
8. Clean shop cloths
9. Masking paper and tape
10. Sandpaper (400A) and sponge rubber sanding block
11. Tack cloth
12. Wax remover
13. Fast-drying reducer (alkyd enamel)
14. Enamel sealer
15. Polyurethane enamel paint
16. Polyurethane activator
17. Polyurethane enamel reducer
18. Hand rubbing compound

Procedure:

1. Clean the panel with wax remover. Apply the product with one cloth and wipe the panel dry with another.
2. Using a 400A abrasive and a sponge rubber sanding block, wet sand the panel's surface.
3. Wipe any sanding residue from the panel with a wet cloth and blow dry.
4. By hand, compound into an adjoining panel for a distance of 8 to 10 inches to expose its true color. Then wipe any compounding residue away with a moistened cloth and blow with a duster gun.
5. Disconnect the battery ground cable and move the vehicle into the spray booth.
6. Using 36-inch paper, mask adjacent panels and/or glass. On the repair panel itself, use masking tape to cover all moldings and trim.
7. Wipe down the panel surface with fast-drying reducer.
8. Mix 2 parts enamel sealer with 1 part alkyd enamel reducer. Strain the mixture into the spray gun cup.
9. Test spray the sealer on a piece of masking paper. Set the transformer-regulator at 45 psi (35 psi at the gun). When properly adjusted, the gun should form an 8-inch pattern that flows well when applied from a distance of 8 to 10 inches.
10. Tack the panel.
11. Apply the sealer in a single wet coat or as the manufacturer's label recommends. Allow 20 minutes of drying time.
12. While the sealer coat is drying, clean the spray gun.
13. Open the paint and, using a wooden stirring stick, stir it by hand for 4 to 5 minutes.
14. Transfer the paint to another container and rinse out the can. Pour in ½ inch of polyurethane reducer, press the lid back in place, and shake so that the reducer is forced against both the bottom and top of the can. Continue shaking until the can's interior is clean and bright.
15. Add the reducer from the can to the paint and stir at least 2 minutes more.
16. To reduce the paint, mix 3 parts polyurethane enamel color with 1

part activator and ½ part polyurethane reducer. Strain into the spray gun cup.

17. Test spray the paint on a piece of masking paper. Set the transformer-regulator between 55 and 60 psi (45 and 50 psi at the gun). When properly adjusted, the gun should form an 8-inch pattern that flows well when applied from a distance of 8 to 10 inches.
18. Tack the sealer coat.
19. Apply two single wet coats of paint to the panel, allowing 20 minutes of drying time between them.
20. Air dry the panel for 2 hours or follow the manufacturer's recommendations on force drying. Unmask.

JOB REPORT SHEET 6-A3

POLYURETHANE ENAMEL PANEL REPAIR

Student Name ______________________ Date ____________

Time Started ____________ Time Finished ____________ Total Time ____________

Specifications

Type of panel ______________________________

Condition of finish (Describe the nature and extent of any damage.) ____________

____

____

____

Make of car ____________ Model ____________ Year ____________

Type of finish ____________ Manufacturer's paint code ____________

Name of color ______________________________

Technique

Wet sanding method: Hose ______ Sponge and bucket ______

Type of sanding block ____________ Abrasive ____________

Surfaces masked ____________ ____________

____________ ____________

____________ ____________

Sealer: Pigmented ______ Clear ______

Sanding ______ Nonsanding ______

Number of applications ______

Polyurethane enamel paint:

Manufacturer ____________ Paint code ____________

Name of color ______________________________

Type of reducer ______________________________

Reduction formula ______

Additives used ______

Drying process:

Air ______ Force drying ______ Total drying time ______

Checkup Questions

1. In what respect does the finished repair look less than professional?

______

______

______

In the space below, write your own procedure for remedying this condition. Then carry out the repair. ______

______

______

______

______

______

______

______

______

2. Describe the results of your procedure. What changes, if any, would you make if you were to redo the repair? ______

______

______

______

______

______

Date Completed ______ Instructor's Signature ______

SPECIAL-USE ENAMELS

Not all vehicle surfaces require a smooth, high-gloss, color finish. Surfaces like truck interiors, for example, contribute little to the vehicle's appearance. They also take much more direct impact abuse than most exterior paints are designed to withstand. For surfaces like these there is a separate category of finishes called special-use enamels.

Chassis Enamel

Chassis enamel is used exclusively to protect a vehicle's frame. Because the frame is directly exposed to the elements and to impacts from road debris, it must be covered with an especially tough material. The element in chassis enamel that gives it the required toughness is the binder. It is specially formulated to resist penetration by water. It also offers an extra measure of protection against heat and abrasion.

The normal drying time for most chassis paints is about 4 hours. Application must be done according to label instructions to achieve the best results.

Aluminum Enamels

Aluminum enamels are metallic paints used on truck interiors, heavy-duty bumpers, trailer hitches, and similar surfaces. Today, given the use of galvanized metals and the ease with which body components can be rechromed, the demand for these finishes is minimal. The painter, however, should be aware that they exist for use in special circumstances and have at least a general idea of how they are applied.

Aluminum enamel comes in three different forms—chrome, hammered, and plain aluminum. The chrome finish is used to restore or simulate the plating on grills, bumpers, or wheels. The hammered finish gives the appearance of a surface that has been roughly metalworked and is used primarily on truck accessories like tool boxes (Fig. 6-12). The plain aluminum is used mainly for painting trailer interiors.

FIG 6-12
Hammered aluminum finish.

All three products require special care in their reduction and handling once mixed. The reason for this precaution is that the aluminum, being heavy, has a tendency to sink. If the paint is allowed to stand for any length of time (either on the shelf or in the spray gun cup), it must be thoroughly stirred (or restirred). Otherwise the material that reaches the panel will not have enough metallic content to provide a satisfactory finish.

SAFETY CHECKLIST

1. Remember not to smoke in areas where paints are being sprayed. Overspray is extremely volatile and the fire danger is great.
2. Always wear a respirator when in or near areas where paint is being sprayed (Fig. 6-13).
3. Disconnecting the battery ground wire on any vehicle you are about to spray before you roll the vehicle into the spray booth has two beneficial results. You will have to roll the vehicle into the booth by hand, meaning the booth's interior will not be polluted by exhaust emissions, and the vehicle's electrical system, thus disconnected, will be rendered spark-free.
4. Thoroughly clean the vehicle and the booth and make sure the booth draft is working properly. This will help prevent nibs and overspray on unpainted areas, minimizing the chances that you will have to expose yourself to sanding dust and a second dose of overspray when having to redo a job that was imperfectly done the first time.
5. Reduce the paint carefully and test the gun, repeatedly, if necessary, to eliminate orange peel. The only way to eliminate orange peel is to wash the painted panel down with reducer while the panel is still wet. Any use of reducer in this way magnifies the risk of this volatile liquid catching fire. It is better to do the job right the first time.
6. Adjust the air pressure carefully to avoid excessive overspray buildup. Such buildup is extremely flammable.
7. Read the directions on all the material cans carefully to minimize the likelihood of having to do the job over, thus having to reexpose yourself to sanding dust and overspray.

FIG 6-13
Spraying chassis enamel.

Student Name ______________________ Date ______________

DIRECTIONS: Circle the best answer to each question.

1. Enamels dry from the
   I. inside out.
   II. outside in.
   A. I only B. II only C. Both I and II D. Neither I nor II

2. Which products are the best suited for spot repairs?
   A. Alkyd and acrylic enamels
   B. Alkyd and polyurethane enamels
   C. Lacquers and polyurethane enamels
   D. Lacquers and acrylic enamels

3. Which of the following must be added to an enamel before it can be force dried?
   A. Activator
   B. Antiwrinkle
   C. Sealer
   D. Oxidizer

4. In the course of a panel repair using slow-drying alkyd enamel, the condition pictured at the right suddenly develops. What should be done?
   A. Let the panel dry and wash with enamel reducer.
   B. Immediately apply a mist coat.
   C. Wait 20 minutes and gently apply masking tape.
   D. Wait 20 minutes and sand.

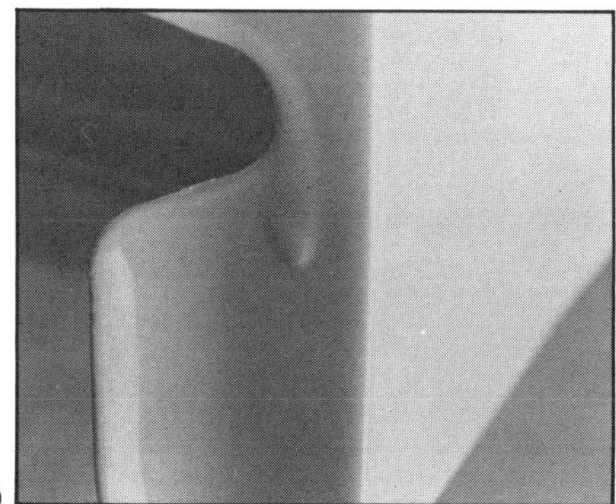

(Jay Storer)

5. The owner of a small fleet of vans used in a hauling business wants all of his vehicles repainted. He wants "the best finish for my money."

   Refinisher I suggests alkyd enamel because it is cheap, durable, and gives good coverage for the amount of paint used.

   Refinisher II suggests polyurethane enamel because it is the strongest finish available, the cheapest, and stretches further than any other product on the market.

   Who is right?
   A. I only B. II only C. Both I and II D. Neither I nor II

6. All of the following could be directions for enamel reduction EXCEPT
   A. Mix 4 parts paint with 1 part reducer.
   B. Combine 1 part paint with 1½ parts reducer.
   C. Reduce paint 25 percent.
   D. Combine activator with color.

7. Which will dry the fastest?
   A. Alkyd enamel with accelerator
   B. Acrylic enamel with oxidizer
   C. Lacquer enamel with hardener
   D. Polyurethane enamel with activator

8. Because of its unusual chemical makeup, polyurethane enamel
   I. requires specially made additives.
   II. can be stored for long periods of time after reducing.
   A. I only   B. II only   C. Both I and II   D. Neither I nor II

9. The finish shown at the right is probably enamel rather than lacquer because
   A. wrinkling is an enamel response to extreme heat.
   B. dry spray is more common in thicker paints.
   C. orange peel seldom occurs in lacquers.
   D. fisheye occurs in all paints.

10. A new enamel spot repair stands out brightly against the old top coat. Refinisher I suggests compounding the new surface to take down its shine. Refinisher II suggests compounding the old surface to bring out its shine. Who is right?
    A. I only   B. II only   C. Both I and II   D. Neither I nor II

11. Aluminum enamels are used on all of the following EXCEPT
    A. grills and bumpers.
    B. tool boxes and truck accessories.
    C. truck interiors.
    D. auto body frames.

12. Enamel refinishing requires a good spray booth air flow because
    I. enamel overspray is light and remains suspended in the air for a long time.
    II. it takes a long time for enamel to become dust-free.
    A. I only   B. II only   C. Both I and II   D. Neither I nor II

13. Polyurethane differs from other enamel paints in all of the following ways EXCEPT
    A. it is packaged in two parts.
    B. it requires only two coats.
    C. it requires sealing.
    D. it is hard to sand.

14. Which product is incorrectly matched with its drying time between coats?
    A. Alkyd enamel—20 to 30 minutes
    B. Acrylic enamel—10 minutes
    C. Polyurethane enamel—20 minutes
    D. Enamel sealer—flash time

15. Which kind of repair requires that paint applications be overlapped and blended with a mist coat?
    A. Whole-vehicle repair using alkyd enamel
    B. Panel repair using polyurethane enamel
    C. Spot repair using acrylic enamel
    D. Any repair using synthetic enamel

16. In the spray booth pictured below, which components are most important in eliminating nibs?
    A. 1 and 2
    B. 2 and 3
    C. 3 and 4
    D. 1 and 4

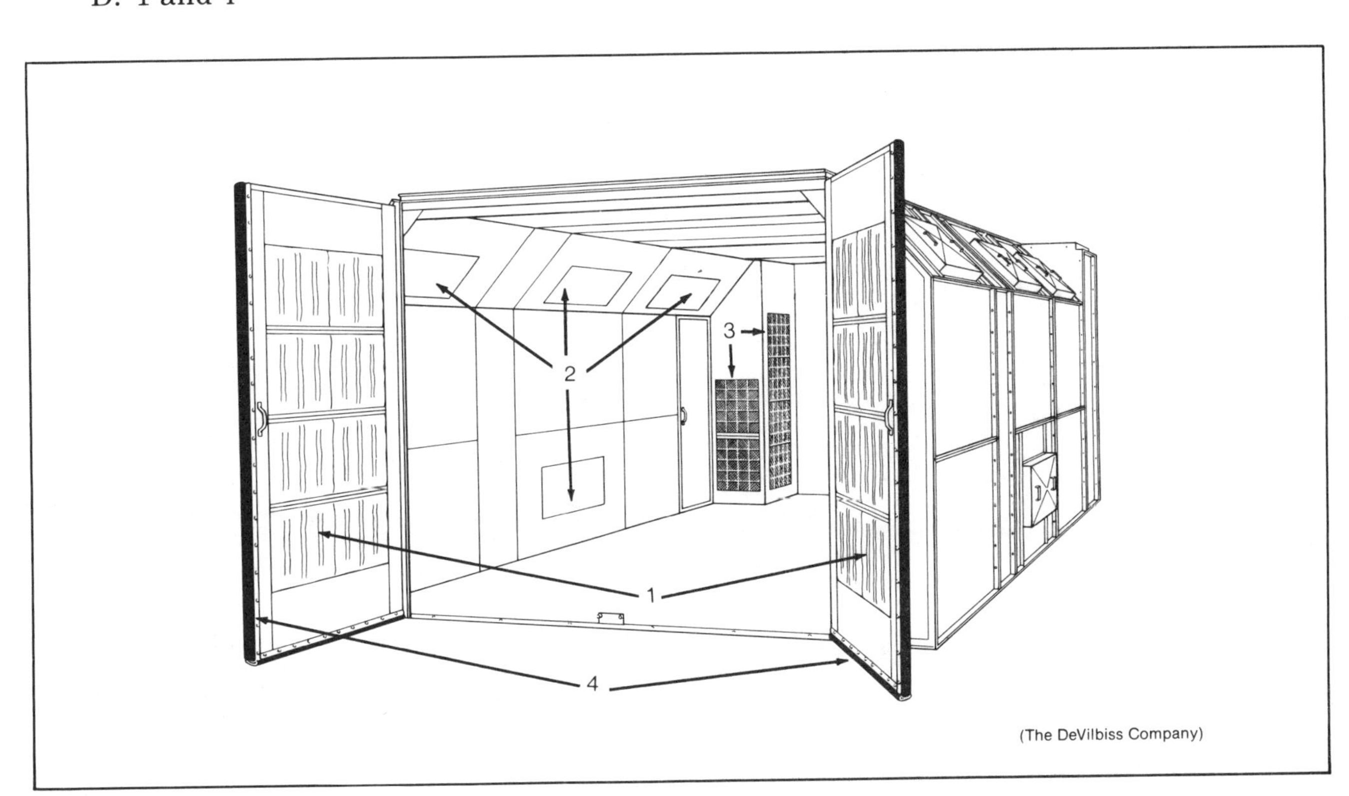

(The DeVilbiss Company)

17. The ideal spraying distance for most enamel products is
    I. 6 to 8 inches.
    II. 8 to 10 inches.

    A. I only   B. II only   C. Both I and II   D. Neither I nor II

18. Which product is matched with an appropriate masking material?
    I. Lacquer primer-surfacer, 36-inch masking paper
    II. Enamel sealer, 12-inch masking paper

    A. I only   B. II only   C. Both I and II   D. Neither I nor II

19. All of the following paints are applied in single wet coats EXCEPT
    A. acrylic lacquer.
    B. acrylic enamel.
    C. alkyd enamel.
    D. polyurethane enamel.

20. All of the following are special problems in enamel refinishing EXCEPT
    A. blushing.
    B. bonding.
    C. dirt in the finish.
    D. wrinkling.

Score ________ Instructor's Signature ______________________________

unit 7

Paint Problems

Following all of the instructions presented thus far cannot guarantee a perfect paint job every time. Refinishing is a complex process. It involves many steps, and each step involves many judgments. Things can go wrong. The condition of an old finish can be misevaluated. A spray gun can be adjusted incorrectly. A job can be rushed and a coat of paint or primer-surfacer applied too soon. When such mistakes are made, a refinisher must know how to recognize the symptoms at the panel.

This ability is doubly valuable. First, if the problem can be caught early enough, in some cases it can be prevented. Second, even if the effects cannot be reversed, at least the problem can be identified. Then the conditions that caused it can be avoided when the work is redone.

This unit presents thirty of the most common paint problems. To help organize them, it is divided into sections according to when particular problems are first likely to appear. Some, like fisheye and bleeding, occur during application of a new finish. Others, like wrinkling, occur as the finish dries. Still others, like cracking and chipping, occur long after a vehicle has been returned to its owner.

To solve refinishing problems, the refinisher studies lists of causes. Usually, one or more of the items on the list will remind the refinisher of something that was not done, or was done incorrectly. By reading the lists before the problems occur, the new refinisher may avoid the more obvious problems and refresh his memory about the correct way to do refinishing.

OBJECTIVE 7-A (written)

After doing the reading and shop exercises, you will be able to answer correctly without reference material a minimum of 14 out of 20 test questions on the following topics:

1. Paint application problems
2. Flow, evaporation, and staining problems occurring during and immediately after drying
3. Long-term refinishing problems, including various forms of cracking and loss of adhesion

Preparation:

1. Study pages 265 through 310.
2. Attend classroom discussions on Objective 7-A.
3. Read the Safety Checklist on pages 305 and 306, items 1 through 3.

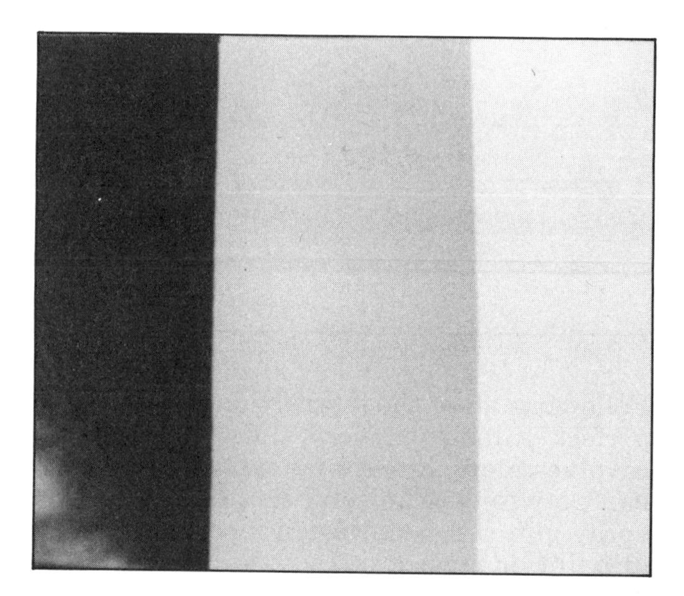

FIG 7-1
Bleeding. (David Keown)

APPLICATION PROBLEMS

Of all the problems discussed in this unit, those appearing during paint application are probably the most familiar. Their causes center mainly on poor surface preparation and faulty spray gun technique. Because they occur while the paint is still wet or when other coats of paint have yet to be applied, some can be corrected without removing and reapplying the new finish.

Bleeding

Bleeding is discoloration of a new top coat that is most likely to occur when a lighter color is applied over a darker one (Fig. 7-1). Only certain colors have a tendency to bleed—mainly reds, maroons, and darker shades of blue. These are usually identified on their containers as bleeders.

Cause

Bleeding happens because the solvent in the fresh paint penetrates the old finish and frees some of its pigment. This then floats to the surface and blends with the new color.

Correction

Once bleeding has occurred, the only solution is to redo the repair. The paint must be allowed to dry fully. Then it must be sanded and bleeder seal applied. Once the sealer has dried, the new color can be resprayed.

Prevention

The only way to prevent bleeding is to apply bleeder seal to the old finish before any painting is done. Like all sealers, bleeder seal operates by blocking a chemical reaction between the top and base coats or, in this case, between the old and new finishes. *Note:* Bleeding is the only reaction bleeder seal will block. It will not, for example, prevent a lacquer top coat from penetrating and lifting old enamel finish.

Bull's-Eye Effect

Shrinkage is normal in both paint and primer-surfacer. Any material that is thinned or reduced will decrease in volume as its solvent evaporates. When the material covers a whole surface, this effect is not apparent. When, however, like primer-surfacer it is used to make spot repairs, the effect can be pronounced. The primed surface sinks below the level of the surrounding finish, cracking the paint applied over it at the featheredge. Since many spot repairs are worked in roughly circular form, the problem is known among refinishers as the bull's-eye effect (Fig. 7-2).

Cause

Bull's-eye has three main causes: (1) failure to apply enough coats of primer-surfacer to compensate for shrinkage, (2) applying primer-surfacer in coats so thick that all of the solvent cannot evaporate in the recommended drying time, and (3) fanning primer coats to speed flashing. The last two procedures trap solvent under a dry outer film—always a mistake. Later, when paint is applied, the fresh solvents penetrate this film and free the trapped ones, thus accounting for the swift shrinkage and cracking.

Correction

Correcting a bull's-eye means filling it, not with plastic but with additional coats of primer-surfacer. Once the cracked paint is dry, the repair area is sanded smooth and the primer-surfacer applied. Special care should be taken to allow ample drying time between coats. Once the spot has been built up to the proper level, it can then be refinished. What the whole procedure amounts to is belatedly completing the original spot repair.

Prevention

To avoid bull's-eye effect, enough overlapping coats of primer-surfacer should be applied to a spot repair to build it up above the surrounding paint film. Then, after drying, the area should be sanded level. *Note:* By this standard, the number of primer-surfacer coats to be applied will vary with the thickness of a vehicle's finish.

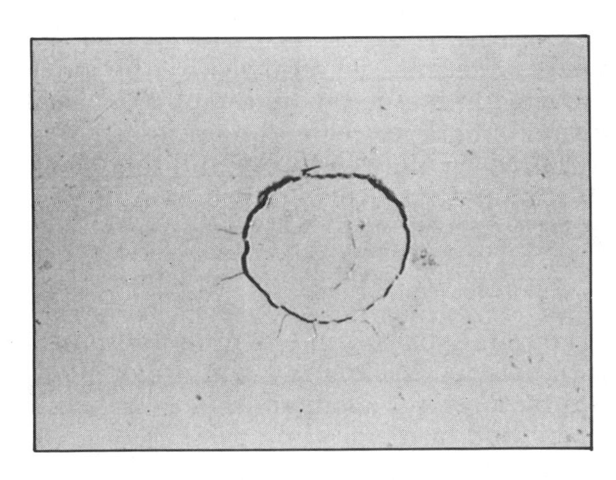

FIG 7-2
Bull's-eye effect. (E. I. du Pont de Nemours & Co., Inc.)

FIG 7-3
Close-up of dry spray. (Jay Storer)

Dry Spray

Dry spray is atomized paint that has too little solvent left in it to flow once it reaches a surface. The effect at the panel is a rough, gritty-looking finish that frequently does not adhere well (Fig. 7-3).

Cause

Dry spray is one of the most common problems in refinishing. It occurs any time that the paint flow in a spray gun cannot keep pace with the air supply. Malfunctions, misadjustments, and poor spray painting technique can all have this effect. Specific causes include (1) blockage of the vent in the spray gun cap assembly; (2) an excessive transformer-regulator setting; (3) an excessive spreader valve adjustment; (4) an inadequately opened fluid valve; (5) a blocked fluid valve; (6) a blocked spray gun nozzle; (7) an excessively fast spray gun stroke; (8) too great a distance between the spray gun and the panel; (9) improper reduction; (10) use of a solvent that is too fast for shop conditions; and (11) application of paint to a hot metal surface (a vehicle that has been left standing in the sun, for example).

Correction

If dry spray is not extreme, it can sometimes be reflowed by the quick application of a mist coat. (The two-gun method of spot repair is based on this technique.) If the condition is both extreme and unintentional, however, the roughened finish should be allowed to dry and then thoroughly sanded. Spray gun adjustment should be checked using a test panel before refinishing proceeds.

Prevention

Dry spray can be avoided by (1) careful spray gun cleaning and maintenance; (2) regular use of test panels to check spray gun adjustment; and (3) observation of the manufacturer's recommendations on paint reduction, including reducing agent and ideal spraying psi.

Fisheye

Fisheye sounds like, and is, a totally descriptive name. The condition is characterized by dark circular openings surrounded by lighter indentations (Fig. 7-4). This eyelike form gives the condition its name. Where the openings are deep, the old finish can actually show through the new.

Cause

Fisheye has one main cause—silicone. Fine, light particles of this material are the major ingredient in polish, and polish is the major source of surface contamination in vehicles. Silicone particles from polish can reach a surface in at least four different ways: (1) they can be absorbed by the old finish over time through numerous polishings; (2) they can be carried onto the finish by contaminated shop cloths; (3) they can be ground into a panel by mechanical sanding that is done without proper cleaning beforehand; and (4) being extremely light, they can float onto the work surface wherever spraying of paint or primer-surfacer is done near sanding or compounding operations.

Correction

Because fisheye is a surface preparation problem, it will generally develop in the initial coat of paint. As soon as the first indentations appear, the refinisher should stop and add a product called fisheye eliminator (or sometimes fisheye killer) to the paint in the spray gun cup. The additive comes in a plastic squeeze bottle (or sometimes in plastic capsules). Usually one squirt (or one capsule) per quart of reduced paint is enough to block the reaction between the fresh paint and the old silicone particles. Once begun, however, use of the additive must be continued through all subsequent coats of paint if the condition is not to reappear.

Prevention

The only effective way to prevent fisheye is to use a good-quality wax remover as the first step in any repair procedure. Remember, this cleaning agent must be applied with one cloth and then—while the surface is still wet—wiped dry with another.

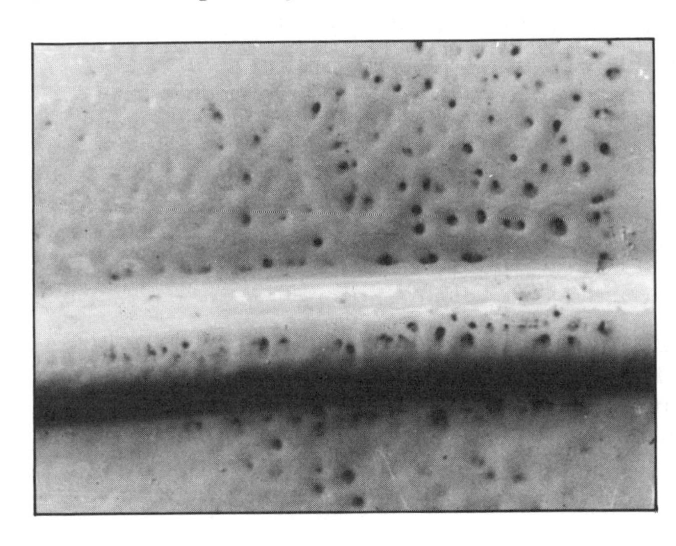

FIG 7-4
Fisheye. (E. I. du Pont de Nemours & Co., Inc.)

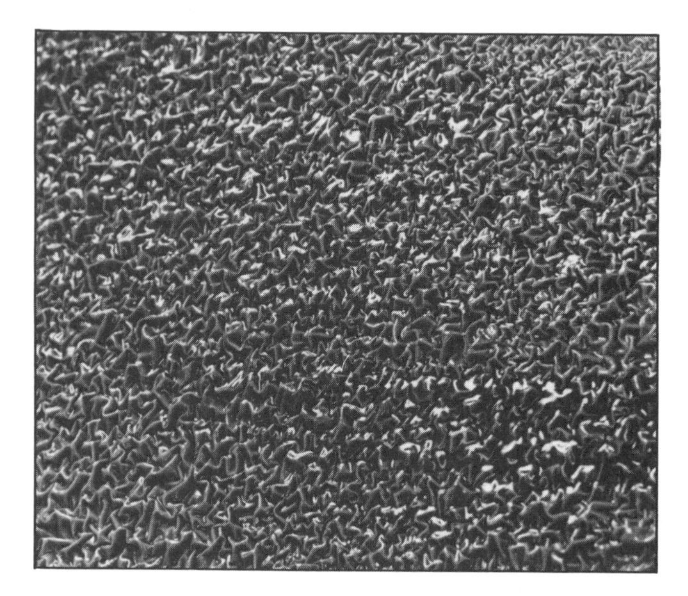

FIG 7-5
Lifting. (E. I. du Pont de Nemours & Co., Inc.)

Lifting

Lifting is a problem that can occur in paint or in both paint and primer-surfacer. It can also develop either immediately on application or later as the material dries. In a wet film, lifting is characterized by swelling that pulls the material up and destroys its bond with the surface. Its appearance at this stage is rough and gritty, much like the surface of cinder block or concrete. Once dry, lifted paint shrivels badly and may actually peel (Fig. 7-5).

Cause

Lifting is usually the result of inadequate drying or incompatibility between the refinishing products being used. Predictably, lacquer top coats figure in most instances of the condition. Lifting frequently occurs, for example, when an acrylic lacquer finish is applied over (1) air-dried, unsealed alkyd enamel; (2) enamel primer-surfacer that has been applied too wet and is not fully cured; and (3) fully cured enamel primer-surfacer that has been applied over an old lacquer top coat (sandwiching the primer-surfacer between two incompatible materials is the problem here). Lacquer finishes will also lift if inadequate flash time is allowed between applications.

Correction

Lifting is such a severe problem that the refinisher has little choice but to remove the affected material. The surface should then be thoroughly cleaned, sanded, and sealed before the top coat is reapplied.

Prevention

Use of the appropriate sealer is the best protection against lifting. Note that most of the causes of the condition would be eliminated if a conservative approach toward sealing were adopted. A standard that requires sealing whenever a lacquer top coat is being applied (except possibly when the old finish is factory-baked lacquer) is one with which most refinishers and paint manufacturers would agree.

Overspray

Like dry spray, overspray is essentially atomized paint that is well on its way to drying before it reaches a panel surface. The difference is in the panel that it eventually reaches. Dry spray is paint deliberately applied to a given surface. Overspray is excess paint that attaches itself to a surface not being painted (Fig. 7-6). Dry spray appears as a rough and gritty finish. Overspray appears as a rough and gritty deposit on an otherwise smooth and glossy coat of paint.

Cause

Overspray has two main causes—a transformer-regulator setting that is too high and poor spray painting technique. The latter includes whipping the spray gun and failing to trigger off promptly at the panel edge (or at all).

Correction

How easily overspray is corrected depends on where it falls. On freshly painted panels, for example, overspray can simply be reflowed with a mist coat. On glass, moldings, and other unpainted surfaces, it can be wiped clean with thinner or reducer. This same technique also works well when enamel overspray attaches itself to old paint, provided the condition is discovered within an hour after spraying. (The wipedown is effective because reducer is a weak solvent and because enamel, once dry, is an insoluble finish. Thus the reducer affects only the fresh overspray, not the old paint.) Lacquer overspray is just as easy to remove. When the panel is dry, the excess paint is compounded away and the gloss restored by polishing.

The only form of overspray that is difficult to remove is enamel that has remained on a painted surface for more than an hour. Being enamel, it cannot be compounded until fully dry. The compounding itself, once begun, is harder. Finally, after compounding, the paint's gloss is difficult, sometimes even impossible, to restore. As a result, failure to discover enamel overspray often leads to additional refinishing.

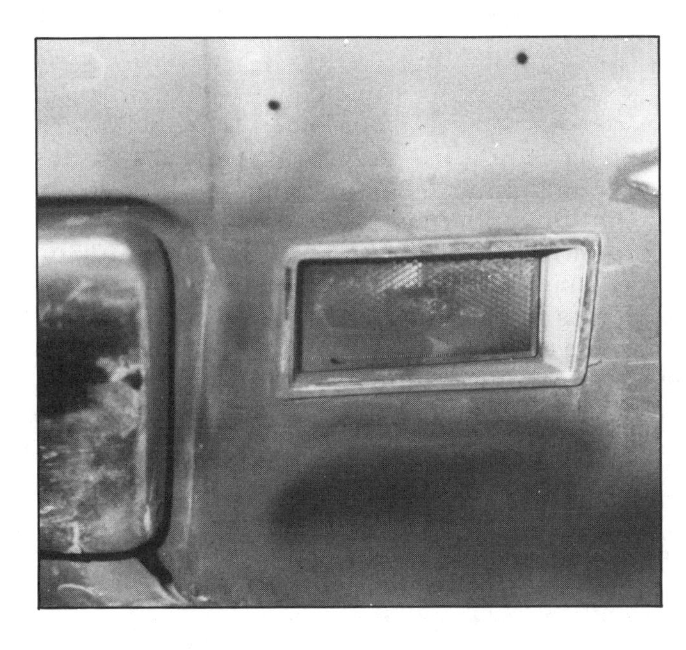

FIG 7-6
Overspray. (David Keown)

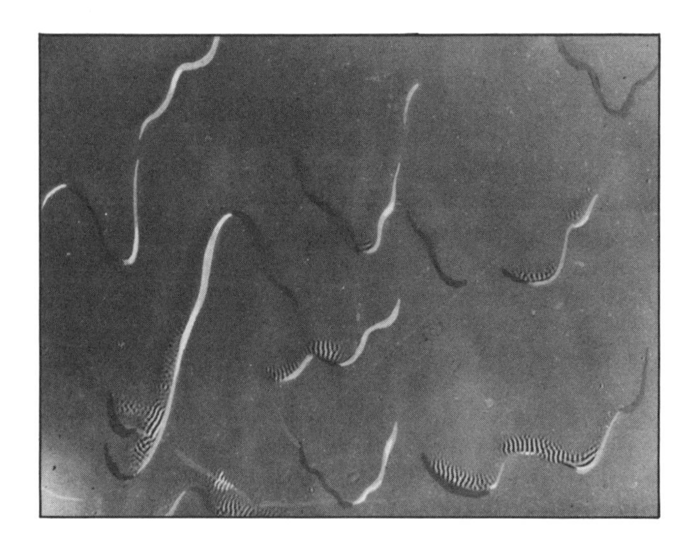

FIG 7-7
Runs and sags. (E. I. du Pont de Nemours & Co., Inc.)

Prevention

Most overspray can be eliminated by a combination of adequate masking and careful spray painting technique. For lacquer refinishing, adequate masking covers everything within 18 to 24 inches of the repair area. For enamel, with its heavier overspray, more extensive protection is required—usually up to 36 inches. Spray painting precautions include (1) observing the manufacturer's recommendations on psi, (2) maintaining proper distance from the work surface, and (3) releasing the trigger promptly at the panel's edge. To the degree that banding discourages overly long spray gun strokes, it also is recommended.

Runs and Sags

Runs and sags occur when more paint is applied than the paint film itself can support. If the condition affects only a small, narrow area, a run forms. If it affects a large area, a whole section of paint may give way, moving down the wet surface in a broad wave. This more extensive failure is called a sag (Fig. 7-7). Sometimes both conditions occur at once.

Cause

Runs and sags develop for one basic reason—overwetting. Overwetting, however, has several causes, including (1) paint that is thinned or reduced too much; (2) paint that is applied with too slow a stroke (thus depositing too much material on the panel); (3) a spray pattern and/or stroke that is not uniform; (4) insufficient flash time between coats; (5) use of a thinner or reducer that is too slow for shop conditions; (6) contamination of the panel surface (which interferes with proper adhesion); (7) a transformer-regulator setting that is too low for the viscosity of the material being sprayed; and (8) holding the spray gun too close to the work surface.

Correction

With a lacquer finish, runs must be sanded out after the surface has had a chance to dry. With an enamel finish, however, they can often be removed with masking tape while they are still wet. (This procedure should be attempted only after the surrounding finish has dried to the point where it will not come off when touched. Enamels, depending on the type, usually reach this stage after about 10 to 20 minutes. A small piece of masking tape is pressed gently onto the run and then pulled away. If it has been caught at the right moment, the excess paint will be lifted off with the tape. Any roughness left behind in the finish can then be flowed smooth with either a mist coat or the next coat of paint.

Clearly, tape removal saves time and materials. It is, however, effective only for isolated runs. When the condition is widespread or accompanied by sagging, the technique should not even be tried. Rather, while it is still wet, the affected panel should be washed with enamel reducer and the new finish reapplied.

Prevention

The best way to avoid runs and sags is to test the spray gun on a scrap panel or masking paper before beginning to apply any new material. In this way, reduction and gun adjustment can be evaluated beforehand and any changes in spray gun technique planned and practiced.

OBJECTIVE 7-A1 (manipulative)

Working as a team with one other student and with the aid of Job Report Sheet 7-A1, you will use a specially prepared practice panel to produce and correct the following paint problems: (1) bleeding, (2) fisheye, and (3) runs. *Note:* The panel should be divided into three equal parts—one finished with a lacquer that is a bleeder, the second finished with a white lacquer and well polished, the third merely primed and sanded.

Time Recommended:

3 hours

Preparation:

1. Review pages 265 through 273.
2. Study pages 273 through 278.
3. Read the Safety Checklist on pages 305 and 306, items 1 through 3.

Tools and Materials:

1. Suction-feed spray guns (two)
2. Prepared practice panel
3. Masking paper and tape
4. Respirator
5. Paint rack and strainers
6. Wooden stirring sticks
7. Clean shop cloths
8. Tack cloth
9. Fast-drying reducer (for wipedowns)
10. Acrylic enamel reducer (for paint)
11. Thinner

12. Acrylic lacquer paint (white)
13. Acrylic enamel paint (any color)
14. Bleeder seal
15. Fisheye eliminator

Procedure:

1. Mask the primed portion of the panel.
2. Give the bleeder-covered portion a final wipedown with fast-drying reducer. *Note:* Do not touch or in any way clean the polished portion.
3. Mix the white lacquer. Combine 1 part paint with 1½ parts thinner and stir thoroughly.
4. Set the transformer-regulator at 45 psi (35 psi at the gun). Test the spray gun on masking paper. Adjust the pattern to 6 inches wide at a distance of 6 inches.
5. Tack the bleeder-covered portion of the panel. Again, do nothing to the polished portion.
6. Apply one coat of paint to the exposed areas of the panel. Note any effects. Describe them on Job Report Sheet 7-A1.
7. Open the spray gun cup and add one squirt (or one capsule) of fisheye eliminator to the paint. Stir well.
8. Be sure the paint on the panel has flashed. Then respray and note any changes on Job Report Sheet 7-A1.
9. Allow the panel to dry 30 minutes.
10. Strain the bleeder seal into the second spray gun's cup. Adjust the gun as in step 4. Make onc or two passes across the top of the panel and stop. Use Job Report Sheet 7-A1 to describe the appearance of the sealer coat.
11. Adjust the sealer mix as necessary and finish spraying.
12. Allow the panel to dry 30 minutes more. *Note:* During this time, thoroughly clean the second spray gun and reserve for use in step 16.
13. Spray the panel a third time and note all effects on Job Report Sheet 7-A1.
14. Allow the panel to dry 30 minutes. Then reverse the masking, exposing the primed side of the panel and covering the painted side.
15. Wipe down the primer with fast-drying reducer.
16. Mix the acrylic enamel color. Combine 2 parts of paint with 1 part of the reducer recommended for conditions in the shop.
17. Set the transformer-regulator at 55 psi (45 psi at the gun). Test the spray gun on masking paper. Adjust the pattern to 8 inches wide at a distance of 8 inches.
18. Tack the primed surface.
19. Apply the paint with a slower stroke than that used when testing the spray gun. Continue in this fashion until the technique produces one or two runs.
20. Allow the paint to dry 6 to 8 minutes. Then test the overspray on the masking by touching it lightly with a finger. Continue testing until the material feels sticky but does not come off. Note on Job Report Sheet 7-A1 how long it took for the paint to reach this state.

21. Tear off a piece of masking tape about the size of one of the runs. Holding it between the thumb and forefinger of one hand, apply the tape, adhesive side down, to the run. Press gently with the forefinger of the other hand. Then slowly pull the tape away. Note the appearance of the panel on Job Report Sheet 7-A1.
22. Remove any other runs in the same manner.
23. To reflow any roughness left by the tape, apply a second coat of paint to the panel. Move fast enough just to wet the surface. *Note:* If extra flowing is necessary, a third coat of paint with a 25-percent overlap or a mist coat can be used.

JOB REPORT SHEET 7-A1

PAINT APPLICATION PROBLEMS

Student Name ______________________________ Date ______________

Time Started ____________ Time Finished ____________ Total Time ____________

Specifications

Panel finish:

Section 1. Acrylic lacquer (bleeder)

Manufacturer ____________ Color name ____________ Number ______

Section 2. Acrylic lacquer (white)

Manufacturer ____________ Color name ____________ Number ______

Section 3. Primer-surfacer

Type ____________ Color ____________

Materials:

Section 1. Bleeder seal

Manufacturer ____________ Color name ____________ Number ______

Section 2. Fisheye eliminator

Manufacturer ____________ Color name ____________ Number ______

Section 3. Acrylic enamel paint

Manufacturer ____________ Color name ____________ Number ______

Technique

First paint coat (white lacquer): Describe any visible effects at the panel.

____

____

____

Second paint coat (white lacquer with eliminator): Describe any changes in the panel surface. ____

Sealer coat: Describe the problem with the sealer application and its solution.

Third paint coat (white lacquer): Describe any changes in the panel surface.

First and second paint coats (acrylic enamel):

Drying time until repair begun ______ minutes

Number of runs removed ______ Number of reflowing coats ______

Checkup Questions

1. Why was the polished portion of the panel never wiped down or tacked?

2. Why was the second coat of acrylic enamel applied with a fast rather than a normal stroke?

3. Why were the lacquer and enamel paints applied at different psi's and different distances from the panel?

Date Completed ____________ Instructor's Signature ____________

DRYING PROBLEMS

The problems in this section all develop either during or immediately after drying. Their causes center on the speed of the drying process itself and on control of shop conditions, including temperature, presence of moisture, and cleanliness. Since the paint is well past flowing by the time they appear, most of these problems are not reversible. Some can be remedied after the fact by compounding or sanding, but most require removal of the finish and reapplication.

Blushing

Blushing is characterized by a milky haze that appears over a new paint film (Fig. 7-8). The condition is especially common in fast-drying paints. It is thus confined almost entirely to lacquer finishes.

Cause

Blushing is the result of moisture being trapped in the paint film. It most commonly occurs when painting is done in hot, humid weather in shops where such conditions cannot be controlled. In these circumstances, the paint absorbs moisture from the air. Then, when the air currents from the spray gun itself cool the vehicle's surface, that moisture condenses out and is trapped beneath the outer layer of paint. The paint films over especially quickly because it is a fast-drying product and because the air in the shop is extremely warm.

Correction

Blushing can be eliminated if the moisture trapped in the paint is somehow released. This objective can be achieved by rewetting the affected surface and arranging for it to dry at a slower rate. The refinisher waits until all coats of paint have been applied and then sprays on a mist coat. The mist coat consists of a small amount of color (approximately 1 inch in the spray gun cup), two or three caps full of retarder, and the rest slow-drying thinner. If one full wet coat of this mixture is applied over the affected area, the blush gradually disappears and the finish takes on its true color. Remember, however, that retarder extends a paint's overall drying time. In the case of a lacquer top coat, for example, the vehicle should dry overnight before any compounding is attempted.

FIG 7-8
Blushing.

FIG 7-9
Dirt in finish.

Prevention

Blushing is a paint problem that can be anticipated. If the weather is warm and a vehicle is to be refinished using acrylic lacquer, observe the following precautions: (1) use a slow-drying thinner or reducer (one recommended for use in a warm shop); (2) avoid excessive air pressure; (3) avoid fanning the vehicle surface to speed flashing; and (4) if at all possible, paint early in the day.

Dirt

Any foreign material in a new finish qualifies as dirt. Most often dirt consists of lint or sanding dust. These are either not cleaned from the vehicle's surface in the first place or settle out as nibs during painting or drying. Once embedded, they stand out against the smooth gloss of the new finish. In other words, even though they are the same color, they are magnified rather than hidden by the new coat of paint (Fig. 7-9).

Cause

Contamination of a new finish with dirt has one major cause—poor cleaning practices. These include failure to (1) wash the vehicle thoroughly before taking it into the spray booth, (2) remove all masking used during application of primer-surfacer, (3) tack all surfaces immediately before painting, (4) inspect and replace booth filters on a regular basis, (5) hose down booth surfaces at least daily if the booth is in constant use, and (6) drain the transformer-regulator before spray painting. Using the spray booth as a storage area also contributes to this paint problem. It gives dust a place to collect and hide as well as interferes with proper and thorough cleaning of the spray booth itself.

Correction

Most dirt can be eliminated from acrylic and polyurethane finishes by allowing them to dry and then wet sanding with an extremely fine abrasive (600A). Compounding and polishing, if done carefully, are usually enough to restore any shine lost in the sanding process. Because of its extremely long drying time, an alkyd enamel finish must be handled differently. While still fresh, it must be removed with reducer and then reapplied. Beforehand, of course, every attempt should be made to identify and eliminate the source of the contamination.

Prevention

The easiest way to avoid dirt in a finish is to avoid accumulating dirt in the spray booth. Specific precautions include (1) not using the spray booth for storage; (2) regularly replacing booth air filters; (3) draining booth transformer-regulators before each use; (4) periodically bleeding booth air hoses to check for contamination; (5) carrying on all sanding and compounding operations well away from the booth; (6) washing the whole vehicle at some point in the preparation process; (7) making regular use of the duster gun, especially during sanding operations; (8) remasking before painting; and (9) tacking thoroughly and systematically.

Hazing

Hazing occurs when a finish goes on wet enough and flows out well enough, but then loses its gloss as it dries. Despite its name, the condition is not marked by any coating or deposit like that found in blushing. Rather, what is visible is a flattening of the new color, a dulling effect with nothing to account for it.

Cause

Even when incomplete flowing is ruled out as the cause of hazing, the choices that remain are still quite varied. They include (1) contamination of the surface with grease or oil, (2) contamination of the surface with soap or a chemical cleaning agent, (3) poor holdout of the undercoat, (4) application of color over a wet undercoat, (5) use of the wrong solvent for shop conditions, (6) use of the wrong additives for the type of color being applied, (7) application of color over a finish already suffering from hazing, (8) application of too few coats of color, (9) insufficient circulation of air during drying or contamination of that air with exhaust fumes, and (10) compounding a surface before it is fully dry.

Correction

With acrylic finishes (either lacquer or enamel), eliminating hazing is a relatively simple matter. The refinisher first allows the surface to dry and then uses an extremely fine abrasive (600A) to wet sand the haze away. With other enamels, the condition is not so easily cured. In some rare instances, it is possible to compound and polish a dull alkyd enamel finish to a high gloss. To have any chance of success, however, this procedure requires waiting at least 30 days until the finish is fully dry. Even then, there is no guarantee that the technique will work. In most such cases, removal of the finish is the only way to achieve a quality repair.

Prevention

Avoiding hazing is mainly a matter of being observant, reading labels, and carrying out repair procedures thoroughly. A refinisher should (1) avoid painting over a surface that is already showing signs of hazing, (2) remove residues of cleaning agents from a vehicle just as carefully as he removes dirt and oil, (3) use materials that are compatible and well suited to shop conditions, (4) observe recommended application and drying procedures for both base and top coats, and (5) regularly check and service the spray booth exhaust system to guarantee maximum circulation of clean air.

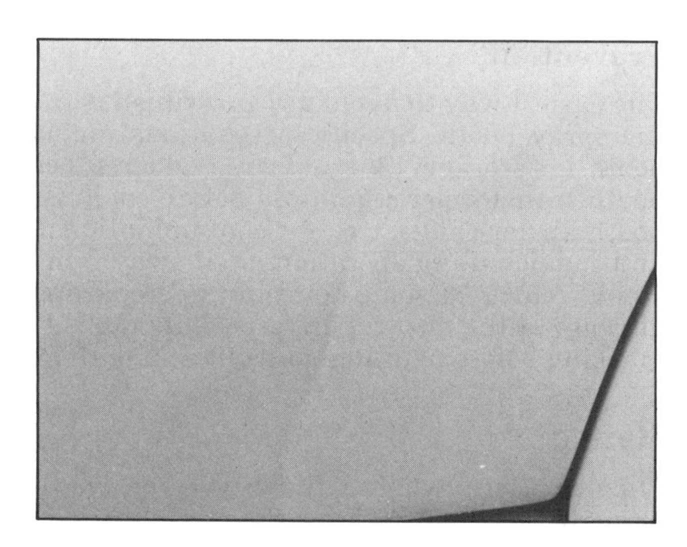

FIG 7-10
Lack of hiding. (Jay Storer)

Lack of Hiding

Lack of hiding occurs when primer-surfacer—usually one of the darker shades—shows through a new top coat. It is particularly noticeable with spot repairs (Fig. 7-10).

Cause

Any color can fail to hide if it is applied too thinly. Where coverage is adequate, however, the main reason for lack of hiding is the nature of the paint itself. Most paints that have this problem are metallics of a type called transparent, or sometimes translucent. (One of these two words usually appears somewhere on the container labels.) Such paints are usually heavy on metallic flake and light on pigment. In other words, they depend more on reflected light than actual color to create their visual effect. It is this absence of color that leads to coverage problems. Typically, maroons, dark blues, chestnut browns, and some shades of bronze are transparent.

Correction

The obvious solution to lack of hiding is to apply more color—one, two, sometimes even three coats. Each of these is allowed to dry thoroughly before the next is sprayed over it. If this procedure does not work, the problem can be approached from the other direction. Instead of trying to hide the primer-surfacer spot, the refinisher can duplicate its shade with paint and blend it in. This new base coat then provides the uniform background that a transparent finish needs.

Prevention

Most paint manufacturers recommend using a sealer under a transparent or translucent paint. When a refinisher wants to avoid either the trouble or the expense of sealing, however, a ground coat can sometimes be substituted. A ground coat is an initial application of color that is allowed to dry thoroughly (rather than merely flash) before any more paint is applied over it. The extra layer of color often provides just enough coverage to prevent primer-surfacer showthrough. It serves, in effect, as a same-shade base coat.

Oily Paint Film

Oil in paint looks and acts very much like oil in water. The two substances do not mix. Rather, the oil floats on top of the finish. Sometimes it is very obvious, forming beads of material that do not dry at the same rate as the rest of the top coat (Fig. 7-11). At other times, it is partially dispersed in greasy smears and streaks pulled through the paint. These reflect in rainbow patterns that detract from the uniform gloss a new finish should have.

Cause

An oily paint film usually results from painting over a contaminated surface. Wet sanding with gasoline, for example, can leave behind a greasy residue. (Gasoline is, of course, a petroleum product.) Using wax remover for final wipedowns can have a similar effect. (Wax remover is a strong, slow-drying solvent that with time can free almost any kind of surface deposit, including accumulated grease and oil.)

Lacquer finishes are far more likely to develop an oily film than enamel. Lacquer's stronger solvents are the reason. Lacquer can lift an old finish and swell sandscratches in bare metal. It therefore has no difficulty freeing and dispersing a surface contaminant like oil that has only recently been applied.

Correction

Oil, once dispersed in paint, cannot be removed. The finish must be sanded away when dry or washed away with solvent when fresh. Then the cleaning that would have prevented the problem in the first place must be done. Wax remover must be applied to remove any traces of oil. Fast-drying reducer must be used to eliminate any traces of wax remover. Once the panel has been cleaned in this manner, it can safely be primed, sanded, and repainted.

Prevention

Oily paint film is a problem that should not exist. Both of its major causes are surface preparation procedures that today no reputable refinisher would use or recommend. For wet sanding, water—not gasoline—is the best way to rinse sanding dust from a surface. Using water also avoids the safety hazards involved in exposing a flammable material in an open container. For final wipedowns, reducer—not wax remover—is the ideal solvent. It is strong enough to dissolve grease and oil and fast enough to evaporate fully before any new finish is applied.

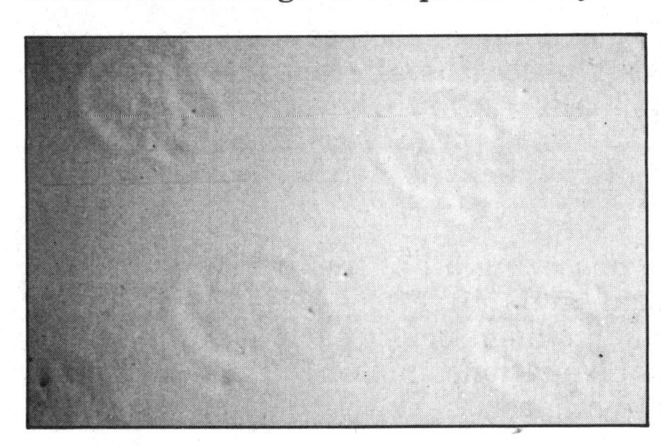

FIG 7-11
Oily paint film. (E. I. du Pont de Nemours & Co., Inc.)

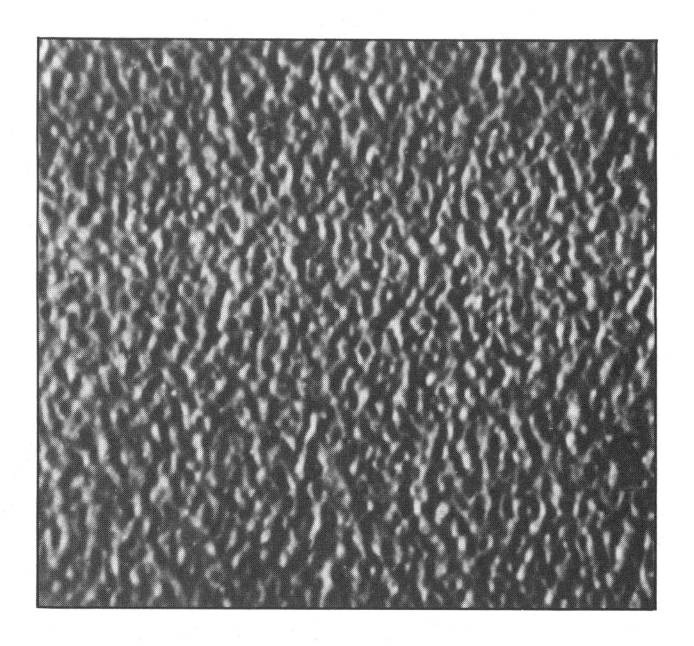

FIG 7-12
Orange peel. (E. I. du Pont de Nemours & Co., Inc.)

Orange Peel

Orange peel looks like what it is—a wetter form of dry spray. The enamel paint films in which it occurs are too thick to become gritty, even when deprived of solvent. Their characteristic irregularity is smoother, less coarse, more dimpled—like the peel of an orange (Fig. 7-12). They have enough wetness to show promise of flowing smooth but never do. That is why orange peel is a problem a refinisher cannot be sure he has until the finish has actually started to dry.

Cause

The causes of orange peel are likewise similar to those of dry spray. They include (1) inadequate reduction, (2) use of the wrong solvent for shop conditions, (3) an excessive transformer-regulator setting, (4) improper spray gun adjustment, (5) improper spray gun technique, (6) poor spray gun maintenance, (7) surface contamination, and (8) spraying material onto an extremely hot or extremely cold surface. Item 8 represents the only real departure from the dry spray listing (page 268). The inability to flow in extremely cold shop conditions or on extremely cold surfaces is a direct consequence of enamel's greater viscosity.

Correction

Since enamel takes so long to dry, sanding or compounding orange peel smooth are not real alternatives. Rather, the affected surfaces should be washed down with fast-drying reducer while they are still relatively wet and refinished.

Prevention

Orange peel can be avoided by observing all of the dry spray precautions: (1) carefully cleaning spray guns after each use; (2) employing test panels to check spray gun adjustment before each use; and (3) following all manufacturer's recommendations on paint reduction, including reducing agent and ideal spraying psi.

Pinholing

Pinholing can occur in paint, primer-surfacer, filler, and putty. A surface affected by the condition looks as though someone has taken a straight pin and poked numerous tiny holes through it (Fig. 7-13). In fact, just the opposite has happened. The surface has not been pushed in by a solid object. It has been pushed out by substances (mostly vapors) trapped in its interior. A pinhole, in other words, is basically a tiny blister that has burst.

Cause

Pinholing has nearly a dozen possible causes. The most common, however, include (1) applying any refinishing material in overly thick, wet coats; (2) fanning a base or top coat to speed its drying; and (3) spray painting with a contaminated air supply or over a contaminated surface. What all of these procedures have in common is that they tend to trap solvents, moisture, or air in whatever material is being applied. By the time these substances break free, the paint, primer-surfacer, or putty has already dried.

Correction

Regardless of the material in which pinholing occurs, the basic correction technique is the same—wet sand smooth and refinish. Under no circumstances should any attempt be made to fill the holes. The condition will simply recur in a slightly less severe form as the solvent evaporates and the filling agent shrinks down into the holes. Clearly, the far better repair is made by getting under the damage.

Prevention

Given the numerous causes of pinholing, the best way to avoid the condition is simply to follow all of the standard recommendations on surface preparation, reduction, and spray painting technique. In particular, (1) regularly check compressed air system filters and drains; (2) clean work surfaces before, during, and after sanding; (3) follow manufacturers' instructions on mixing or reducing any refinishing materials; (4) adjust spray gun technique to the materials being applied; and (5) resist the temptation to speed air drying by any means other than the application of heat or the use of proper additives.

FIG 7-13
Pinholing. (E. I. du Pont de Nemours & Co., Inc.)

FIG 7-14
Sandscratch showthrough.
(The Martin-Senour Company)

Sandscratch Showthrough

Sandscratch showthrough occurs when marks made by abrasives remain visible through the new coat of paint (Fig. 7-14). The condition thus contrasts with hazing, where the effect (lack of gloss) is apparent but the imperfection causing it is not.

Cause

Sandscratch showthrough results mainly from rushing a repair. In an effort to speed removal of the old paint, for example, the refinisher uses too coarse an abrasive. The abrasive cuts the surface so deeply that sanding with finer grits cannot eliminate the marks. Alternatively, in an effort to shorten the preparation process, the refinisher fails to (1) apply enough coats of primer-surfacer or putty, (2) wait until either product is fully cured before sanding, or (3) use a sealer to prevent sandscratch swelling.

Correction

Ultimately none of these shortcuts saves any time. At a minimum, a finish marked by sandscratches must be resanded with a finer abrasive, sealed, and then painted again. If the scratches are especially deep, additional coats of primer-surfacer and perhaps even putty will have to be applied. A large portion of the repair, in other words, will have to be redone—this time without leaving out or rushing any of the steps.

Prevention

Preventing sandscratch showthrough is thus mainly a matter of doing things right the first time. It means (1) avoiding the coarsest abrasive grits for paint removal; (2) applying an adequate number of primer-surfacer coats; (3) using putty where necessary; (4) allowing all base coat materials to dry thoroughly before sanding; (5) finish sanding for alkyd enamel with at least a 320-grit abrasive, for acrylic or polyurethane with a 400-grit abrasive, and for acrylic lacquer with a 500-grit abrasive; and (6) sealing to hold down sandscratches whenever a strong solvent is used for reduction.

Solvent Popping

Solvent popping is basically a lacquer problem. A surface affected by this condition appears to be covered with widely spaced blisters, or bubbles. Compared to the blisters found in pinholing, these are fairly large (Fig. 7-15). They too, however, are raised by vapors trapped beneath an outer film of paint or primer surfacer.

Cause

Like all paint problems involving trapped vapors, solvent popping is caused mainly by excessively fast filming over of a top or base coat material. This condition, in turn, results from (1) using a solvent that is too fast for shop conditions, (2) applying too many coats of material with too little drying time between them, and (3) force drying without use of the proper additives or at excessive temperatures.

Correction

As with pinholing, repairing a surface marred by solvent popping means getting under the damage rather than filling it. The refinisher uses wet sanding to remove the raised portions of the blisters and to determine how deep the damage extends into the surface. In severe cases of solvent popping, the entire top coat or both the top and base coats might have to be removed. Once the surface has been leveled and smoothed, it should be refinished, this time using a slower-drying solvent.

Prevention

Preventing solvent popping is mainly a matter of not rushing the refinishing process. It means (1) allowing adequate flash and drying times between coats of paint and primer-surfacer; (2) using the slowest solvent that shop conditions and job requirements will allow; and (3) force drying only at recommended temperatures, after recommended evaporation times, and with recommended additives.

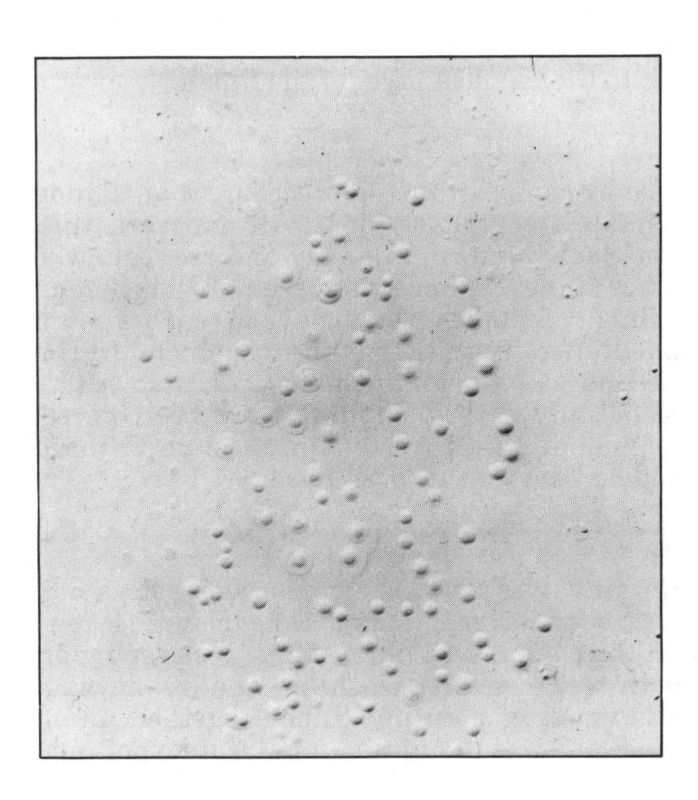

FIG 7-15
Solvent popping. (E. I. du Pont de Nemours & Co., Inc.)

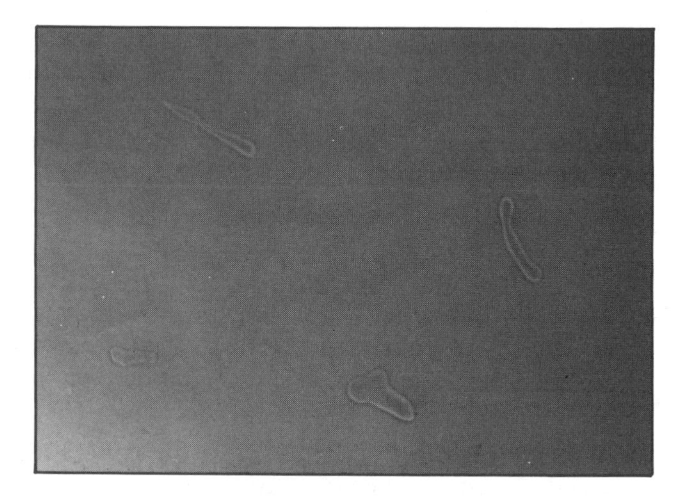

FIG 7-16
Water spotting. (E. I. du Pont de Nemours & Co., Inc.)

Water Spotting

Water spots are imprints left on a vehicle's finish by evaporated moisture (Fig. 7-16). When this condition occurs on a dry or waxed surface, the spots are temporary. They can be removed by buffing with a damp cloth. When the condition occurs in wet or newly applied paint, however, it does real damage. Simply wiping the finish once it is dry cannot remove the spots. The presence of the water at a critical time in the drying cycle physically alters the paint.

Cause

The water used in paint shops for washing down both vehicles and spray booths is usually not distilled. It has a substantial mineral content. When drops of this water are allowed to air dry on a surface, the water evaporates, but the minerals remain. They form a dull, chalky deposit. If the surface is a freshly painted body panel, this deposit not only remains but is locked into the topmost layer of the finish.

Correction

Water spots must be removed by compounding, a procedure that cannot be employed until a new finish is completely dry. With lacquers, this restriction poses no problem. Such paints dry quickly and are regularly compounded to bring out their shine. Enamels, however, are a different story. An air-dried enamel finish can take up to 30 days to reach a point where it can be compounded effectively. (Remember, enamels dry in two steps, and it is the second step—oxidation—that takes so long.) When water spotting is especially severe, sanding may be required before the damage will compound out properly. Only the very finest sandpaper grit, 600A, should be used for this procedure.

Prevention

Prevention of water spotting involves first seeing that water does not reach the vehicle in the spray booth. Precautions to take include (1) regularly opening all drains in the compressed air system, (2) sweeping or wiping down all spray booth surfaces after washing, and (3) blowing out all vehicle crevices in advance of painting. Taken together, all of these procedures should reduce chances of unintentional water spotting.

Outside the spray booth, care should be taken when intentionally wetting down a vehicle. Cars recently painted with enamel are particularly sensitive. They should be washed away from direct sunlight and all surfaces hand rather than air dried.

Wrinkling

Wrinkling is characterized by swelling and puckering of a finish into minute, closely spaced ridges (Fig. 7-17). These may form linear or mazelike patterns and extend over large or small areas. Traces of the condition, for example, can be seen along the bottom edges of the sags in Figure 7-7.

Cause

Wrinkling occurs mainly in enamels that are (1) applied in extremely thick, wet coats and (2) force dried either intentionally (as with a heat lamp) or unintentionally (as when a newly finished vehicle is parked in the hot sun).

Correction

Wrinkling is too severe a problem to be corrected by sanding. Usually the entire finish must be removed. Since the paint is still relatively fresh, however, it can be washed from the vehicle's surface with enamel reducer. In this fashion, at least the base coat is preserved and can be repainted almost immediately.

Prevention

The best way to prevent wrinkling is to add baking resin to the paint when it is being reduced. Baking resin keeps the outermost layer of paint wet even when it is subjected to heat. The solvents in the interior thus have a chance to evaporate. Use of the additive is recommended whenever enamel is being applied in extremely warm shop conditions. It is essential when enamel is force dried.

Baking resin, however, cannot do all the work itself. It must be used with a high-grade reducer and the reduced mixture applied with a fast enough stroke to avoid excessive film buildup.

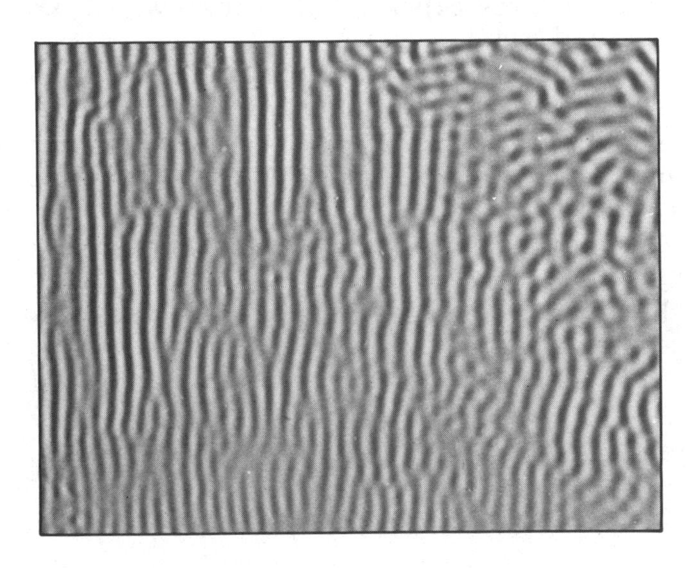

FIG 7-17
Wrinkling. (E. I. du Pont de Nemours & Co., Inc.)

OBJECTIVE 7-A2 (manipulative)

Working as a team with one other student and with the aid of Job Report Sheet 7-A2, you will use a primed and sanded practice panel to produce and correct the following paint problems: (1) solvent popping, (2) water spotting, and (3) blushing.

Time Recommended:

4½ hours

Preparation:

1. Review pages 265 through 289.
2. Study pages 290 through 294.
3. Read the Safety Checklist on pages 305 and 306, items 1 through 3.

Tools and Materials:

1. Suction-feed spray gun
2. Prepared practice panel
3. Heat lamp
4. Respirator
5. Masking paper and tape
6. Paint rack and strainers
7. Wooden stirring sticks
8. Clean shop cloths
9. Tack cloth
10. Selection of sandpapers (320A, 500A, 600A)
11. Thinner (both high and low grades)
12. Acrylic lacquer paint (dark color)
13. Retarder
14. Fast-drying reducer
15. Hand rubbing compound

Procedure:

1. Mask half of the panel. Give the exposed half a final wipedown with fast-drying reducer and tack.
2. Pour 1 inch of acrylic lacquer paint into the spray gun cup. Add 1½ inches of high-grade thinner and stir thoroughly.
3. Set the transformer-regulator at 45 psi (35 psi at the gun). Test the spray gun on masking paper. Adjust the pattern to 6 inches wide at a distance of 6 inches.
4. Apply four coats of lacquer to the panel. Allow no more than 3 minutes between applications.
5. After all four coats have been applied, use the partially triggered spray gun to fan the panel. As soon as a dry film forms over the fresh paint, apply heat. Force dry for the time recommended on the paint container label.
6. Note if and when solvent popping or a similar condition develops. Mark this information on Job Report Sheet 7-A2.
7. When the panel is cool, wet sand to remove all signs of solvent

popping. Start with a 320-grit abrasive and follow up with a 500-grit. Then clean the panel and repaint. This time, apply only two coats of color and allow adequate flash time between them.

8. After the new finish has had 10 minutes of drying time, place the panel in a horizontal position and flick some drops of water onto it. Allow the water to dry on the panel surface.
9. When the paint has fully dried and the water evaporated, note any effects at the panel. Describe these on Job Report Sheet 7-A2.
10. Using a 600-grit abrasive, sand the panel lightly to remove any water spots and then compound. *Note:* If the marks are not deep, they may be removed by compounding only.
11. Remove the masking, exposing the primed half of the panel. Remask to cover the painted half. Place a sponge or wet cloth over the masking, right next to the area that is to be painted.
12. Give the primer-surfacer a final wipedown with fast-drying reducer.
13. Mix a small amount of lacquer, using the same technique described in step 2. This time, however, substitute the low-grade solvent for the high-grade product.
14. Working with the same psi as before, test the spray gun.
15. Tack the panel and apply two coats of paint. Allow adequate flash time between coats.
16. After 15 minutes of drying time, examine the panel and note its appearance on Job Report Sheet 7-A2.
17. Remove the cloth or sponge and wipe up any moisture left on the masking.
18. Remove all of the paint from the spray gun cup except for ¼ inch. To this add 2 inches of high-grade thinner and two caps full of lacquer retarder. (*Note:* Had the correct thinner for shop conditions been used, much less retarder would have been necessary for this small amount of paint.)
19. Tack the panel and apply one wet coat of this mixture from a distance of 8 inches. If the blushing does not disappear within 10 minutes, spray the panel a second time. *Note:* The mixture is extremely thin. Avoid the kind of sharp movements that might cause it to drip onto the panel surface.

JOB REPORT SHEET 7-A2

PAINT DRYING PROBLEMS

Student Name ______________________________ Date ______________

Time Started ____________ Time Finished ____________ Total Time ____________

Specifications

Primer-surfacer type ________________ Color ________________

Acrylic lacquer paint: Manufacturer ______________________________

Color name ________________ Number _____

Technique

Solvent popping:

Drying time until problem appeared _____ minutes

Total force-drying time _____ minutes

Description of condition ______________________________

____

____

Removed by sanding with ________________ -grit abrasive(s)

Water spotting:

Description of condition ______________________________

____

____

Removed by ______________________________

Blushing:

Description of condition ______________________________

____

____

Removed by application of _____ mist coat(s)

Checkup Questions

1. Was the attempt to remedy any paint problem unsuccessful? If yes, explain why.

____

____

____

2. Why were the following items changed?

   a. The type of thinner in step 13 ______________________________

   ____

   ____

   b. The drying time between coats in step 4 ______________________________

   ____

   ____

   c. The spraying distance in step 19 ______________________________

   ____

   ____

3. How soon could the panel used for this job sheet be worked on again? Explain why. ______________________________

____

____

Date Completed ____________________ Instructor's Signature ______________________________

LONG-TERM PROBLEMS

The problems in this section usually occur long after the vehicle has left the paint shop—six or more months later, in fact. This time lapse suggests that the customer might be in part responsible for their occurrence, but that is not the case. Most of the problems discussed here start in the shop with too much paint, too little drying time, or an unfortunate combination of materials.

Because the refinisher must deal with a fully cured surface, correcting such problems almost always means removal of the finish. The nearest thing to a halfway measure is removal down to the primer-surfacer. Severe damage requires stripping to the bare metal.

Blistering

Blistering covers a surface with small, closely spaced, irregularly shaped bubbles. These make it appear that sand or grit is caught in the paint (Fig. 7-18). In fact, what is below the surface is more likely to be solvent, moisture, air, oil, or the beginnings of rust.

Cause

The foreign substances that cause blistering generally reach the surface in three ways: (1) through contaminated air lines, (2) from the passageways of a poorly cleaned spray gun, and (3) as residues from cleaning or sanding procedures. Moisture and the kind of dirt that can hold moisture are special hazards here. They can give rust a toehold on an otherwise good surface. The air and solvents get trapped in a blistered film predictably, through use of excessively fast thinners and excessively high air pressures.

Correction

If blistering is not deep, it can be sanded out. The old finish is then sealed and repainted. If the damage extends into the primer-surfacer, however, both base and top coats must be removed and the area entirely refinished.

FIG 7-18
Blistering. (E. I. du Pont de Nemours & Co., Inc.)

FIG 7-19
Chalking. (E. I. du Pont de Nemours & Co., Inc.)

Prevention

The two most important factors in preventing blisters are cleaning and maintenance. Any substance is a potential contaminant if proper precautions are not observed in handling it. Even the water used in wet sanding can leave behind a residue (mineral salts) that can cause blistering. The only sure way to avoid such commonplace hazards is to clean at all stages of the refinishing process. Specifically, (1) on a daily basis, check filters and open all drains in the air supply system; (2) before beginning any repair, remove all wax and road film from the old finish; (3) immediately air and hand dry all surfaces that are wet sanded; (4) give all surfaces to be painted a final wipedown with fast-drying reducer; and (5) clean all spray guns after each use. If the previous finish was blistered, sealing is also a wise precaution.

Chalking

Chalking is part of the natural aging process that all finishes go through. With time, the resin in the paint binder shrinks, freeing particles of pigment. These form a powdery deposit on the vehicle's surface, robbing it of its shine (Fig. 7-19). The color itself remains recognizable, but it looks washed out, as though someone has mixed it with bleach. This combination of dust and fading are what give the condition its name.

The small amount of chalking that occurs gradually in all finishes is removed by regular washing and polishing. Chalking becomes a paint problem when it occurs extensively and resists removal by such simple means.

Cause

Chalking is essentially a failure of holdout. Something in the reduction process, the preparation of the surface, or the spray painting technique deprives the finish of the balance it needs for durability. Typically it is a matter of (1) overreducing, (2) using the wrong solvent for shop conditions, (3) applying primer-surfacer coats too dry, (4) applying too few coats of paint too thinly, or (5) not sealing a surface that is already showing signs of chalking.

Correction

Since it is not possible to restore a proper balance of materials to any finish that has already dried, the best the refinisher can hope to do is keep the defective paint from reacting with any new top coat applied over it. He accomplishes this objective by wet sanding the affected surfaces and sealing them before proceeding with the repair.

Prevention

Three basic precautions will eliminate most cases of chalking: (1) always follow the manufacturer's recommendations on reduction and application of both paint and primer-surfacer; (2) apply both materials wet enough to flow; and (3) when in doubt about the holdout capabilities of any finish or base coat, apply sealer.

Chipping

Chipping is a loss of adhesion brought about by a sharp impact. The most common forms of the condition are stone bruises and so-called parking lot damage (Fig. 7-20). The latter results when car doors are carelessly swung open and strike neighboring vehicles.

Cause

Not all impacts to a vehicle's finish cause chipping. A panel can be severely dented, and yet the paint film will remain intact. What causes chipping is a blow whose force is concentrated in a small area. If the impact of a car door could be spread over an entire panel, for example, damage to the finish would be slight. It is concentrating that force at a single point no wider than the door's edge that dislodges the paint film.

Correction

There are two ways to correct chipping. If the amount of damage is small or isolated, a touch-up (or striping) brush can be used to deposit small amounts of paint into the chip. After drying, the area is sanded and compounded smooth. If chips are fairly large or numerous, a full spot repair can be done. The damaged paint is featheredged, the chips filled to the proper level with primer-surfacer, and the whole area sanded and painted.

FIG 7-20
Chipping. (Jay Storer)

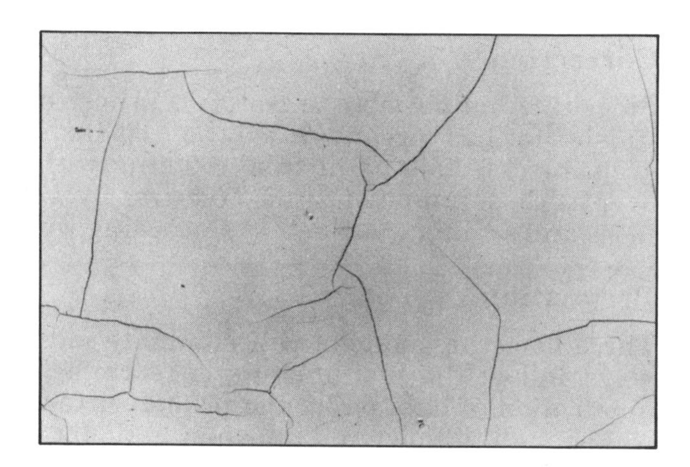

FIG 7-21
Cracking. (E. I. du Pont de Nemours & Co., Inc.)

Prevention

There is no realistic way to prevent chipping, but some precautions can help keep it to a minimum. When parking, always position a vehicle in the center of the space. When driving, avoid roadways paved with crushed rock or gravel. When purchasing a vehicle, order protective moldings as an option.

Cracking

Cracking in an automobile finish can take nearly a half dozen different forms. The term *cracking* itself is reserved for the longest and deepest of these. Such breaks in a finish are usually widely spaced and occur in no overall pattern. It is not uncommon, however, for two or three lines to radiate out from a single point, at angles to each other rather than parallel (Fig. 7-21).

Cause

When old paint cracks, it is usually because it is old. The finish has had years of exposure to the elements, particularly to extremes of temperature and moisture. When new paint cracks, the refinishing process itself is probably at fault. Common causes include (1) using incompatible materials, (2) using the wrong solvent for shop conditions, (3) allowing no flash time between coats, and (4) applying coats so wet and thick that solvents cannot escape before the paint films over.

Correction

Old paint that is cracked should be removed down to the bare metal. New paint can simply be sanded smooth and refinished—unless, of course, the cracking extends into the primer-surfacer. In that case, both top and base coats should be replaced.

Prevention

Preventing cracks is mainly a matter of using the right materials and letting them work at their own pace. It means, among other things, (1) allowing one coat of paint to flash before applying the next, (2) allowing paint to flash naturally rather than forcing the process with heat or fanning, (3) using the correct solvent for shop conditions, and (4) avoiding excessive film buildup.

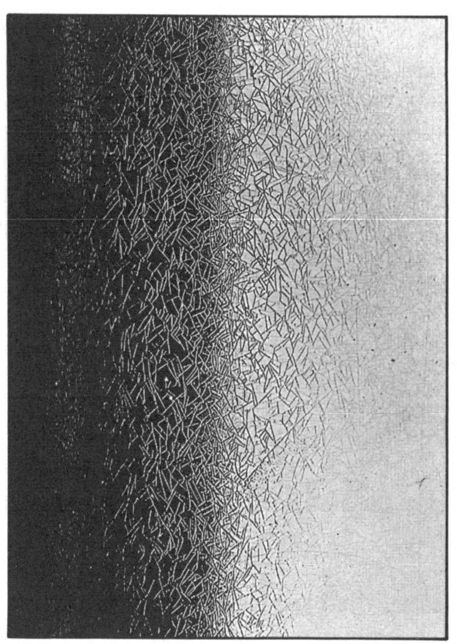

FIG 7-22 Crazing. (E. I. du Pont de Nemours & Co., Inc.)

Crazing

Crazing is the finest form of cracking. It consists of thousands of tiny breaks that link up with each other at irregular angles, giving the finish a texture like that of a frosted glass (Fig. 7-22).

Cause

Crazing is a lacquer problem. It occurs when extreme shop conditions and strong lacquer solvents so stress an old finish that it shatters. Eventually the damage is reflected in the new top coat as well.

Correction

When old lacquer shows evidence of crazing, it should be removed down to the bare metal and the surface reprimed before refinishing. When crazing occurs in new lacquer, only the color coat need be removed. This operation can be performed either by sanding or by applying lacquer-removing solvent. Before repainting, the base coat should be sealed.

Prevention

If all of the standard precautions for applying a lacquer finish are observed, crazing should not be a problem. These precautions include (1) applying sealer when painting over enamel or air-dried lacquer, (2) using the correct solvent for shop conditions, (3) allowing adequate flash time between coats, (4) allowing the recommended evaporation time before force drying, and (5) sanding or chemically removing any top coat material that is already showing signs of crazing.

Crow's-Feet

Crow's-feet occur most often around spot repairs, specifically along the feathered edge of the old paint. They are breaks that fall in size mid-

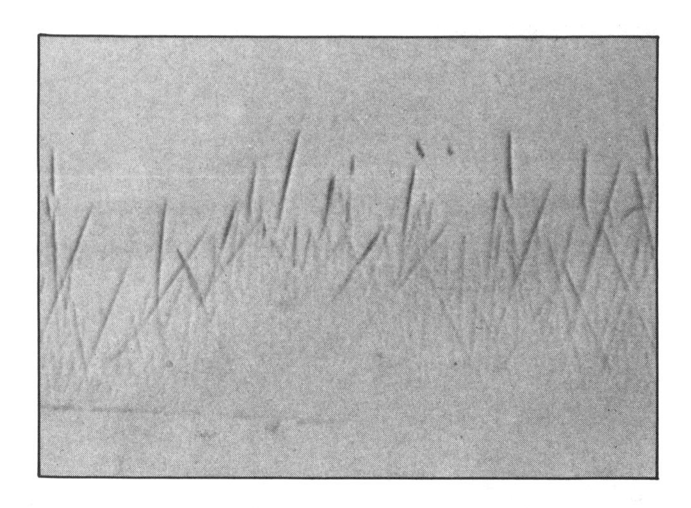

FIG 7-23
Crow's-feet. (E. I. du Pont de Nemours & Co., Inc.)

way between full-length cracks and crazing. They often take a three-toed, footprintlike form that accounts for their name (Fig. 7-23).

Cause

Crow's-feet are the result of stress set up in a repair when it absorbs solvents from fresh paint. The solvents first swell and then, as they evaporate, contract the primer-surfacer and with it the new top coat. In the end, the surface returns to its original level. There is thus no general collapse as in bull's-eye effect. The repair area, however, has been severely stressed, especially at its edges, which is where crow's-feet tend to appear.

Correction

As with most forms of cracking, the only sure correction is to sand out the damage. The surface should then be sealed to hold down swelling of both the sandscratches and the primer-surfacer.

The sealing is extremely important in this case, given the distinctive appearance of the damage. The fact that the scratches outline the repair rather than cover the whole surface calls attention to them. Even their faint reappearance could make the whole refinishing effort a waste.

Prevention

Sealing is likewise the most important measure a refinisher can take to prevent crow's-feet. When sealer is not applied, the refinisher should at least use a ground coat as a substitute. Other precautions that should be observed include (1) using the correct solvent for shop conditions and (2) allowing each color coat to flash before applying the next. Both of these measures speed evaporation and thus give paint solvents less time to penetrate primer-surfacer and other fillers.

Fading

Fading occurs when a finish loses the brightness and clarity of its color. It is often accompanied by hazing, or loss of gloss. All paint fades to some extent after a period of years. Fading that occurs in a matter of months, however, is a symptom of a poorly done repair.

Cause

A finish usually fades because the paint film is too thin. In other words, not enough coats of color have been applied. The fact that a spot repair matches an old finish after three coats of paint, for example, does not mean that the refinisher should stop at three coats. He must consider the thickness of the paint film after the solvents have evaporated. At three coats, the film that remains would lack the depth necessary to last and protect over time.

Correction

Whether a surface has faded from age and exposure or improper refinishing, the correction is the same: remove any wax or polish, wet sand, and repaint.

Prevention

Prevention is equally simple. Read the paint can label and apply the recommended number of color coats.

Line-Checking

Line-checking is the term used to describe a series of straight, parallel cracks (Fig. 7-24). From a distance, these may seem to extend the entire length or width of the panel on which they appear. However, closer inspection usually reveals a pattern of shorter film breaks, one taking up and continuing where the other leaves off. The minimum crack length is usually 2 to 3 inches; the maximum, up to 18.

Cause

Line-checking is a symptom of excessive paint buildup: (1) the vehicle has been refinished too many times without paint removal; (2) too many coats of paint have been applied at one time; or (3) the required coats have been sprayed on too thick and wet.

Correction

When line-checking occurs in a new finish, the color should be removed down to the primer-surfacer, a sealer applied, and the surface repainted. When the condition occurs in an old finish, the paint must be removed down to the bare metal.

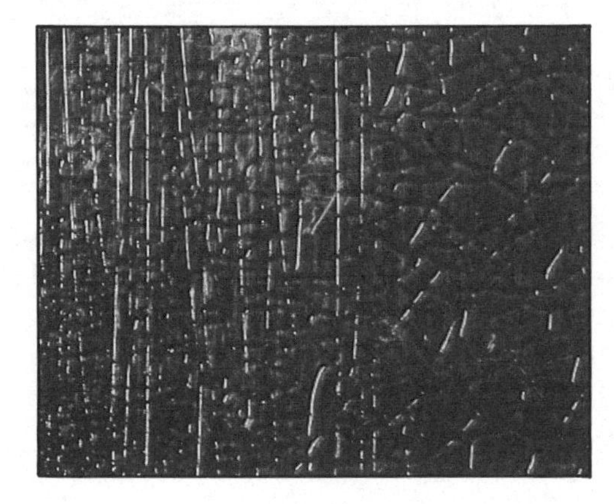

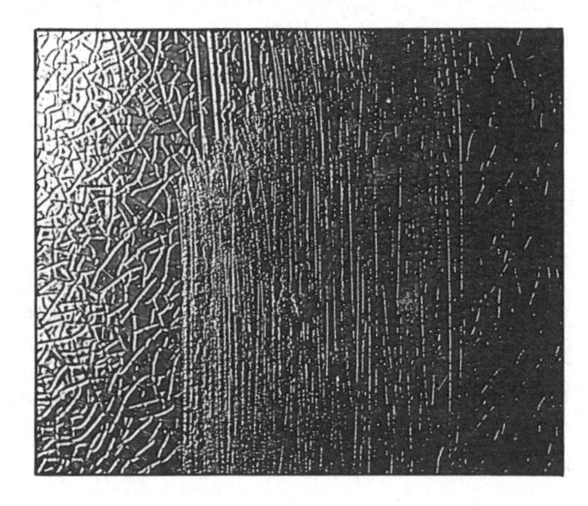

FIG 7-24
Line-checking. (E. I. du Pont de Nemours & Co., Inc.)

FIG 7-25
Peeling. (E. I. du Pont de Nemours & Co., Inc.)

Prevention

To avoid line-checking, (1) always measure the existing paint film on a vehicle before proceeding with any repair; (2) use the proper reducing agent for both the paint and shop conditions; (3) adjust, position, and move the spray gun to avoid excessive film buildup; and (4) allow ample flash time between coats of paint.

Micro-Checking

Micro-checking is a shorter, finer, more shallow version of line-checking. The individual cracks are so small, in fact, that often they can only be seen with a magnifying glass. Micro-checking is considered to be the first step in the breakdown of a paint film. The virtually invisible cracks first rob a finish of its gloss, then gradually develop into more severe breaks. Finally they allow rust and corrosion to work their way under the paint, thus destroying the finish.

Cause

Micro-checking occurs mainly when a refinisher cuts corners or rushes a repair. He (1) overreduces, (2) uses a solvent that is too fast for shop conditions, (3) applies too few coats of paint, (4) applies those coats too thinly, or (5) fails to seal when applying lacquer over enamel. His haste creates a finish that dulls prematurely and has low resistance to extremes of weather.

Correction

There is no such thing as strengthening a thin, weak finish. By the time micro-checking appears, the damage is done and any paint or refinishing material applied over it will sooner or later be undermined. The only option is to sand the micro-checks out of the paint, seal the surface, and refinish—this time with enough coats of paint.

Prevention

To avoid micro-checking, exercise special care when painting over surfaces that are either already micro-checked or potentially incompatible. Specifically, in such circumstances, always (1) sand and seal the old finish, (2) use the correct solvent for shop conditions, (3) follow the manufacturer's recommendations on reduction, and (4) apply enough coats of paint uniformly and with adequate flash time between them.

Peeling

Peeling is a loss of adhesion. The paint separates from the base coat and falls away, usually in flakes (Fig. 7-25).

Cause

Most adhesion problems can be traced to errors in surface preparation. Chief among these are (1) using incompatible materials without first applying a sealer, (2) using the wrong sealer, (3) inadequately sanding either the old finish or the new primer-surfacer, (4) painting over a wet surface or contaminating a dry one with moisture from air lines, and (5) failing to give a surface a final wipedown with enamel reducer. Spray painting technique is a secondary cause of peeling. Any practice that produces dry spray is also likely to produce a finish that does not adhere well.

Correction

To correct peeling, all of the affected paint must first be removed. In extreme cases, it may simply be pulled from the surface by hand. If there is still some bonding, sanding or use of a chemical paint remover may be necessary. At this point, the base coat should be carefully checked. If there is any sign that it may have contributed to the problem, it too should be removed. (Examples of such signs would include lack of a good sandscratch or the presence of a sealer coat that has obviously failed to do its job.) Once all of this material has been removed, the surface should be thoroughly cleaned, resanded if a good sandscratch is not evident, reprimed, sealed, and finally repainted.

Prevention

Virtually all preparations for spray painting are in some way designed to create or improve adhesion. To insure the best possible bond, however, special attention should be given to (1) thorough cleaning, (2) adequate sanding, and (3) proper sealing.

Rust

Rust occurs when moisture attacks the sheet metal from which many vehicle panels are made. The oxygen in the water combines with the iron to form a swollen, reddish crust (Fig. 7-26). This material has none of the strength and flexibility of the sheet steel it replaces.

FIG 7-26
Rust. (David Keown)

Rust develops quickly on any unprotected metal surface. Panel interiors, which are seldom painted, are a frequent starting point. From there the condition works its way out to the surface, where it blisters and finally dislodges the paint from below. Rust that works its way inward usually starts with a defective or damaged top coat. A chip or crack allows moisture to reach the metal, and the condition then eats through to the back of the panel.

Cause

Rust most often occurs because a vehicle (1) is not undercoated; (2) has unrepaired body damage; (3) has been repaired but without application of metal conditioner; (4) has partial repairs of long standing (like body panels that are primed but not painted); (5) is not washed or waxed regularly; and (6) has leaks that allow moisture to collect along the frame or inside body panels. Climate is another important (though uncontrollable) factor in the formation of rust. Vehicles used in dry climates rust slowly. Those used in coastal areas or wet climates tend to rust more quickly.

Correction

The only correction for rust is its complete and thorough removal. No trace of the condition can remain, or it will continue to attack the metal regardless of any protective measures taken. Surface rust can usually be removed with a grinder and a 24-grit abrasive. Rust that has pitted or worked its way into a metal surface, however, must be removed by sandblasting. (*Note:* If rust is advanced, the latter process may leave holes in the metal. These will require brazing or metal patching for full repair.) Once all rust is removed, the surface must be treated with metal conditioner and refinished as quickly as possible.

Prevention

Preventing rust is mainly a matter of giving a car's body the same kind of regular care and attention its motor receives. Recommended procedures include (1) undercoating; (2) regular washing and waxing; (3) prompt repair of all body and finish damage, no matter how slight; and (4) where possible, garaging the vehicle.

FIG 7-27
Stain spotting.
(E. I. du Pont de Nemours & Co., Inc.)

Stain Spotting

Stain spotting is in the same category as chipping. It is not a problem that the painter causes. Rather, it is one he is often called upon to correct. It occurs when foreign substances fall on a finish and leave it permanently marked (Fig. 7-27). Examples of materials that cause such damage include automotive products like transmission fluid, brake fluid, and battery acid; industrial fallout like cement dust and acid rain; and natural substances like tree sap, bird droppings, wet leaves, and the remains of insects and fruit pulps.

Cause

What ties all of these substances together is the fact that they have solventlike properties. They soften, dissolve, or actually eat into other materials, including automotive paints. Chemically, in fact, many of them are acids. As such, they continue to do damage until diluted or neutralized.

Correction

Correction, therefore, begins with a neutralizing solution of baking soda and water. If any of the damaging substance remains on or embedded in the spotted area, washing with this mixture stops its solvent action. (In other words, it renders the material chemically neutral.) After this procedure, the stain can be rubbed out. If it is only in the outermost layer of the paint film, compounding should eliminate it and a follow-up polishing restore the uniformity of the finish. If the damage is deeper, however, a full spot repair will have to be done, complete with sanding, priming, and repainting.

Prevention

Preventing stain spotting is largely a matter of protecting a vehicle's finish. Recommended precautions include (1) regular washing and waxing; (2) garaging the vehicle or, if this is not possible, using a car cover; and (3) avoiding parking spaces under trees, wires, pipes, overhangs, and gutters. (All of these locations could provide roosting places for birds and serve as sources of corrosive runoff.)

Whenever a potentially damaging material does fall on the finish, wash it away promptly. In certain situations, assume contamination even when it is not visible. Always, for example, wash a vehicle thoroughly after it has been in the shop for major repairs or regular service and maintenance.

SAFETY CHECKLIST

Causes and Prevention:

1. It should be obvious from the various discussions in this unit that doing things the right way (the way that avoids paint problems) also amounts to doing things the safe way. Consider some examples.
   a. Wet sanding with gasoline produces an oily paint film. It also produces one of the most glaring violations of commonsense

safety rules in all of refinishing—exposing an extremely flammable substance in an open container. Doing the job the right way—with water—avoids both the problem and the safety hazard.

b. Excessive air pressure increases the possibility of dry spray, overspray, and orange peel. It also scatters larger amounts of atomized paint and primer-surfacer in the air. With time, these particles can overburden both the exhaust system and the refinisher's respirator. A lower pressure setting does the job, avoids the problems, and spares the safety equipment.

c. Driving a vehicle into the spray booth introduces exhaust fumes into the air in which the paint must be applied and dry. This kind of contamination can cause hazing. The electrical system that allows the vehicle to be driven in the first place, however, is a safety hazard. It brings a potential source of sparks into an area where paint is being stored and where paint fumes and vapors are concentrated. Disconnecting the battery cable and pushing the car into the booth both saves the gloss and eliminates the fire hazard.

d. Failure to read container labels can lead to mistakes in reduction, drying time, number of coats, and compatibility. These factors figure in nearly a third of all the conditions listed here, including bleeding, lifting, lack of hiding, solvent popping, cracking, fading, and micro-checking. Correcting most of these problems means redoing the job—and re-exposing the painter to sanding dust and harmful product vapors. Reading the label and getting the details right thus does more than save time and materials. It cuts the refinisher's exposure to potentially harmful contaminants.

e. Puddles left from washing down the spray booth can be a source of water spotting in a new top coat. They can also be a hazard to the refinisher who might slip as he moves around a vehicle during spray painting. Sweeping out the booth before use thus protects both the refinisher and his work.

Correction:

2. Often, to correct a paint problem or guarantee that it will not recur, the refinisher must apply sealer. Spraying this product calls for the same precautions as spraying paint or primer-surfacer. These include use of a respirator. Remember, sealer keeps solvents from passing through layers of paint. It is therefore not a substance that belongs in human lungs, which function by passing oxygen and waste gases back and forth through layers of tissue.
3. Washing down a surface with thinner or reducer is a correction technique that is used less frequently. It too, however, has hazards. It amounts to using straight the most volatile component in paint and primer-surfacer. The procedure should therefore be done only outside or in a well-ventilated spot away from sanding operations, compressor motors, smoking areas, and any activity that might produce sparks.

Working as a team with three other students and with the aid of Job Report Sheet 7-A3, you will see how many of the paint problems discussed in this unit you can identify in cars parked in the school lot.

OBJECTIVE 7-A3 (manipulative)

Time Recommended:

30 minutes

Preparation:

1. Review pages 265 through 306.
2. Study pages 307 through 310.

Tools and Materials:

None

Procedure:

1. On a separate sheet of paper, draw a rough outline of the parking lot and insert a few key landmarks as reference points. As the various paint problems are identified, note the location of each vehicle on this map.
2. Write in the starting time at the top of the job report. Plan on returning to the classroom or shop area within 30 minutes.
3. With the other members of your team, spread out around the lot and carefully examine the finishes of as many vehicles as possible in the allotted time. When a paint problem is found, identify the vehicle by make, model, color, and license plate number. Mark its location on Job Report Sheet 7-A3. Then name the problem and describe its extent.
4. At the end of a half hour, return to the classroom or shop. Be prepared to lead the class as a group to any vehicle on your list and indicate which areas of the finish are affected by the named problem.

IDENTIFYING PAINT PROBLEMS

Student Name ______________________ Date ____________

Time Started ____________ Time Finished ____________ Total Time ____________

Specifications

Attach the parking lot/search area diagram with marked vehicle locations to this job report sheet.

Observed Finish Defects

Vehicle 1: Make ____________ Model ____________ Color ____________

License number ____________

Paint problem(s) (Describe nature and extent.) ____________

Vehicle 2: Make ____________ Model ____________ Color ____________

License number ____________

Paint problem(s) (Describe nature and extent.) ____________

Vehicle 3: Make ____________ Model ____________ Color ____________

License number ____________

Paint problem(s) (Describe nature and extent.) ____________

Vehicle 4: Make ____________ Model ____________ Color ____________

License number ____________

Paint problem(s) (Describe nature and extent.) ____________

____

Vehicle 5: Make ____________ Model ____________ Color ____________

License number ____________

Paint problem(s) (Describe nature and extent.) ____________

____

____

Vehicle 6: Make ____________ Model ____________ Color ____________

License number ____________

Paint problem(s) (Describe nature and extent.) ____________

____

____

Checkup Questions

1. Which problems, if any, seemed to occur together? ____________

   ____

   ____

   ____

2. Were the causes of any of the problems apparent? If yes, indicate which and describe the cause(s) briefly. ____________

   ____

   ____

   ____

   ____

   ____

Date Completed ____________ Instructor's Signature ____________

Student Name ______________________ Date ______________

DIRECTIONS: Circle the best answer to each question.

1. The paint problem shown at the right is
   A. orange peel.
   B. sagging.
   C. sandscratch swelling.
   D. wrinkling.

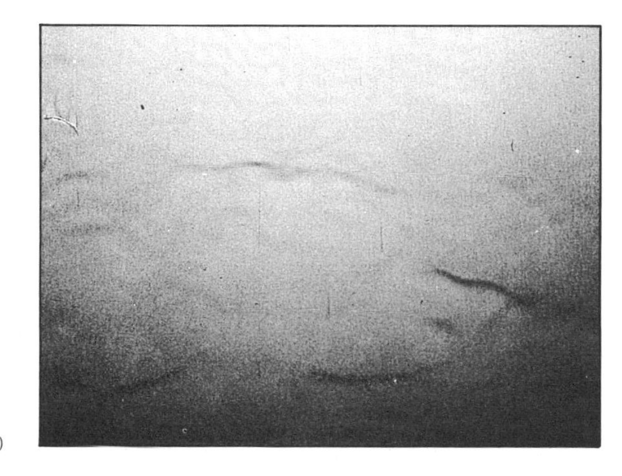

(E. I. du Pont de Nemours & Co., Inc.)

2. All of the following are practices that produce paint problems. One, however, is also a safety hazard. Which?
   A. Failing to clean and maintain spray guns
   B. Fanning surfaces to speed drying
   C. Not sealing under fresh lacquer
   D. Wet sanding with gasoline

3. Which can lead to adhesion problems if trapped under a paint film?
   I. Air
   II. Water
   A. I only B. II only C. Both I and II D. Neither I nor II

4. Which condition can be corrected by filling spaces left in the paint or primer-surfacer?
   I. Pinholing
   II. Blistering
   A. I only B. II only C. Both I and II D. Neither I nor II

5. When primer-surfacer shows through a new top coat, the condition is called
   A. bleeding.
   B. chalking.
   C. lack of hiding.
   D. stain spotting.

6. In appearance, each pair below represents the large and small versions of the same condition EXCEPT
   A. cracking and crazing.
   B. line-checking and micro-checking.
   C. overspray and dry spray.
   D. sags and runs.

7. Chipping and stain spotting are alike in that both
   I. are not caused by poor refinishing technique.
   II. require a baking soda and water rinse for correction.

   A. I only   B. II only   C. Both I and II   D. Neither I nor II

8. Which condition could be prevented by using a slower solvent?
   I. Blushing
   II. Dry spray

   A. I only   B. II only   C. Both I and II   D. Neither I nor II

9. All of the following paint problems can be prevented with additives EXCEPT
   A. blushing.
   B. fisheye.
   C. hazing.
   D. wrinkling.

10. The problem shown at the right appears in the first coat of paint. The refinisher eliminates it in the second coat, but it reappears in the third. The most likely reason is failure to
    A. clean the surface before applying the third coat.
    B. add fisheye killer to the paint.
    C. use the right solvent for shop conditions.
    D. allow enough drying time between coats.

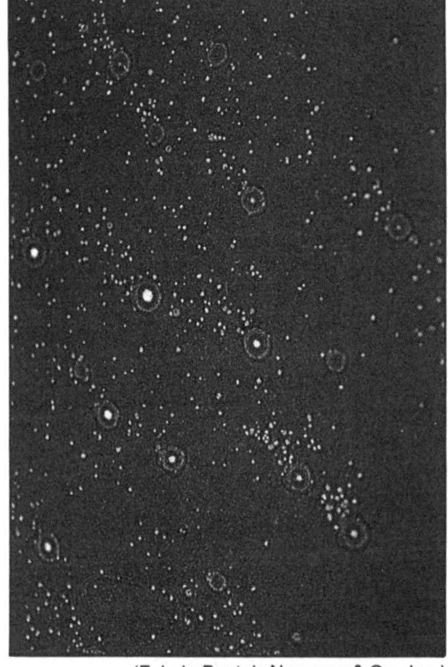

(E. I. du Pont de Nemours & Co., Inc.)

11. All of the following are special problems of spot repairs EXCEPT
    A. bull's-eye effect.
    B. chipping.
    C. crow's-feet.
    D. lack of hiding.

12. A white convertible is being painted red. The old finish and the new color are compatible, but the label on the can of red paint warns that it is a bleeder.

Refinisher I tells the customer that the warning is nothing for him to worry about because it does not apply in this case.

Refinisher II tells the customer that the warning means he will need bleeder sealer under the new top coat.

Who is right?

A. I only B. II only C. Both I and II D. Neither I nor II

13. Which is an early symptom of paint failure?

A. Micro-checking
B. Rust
C. Sandscratch showthrough
D. Water spotting

14. Using wax remover for the final wipedown before painting can lead to all of the following conditions EXCEPT

A. blistering.
B. oily paint film.
C. peeling.
D. stain spotting.

15. Which condition always requires removal of the paint film down to the bare metal?

A. Runs in lacquer
B. Runs in enamel
C. Cracking in an old finish
D. Crazing in a new finish

16. A customer brings in a vehicle that, he claims, was refinished eight months before. "The paint used to be glossy," he states, "a warm chestnut brown." Now the finish is dull and the color muddy.

Refinisher I suggests that the car is weathering prematurely because not enough paint was applied.

Refinisher II suggests that compounding will bring the finish back to life.

Who is right?

A. I only B. II only C. Both I and II D. Neither I nor II

17. All of the following can be caused by trapped solvents EXCEPT

A. blistering.
B. bull's-eye effect.
C. pinholing.
D. orange peel.

18. All of the following can be caused by poor spray painting technique EXCEPT

A. dry spray.
B. hazing.
C. orange peel.
D. wrinkling.

19. Applying too many coats of paint too quickly can result in
   I. bull's-eye effect.
   II. solvent popping.

   A. I only B. II only C. Both I and II D. Neither I nor II

20. The condition shown at the right was probably caused by
   A. applying lacquer over enamel without sealing.
   B. applying too few coats of color.
   C. flooding the surface with paint.
   D. allowing water to air dry on fresh paint.

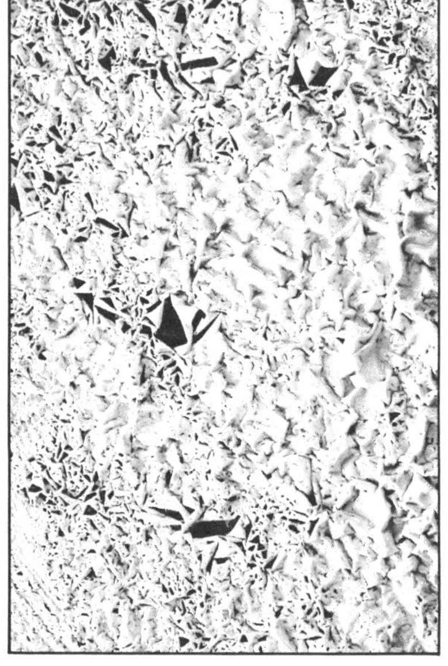

(E. I. du Pont de Nemours & Co., Inc.)

Score ________ Instructor's Signature ______________________________

unit 8

Special Finishes

Most of the finishes discussed thus far have been flat colors. They are so called because they are visually and physically flat. They have no reflective properties other than the luster that is often compounded or polished into them. They have no texture. If properly applied, they have no variations in shade. It is possible, however, to produce automotive finishes that do have all of these traits.

The most popular of these special finishes are the metallics. Like flat colors, they are combinations of pigment, binder, and solvent but with an added ingredient—aluminum flakes. The flakes give the finish a reflective quality and, depending on the angle of the viewer, a variety of hues.

Metallics, in turn, are the basis for many other special finishes. Some of these merely vary the basic ingredients. A metal flake finish, for example, has flakes that are tinted and a binder that is clear. Other finishes combine metallics with more common materials. A pearlescent finish starts with a flat color coat (white) over which is applied a metallic material (mother-of-pearl).

Mixing metal flakes into paint is only one alternative to flat colors. A less dramatic technique involves suspending flecks of two or three different colors in a neutral gray, beige, or black carrying coat. In the 1960s, such spatter finishes were used extensively for trunk interiors. Today spatter paint is a popular refinishing material for truck beds.

Another alternative to flat colors is a paint that actually has a texture, not just the appearance of one. Vinyl finish looks very much like the vinyl roofing material installed on vehicles at the factory. Its rough, dimpled pattern, however, is produced by a spray gun.

This unit discusses all three of these product groups. The emphasis, however, is on the metallics. Metallic color effects are explained along with color control problems and techniques. Detailed procedures are provided for applying plain metallic, metal flake, candy apple, and pearlescent finishes. The unit concludes with briefer discussions of water-based paints (of which spatter finish is one) and imitation vinyl top coats.

OBJECTIVE 8-A (written)

After doing the reading and shop exercises, you will be able to answer correctly without reference material a minimum of 14 out of 20 test questions on the following topics:

1. Metallic characteristics and application techniques
2. Differences between the various metallic finishes
3. Interior vs. exterior water-based paints
4. Dying and simulating vinyl-covered panels and trim

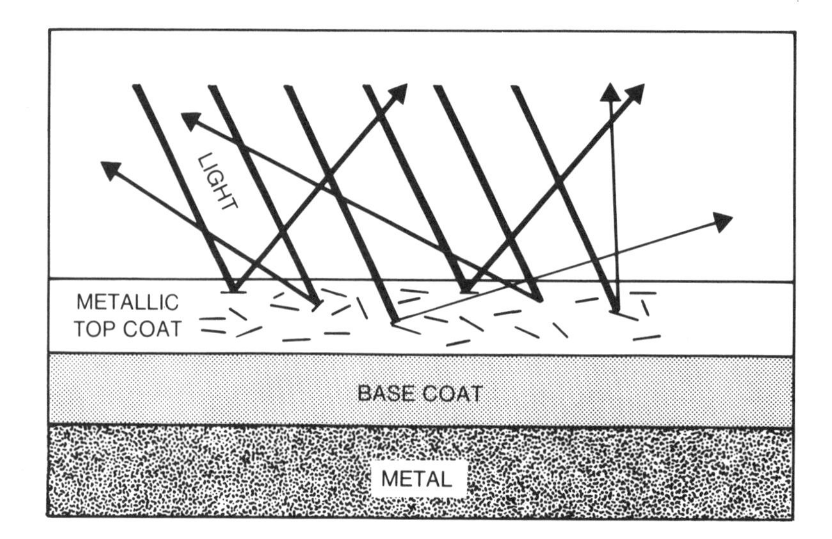

FIG 8-1
Aluminum flakes in metallic paint reflect light at different angles.

METALLIC PAINT

Today metallic colors are extremely popular for passenger cars. Such finishes get their distinctive look from aluminum flakes. Having no color other than their own natural metallic, the flakes can be added to virtually any shade of paint. They come in three grinds—fine, medium, and coarse. Which grind is used depends on the effect desired and the color selected. Generally, the fine grind is used in light colors and the coarse grind in dark ones.

When metallic paint is properly applied, the flakes are suspended randomly throughout the paint film. Light passes through the pigment and bounces back off the flakes at different angles. Thus the finish seems to contain multiple points of color and a variety of hues (Fig. 8-1). These shift back and forth as the viewer changes his position. This appearance is the classic metallic effect.

Color Effects

The flakes, however, make metallic colors extremely sensitive to spray painting technique. If a flat color is applied too wet, the refinisher can

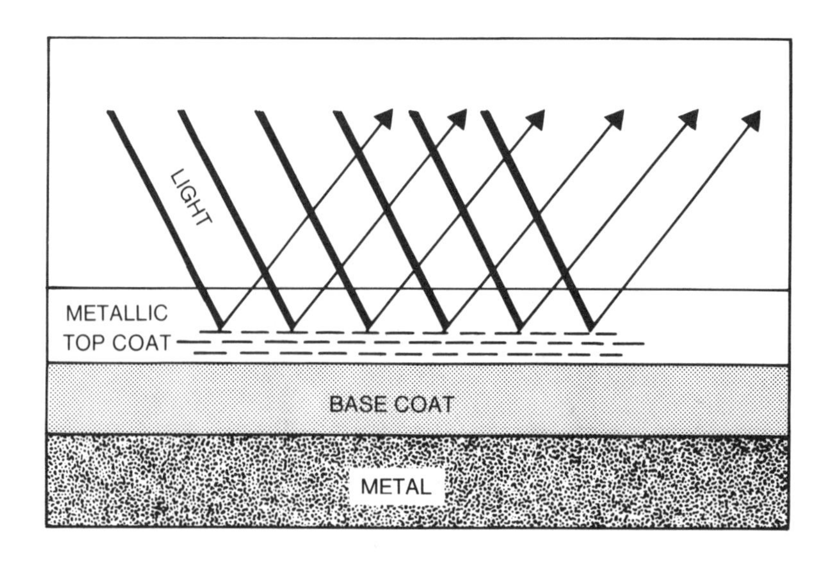

FIG 8-2
When applied too wet the metal flakes sink into the paint and the color becomes darker.

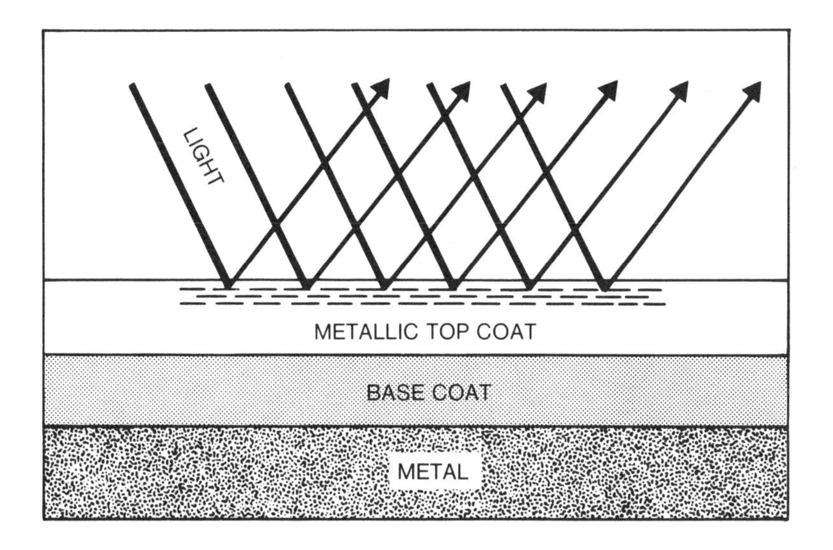

FIG 8-3
When applied too dry the metal flakes stay near the surface and the color is lighter.

compensate by allowing more time between coats for the additional solvent to evaporate. If he makes the same mistake and tries the same solution with a metallic, however, he will change the color of the finish. The change occurs because, in the time that it takes for the extra solvent to evaporate, the metallic flakes sink to the bottom of the paint layer. There they arrange themselves uniformly, flat to the panel surface. As a result, light has to travel farther both to reach the flakes and to escape again once it has bounced off them. In the process, much of it is absorbed. The finish thus appears darker (Fig. 8-2).

Just the opposite results occur if a metallic finish is applied too dry. The little solvent that there is evaporates quickly, before the flakes can disperse themselves evenly throughout the paint film. Most are trapped near the surface. Thus light barely penetrates the color coat before it is bounced back toward the viewer. Very little is absorbed, and the color coat appears lighter (Fig. 8-3).

Metallic Control Techniques

These facts form the basis of metallic control, a group of techniques that refinishers use to make midrepair color corrections. Basically four options are involved: (1) changes in reduction, (2) changes in spray gun adjustment, (3) changes in spray gun movement and positioning, and (4) the use of mist coats. When applying a metallic finish, any one or any combination of these techniques will have an immediate and noticeable effect at the panel.

Spray Gun Adjustment and Movement

The easiest way to correct a color mismatch is to make some adjustments in spray painting technique. If a metallic color is going on too dark, for example, the refinisher has five quick remedies at hand. He can (1) close the fluid valve slightly, (2) use a faster stroke, (3) hold the gun farther from the panel, (4) open the spreader valve a little more, or (5) increase the pressure at the transformer-regulator. What all of these adjustments do is speed the drying process by increasing the amount of air mixed with the paint. Remember, if a metallic dries faster, its flakes will settle less and its color take on a lighter hue. (*Note:* The suggested adjustments are listed in order of preference. Items 4 and 5 are the least desirable because, while they speed drying, they also increase the possibility of overspray. This result does not so clearly follow from the other choices.)

To darken a repair area that is too light, the refinisher would use just the opposite techniques. He would (1) open the fluid valve, (2) use a slower stroke, (3) hold the gun closer to the surface, (4) close the spreader valve, or (5) decrease the transformer-regulator pressure. All of these things would produce a wetter finish. The metallic flakes would sink farther into the paint film, thus reducing its extremely metallic appearance.

Mist Coating

It is also possible to control the dispersal of metallic flakes by using mist coats. These may be purely corrective, as where a mist coat or two is used to reflow a finish that has dried too light. Mist coats may also be a regular part of an application procedure. In such a case, the color is deliberately sprayed on dry, then followed up with a mist coat to distribute its metallic more evenly. This technique, of course, is the same as that used in the two-gun method of spot repair. The only difference is in the area covered, which is larger. In fact, the two-gun procedure is frequently called the metallic control method.

Mottling

Besides mismatching, metallics have at least one other characteristic problem. Called mottling, it is the metallic equivalent of zebra effect. Instead of smooth and rough areas forming stripes, however, there are light and dark ones (Fig. 8-4).

Despite the difference in appearance, the two conditions have the same causes. Alternate areas of overwetting and dry spray are formed by (1) poor spray gun adjustment, (2) poor spray gun cleaning and maintenance, (3) arcing or tilting the spray gun, (4) variations in stroke speed, and (5) uneven overlaps between successive strokes. All of these practices can be aggravated by failure to mix or reduce the paint properly or to allow adequate drying time between coats. In such circumstances, a finish can break down further into spots and patches of light and dark (Fig. 8-5).

FIG 8-4 Mottling in a metallic finish. (E. I. du Pont de Nemours & Co., Inc.)

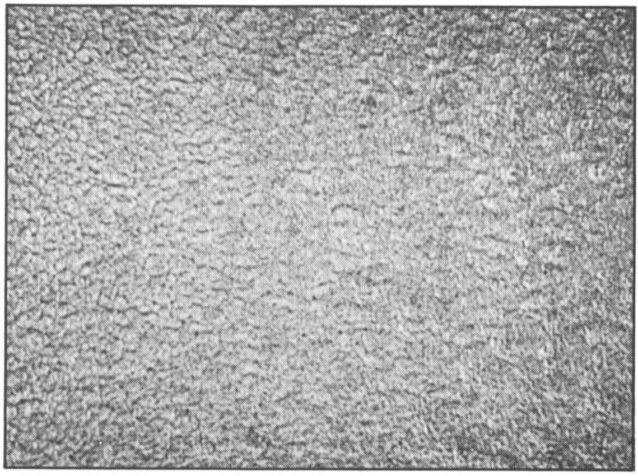

FIG 8-5 Extreme mottling in a metallic finish. (E. I. du Pont de Nemours & Co., Inc.)

Mottling can be corrected by applying a medium wet coat of color across the stripes and then mist coating the entire area. The finish must be allowed to flash thoroughly before any corrective coats are applied, however. *Note:* Where an enamel metallic is being used, the color coat may require additional reduction.

OBJECTIVE 8-A1 (manipulative)

Working as a team with one other student and with the aid of Job Report Sheet 8-A1, you will use the two-gun method to apply a metallic finish to a bare metal practice panel.

Time Recommended:

2 hours

Preparation:

1. Review pages 315 through 319.
2. Study pages 319 through 322.
3. Read the Safety Checklist on pages 347 and 348, items 1 through 3.

Tools and Materials:

1. Suction-feed spray guns (three—two for paint, one for primer-surfacer)
2. Duster gun
3. Polisher with both compounding and polishing pads
4. Respirator and safety goggles
5. Rubber gloves
6. Paint rack and strainer
7. Wooden stirring sticks
8. Hose (or sponge and bucket)
9. Sponge rubber sanding block
10. Clean shop cloths
11. Metal conditioner
12. Lacquer primer-surfacer
13. Thinner
14. Acrylic lacquer paint (medium blue or green metallic)
15. Fast-drying reducer
16. Machine rubbing compound
17. Liquid polish
18. Selection of sandpapers (500A, 600A)
19. Tack cloth

Procedure:

1. Treat the panel with metal conditioner.
2. Mix and test spray the primer-surfacer. Apply three coats to the panel, allowing each to flash before applying the next one. Allow the primer-surfacer to dry for 30 minutes.

3. Using a 500A abrasive, wet sand the primer-surfacer. Wipe away any sanding residue with a moistened cloth and blow the panel dry.
4. Remove the panel to the spray booth. Give the primer-surfacer a final wipedown with fast-drying reducer.
5. Prepare the remaining two spray guns. For the first, strain 1 part paint followed by 1½ parts thinner into the spray gun cup and mix well. Label this cup *P* for *paint.* For the second gun, place ½ inch of paint in the cup and fill with thinner to the 1-quart mark. Label this gun *T* for *thinner.*
6. Set the transformer-regulator at 35 psi (25 psi at the gun) and test spray the two mixtures.
7. Tack the panel.
8. Apply one coat of the thinner to the panel. *Note:* Overlap each stroke only 25 percent into the previous one.
9. Disconnect the air hose and attach it to the gun with the paint. Immediately apply a single coat of color, using the standard 50-percent overlap.
10. Continue in this fashion until at least five color coats and six mist coats have been applied. Then allow 10 minutes of drying time.
11. Check the panel for proper flowing and uniformity of finish. If any mottling is apparent, cross-spray with the paint mixture and then apply one mist coat with the thinner.
12. Allow the panel to air dry a minimum of 4 hours or force dry for 1 hour at a temperature of 165 degrees Fahrenheit.
13. Using a 600A abrasive and a sponge rubber sanding block, wet sand the panel. Rinse with water, wipe, and blow dry.
14. Machine compound the surface until a smooth gloss is visible. Then, to remove any trace of the compound, wash the panel with water, wipe dry, and polish.

METALLIC FINISH

Student Name ______________________ Date ____________

Time Started ____________ Time Finished ____________ Total Time ____________

Specifications

Metallic paint: Type ____________ Color code ____________

Name of color ______________________

Metallic flake: Fine ______ Medium ______ Coarse ______

How was the flake grind determined? ______________________

____

____

Technique

Primer-surfacer: Type ____________ Color ____________

Reduction formula ______________________

Total number of coats ______ Psi ____________

Paint reduction: Type of thinner ______________________

Formula ______________________

Paint application:

Total number of color coats ______ Psi ____________

Total number of mist coats ______ Psi ____________

Mottling ______ Yes ______ No

Other problems (Describe.) ______________________

____

____

Drying process:

Air ______ Force drying ______ Total drying time ____________

Checkup Questions

1. What standard was used for the test sprayings in steps 2 and 6? Why?

____

____

____

2. In step 5, why was it important to strain the paint into the spray gun cup first, before the thinner? ____

____

____

3. In step 8, why was the thinner mixture applied with only a 25-percent overlap?

____

____

____

Date Completed ____________________ Instructor's Signature ______________________________

METAL FLAKE FINISH

The terms *metal flake* and *metallic* are sometimes confused. They are, in fact, two different materials. A metallic finish consists of aluminum flakes suspended in a pigmented binder. A metal flake finish consists of pigmented particles suspended in a clear binder.

Use of Clear

Of the two finishes, the metal flake has the more three-dimensional look. This appearance is the result of the numerous coats of clear that are applied over the flaked material.

Clear is binder without color. When applied in multiple coats, it protects and provides great depth and gloss. Metal flake finishes have been known to carry as many as fifteen coats of clear.

Even when properly reduced, clear is an extremely thick material that builds very quickly. This quality means that a paint film covered with clear can very easily reach a critically thick level. This condition, in turn, can lead to early paint failure. If exposed regularly to sun and rain, for example, a metal flake finish soon dulls, cracks, and peels. For this reason, metal flake finishes are seldom seen on general-use vehicles. They are confined mainly to show cars and motorcycles (Fig. 8-6).

Effect of Ground Coat

The flakes used in a metal flake finish are purchased separately, in packets. They come in a variety of everyday colors (like red, green, and blue) plus gold and silver. Their shade on a vehicle, however, depends on the ground coat over which they are applied. White or silver ground coats are favored because they reflect the most light. When applied directly over sealer, which is usually a shade of gray, metal flake looks darker.

Metal flake is sprayed onto a surface in single passes. The 50-percent overlap that is normal for flat and metallic colors is not used. If it were, the metal flakes would totally hide the ground coat. No reflected light would reach the viewer, and an important part of the metal flake effect would be lost. Rather, the tinted flakes are spread thinly across the surface so that they can pick up light bounced off the ground coat.

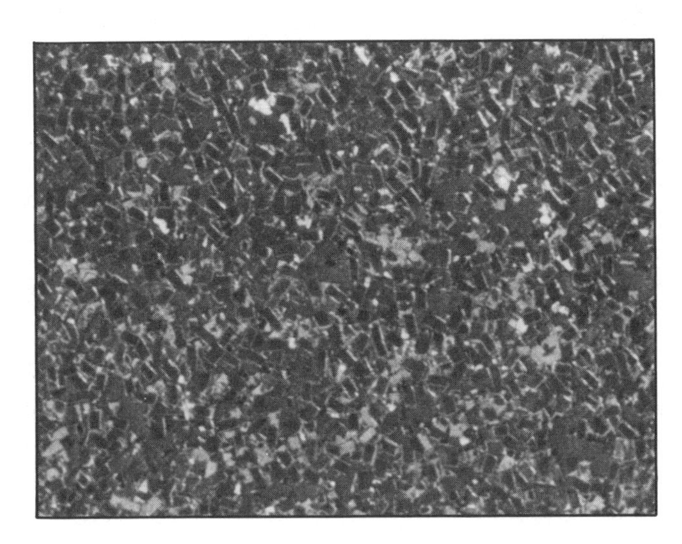

FIG 8-6
Metal flake finish. (Jay Storer)

OBJECTIVE 8-A2 (manipulative)

Working as a team with one other student and with the aid of Job Report Sheet 8-A2, you will apply a metal flake finish to a bare practice panel.

Time Recommended:

6 hours

Preparation:

1. Review pages 315 through 323.
2. Study pages 324 through 328.
3. Read the Safety Checklist on pages 347 and 348, items 1 through 3.

Tools and Materials:

1. Suction-feed spray guns (two—one for paint, one for primer-surfacer)
2. Duster gun
3. Polisher with both compounding and polishing pads
4. Respirator and safety goggles
5. Rubber gloves
6. Paint rack and strainer
7. Wooden stirring sticks
8. Hose (or sponge and bucket)
9. Sanding blocks (hard and sponge rubber)
10. Clean shop cloths
11. Metal conditioner
12. Lacquer primer-surfacer
13. Thinner (medium and high grades)
14. Acrylic lacquer paint (white, silver, or some other light color suitable as a ground coat)
15. Acrylic lacquer clear
16. Metal flake (color of choice)
17. Fast-drying reducer
18. Machine rubbing compound
19. Liquid polish
20. Selection of sandpapers (500A, 600A)
21. Tack cloth

Procedure:

1. Treat the panel with metal conditioner.
2. Mix and test spray the primer-surfacer. Apply three coats to the panel, allowing each to flash before applying the next one. Allow the primer-surfacer to dry for 30 minutes.
3. Using a 500A abrasive, wet sand the primer-surfacer. Wipe away any sanding residue with a moistened cloth and blow the panel dry.
4. Remove the panel to the spray booth. Give the primer-surfacer a final wipedown with fast-drying reducer.

5. Mix the color for the ground coat. Use the medium-grade thinner.
6. Set the transformer-regulator at 45 psi (35 psi at the gun) and test spray the mixture.
7. Tack the panel.
8. Apply two single coats of paint, allowing the first coat to flash before applying the second. Allow the panel to dry for 30 minutes.
9. While the ground coat is drying, clean the spray gun.
10. Prepare the metal flake mixture. Strain 1 inch of clear and 2 inches of high-grade thinner into the spray gun cup. Then add ¼ ounce of metal flake and stir thoroughly. *Note:* To avoid breaking the flakes, take care not to press them against the sides or bottom of the cup.
11. Using the same transformer-regulator setting as before, retest the spray gun and adjust the pattern as necessary. *Note:* If not enough flakes are reaching the test surface, the transformer-regulator setting can be raised by up to 10 psi.
12. Tack the ground coat.
13. Apply one thin coat of metal flake to the panel. Lap the strokes 1 to 1½ inches, not the normal 50 percent. Between strokes, shake the spray gun to keep the flake material from settling out in the cup. Allow the panel to dry to the touch (usually about 30 minutes).
14. While the panel is drying, clean the spray gun.
15. After 30 minutes, use a bare hand to wipe any loose or protruding flakes from the panel. Between hand strokes, wipe the dislodged flakes off on a tack cloth.
16. Mix 1 part clear with 2 parts high-grade thinner.
17. Set the transformer-regulator at 45 psi (35 psi at the gun) and test the clear coat.
18. Apply six single coats of clear to the panel. Spray each coat very wet or use double coats to achieve the necessary film depth. *Note:* No more than 10 minutes of drying time should be allowed between coats, single or double.
19. Allow the panel to air dry overnight or force dry for 1 hour at a temperature of 165 degrees Fahrenheit.
20. Using a 500A abrasive and a hard rubber sanding block, wet sand the panel. Rinse with water, blow dry, wipe, and tack.
21. Mix and spray at least two more coats of clear, once again keeping them very wet.
22. Allow the panel to air dry three or more days or force dry for 1 hour at a temperature of 165 degrees Fahrenheit.
23. Using a 600A abrasive and a sponge rubber sanding block, wet sand the panel. Rinse with water, wipe, and blow dry.
24. Machine compound the surface until a smooth gloss is visible. Then, to remove any trace of the compound, wash the panel with water, wipe dry, and polish.

METAL FLAKE FINISH

Student Name ______________________ Date ______________

Time Started ______________ Time Finished ______________ Total Time ______________

Specifications

Ground coat: Type ______________ Color code ______________

Name of color ______________________________

Metal flake: Color ______________________________

Technique

Primer-surfacer: Type ______________ Color ______________

Reduction formula ______________________________

Total number of coats ______ Psi ______________________

Paint reduction:

Ground coat formula (including thinner type) ______________________

____

Flake mix formula (including thinner type) ______________________

____

Clear coat formula (including thinner type) ______________________

____

Paint application:

Total number of color coats ______ Psi ______________________

Total number of flake coats ______ Psi ______________________

Total number of clear coats ______ Psi ______________________

Drying process:

Air ______ Force drying ______ Total drying time ______________

Checkup Questions

1. Which finish takes a higher application psi—a metallic or a metal flake? ______

   Why? ____

   ____

   ____

2. Why was step 15 necessary? ____

   ____

   ____

3. Describe the appearance of the panel both before and after the clear coats.

   ____

   ____

   ____

Date Completed ______________ Instructor's Signature ______________________

CANDY APPLE FINISH

Candy apple is an effect created by applying transparent color over a highly reflective ground coat, usually white or a metallic like gold or silver. The transparent material is the candy apple color. Basically it is clear mixed with a small amount of pigment. This minimal coloring allows light to pass through the top coat and bounce off the metallic or white surface below. The reflection through a clear tint is what gives a candy apple finish its distinctive look.

Candy apple comes in a half dozen different colors, not just red. It is applied in two extremely thin coats. These are cross-sprayed to insure uniformity (that is, the first coat is sprayed on from side to side, the second from top to bottom). The coats are kept to a minimum to avoid color buildup, which can occur very quickly even when such small amounts of pigment are involved. Three coats of candy apple, for example, contain enough color to interfere with light reflection off the ground coat.

To make a candy apple finish more candylike, a half dozen coats of clear are applied over the color. They are sprayed on not after the top coat has dried (as in the case of a metal flake finish) but right after it has flashed. Once the clear coats have been applied, however, the candy apple and metal flake procedures are basically the same.

OBJECTIVE 8-A3 (manipulative)

Working as a team with one other student and with the aid of Job Report Sheet 8-A3, you will apply a candy apple finish to a bare metal practice panel.

Time Recommended:

6 hours

Preparation:

1. Review pages 315 through 329.
2. Study pages 329 through 334.
3. Read the Safety Checklist on pages 347 and 348, items 1 and 3.

Tools and Materials:

1. Suction-feed spray guns (two—one for paint, one for primer-surfacer)
2. Duster gun
3. Polisher with both compounding and polishing pads
4. Respirator and safety goggles
5. Rubber gloves
6. Paint rack and strainers
7. Wooden stirring sticks
8. Hose (or sponge and bucket)
9. Sanding blocks (hard and sponge rubber)
10. Clean shop cloths
11. Metal conditioner

12. Lacquer primer-surfacer
13. Thinner (medium and high grades)
14. Acrylic lacquer paint (silver or gold metallic for ground coat)
15. Candy apple finish (color of choice)
16. Acrylic lacquer clear
17. Fast-drying reducer
18. Machine rubbing compound
19. Liquid polish
20. Selection of sandpapers (500A, 600A)
21. Tack cloth

Procedure:

1. Treat the panel with metal conditioner.
2. Mix and test spray the primer-surfacer. Apply three coats to the panel, allowing each to flash before applying the next one. Allow the primer-surfacer to dry for 30 minutes.
3. Using a 500A abrasive, wet sand the primer-surfacer. Wipe away any sanding residue with a moistened cloth and blow the panel dry.
4. Remove the panel to the spray booth. Give the primer-surfacer a final wipedown with fast-drying reducer.
5. Mix the color for the ground coat. Use the medium-grade thinner.
6. Set the transformer-regulator at 45 psi (35 psi at the gun) and test spray the mixture.
7. Tack the panel.
8. Apply two double coats of paint, allowing at least 4 minutes of flash time between them.
9. Allow the panel to air dry 1 hour or force dry for 30 minutes at a temperature of 165 degrees Fahrenheit. During this time, clean the spray gun.
10. Check the ground coat for imperfections. If any are found, wet sand with a 600A abrasive and a sponge rubber sanding block.
11. Compound the panel as needed to achieve a smooth, high gloss.
12. To remove all traces of the compounding and sanding operations, rinse the panel with water, wipe dry, and blow with a duster gun.
13. Mix the candy apple finish according to the directions on the container label.
14. Set the transformer-regulator at 45 psi (35 psi at the gun) and test spray the mixture.
15. Tack the ground coat.
16. Apply one single wet coat of the candy apple finish, moving from left to right across the panel and back again. Cross-spray the second coat immediately, while the first is still wet. Allow the panel to dry for 30 minutes.
17. While the candy apple tint is drying, clean the spray gun.
18. Mix 1 part clear with 2 parts high-grade thinner.
19. Using the same transformer-regulator setting as before, retest the spray gun and adjust the pattern as necessary.

20. Apply six coats of clear to the panel, allowing only flash time between them.
21. Allow the panel to air dry three days or force dry for 1 hour at a temperature of 165 degrees Fahrenheit.
22. Using a 600A abrasive and a sponge rubber sanding block, wet sand the panel. Rinse with water, wipe, and blow dry.
23. Machine compound the surface until a smooth gloss is visible. Then, to remove any trace of the compound, wash the panel with water, wipe dry, and polish.

JOB REPORT SHEET 8-A3

CANDY APPLE FINISH

Student Name ____________________ Date ____________

Time Started ____________ Time Finished ____________ Total Time ____________

Specifications

Ground coat: Type ____________ Color code ____________

Name of color ____________________

Candy apple coat: Color ____________________

Technique

Primer-surfacer: Type ____________ Color ____________

Reduction formula ____________________

Total number of coats ______ Psi ____________

Paint reduction:

Ground coat formula (including thinner type) ____________________

____

Candy apple formula (including thinner type) ____________________

____

Clear coat formula (including thinner type) ____________________

____

Paint application:

Total number of metallic coats ______ Psi ____________

Total number of candy apple coats ______ Psi ____________

Total number of clear coats ______ Psi ______

Drying Process:

Air ______ Force drying ______ Total drying time ____________

Checkup Questions

1. The ground coat for a candy apple finish consists of twice as many applications of paint as the ground coat for a metal flake finish. Why? ______________________

____

____

2. Why were steps 10 through 12 necessary? ______________________

____

____

Why weren't these same steps included in the metal flake procedure?

____

____

____

Date Completed ______________ Instructor's Signature ______________________

FIG 8-7
Pearlescent concentrate.
(Badger Air-Brush Co., *Air-Brushing Techniques for Custom Painting, Volume II*)

PEARLESCENT FINISH

A pearl, or pearlescent, finish is iridescent. Its basic color is white, but swirled through it are rainbowlike bands. These shift in pattern and hue as the viewer changes his position.

Pearlescent finishes come in two forms. One is a pastelike concentrate that must be thinned before use (Fig. 8-7). The other is a ready-to-spray liquid. The metallic element in both products is pearl dust suspended in binder. This ingredient makes a pearlescent finish the most expensive that can be applied to a vehicle.

Like most metallics, pearl is sprayed on over a ground coat. Usually this coat is white, although it need not be. Some interesting effects can be achieved by using darker colors. A red base coat, for example, gives the pearl a pink hue that shifts in intensity with the mother-of-pearl patterns. Adding a small amount of red to the pearl itself results in a more uniformly pink top coat.

Because pearl is so expensive, special pains must be taken to prepare a surface for its application. An old finish must be entirely removed if there is any concern about its durability. A good finish must be sealed if there are any doubts about its compatibility. The ground coat, once dry, must be carefully inspected and any trace of overspray or other imperfections eliminated. Before the pearl is applied, in other words, the surface must be as perfect as it is humanly possible to make it.

OBJECTIVE 8-A4 (manipulative)

Working as a team with one other student and with the aid of Job Report Sheet 8-A4, you will apply a pearlescent finish to a bare practice panel.

Time Recommended:

4 hours

Preparation:

1. Review pages 315 through 335.
2. Study pages 336 through 340.
3. Read the Safety Checklist on pages 347 and 348, items 1 and 3.

Tools and Materials:

1. Suction-feed spray guns (two—one for paint, one for primer-surfacer)
2. Duster gun
3. Polisher with both compounding and polishing pads
4. Respirator and safety goggles
5. Rubber gloves
6. Paint rack and strainer
7. Wooden stirring sticks
8. Hose (or sponge and bucket)
9. Sanding blocks (hard and sponge rubber)
10. Clean shop cloths
11. Metal conditioner
12. Lacquer primer-surfacer
13. Thinner (medium and high grades)
14. Acrylic lacquer paint (white for ground coat)
15. Pearl finish (either paste or ready-to-spray form)
16. Acrylic lacquer clear
17. Fast-drying reducer
18. Machine rubbing compound
19. Liquid polish
20. Selection of sandpapers (500A, 600A)
21. Tack cloth

Procedure:

1. Treat the panel with metal conditioner.
2. Mix and test spray the primer-surfacer. Apply three coats to the panel, allowing each to flash before applying the next one. Allow the primer-surfacer to dry for 30 minutes.
3. Using a 500A abrasive, wet sand the primer-surfacer. Wipe away any sanding residue with a moistened cloth and blow the panel dry.
4. Remove the panel to the spray booth. Give the primer-surfacer a final wipedown with fast-drying reducer.
5. Mix the color for the ground coat. Use the medium-grade thinner.
6. Set the transformer-regulator at 45 psi (35 psi at the gun) and test spray the mixture.
7. Tack the panel.
8. Apply two single coats of paint, allowing the first coat to flash before applying the second. Allow the panel to dry for 30 minutes.
9. While the ground coat is drying, clean the spray gun.
10. Check the ground coat for imperfections. If any are found, wet sand with a 600A abrasive and a sponge rubber sanding block.

11. Compound the panel as needed to achieve a smooth, high gloss.
12. To remove all traces of the compounding and sanding operations, rinse the panel with water, wipe dry, and blow with a duster gun.
13. Mix the pearl finish. Strain 2 ounces of clear and 4 ounces of medium-grade thinner into the spray gun cup. Add ¼ ounce of pearl paste and stir well. *Note:* Omit this step if using ready-to-spray pearl.
14. Set the transformer-regulator at 45 psi (35 psi at the gun) and test spray the mixture.
15. Tack the ground coat.
16. Apply one single wet coat of the pearl finish, moving from left to right across the panel and back again. Allow 30 minutes of drying time. Then cross-spray a second coat. *Note:* Between strokes, shake the spray gun to keep the pearl from settling out in the cup.
17. Allow the panel to air dry for 20 minutes. During this time, clean the spray gun.
18. Mix 1 part clear with 2 parts high-grade thinner.
19. Using the same transformer-regulator setting as before, retest the spray gun and adjust the pattern as necessary.
20. Apply four coats of clear to the panel, allowing 10 minutes of drying time between coats.
21. Allow the panel to air dry two days or force dry for 1 hour at a temperature of 165 degrees Fahrenheit.
22. Using a 600A abrasive and a sponge rubber sanding block, lightly wet sand the panel. Be sure not to cut through the clear. Rinse with water, wipe, and blow dry.
23. Machine compound the surface until a smooth gloss is visible. Then, to remove any trace of the compound, wash the panel with water, wipe dry, and polish.

JOB REPORT SHEET 8-A4

PEARLESCENT FINISH

Student Name ______________________________ Date ______________

Time Started ______________ Time Finished ______________ Total Time ______________

Specifications

Ground coat: Type ______________ Color code ______________

Name of color ______________________________

Pearl finish: Paste ______ Ready to spray ______

Manufacturer ______________ Product name ______________

Technique

Primer-surfacer: Type ______________ Color ______________

Reduction formula ______________________________

Total number of coats ______ Psi ______________

Paint reduction:

Ground coat formula (including thinner type) ______________________________

____

Pearl formula (including thinner type) ______________________________

____

Was the pearl tinted? ______ If yes, with how much color? ______________

____

Clear coat formula (including thinner type) ______________________________

____

Paint application:

Total number of color coats ______ Psi ______________

Total number of pearl coats ______ Psi ______________

Total number of clear coats ______ Psi ______________

Drying Process:

Air ______ Force drying ______ Total drying time ______________________

Checkup Questions

1. Why does pearl, unlike candy apple, require drying time between cross-sprayed coats? ____

____

____

2. Why does a pearl finish take fewer coats of clear than either a metal flake or a candy apple finish? ____

____

____

3. What was the price of the pearl material? ______________________

How does this figure compare with the cost of candy apple and metal flake?

____

____

____

Date Completed __________________ Instructor's Signature ______________________

FIG 8-8
Spatter finish.

WATER-BASED PAINT

Water-based paints are different from lacquers and enamels. They are, in fact, a separate family of products. What sets them apart, as their name implies, is their use of water as a reducing agent.

Exterior Finish

Water-based paints for vehicle exteriors were developed in the early 1970s. They had two main advantages.

1. *Water-based paints sharply reduced the fire hazard in the paint shop.* Mixing paint no longer required the use or storage of large amounts of thinner and reducer. The fumes from both of these products were thus eliminated and with them the risk of explosion.
2. *Water-based paints dried extremely fast.* A panel finished with water-based paint could be unmasked and the vehicle returned to its owner after only 1½ hours. This was an air-drying rate that compared favorably with acrylic lacquer.

In other respects, however, water-based paints proved unsatisfactory. They could not, for example, be used for spot repairs. The manufacturers recommended that a water-based finish itself be repaired with acrylic lacquer. As a result, by the early 1980s exterior water-based paints were no longer in general use.

Spatter Finish

The water-based paint developed for vehicle interiors has been more successful. Called spatter finish, it has a very distinctive appearance. It consists of a neutral carrying coat (usually gray, beige, or black) in which are suspended flecks of two or three contrasting colors (Fig. 8-8). For example, a gray spatter finish may have spots of red, green, and white pigment running through it.

Characteristics and Use

Spatter paints were designed for use in trunk interiors in the early 1960s and continued to be used for that purpose through the early 1970s. Today the finish is still available and is frequently employed for resurfacing truck beds. Although auto manufacturers no longer use it in new cars, the material continues to be popular for two reasons. First, it resists chipping. (When impacted, it tends to smudge rather than chip.) Second, when damage does occur, it is difficult to see in the speckled pattern of the finish.

Application Technique

Spatter paint comes in two forms—ready to spray in aerosol cans and concentrated for reduction in 1-quart containers. The reducing agent, of course, is water. A frequently used reduction formula is 2 parts paint to 1 part water. Under no circumstances should the material be strained. This procedure would break up or remove the pigmented particles floating in the carrying coat.

To match or make a spot repair to a spatter painted interior, the refinisher must consider two factors that do not enter into most other refinishing jobs.

1. *Spatter match.* All spot repairs require color matching, but in the case of a spatter finish there is more than one color to be matched. The shade of the carrying coat must be the same, of course; but then the refinisher must determine by visual inspection which spatter colors are present. As already noted, combinations of two or three are possible.
2. *Distance.* The size of the spatter pattern must be matched as well. This factor is controlled by the distance from which the paint is applied. Normally the spray gun is adjusted for maximum fluid and air flows. (In other words, both the fluid and the spreader valves are fully open.) If the gun is held too close under these circumstances (any distance under 12 inches), so much material hits the surface with such force that the specks of pigment are either driven into the carrying coat or pulverized. In either case, they disappear from view. To match most spatter finishes, therefore, the spray gun must be held between 12 and 16 inches from the panel.

OBJECTIVE 8-A5 (manipulative)

Working as a team with one other student and with the aid of Job Report Sheet 8-A5, you will apply a spatter finish to a bare metal practice panel.

Time Recommended:

1 hour

Preparation:

1. Review pages 315 through 342.
2. Study pages 342 through 346.
3. Read the Safety Checklist on pages 347 and 348, items 1 and 3.

Tools and Materials:

1. Suction-feed spray guns (two—one for paint, one for primer-surfacer)
2. Duster gun
3. Respirator and safety goggles
4. Rubber gloves
5. Wooden stirring sticks
6. Hose (or sponge and bucket)
7. Clean shop cloths
8. Metal conditioner
9. Lacquer primer-surfacer
10. Thinner
11. Water-based spatter paint
12. Fast-drying reducer
13. Sandpaper (400A)
14. Tack cloth
15. Masking paper or test panel
16. Lacquer solvent or gun cleaner

Procedure:

1. Treat the panel with metal conditioner.
2. Mix and test spray the primer-surfacer. Apply three coats to the panel, allowing each to flash before applying the next one. Allow the primer-surfacer to dry for 30 minutes.
3. Using a 400A abrasive, wet sand the primer-surfacer. Wipe away any sanding residue with a moistened cloth and blow the panel dry.
4. Remove the panel to the spray booth. Give the primer-surfacer a final wipedown with fast-drying reducer.
5. Mix 1 part water with 2 parts spatter paint. *Note:* Do not strain the paint.
6. Set the transformer-regulator at 45 psi (35 psi at the gun) and test spray the mixture. The fluid and spreader valve adjustments should be fully open and the gun positioned between 12 and 16 inches from the masking paper or test panel surface.
7. Once the gun is adjusted, use a fresh piece of masking paper to test the spatter effect. Hold the gun more than 16 inches from the test surface and spray the finish. Then reposition the gun 8 to 10 inches from the paper and do another test spraying. Note the results of both tests on Job Report Sheet 8-A5.
8. Tack the panel.
9. Apply the spatter finish in a single coat, using the ideal spraying distance of 12 to 16 inches. Move the gun slowly so that the material can build and the spatter effect be observed easily.
10. Allow the panel to dry 1½ hours.
11. Use water to clean all paint from the spray gun interior and exterior. Then backwash with solvent to force any moisture from the spray gun's passages.

JOB REPORT SHEET 8-A5

WATER-BASED PAINT (SPATTER FINISH)

Student Name ______________________ Date ______________

Time Started ______________ Time Finished ______________ Total Time ______________

Specifications

Spatter finish: Carrying coat color ______________________

Spatter color(s) ______________________

Technique

Primer-surfacer: Type ______________ Color ______________

Reduction formula ______________________

Total number of coats ______ Psi ______________________

Paint reduction: Reducing agent ______________________

Formula ______________________

Test spraying:

Results at more than 16 inches ______________________

____

____

Results at 8 to 10 inches ______________________

____

____

Paint application: Number of coats ______ Psi ______________________

Drying process:

Air ______ Force drying ______ Total drying time ______________

Checkup Questions

1. From what distance within the ideal 12- to 16-inch range was the spatter finish applied? ____________ Why was this distance selected? ____________

   ____

   ____

2. Why was water instead of solvent used to clean the spray gun (step 11)?

   ____

   ____

   ____

   Why was it necessary to follow the water cleaning with a solvent backwash?

   ____

   ____

   ____

Date Completed ____________ Instructor's Signature ____________

FIG 8-9
Sprayed vinyl finish.

VINYL FINISH

Vinyl finish is sprayed onto panels to make them look as though they are vinyl covered. When used in this manner, the material is not reduced. This procedure makes it possible for the finish to hold its application texture rather than flow smooth. Thus the finish goes on dimpled and dries that way (Fig. 8-9).

The dimpling is controlled entirely by spray painting technique. By holding the spray gun closer to the panel or increasing the pressure at the transformer-regulator, the refinisher can make the pattern smaller. By holding the gun farther from the panel or decreasing the pressure, he can make it larger. The illusion of real vinyl can be increased by applying the material over a special tape that looks like a sewed seam.

Being a lacquer product, vinyl finish dries quickly—in about 30 minutes. It also dries dull. Unlike other lacquer top coats, however, it is never sanded or compounded to bring it to a high gloss. Such efforts would destroy an essential part of its vinyl look. They would also level the texture so carefully created during spray painting.

In all other respects, simulated vinyl can be treated like the real thing. It can (and should) be washed regularly and waxed. When so cared for, it is as durable as true vinyl.

Vinyl finish can also be used to restore or dye vinyl installed by vehicle manufacturers. In such cases, it is not necessary for the paint to provide the texture. The existing vinyl already does that. When used in this manner, therefore, vinyl finish is reduced. The normal rate of reduction is 1 part paint to 2 parts thinner.

SAFETY CHECKLIST

Metallic Finishes:

1. The application of a special finish to a bare metal surface requires minimal sanding. All sanded surfaces, however, must at some point be blown with a duster gun. This procedure, no matter how minor the actual amount of cleaning to be done, requires the use of safety gear. Specifically, safety goggles must be worn whenever a duster gun is applied to a surface. Remember, any particle propelled by compressed air can do serious eye damage.

2. The flaked material used for a metal flake finish is extremely light. During application, a certain amount of it will scatter and attach itself to the clothes and skin of the person doing the spraying. In most cases, this situation is more inconvenient than hazardous. Special care, however, should be taken when removing flakes from the eye area. (They have a tendency to cling to the eyelashes and eyebrows.) Stray flakes here should be lifted rather than brushed off and the removal done in circumstances where the refinisher can see clearly what he is doing.

Other Finishes:

3. A respirator should be worn at all times when spray painting. This precaution is especially important, however, when applying vinyl finish. Vinyl paint contains ketones. These are extremely hazardous if inhaled even in small amounts and even over short periods. Therefore, exposure time should be kept to a minimum when working with vinyl finish. Ventilation should be kept at a maximum. A respirator must be worn during spraying, and its use during mixing and cleanup procedures is also recommended.

OBJECTIVE 8-A6 (manipulative)

Working as a team with one other student and with the aid of Job Report Sheet 8-A6, you will apply vinyl finish to a bare metal practice panel. *Note:* If the necessary materials are available, you will create two seams either across the body of the panel or along two of its edges.

Time Recommended:

2 hours

Preparation:

1. Review pages 315 through 348.
2. Study pages 348 through 352.
3. Read the Safety Checklist on pages 347 and 348, items 1 and 3.

Tools and Materials:

1. Suction-feed spray guns (two—one for paint, one for primer-surfacer)
2. Duster gun
3. Respirator and safety goggles
4. Rubber gloves
5. Wooden stirring sticks
6. Hose (or sponge and bucket)
7. Clean shop cloths
8. Knife or single-edged razor (optional)
9. Metal conditioner
10. Lacquer primer-surfacer
11. Thinner
12. Vinyl finish

13. Fast-drying reducer
14. Sandpaper (400A)
15. Seam tape (optional)
16. Tack cloth
17. Masking paper or test panel
18. Masking tape (optional)

Procedure:

1. Treat the panel with metal conditioner.
2. Mix and test spray the primer-surfacer. Apply three coats to the panel, allowing each to flash before applying the next one. Allow the primer-surfacer to dry for 30 minutes.
3. Using a 400A abrasive, wet sand the primer-surfacer. Wipe away any sanding residue with a moistened cloth and blow the panel dry.
4. Remove the panel to the spray booth. Give the primer-surfacer a final wipedown with fast-drying reducer.
5. If seam tape is available, apply it across the panel or along two of its edges. Measure and mark with masking tape the beginning and end points for each seam. Apply the tape at one end of the panel and, without stretching it, extend it to the other end. Cut the tape with a knife or single-edged razor and apply it at the second mark. Then press the tape in place along its full length. Remove the pieces of masking tape used as guides.
6. Open and stir the vinyl paint. Then pour the material, without reduction or straining, into the spray gun cup.
7. Set the transformer-regulator at 55 psi (45 psi at the gun) and test spray the paint. The fluid and spreader valve adjustments should be fully open and the gun positioned between 10 and 12 inches from the masking paper or test panel surface.
8. Once the gun is adjusted, use a fresh piece of masking paper to test the dimple effect. Hold the gun more than 12 inches from the test surface and spray the finish. Then reposition the gun so that it is 6 to 8 inches from the paper and do another test spraying. Note the results of both tests on Job Report Sheet 8-A6.
9. Tack the panel.
10. Apply the vinyl finish in one even coat, using the ideal spraying distance of 10 to 12 inches. Overlap each stroke only 1 to 1½ inches, not the standard 50 percent.
11. Allow the panel to dry 30 minutes.

VINYL FINISH

Student Name ______________________ Date ____________

Time Started ____________ Time Finished ____________ Total Time ____________

Specifications

Vinyl finish: Type ____________ Color code ____________

Name of color ______________________

Seam tape: Yes ______ No ______

Technique

Primer-surfacer: Type ____________ Color ____________

Reduction formula ______________________

Total number of coats ______ Psi ____________

Test spraying:

Results at more than 12 inches ______________________

____

____

Results at 6 to 8 inches ______________________

____

____

Paint application: Number of coats ______ Psi ____________

Drying process:

Air ______ Force drying ______ Total drying time ____________

Seam tape (optional):

In the space below, sketch the panel and, using a dotted line, show the placement of the false seams.

Checkup Questions

1. Compare the finished panel with a factory-installed vinyl roof. In what, if any, ways are the two surfaces different? ______________________________

____

____

____

2. The application psi for vinyl paint is higher than that for any other finish in the unit. Why? ______________________________

____

____

Date Completed ______________ Instructor's Signature ______________________

Name ______________________________ Date ______________

DIRECTIONS: Circle the best answer to each question.

1. All of the following colors make good ground coats EXCEPT
   A. white.
   B. gold.
   C. silver.
   D. gray.

2. Which technique makes controlling metallic easy?
   I. One-gun method of spray painting
   II. Two-gun method of spray painting
   A. I only B. II only C. Both I and II D. Neither I nor II

3. The owner of a van with a custom interior brings the vehicle into the paint shop. He wants a metal flake finish applied to the exterior.
   Refinisher I suggests that this finish is the most expensive he could have chosen and advises him to settle for something cheaper.
   Refinisher II suggests that this finish is not intended for use on a road vehicle and advises him to choose something more durable.
   Who is right?
   A. I only B. II only C. Both I and II D. Neither I nor II

4. The material shown at the right must be
   A. stirred carefully to avoid breakage.
   B. stirred between coats to avoid settling.
   C. applied very wet in double coats.
   D. applied at a distance of 14 to 16 inches.

5. Which could probably not exist in green?
   A. A convertible refinished in metallic paint
   B. A display model motorcycle finished in metal flake
   C. A truck bed repainted with a spatter finish
   D. A simulated vinyl roof

6. All of the following claims for exterior water-based paint were true EXCEPT
   A. easy to use for spot repairs.
   B. reduced fire hazards in the shop.
   C. cleaned up with water.
   D. dried like lacquer.

7. Which requires no compounding?
   I. Spatter paint
   II. Vinyl finish
   A. I only B. II only C. Both I and II D. Neither I nor II

8. Which terms are incorrectly paired?
   A. Metallic—tinted flakes
   B. Candy apple—tinted clear
   C. Water-based paint—specks of color
   D. Pearlescent finish—rainbow colors

9. All of the following finishes require a reflective ground coat EXCEPT
   A. metallic.
   B. metal flake.
   C. candy apple.
   D. pearlescent.

10. In the course of refinishing the right front fender of a vehicle in metallic blue, it is found that the color is going on too light.
    Refinisher I insists that the only way to correct the problem is by using a slower stroke.
    Refinisher II insists that the only way to correct the problem is by opening the spreader valve a little more.
    Who is right?
    A. I only B. II only C. Both I and II D. Neither I nor II

11. Which is cross-sprayed onto a surface?
    I. Candy apple
    II. Pearl
    A. I only B. II only C. Both I and II D. Neither I nor II

12. To make a spot repair to a trunk interior finished with spatter paint, the refinisher must match all of the following EXCEPT
    A. the color of the carrying coat.
    B. the colors of the flecks suspended in the carrying coat.
    C. the angle at which the original finish was sprayed.
    D. the distance at which the original finish was sprayed.

13. The purpose of applying several coats of clear over a new finish is to
    I. add depth and gloss.
    II. eliminate compounding and polishing.
    A. I only B. II only C. Both I and II D. Neither I nor II

14. Which combines a small amount of color with a binder?
   A. Clear
   B. A mist coat
   C. Candy apple
   D. Metal flake

15. All of the following are applied with a standard 50-percent overlap EXCEPT
   A. a gold metallic finish.
   B. a silver metal flake finish.
   C. a red pearlescent finish.
   D. a gray spatter finish.

16. A metallic finish with the flake distribution shown at the right would be
   A. too dark.
   B. too light.
   C. just right.
   D. mottled.

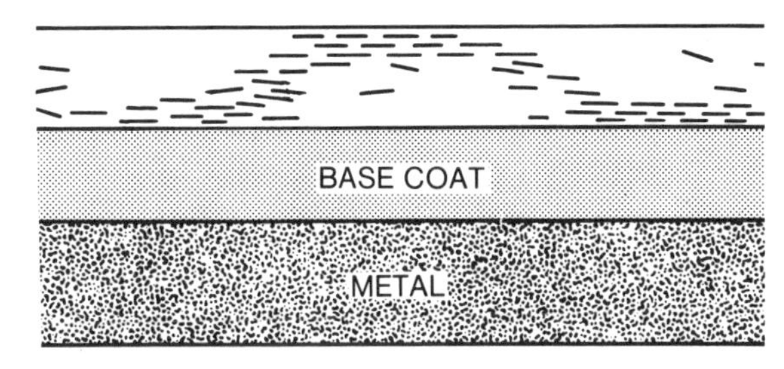

17. Which material is applied in the fewest coats?
   A. Candy apple
   B. Pearl
   C. Metallic
   D. Metal flake

18. A pearlescent finish owes its effect to
   I. light reflecting off a mother-of-pearl ground coat.
   II. pearl dust suspended in clear.

   A. I only   B. II only   C. Both I and II   D. Neither I nor II

19. If a spatter finish is sprayed onto a trunk interior from a distance of less than 10 inches, the result will be
   A. mottling.
   B. a flat color.
   C. a light color.
   D. a rough, dimpled texture.

20. Which finish takes the largest number of clear coats?
   A. Metallic
   B. Candy apple
   C. Pearlescent
   D. Vinyl

Score ______________ Instructor's Signature ______________________

unit 9

Custom Finishes and Effects

The refinisher may apply a large variety of creative finishes and decals. These designs are applied over a completely finished and compounded paint job. To protect and hold down the custom finish, multiple coats of clear are applied over the top. This gives the completed finish the look of one smooth, continuous coat of paint.

This unit introduces customizing techniques. The first section consists of simple effects such as decaling, some kinds of striping, and two-tone work. Some of these effects are available as options from automobile manufacturers. They also can be added to any vehicle at any time by a refinisher.

The second category consists of the more unusual and imaginative effects. Many of these involve the use of a stencil of some kind to create a design. The lace effect is a particularly striking example of this technique.

The remaining effects are done freehand. They include the application of cobwebbing, custom wood-graining, and smoke.

The techniques included here are within the reach of any student of automobile refinishing. If used with imagination and a willingness to experiment, they can produce effects of remarkable beauty.

When you master the techniques in this unit, you will be ready to attempt a mural. Murals are pictures that are painted on body panels with a combination of stencil and freehand airbrush techniques.

OBJECTIVE 9-A (written)

After doing the reading and shop exercises, you will be able to answer correctly without reference material a minimum of 14 out of 20 test questions on the following topics:

1. Custom painting equipment and materials
2. Vinyl decals and their application
3. Lace and other stenciling effects
4. Striping
5. Two-tone finishes
6. Freehand rendering of wood-grain, smoke, and cobwebbing patterns.

EQUIPMENT USED FOR CUSTOM WORK

Custom paint work frequently is accomplished, when working on large areas, by the use of a regular suction-feed spray gun or a small touch-up gun. More delicate spraying is done with an airbrush (Fig. 9-1).

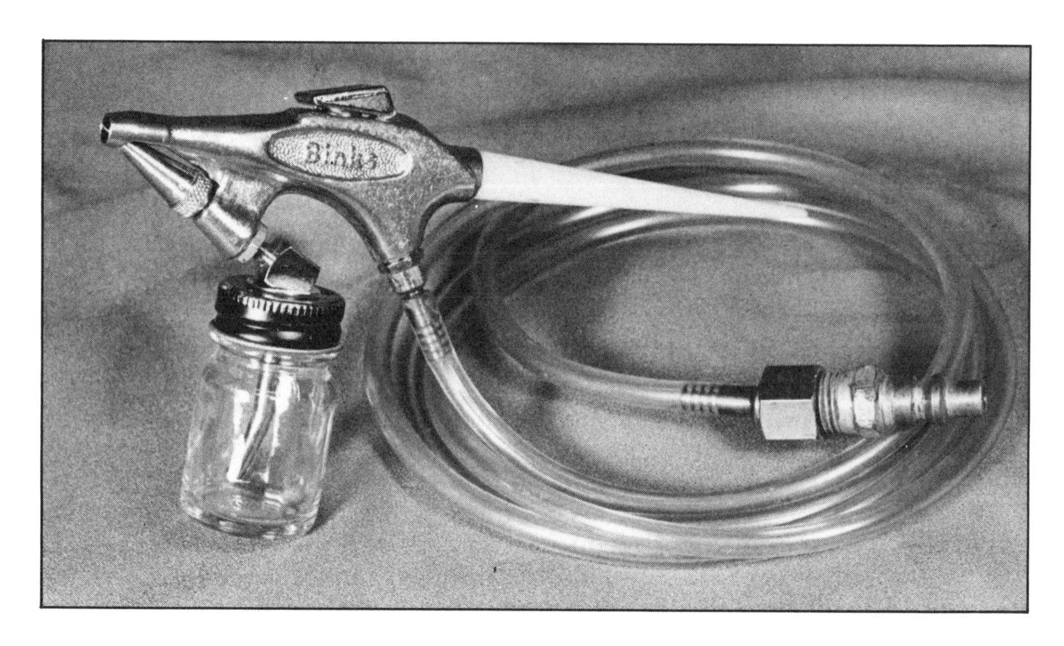

FIG 9-1
Custom-painting airbrush.
(Binks Manufacturing Company)

Using an Airbrush

The airbrush is a versatile piece of equipment which sprays a round pattern as small as a sixteenth of an inch or as large as an inch and a half. The gun is adjustable by turning the spray regulator near the tip of its head.

The airbrush is in fact a small suction-feed spray gun which uses either a small metal color cup or several sizes of glass color bottles with suction-vented caps. The metal cup is used to deposit very small amounts of color, as in photo retouching and fine artwork. The glass jars are used to apply larger amounts of color.

The airbrush trigger controls the amount of material applied to the work surface. Less pressure on the trigger gives a lighter spray. Adding pressure gives a heavier spray.

With trigger control, the airbrusher can apply various shades of the color in the cup. For example, if you are airbrushing blue over a white surface, you can achieve light blue with a lighter spray. This saves the time of mixing separate shades of blue. You may use trigger control for unlimited special effects, including the following:

1. To soften the edges of an airbrushed design.
2. To give a transparent look, such as looking through a window, water, clouds, or fog.
3. To shade a three-dimensional object.
4. To gradually change colors; for example, from blue to green, the transition area has both light blue and light green spray.

Airbrush Maintenance

You must clean the airbrush as soon as you finish using the tool to keep the paint from drying in the tool's passages.

The airbrush is back-washed in the same manner as any suction-feed spray gun. Simply placing a finger over the spray tip forces the solvent back through the brush and out the vent on the color bottle's cap. There is no need to disassemble the airbrush for cleaning if enough solvent is back-washed through it after every use.

The bottles, caps, spray tips, and metal color cup may be brushed clean of material with the paint gun brush filled with solvent before the airbrush is back-washed.

Remember that the airbrush is a delicate tool. All filling, cleaning, and maintenance of the airbrush is done over a cloth spread on a worktable. This helps keep track of the small parts and helps avoid damage to the spray head, tip, plastic body, or trigger.

Airbrush Practice Procedure

1. Using acrylic lacquer or acrylic enamel thinned one part paint to two parts solvent, set regulator pressure at 15 psi.
2. Spray a test pattern on masking paper. If the pattern is grainy, add a little more solvent and check the pattern again.
3. On a piece of 36-inch-wide paper taped to the side of the spray booth, practice spraying straight strokes to produce straight lines.
4. Practice spraying curved lines, making each successive curved line nest outside, or around, the previous curved line.
5. Make a series of circles, shading their inside edges to make them look like spheres.
6. Draw a pipe by connecting two parallel lines, painted 4 inches apart with a half circle at one end and a complete circle at the other.
7. Apply dark shading to the lower edge of the pipe and shade the upper edge lightly. Do this by using variable trigger pressures.
8. Shade the circle end of the pipe, heavily in the lower part of the circle, and more lightly as you move upward, ending the shading as you reach the half-way point of the circle.
9. Clean the airbrush.

PREPARING SURFACES FOR CUSTOM PAINT

No matter what sort of custom effect you plan to apply, always begin with a completely rubbed out and finished surface. Clean the panel thoroughly with grease and wax remover if the panel has not been freshly painted.

Never touch the clean panel with your hands. Oil from your skin and hair will cause disruptions in the paint surface called fisheyes. If these appear you must wipe the panel clean and start over.

Remove trim and nameplates using a small screwdriver or a wrench. Mask off the areas that will not receive the custom treatment.

PAINT USED IN CUSTOM WORK

Because custom painting almost always requires the use of more than one color of paint, fast-drying materials are highly favored. They allow color changes to be made rapidly, without the painter having to resort to force-drying.

Acrylic lacquer and acrylic enamel both are favored by custom paint artists. Both dry rapidly and are available in clear that can be applied over custom work.

For some custom work the painter may use an artist's acrylic paint to achieve certain effects. This material is reduced with water and dries fast. It is top sealed with clear acrylic lacquer or acrylic enamel.

Acrylic lacquer, when used over lacquer for custom work, has excellent durability. The thinner used for the color has high solvency and forms an ideal bond between the existing paint and the custom work. When acrylic lacquer is applied over factory-baked enamel, however, it does not have ideal bonding, because the solvent will not soften the factory-baked enamel.

If acrylic lacquer is applied over air-dried enamel such as that on a newly refinished vehicle, the enamel must be completely cured. If not, lifting will occur when the solvent is absorbed into the enamel.

Acrylic enamel, when used for custom work, has ideal bonding with all types of automotive enamels. A true acrylic enamel is made with some materials similar to those in lacquer. It bonds to lacquer well enough to be durable for a long time.

Artist's acrylic color bonds well and has good durability when applied to any clean surface.

Sealing Custom Work with Clear

When one or two thin color coats are used in the custom job, use two to four coats of clear of the same type material as the color. The clear acts as a sealer for the color and increases its durability and gloss.

For the best results, the clear used must be made especially for use over the type of color used for the custom work—lacquer over lacquer color, acrylic enamel over acrylic enamel color, etc.

Clears are compounded to achieve extra gloss. As long as the clear coat is thick enough, the fragile custom color is not disturbed by this compounding. As we will see, the clear must be thinned or reduced properly and sprayed on in even, medium-wet coats with a perfectly clean spray gun.

The recommended drying time between coats for the clear must be followed. Overwetting of clear lacquer over lacquer color can damage the custom color work.

Baking Custom Painting

There is no great advantage to force drying custom work with a heat lamp or baking oven, unless there is a deadline by which the clear must be compounded.

Force drying allows compounding as soon as the panel has cooled to room temperature.

If either acrylic enamel or acrylic lacquer is to be baked, no additives should be used with the color or the clear. When baking either of these materials, follow these steps:

1. Allow the clear at least 5 minutes flash time before applying heat when the ambient temperature is between 70 to 90 degrees, and 10 minutes if the temperature is below 70.
2. Heat custom work for 20 minutes if the temperature is 70 degrees or more, 30 minutes if it is less than 70 degrees. If the heating element being used has a temperature setting adjustment, it should be set for 165 degrees.

Acrylic materials force dried in this manner will be as dry as similar materials subjected to 24 hours of regular drying time in the open air. The finish force dried in this manner may be compounded without worry of damage to the finish.

DECALS

Decalcomania is a term used to describe the many types of decals or transfer materials used on automobiles. These materials may render a wood-grain, flames, eagles, or a blend of many colors in large stripes. They may be relatively small; they may be large enough to cover an entire fender, door, or hood panel.

As with other types of custom application, the first step is to thoroughly clean the panel(s) being worked on with wax and grease remover. If the panel has just been painted and compounded, it must be cleaned well with water and wiped dry with a clean cloth.

There are three types of decals. The first type has a white paper covering the finished side, the second has a peel-off covering on its back side, and the third is the old-fashioned type that has the white paper on the back side.

Applying Paper-Covered Decals

To install the first type, start with a large container of water to which has been added a liberal amount of liquid dish soap. Spread this soapy water on the area where you intend to apply the decal. Put the decal on the panel where you want it. The soapy water will help you move the decal around so that you get it perfectly positioned. Keep the outer paper film wet by applying soapy water to it with a squeegee. As the work progresses, the paper dissolves and its fragments are removed.

When the paper is gone, make sure the decal is pulled straight, is positioned properly, and is still being kept wet. Use the squeegee to work any remaining bubbles out from under the decal. Any bubbles that cannot be removed with the squeegee should be popped with a pin and smoothed down.

The decal is now given a final once-over with the squeegee and allowed to dry.

Applying Peel-Off Decals

The second type of decal, also called the "glue-on" type, is frequently used for wood-grain (Fig. 9-2). Be sure to apply this type of decal carefully and accurately the first time. It is almost impossible to remove the decal for a second try.

FIG 9-2
Wood-grain station wagon panels. (Chrysler Corporation)

First, unroll the decal and lay it against the panel. Make light reference marks on both decal and panel, top and bottom, every few inches. Then, starting at one edge of the decal, begin peeling back a small area of the material covering the decal's sticky back side. Make sure the decal is properly positioned, especially as you begin. As you peel the back, apply a small area of the decal to the panel. Press it smoothly into place with a rubber squeegee. When the first area of the decal is in place, roll 3 or 4 more inches of the back side material off the decal and press more of the decal into place. Make certain you work without stretching the decal or causing wrinkles. Continue until you have applied the entire decal.

Clear may be applied over this second type of decal to tack down its edges and give it depth.

Wood-grain transfers may also be installed using detergent to slow down the sticking of the glue and allow getting the transfer into position before it sticks firmly to the car. To use this method, rub the surface of the car with a cloth soaked in liquid dishwashing detergent. The surface should be slippery, but not soaked. Remove the backing from the transfer and put it into position on the door. As the detergent dries, the transfer will start to stick in place. With the right amount of detergent, the transfer should start to stick in place by the time you have it in the correct position. Some wood-grain transfers require a heat gun to shape them around door edges or make them conform to body contours.

Applying Paper-Backed Decals

The third type of decal is familiar to anyone who has ever built a model car, boat, or plane from a kit. This decal is usually soaked in water until the design loosens from the paper backing. Then slide the design carefully off the backing into place on the car. Smooth it and get all the air bubbles and wrinkles out without tearing the design. After it dries, spray it with clear to prevent water from washing it off. This original type of decal is not used much because the design is on a very thin film that damages easily.

Do not apply heat to force dry decals. Heat may damage the decal material and cause blisters.

OBJECTIVE 9-A1 (manipulative)

Working as a team with two other students and with the aid of Job Report 9-A1, you will apply a wood-grain decal to a body panel.

Time Recommended:
3 hours

Preparation:

1. Review pages 357 through 362.
2. Study pages 362 through 365.
3. Attend classroom discussion.

Tools and Materials:

1. Socket set ¼ or ⅜ drive
2. Screwdrivers: Phillips, plain, and/or posi-drive

3. Vibrator or orbital sander
4. Sandpaper selection 80D, 280A, 320A, 500A, 600A
5. Enamel reducer
6. Tack cloth
7. Primer-surfacer (mixed in spray gun)
8. Suction-feed spray gun, for color
9. Acrylic lacquer color (to match vehicle)
10. Sanding bucket, or water hose
11. Clean shop cloths, and masking materials
12. Wood-grain decal material
13. Squeegee (thick rubber block)
14. Sewing needle, or long straight pin
15. Clear acrylic lacquer (or clear that may be included in the decal package)
16. Lacquer thinner

Procedure:

1. Remove mouldings and clips if decal is bordered by mouldings.
2. Use normal sanding and priming steps as required for lacquer, including final wipe down with reducer, and tacking.
3. After panel has been properly filled with primer-surfacer and sanded smooth, apply the lacquer color using the normal methods.
4. After the recommended air dry, or after force drying is complete, scuff sand the panel with 600A and machine compound it to a smooth gloss.
5. With a cloth moist with water, wipe the panel clean. Then dry it with a clean cloth.
6. Place the decal on the panel with the backing still on it. Align the decal to the panel, marking decal and panel top and bottom every few inches.
7. With the decal held in place, apply masking tape on the panel next to the upper edge of the decal if you need a horizontal reference. *Note:* Do not allow the tape to stick to the decal, but make sure that it is at the edge of the decal.
8. Remove two to three inches of the backing from decal at one end. Allow ¼ inch of the decal to extend past the end of the panel. Make sure it is aligned with the tape on the panel. Press the end of it smoothly to the panel.
9. Work out any wrinkles with a rubber squeegee as you work toward the other end of the panel. Keep the backing removed just ahead of the work as you progress along the panel.
10. With a pin or needle, puncture any bubbles in the decal and work the air from them by pressing with the squeegee until they are smooth.
11. Make sure that the decal is clean and dry. Then tack and spray it with clear.
12. Clear may be scuff sanded with 600A and compounded for extra gloss, if needed, after it is dry.
13. Install moulding clips and mouldings. Wipe the moulding clean when installation is complete.

DECAL INSTALLATION

Student Name ______________________________ Date ______________

Time Started ______________ Time Completed ______________ Total Time ______________

Specifications

Type of panel ______________________________

Type of paint on panel ______________________________

Type of decal (wood-grain or other) ______________________________

____

Type of clear ______________________________

Technique

Method used for cleaning panel ______________________________

____

Method of marking edge of decal location ______________________________

____

Were air bubbles removed by pin? ______ Yes ______ No

Was rubber squeegee used? ______ Yes ______ No

Checkup Questions

1. Was decal alignment correct? ______ Yes ______ No
2. Were all air bubbles removed? ______ Yes ______ No
3. How many clear coats were used? ______
4. Was compounding used? ______ Yes ______ No

Date Completed ______________ Instructor's Signature ______________________

FIG 9-3
Body stripe. (Chrysler Corporation)

STRIPING

Striping—both with paint and with vinyl tape—is used in custom work and in refinishing operations. New cars and light trucks have been rolling out of the factories for several years now wearing stripes (Fig. 9-3). Custom-painted pin stripes also are being applied both to new cars and to custom-refinished older cars.

There are advantages to the painted stripe over the vinyl tape stripe. The painted stripe does not expand and contract and break as the vinyl stripe can when subjected to extreme temperature differences. In most painted stripe jobs, it is not necessary to apply clear over the stripes. Also, most refinishers can apply painted stripes in approximately the same time it would take to apply the factory kit of vinyl striping. Finally, vinyl stripes in original factory designs must be ordered through a car dealer who sells the kind of car you're working on.

Vinyl stripes, on the other hand, are handy and effective because applying paint stripes requires a good deal of practice and skill. To apply tape stripes, you need the skill to apply the tape and the ability to apply clear over the tape.

If clear is not applied over vinyl tape, breaking or lifting of the ends of the tape can occur after it has been exposed to the elements.

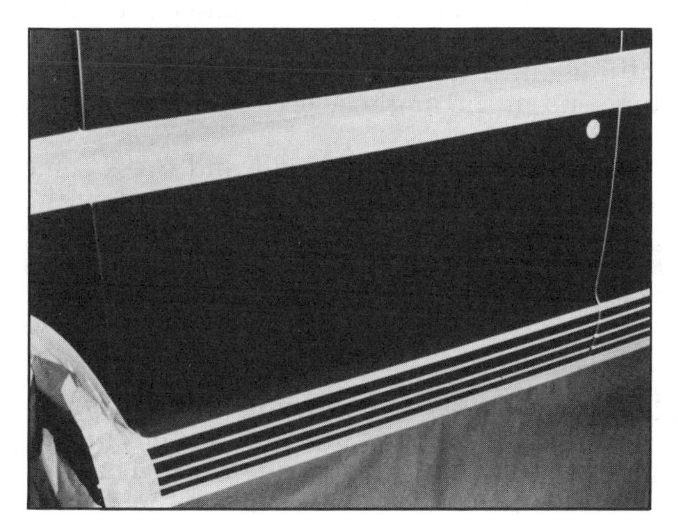

FIG 9-4
Rocker panel striping. (Badger Air-Brush Co., *Air-Brushing Techniques for Custom Painting, Volume II*)

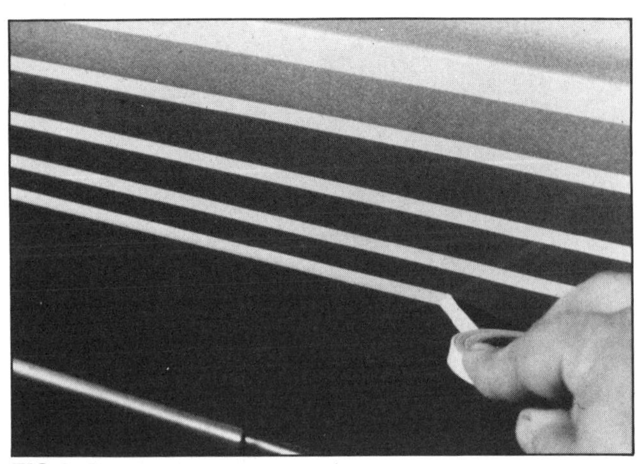

FIG 9-5 Applying tape to panel.
(Badger Air-Brush Co., *Air-Brushing Techniques for Custom Painting, Volume II*)

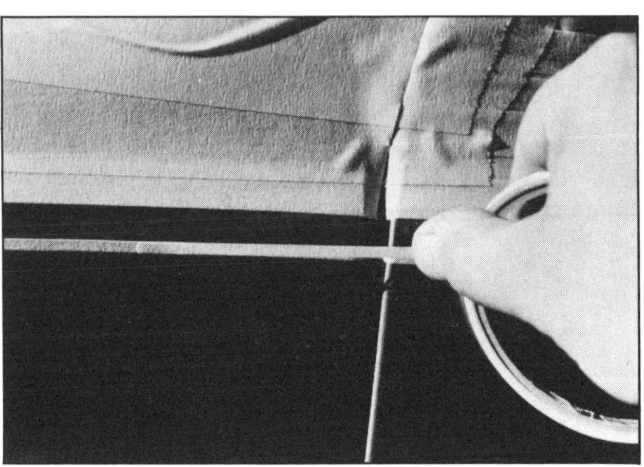

FIG 9-6 Pressing tape to panel.
(Badger Air-Brush Co., *Air-Brushing Techniques for Custom Painting, Volume II*)

The stripes can be in the form of the LeMans or "racing" stripe—one or two bold stripes running down the entire length of the car. They can run along the rocker panels between the wheel wells (Fig. 9-4). They can be, as mentioned, pin stripes which accent the car's lines and styling. Stripes should always complement the car's body style. They should never run in opposing directions to the creases that make up the sheet metal styling.

When stripes are applied to an original factory finish, the area to be striped must be thoroughly cleaned with grease and wax remover, compounded, wiped down with a fast-drying enamel reducer, and dusted with a tack cloth.

Tape Stripes

Tape stripes nearly always are applied in straight lines which follow body contours. They are extremely easy to apply. First, cut one end of the tape to the angle desired—square or diagonal, as best suits your customizer's eye—and attach that end of the tape firmly where you want the stripe to begin. Unroll a section of tape several feet long and pull it taut—but not so taut as to stretch it. With the tape pulled taut and held close to the panel, gently apply it to the panel (Fig. 9-5). Gently go back over it, rubbing it with a finger, to make sure it is stuck to the panel securely. Continue on in the same fashion until the tape line is complete. Cut the tape end at the angle desired and firmly affix it to the panel.

Following curves with tape stripes is more difficult and takes some practice. Work with just a short section of tape at a time. Follow the curve with the tape, pressing the tape onto the panel with a finger every quarter inch or so (Fig. 9-6). Make sure that the tape curve follows a smooth line, and that the tape surface itself does not bend or buckle.

Painted Stripes

Painted stripes can be applied in straight lines by using pre-cut striping tape. This is like regular masking tape, but it has been die-cut at several different widths. Apply the full-width tape to a surface. Then lift and remove a die-cut section of tape to expose a stripe of the desired width. The areas on either side of that now exposed stripe of base color should be masked. Then wipe the exposed area with enamel reducer, tack, and spray with two coats of the desired color.

An alternative method is to spray the panel the color of the finished stripe. Let it dry completely and compound it. Apply masking tape in the desired width along the panel. Pull the tape tight and make sure the edges of the tape are fully stuck down. Now wipe with enamel reducer, tack, and spray the panel with two coats of a color that contrasts with the base color (Fig. 9-7). Allow it to dry and remove the tape.

One form of pinstriping is done in a similar way, using eighth-inch or thinner masking tape. Spray the entire panel with the desired base color. Dry and compound the panel. Then use eighth-inch or thinner masking tape to mask a straight or curved line (Fig. 9-8). Spray two coats of the desired color coat over the panel. When the tape is removed, the undercoat, or base coat, will shine through as a stripe.

Using a Sword Brush for Pinstripes

The classic method of applying pinstripes involves use of some specialized materials. One is a *sword brush*—a short, small brush with long, soft bristles that when wet come to a fine point. The other is a paint such as One Shot lettering paint that covers in one coat. It also involves use of some sort of painter's palette, necessary because you will mix the paint and the thinner on the palette with the brush. Holding the sword brush as you'd hold a pencil, dip it into a small container of the paint you're using and deposit that paint onto the palette. By the same method deposit some thinner into the paint on the palette. Mix the two so that the paint is neither so thin that it runs easily nor so thick that it causes the brush to drag excessively or skip on a test panel. When the paint is the proper consistency—and this is something that can only be determined through trial and error—draw the brush along a test panel to make a stripe, holding the brush between your thumb and first two fingers, just as you would hold a pencil. Steady your hand and control your hand's distance from the panel by extending your little finger and, using it as a guide, pulling it along the panel. The more pressure you put on the brush, the wider the stripe will be.

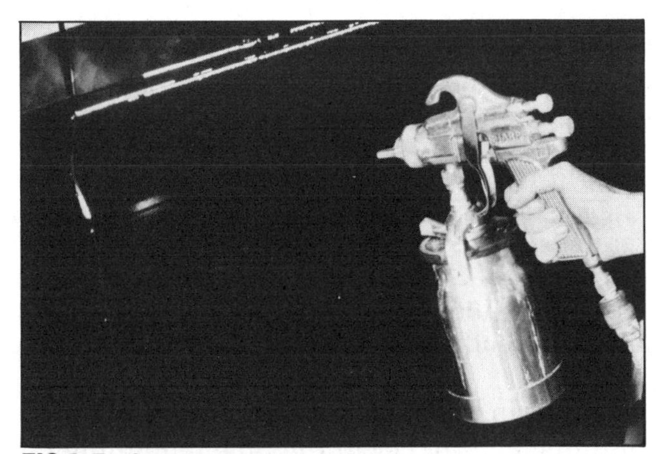

FIG 9-7 Spraying over tape to create stripe. (Badger Air-Brush Co., *Air-Brushing Techniques for Custom Painting, Volume II*)

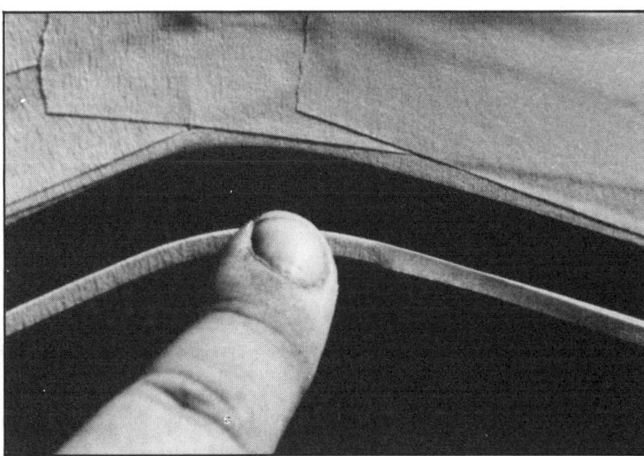

FIG 9-8 Masking a curved line. (Badger Air-Brush Co., *Air-Brushing Techniques for Custom Painting, Volume II*)

A striping (sword) brush filled with properly reduced paint can make an eighth-inch stripe 36 inches or more long in the hands of a skilled striping artist. The advantages of this method are that each stripe job is unique. The paint is very durable and does not need coats of clear over it.

OBJECTIVE 9-A2 (manipulative)

Working as a team with one other student and with the aid of Job Report 9-A2, you will use pre-cut striping tape to make a curved pinstripe border along two edges of a practice panel. Then you will fill in the center of the panel with painted stripes that are straight, of gradually decreasing widths, and rendered in at least two colors.

Time Recommended:

2 hours

Preparation:

1. Review pages 357 through 370.
2. Study pages 370 through 373.
3. Attend classroom discussion.
4. Observe demonstration of masking for stripes.

Tools and Materials:

1. Practice panel already painted with lacquer paint
2. Roll of pre-cut striping tape
3. Roll of regular ¾-inch masking tape
4. Masking paper
5. Airbrush, small touch up gun or regular paint spray gun
6. Two colors of lacquer paint
7. Enamel reducer
8. Tack cloth

Procedure:

1. Apply the end of the pre-cut tape 2 inches from the top of the panel. Allow the end to extend slightly past the edge of the panel where you start. Press the end firmly into place and unroll the tape, holding it in a straight line. Pull the tape taut with one hand, and press it down to the surface of the panel with the other hand. As you approach the panel's opposite edge, curve the tape so that it follows the second edge.
2. Remove the ⅛-inch pre-cut section from the tape you've just applied by separating it at the end you extended past the panel's edge.
3. Remove the 1/16-inch pre-cut strip in the same manner.
4. Apply masking tape and masking paper to the tape remaining on the panel on both sides of the stripe masking.
5. Wipe the exposed area to be painted with enamel reducer, dry it, and tack it.

6. Set the regulator at 20 psi. Reduce the material one part paint to two parts thinner. Apply two coats of lacquer color, allowing the first coat to flash before application of the second.
7. Make larger, parallel stripes on the same panel by removing additional parts of the pre-cut tape or by masking with ¼-, ½- or ¾-inch tape.
8. Mask over the painted areas, change color, and make straight, wide stripes.
9. Apply a piece of pre-cut tape. After removing the pre-cut section, curve the outer pieces so they meet each other, so the stripe will come to a point. Use a single-edged razor blade or a frisket knife to remove any tape necessary.
10. Apply clear lacquer, dry, and compound it. This will help remove any undesirable rough edges from a stripe. Use regular lacquer drying times.

APPLICATION OF PIN STRIPES

Student Name ______________________ Date ______________

Time Started ______________ Time Finished ______________ Total Time ______________

Specifications

Size of panel ______________ Background color ______________

Color of stripe: ______________ First color ______________ Second color

Psi of air: at regulator ______________ at gun ______________

Technique

Number of color coats used for stripe ______________________

Paint number of stripe colors ______________________

Was enamel reducer used? ______ Yes ______ No

Number of stripes on the panel: ______ Curved ______ Straight

Checkup Questions

1. Were stripe edges smooth and well-defined? ______ Yes ______ No
2. Which of the tapes worked best for you for striping? ______________
3. Were curves and points made uniformly? ______ Yes ______ No
4. Which of the choice of spray equipment given was used? ______________

   ______________________ Why? ______________________

   ____

Date Completed ______________ Instructor's Signature ______________________

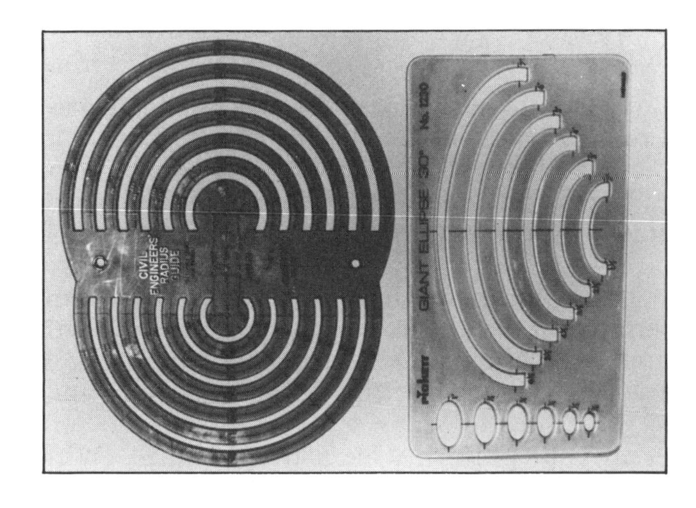

FIG 9-9
Drafting stencils. (Badger Air-Brush Co., *Air-Brushing Techniques for Custom Painting, Volume II*)

STENCILS

Stencils can play a large role in custom refinishing. Commercially made number and letter stencils are available at your paint jobber's, as are those that yield some geometric designs and effects. But special designs and custom scenes must be handmade.

Using Common Items as Stencils

Many common items can be used as stencils. One example is pressing a grinding disc's smooth back side against a panel and spraying through the center of the disc to make a dot. An entire stick-on sanding disc applied to a panel will render a circle.

Drafting stencils (Fig. 9-9) will render ellipses and a variety of other designs and effects. Drafting stencils typically are made of sturdy material and may be reused for custom paint work many times.

To apply a fish scale effect (Fig. 9-10), a row of quarter-sized Avery dots, with half their hemispheres exposed and the other half uniformly stuck to a card (Fig. 9-11), can be used. What you use and how you use it is limited only by your imagination.

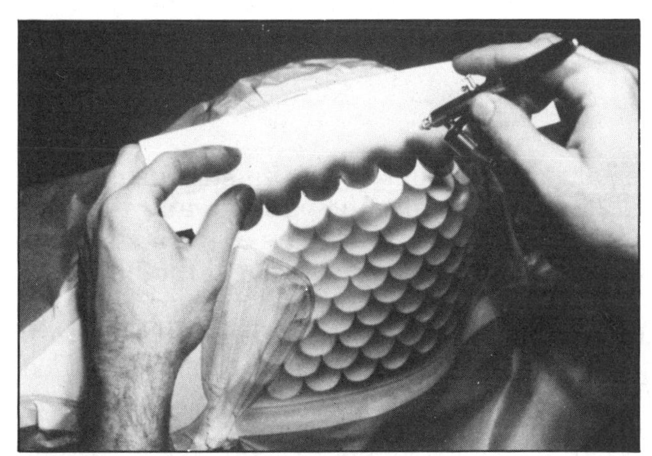

FIG 9-10 Using airbrush and stencil for fish scale effect. (Badger Air-Brush Co., *Air-Brushing Techniques for Custom Painting, Volume II*)

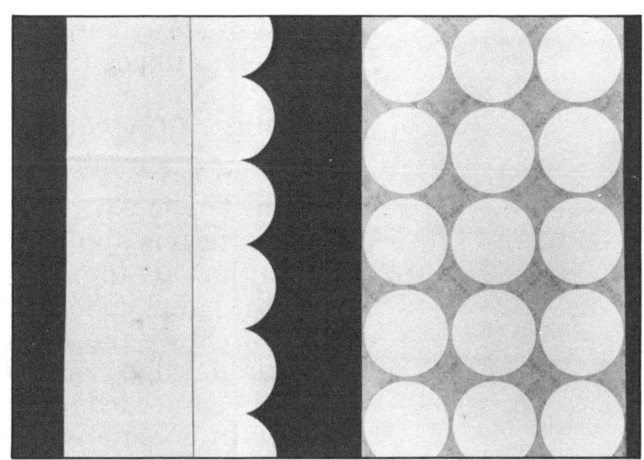

FIG 9-11 Fish scale stencil made from self-stick dots and a card. (David Keown)

Making Your Own Stencils

Stencils can be handmade in several ways. Carefully sketch the desired design in pencil on stencil paper. Then cut it out with a frisket knife or single-edged razor blade. Instead of sketching, you may trace a photo or picture onto tracing paper. Use an opaque or slide projector to project the design in the proper size onto the paper. Then trace the projected image.

To stencil a design of several colors, sketch your design on the non-sticky side of frisket paper available at art supply stores. This will serve as a pattern. Then apply the sticky side of the frisket paper to a panel that has been prepared for custom painting. Mask the surrounding area.

Carefully cut all outlines in your pattern. Use a frisket knife. (With much practice, you will learn to cut the paper and not the finish.) Then remove the frisket paper for the color that covers the largest area, such as the sky. Paint the area. When the paint is absolutely dry, replace the frisket paper over the paint. Next, remove the frisket paper from the second-largest color area. Paint that area, let it dry, and replace the frisket paper.

Repeat this process until you have painted all colors. You may wish to add more details. For example, you may add clouds to a sky by cutting out cloud shapes from the original sky area, removing the shapes, and painting clouds.

You also may remove the frisket paper and add freehand details. One method is to spray a small area and remove the excess with a cotton swab dipped in thinner.

Attaching Stencils to the Panel

When stencils are attached to a panel, they are affixed with masking tape or with their own adhesive backing. Some stencils such as fan stencils are held in the painter's hand. The painter sprays the stencils, moves it a few inches, sprays it again, moves it again, and so on.

When stencils are fastened to the panel, regular masking tape is used. On some curved surfaces, however, the edges of the stencil may not lie flat against the panel surface. When this happens, apply a slight mist of spray can sanding disc adhesive to the back side of the stencil to hold it in position.

Using Spray Mastic

The preferred stencil material is paper, but spray mastic also can be used. The mastic is sprayed onto the panel to be painted, and the stencil pattern is applied to the mastic surface. The areas of the stencil pattern that are to receive paint are then cut away to reveal the base coat on the panel underneath.

To remove these carefully, cut away these areas with a frisket knife or single-edged razor blade so there is no damage to the base coat. Peel off the unneeded section of mastic.

Spray mastic is thin so the paint lines at its edges are smooth and neat. It also usually clings well to the panel surface while the work is in progress. When properly applied, it is easy to remove when the work is complete. Remove it by rubbing an edge with a finger to turn up the edge. Then peel it off. Wash away any residue with clean water.

The disadvantages of spray mastic are that sometimes it will not cover very well, will peel up at its edges, or will be very difficult to peel off after the paint has dried. If it has been applied in too thin a coat, it is especially difficult to remove. Masking paper remains, for most uses, a better choice.

Applying Color

General stencil color application consists of one or two thin coats of color applied in such a way as to avoid paint buildup at the edges of the stencil. To begin, thoroughly clean the panel with wax and grease remover, compound, and tack it. Wipe it down with enamel reducer and dry it. Use 20 to 30 psi with a regular gun or 15 to 25 psi with an airbrush. Use a test panel to determine what pressure works best with the gun you're using. You will find that the amount of material you deposit on the panel is more difficult to control with a regular spray gun or a touch-up gun than it is with an airbrush.

Apply your stencil to the panel. Use color reduced one part color to two parts reducer. Spray the stencil, fogging the edges (Fig. 9-12) to avoid build-up and then spray the entire area. If you're using a hand-held stencil, change the position of the stencil as you spray (Fig. 9-13), overlaying and overlapping its edges to create the effect that you want. Spray the inside of the stencil for a negative image, the outside edges for a positive image. If you're using round stick-on labels to make fish scaling, fog just the edges of this makeshift stencil.

Allow the panel to dry for 4 hours. Carefully remove the stencil. Apply two coats of clear acrylic enamel or lacquer 5 minutes apart, thinned one part clear to two parts reducer. These materials should be sprayed at 45 psi with the gun 6 to 8 inches from the panel.

Air dry the result for 18 hours and compound it.

Avoiding Problems with Stencils—

1. Make sure the stencil is firmly against the panel.
2. Clean the surface to be sprayed with enamel reducer before applying the stencil.
3. Be careful during spraying to avoid material build-up at the stencil edges.
4. Allow the material to dry completely before removing the stencil.

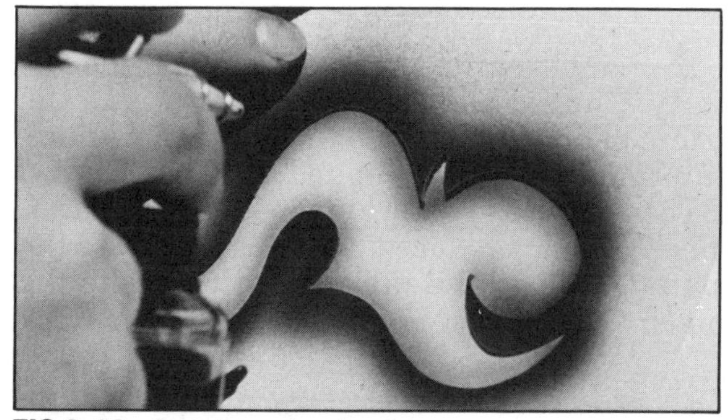

FIG 9-12 Spraying a stencil. (Badger Air-Brush Co., *Air-Brushing Techniques for Custom Painting, Volume II*)

FIG 9-13 Spraying hand-held stencil. (Badger Air-Brush Co., *Air-Brushing Techniques for Custom Painting, Volume II*)

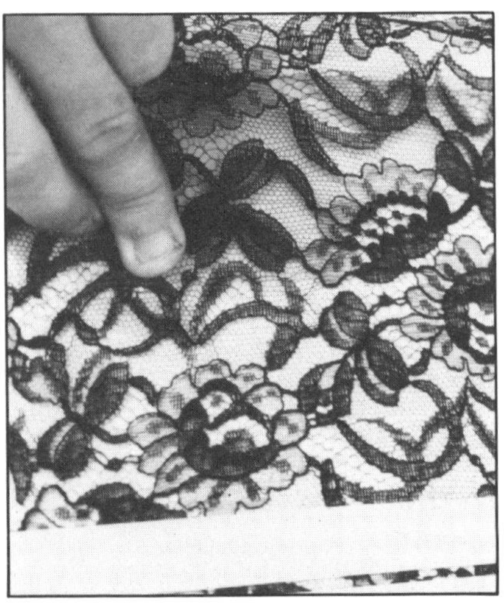

FIG 9-14 Applying lace to panel. (Badger Air-Brush Co., *Air-Brushing Techniques for Custom Painting, Volume II*)

FIG 9-15 Spraying lace. (Badger Air-Brush Co., *Air-Brushing Techniques for Custom Painting, Volume II*)

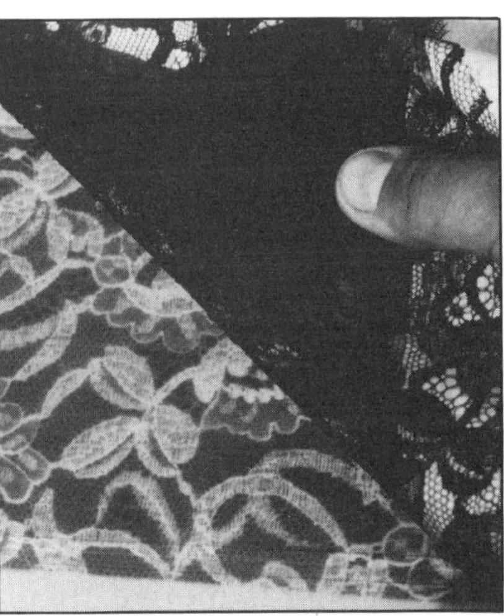

FIG 9-16 Removing lace after spraying. (Badger Air-Brush Co., *Air-Brushing Techniques for Custom Painting, Volume II*)

The Lace Effect

One particularly popular and striking stencil effect involves use of lace as a stencil. First, select a lace pattern at a yardage store and buy an amount appropriate for your needs. The more difficult the lace, the more effective the pattern is. Thoroughly clean the panel with grease and wax remover, tack it, and wipe it with enamel reducer. Mask all adjacent panels. Dampen the lace with clean water. Make sure it is just damp, not wet enough to drip. The moist lace will tend to cling to the base paint when it is laid onto the panel being painted. Lay the lace out and carefully pull it taut (Fig. 9-14), being careful not to distort its pattern, and tape down its edges with masking tape. Make sure the piece of lace you're using is bigger than the area you wish to paint with the lace effect. Spray a coat of clear, three parts thinner to one part acrylic lacquer, on the lace to help hold it in place using 20 to 25 psi. Allow the clear coat to flash 5 minutes before applying the color coats.

An alternative method of applying the lace to the panel is as follows: Spread the lace upside down on a table covered with clean cloth or paper. Using sanding disc spray adhesive, lightly spray the lace. Carefully apply the adhesive side of the lace to the panel, keeping the lace taut as you work and making sure that when you finish, the lace pattern isn't distorted.

After applying the lace to the panel, spray on two coats of acrylic lacquer in a color that will clearly contrast with the base color (Fig. 9-15). These coats should be a mixture of one and three-fourths parts medium-grade thinner to one part paint and should be applied at 20 psi. As you spray, use a light coating. Be careful not to saturate the lace with paint. Too heavy a coat, or paint insufficiently reduced, will not penetrate the lace pattern, will mar the pattern edges, and may stick the lace to the panel. If the paint has too much thinner in it and is applied too heavily, it will run.

After allowing the two coats to flash, carefully remove the lace (Fig. 9-16). Let the work dry overnight and apply the final clear coats, thinned two parts thinner to one part paint. Apply a total of six coats, allowing each to flash before the next is applied. After the final coat, allow a total drying time of 18 hours before compounding.

Working as a team with one other student and with the aid of Job Report 9-A3, you will produce the following effects on a practice panel by using both improvised (straight) and handmade (free-form) stencils: (1) positive image; (2) negative image (free-form only); (3) repeating pattern; and (4) overlapping pattern. You will then use masking paper to plan a design combining some or all of these techniques and reproduce it on the reverse side of the panel.

OBJECTIVE 9-A3 (manipulative)

Time Recommended:

2 hours

Preparation:

1. Review pages 357 through 378.
2. Study pages 379 through 381.
3. Attend classroom discussion.

Tools and Materials:

1. Panel painted on both sides
2. Choice of standard size spray gun, touch-up gun, or airbrush
3. Choice of material to be used to create the different effects
4. Easel, or stand suitable for holding pane, while work progresses
5. Lacquer paint or acrylic enamel paint, thinned or reduced one part to two parts thinner, or reducer (dependent on the background paint that was used on the panel).

Procedure:

1. Select the item that you plan to use for a stencil to make the straight effect.
2. Set the pressure at 15 to 30 psi at the regulator (find the psi that works best with the gun or airbrush you have chosen). Tack the panel and apply the improvised straight stencil to it. Create a straight edge effect by spraying lightly along its edge.
3. Continue to use the edge to make your own design. Change the position of the stencil as desired.
4. Use handmade stencils to create a negative image and a positive image by spraying the inside edges or outside edges of your stencil.
5. Make repeating patterns in a line with each other. Then make overlapping patterns across the panel.
6. Practice the same kinds of effects on the other side of the panel by drawing and cutting out patterns on masking paper.
7. After the practice is completed, clean all equipment well while the paint dries.
8. Any panel on which the effects are poor may be water sanded and used for practice again. Panels that have very good effects may be sprayed with clear to give them protection and more depth.
9. Application of clear for the panel should be two coats sprayed 10 minutes apart with acrylic enamel, reduced one part clear to two parts reducer, or one part lacquer to two parts thinner sprayed 5 minutes apart. Use 45 psi with a gun distance of 6 to 8 inches and

a 6-inch pattern. The speed of stroke is normal as in all panel painting with an overlap of not less than 3 inches.

10. The panel may be force dried for one hour at 165 degrees before compounding to obtain extra gloss, or air dried 4 hours. After compounding, polish may be applied.

JOB REPORT SHEET 9-A3

EFFECTS WITH STENCILS

Student Name ______________________ Date ______________

Time Started ____________ Time Finished ____________ Total Time ____________

Specifications

Color of panel base coat ______________________________

Type of paint sprayed: Acrylic enamel_____ Lacquer _____

Color selection for effect ______________ Base color ______________

Large spray gun _____ Touch-up gun _____ Airbrush _____

Technique

Psi at regulator _____ with what spray equipment______________

______________________ Type material ______________________

Type of stencil ______________________________

____

Material application: One coat _____ Two coats _____

Clear application _____ Yes _____ No

Checkup Questions

1. Were the effects produced on the front side of the panel reproduced on the other side? _____ Yes _____ No
2. Was clear applied to the panel? _____ Yes _____ No

   If yes, how many coats? _____
3. Was more than one color used to produce the effect? _____ Yes _____ No
4. If clear was applied, was compounding done to achieve extra gloss? _____ Yes _____ No

Date Completed ______________ Instructor's Signature ______________________

Working alone under supervision of the instructor, you will compound, clean, and apply lace effect to an assigned panel. Use Job Report 9-A4 and obtain the instructor's approval upon completion of the assignment.

OBJECTIVE 9-A4 (manipulative)

Time Recommended:

2½ hours

Preparation:

1. Review pages 357 through 381.
2. Study pages 383 through 385.
3. Attend classroom discussion.

Tools and Materials:

1. Painted panel
2. Wax remover
3. Suction-feed spray gun, touch-up gun, or airbrush
4. Tack cloth, clean shop cloths, and masking materials
5. Lace
6. Disc adhesive
7. Clear lacquer
8. Lacquer thinner
9. Acrylic enamel or lacquer color

Procedure:

1. Compound the panel that is to receive the lace effect and clean with grease and wax remover.
2. Dry the panel thoroughly, blow, and tack it with a tack cloth.
3. Select and cut lace to proper length for the panel.
4. Mask adjacent areas.
5. Moisten lace with water, or spray a light mist of disc adhesive on the back side of the lace.
6. Place the lace on the panel with care to avoid stretching the lace.
7. Mask down all edges of the lace with ¾-inch masking tape, pressing it firmly.
8. Mist on one coat of clear lacquer mixed one part clear to three parts thinner.
9. Apply two coats of lacquer mixed one part of lacquer color to one and three-fourths parts medium-grade thinner.
10. Allow color coats to flash. Remove the lace and masking carefully.
11. Allow overnight drying. Apply four to six coats of clear mixed one part clear lacquer to two parts thinner, allowing flash time between coats.
12. The lace effect area may be compounded after overnight air drying or force drying. All compound traces should be removed with water and a polish applied to the lace area.

APPLICATION OF LACE EFFECT

Student Name ______________________________ Date ______________

Time Started ____________ Time Finished ____________ Total Time ____________

Specifications

Color of panel base coat ______________________________

Type of paint sprayed: Acrylic enamel______ Lacquer ______

Color selection ______________ Base color ______________

Gun used: Large ______ Touch-up ______ Airbrush ______

Technique

Psi at regulator ______ with what spray equipment______________

Material application: One coat ______ Two coats ______

Clear application ______ Yes ______ No

Checkup Questions

1. Was the lace pattern cleanly produced on the panel? ______
2. Was the paint properly reduced? ______________
3. Did the lace pull cleanly away from the panel? ______________

Date Completed ______________ Instructor's Signature ______________

FIG 9-17
Two-tone paint.
(Davenport Photography)

TWO-TONE AND STYLE TONE PAINT JOBS

Any of the different types of automotive paints can be used to do a variety of two-tone painting (Fig. 9-17). These are sometimes called style tones, and can involve use of more than two colors.

The most common two-tone paint job is to paint the roof one color and the body another. This is a straightforward procedure. The most important element is that the area painted first is fully masked so that overspray from the second area painted cannot mar the first area. In most of such jobs the smallest area to be painted is sprayed first to reduce masking time and material used.

After deciding which colors will be used and how the different colors will be divided over the automobile, complete all steps of preparation for the material you have chosen to use. Mask the chrome and glass as needed. When masking for the first color, do not mask a line dividing the first color from the second. Clean the panels thoroughly with grease and wax remover. Tack the panels and spray on the first color, lapping into the area of the second color. Apply the number of coats and allow the drying time appropriate for the material you are spraying.

Pull all masking tape as soon as the paint has become tacky and won't run. This will yield a sharp, clean edge on the paint. Pull the tape straight, at a 90-degree angle or less. With enamel, the tape must not be removed until the top of the paint coat has set up and hardened. With lacquer, the tape can be pulled almost immediately.

Allow the first color to dry overnight and mask the fresh paint so that your second color won't mar it. Mask it carefully, including the line where the color will change. Make sure you leave no rough edges.

Apply the second color, spraying the number of coats and allowing the amount of drying time appropriate for the material you are spraying. Be sure to pull the masking tape between the two colors to leave the cleanest, sharpest line possible between them. This dividing line should require no further attention, but some painters prefer to apply a pin stripe in a complementary color over this line after the two basic colors are dry and completely finished.

OBJECTIVE 9-A5 (manipulative)

Working as a team with three other students, and with the aid of Job Report Sheet 9-A5, you will prepare and apply a two-tone refinish to an automobile.

Time Recommended:

40 hours

Preparation:

1. Review pages 357 through 387.
2. Study pages 388 through 391.
3. Attend classroom discussion.
4. Observe demonstration on masking for two-tone work.

Tools and Materials:

1. Selection of sandpapers to accommodate type of material to be used
2. Respirator
3. Vibrator, and/or dual action sander
4. Primer-surfacer ready mixed in spray gun
5. Suction-feed spray gun
6. Two colors of paint
7. Sealer if a job requirement
8. Clean shop cloths
9. Tack cloth
10. Enamel reducer
11. Wax remover

Procedure:

1. Remove any wax from the painted surface of the car with wax remover.
2. Featheredge any chips or broken paint and apply primer-surfacer as needed until the surface is filled properly.
3. Water sand the car and rinse it clean. Allow it to drip for a few minutes to avoid making puddles in the spray booth. Disconnect the battery ground cable and roll the car into the booth.
4. After blowing and wiping away all water from the vehicle, mask all glass and chrome. Do not mask a line at this time where the color is supposed to change.
5. Do a final wipe down with a fast-drying enamel reducer.
6. Mix the paint for the smallest portion of the vehicle that is to receive that color. Viscosity should be in the range of 18–21 seconds regardless of the type of material.
7. Tack the vehicle and apply the paint by the use of normal technique used in overall refinishing with the type of material being used. Allow paint to slightly lap the area where the color is to change.

8. After force drying the recommended time, or overnight drying, apply a strip of ¾-inch tape to the area where the two-tone edge is to be.
9. Attach masking to the strip of tape. Completely cover and seal the newly painted area.
10. Lightly scuff away any roughness exposed on the surface to be painted with a grit abrasive recommended for the type of material being used.
11. Blow and wipe down the surface again with enamel reducer. Mix the color for that part of the vehicle.
12. Tack the surface to be painted and apply the paint with the normal technique recommended for that type of paint.
13. Remove tape used for two-tone work as soon as the paint is dry enough to avoid being stringy at the edge. Do not allow tape to remain on a freshly painted surface more than 12 hours, or the paint may be damaged when it is removed.
14. As masking is removed from one color it is pulled away from the other color and not allowed to touch the painted surface.

TWO-TONE PAINTING

Student Name ______________________ Date ______________

Time Started ______________ Time Finished ______________ Total Time ______________

Specifications

Type of vehicle ______________ Year model ______________

Type of two-tone (give location on vehicle of color change) ______________

____

Type of two-tone (give location on vehicle of color change ______________

First color applied ______________________________

Second color applied ______________________________

Vehicle original paint number, if not the same ______________

Technique

Abrasive used in preparation (give numbers) ______________

____

Type of paint used for job ______________________________

Was a sealer used? ______ Yes ______ No

Checkup Questions

1. Was any second color paint visible on the first color? ______ Yes ______ No
2. Was the area of color change a smooth, straight line? ______ Yes ______ No
3. Were there any problems with tape removal? ______

Date Completed ______________ Instructor's Signature ______________

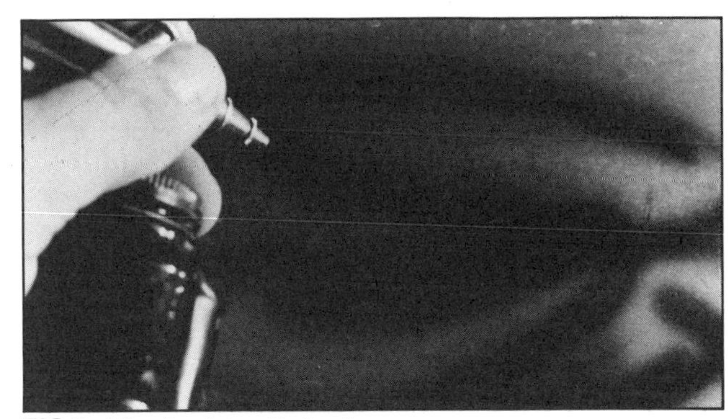

FIG 9-18 Applying Badger's Eerie-Dess. (Badger Air-Brush Co., *Air-Brushing Techniques for Custom Painting, Volume II*)

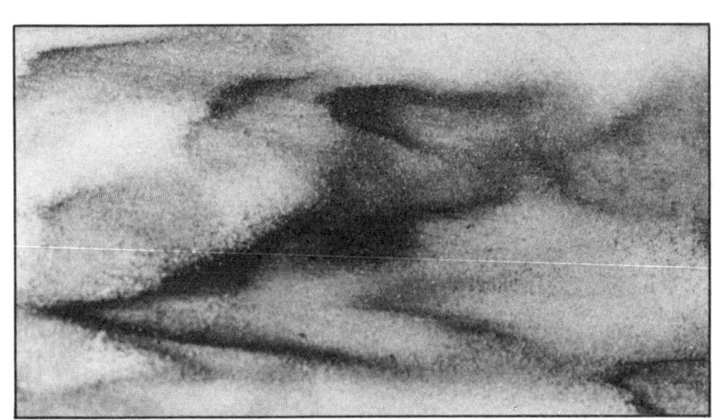

FIG 9-19 Wood-grain results after using squeegee on Eerie-Dess. (Badger Air-Brush Co., *Air-Brushing Techniques for Custom Painting, Volume II*)

WOOD-GRAINING

The wood-grain finish was used extensively on early automobiles, and is a custom effect that can yield very pleasing results.

In the old days it was done with a wood-graining kit consisting of nitrocellulose-lacquer base color and several different colors of graining ink.

These days refinishers use an acrylic lacquer base coat in a light tone and an artist's oil paint in a contrasting dark earth or brown tone. Raw umber or burnt umber oil paint works especially well over a light base coat.

Clean the panel thoroughly with grease and wax remover, wipe it with a fast-drying enamel reducer, and tack it. Spray on the base coat of acrylic lacquer and allow it to dry thoroughly. The artist's oil is applied with a brush that has coarse bristles, or with a special wood-grain squeegee available from your paint jobber. Some painters trim old brushes down fairly short to get stiff bristles for this purpose.

The idea is that the contrasting top coat should not flow. It should streak, and the base color should be visible through it. Squirt the artist's paint out of its tube onto a dry, clean palette. Thin it, as necessary, with either linseed oil or turpentine. Some trial and error will be necessary here. Apply the slightly thinned paint with the graining brush, pressing heavily enough on it to streak the top coat and reveal the base coat. Real wood-grain is irregular, so rock the brush or squeegee from side to side, move it in a slight curve to make irregular grain, or rotate it to make a knot effect. Again, this requires some experimentation.

An alternative wood-graining method uses Badger's Eerie-Dess, applied to the panel over a contrasting base coat with an airbrush or touch-up gun (Fig. 9-18). Using the squeegee, begin the graining process immediately, drawing the squeegee across the wet Eerie-Dess with a rocking, side-to-side motion to simulate wood-grain. Rapid rocking yields a tighter grain, and slower rocking yields a looser grain (Fig. 9-19).

Artist's oils tend to dry slowly, particularly those of the umber family because of the amount and kind of pigment they contain. Let the panel dry for a full 12 to 18 hours. Spray on two coats of clear acrylic lacquer. Air drying time will vary according to the climate. To force dry the clear, use heat lamps for 60 minutes, 40 inches from the panel. When dry, the clear can be hand-compounded and polished for extra gloss.

OBJECTIVE 9-A6 (manipulative)

Working as a team with one other student and with the aid of Job Report Sheet 9-A6, you will apply a freehand wood-grain pattern to a practice panel.

Time Recommended:

2½ hours

Preparation:

1. Study pages 394 through 395.
2. Attend classroom discussion.

Tools and Materials:

1. Practice panel painted white with lacquer
2. Artist oil
3. Paintbrush, 1½- to 2-inch width
4. Palette
5. Small container of water
6. Masking paper to check thinness, or flowing on
7. Tack cloth
8. Spray gun
9. Clear lacquer
10. Machine rubbing compound
11. Polish
12. Clean cloths

Procedure:

1. Apply a ribbon of acrylic color on the palette.
2. Tack the panel to be grained with a tack cloth and place the masking paper in easy reach of the panel.
3. Touch the tip end of the brush to the acrylic color, and then dip it lightly into the water. Check the thinness and flow of the color on the masking paper. If material does not flow into light brown grains, it is too thick. If the material flows until it looks like a solid color, it is too thin. The brush will have to be touched to the color again to make the paint thicker.
4. Apply the brush to the panel with a continuous stroke—straight for making straight grains, or from side-to-side slightly to make curved grains. Knots may be made with the bristles of one edge of the brush by turning the brush. They also may be applied freehand with a smaller brush. You may need to rewet the brush often because the acrylic color dries fast.
5. Clean the brush or brushes while the panel dries for one-half hour. Then apply four coats of clear lacquer with a spray gun, after tacking the panel again.
6. Force dry the panel for one hour at 165 degrees, or allow the panel to air dry at least 4 hours before compounding.
7. After compounding, polish the panel to increase the gloss.

JOB REPORT SHEET 9-A6

APPLICATION OF WOOD-GRAIN

Student Name ______________________________ Date ______________

Time Started ______________ Time Finished ______________ Total Time ______________

Specifications

Color of ground coat on panel ______________ Paint number ______________

Type of paint ______________ Type of graining material ______________

______________________________ Color ______________________________

Technique

Width of paintbrush ______________________________

If clear applied, give number of coats ______________________________

Times tack cloth used _____ One _____ Two

Type of thinner used for graining material ______________________________

Checkup Questions

1. Were both straight and curved grains produced on the panel?

   _____ Yes _____ No

2. Were knots made in the grain effect on the panel? _____ Yes _____ No

3. Was clear coat allowed to air dry? _____ Yes _____ No

4. If a force dry was used for the clear, what time and temperature was used?

   ____

Date Completed ______________ Instructor's Signature ______________________

FIG 9-20
Cobwebbing or spiderwebbing. (Badger Air-Brush Co., *Air-Brushing Techniques for Custom Painting, Volume II*)

COBWEBBING

Cobwebbing, otherwise known as spiderwebbing (Fig. 9-20), consists of long, stringy lines of one or more colors that criss-cross each other on the panel in a random manner. The effect is obtained by spraying unthinned acrylic lacquer through a spray gun. Pressure should be 40–70 psi. The effect is variable at different pressures. As with other custom effects, experimentation is called for. Note that if the paint is sprayed at too high a pressure it will break up and lose its string effect. If not enough pressure is used, the material will not come out of the gun.

To obtain the cobweb effect, thoroughly clean the panel with wax and grease remover. Strain the unthinned acrylic into a regular suction-feed spray gun. Use a larger-than-usual fluid nozzle, such as a 36, and set the gun's needle back a bit. Holding the gun 12 to 18 inches from a test panel or piece of masking paper, spray a test pattern. Adjust distance, pressure, and needle until you obtain the effect you want (Fig. 9-21). Spray the string of paint until you get the coverage and effect you want. If the paint is not thick enough, allow it to stand in an open can for an hour or two.

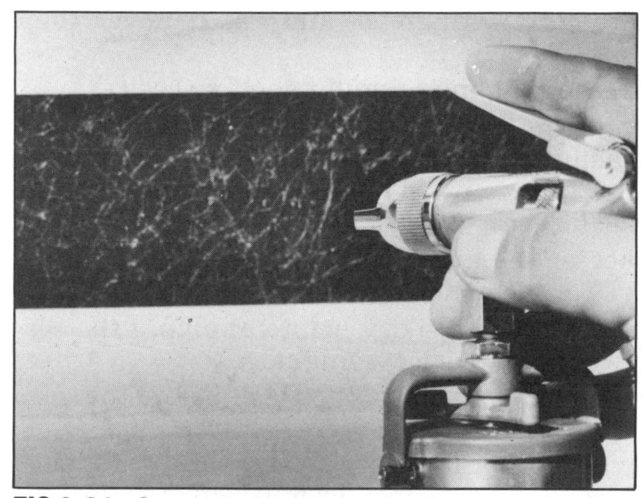

FIG 9-21 Spraying cobwebbing. (Badger Air-Brush Co., *Air-Brushing Techniques for Custom Painting, Volume II*)

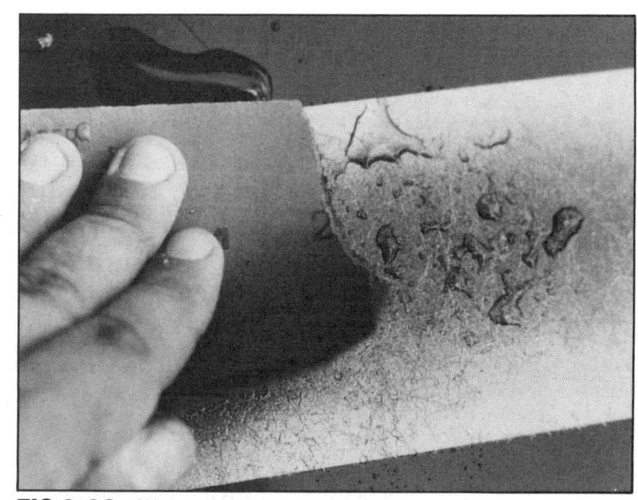

FIG 9-22 Wet sanding clear acrylic on cobwebbing. (Badger Air-Brush Co., *Air-Brushing Techniques for Custom Painting, Volume II*)

When spraying more than one color of webbing, allow the first color to dry for at least 30 minutes before applying the second color.

Allow the cobwebbing to dry overnight and apply at least six coats of clear acrylic, allowing each coat to flash before applying the next coat. The final clear coatings must be thick enough to cover the string-like cobwebbing so that final wet sanding (Fig. 9-22) and compounding can be accomplished without cutting into the webbing.

Some painters use as many as eight or nine coats of clear, sanding and compounding many of them away to make certain of a completely smooth, glossy finish over the cobwebbing.

OBJECTIVE 9-A7 (manipulative)

Working alone under the supervision of the instructor, prepare a panel, apply cobwebbing, in two colors, and cover the cobwebbing with clear acrylic lacquer. Use Job Report Sheet 9-A7. Obtain instructor's approval upon completion of the assignment.

Time Recommended:

2 hours

Preparation:

1. Study pages 398 through 399.
2. Attend classroom discussion.

Tools and Materials:

1. Panel cleaning materials
2. Regular suction-feed paint spray gun and air supply
3. Painted panel and painted trial panel
4. Acrylic lacquer in two colors
5. Clear acrylic lacquer and thinner
6. Sanding and compounding materials

Procedure:

1. Clean the test panel thoroughly with grease and wax remover, then compound and tack it.
2. Add acrylic lacquer to the spray gun at regular shelf viscosity.
3. Using a large piece of masking paper, adjust the spray pattern and air pressure until you achieve the pattern you desire. At higher pressures the thickness of the paint string is made smaller, and at lower pressures it is made larger.
4. Apply in uniform strokes of the gun, swirling the string of paint and overlapping the edges of the panel slightly.
5. Allow the first color of cobwebbing to dry before applying the second color. Allow the cobwebbing to dry overnight.
6. Apply six coats of clear, allowing each coat to flash before the next is applied.
7. Allow clear to air dry overnight or force dry. Water sand with 600A sandpaper, being very careful not to cut too deeply into the clear.
8. Machine compound the clear until a suitable gloss is obtained. Then polish and hand buff the panel.

APPLICATION OF COBWEBBING

Student Name ______________________ Date ____________

Time Started ____________ Time Finished ____________ Total Time ____________

Specifications

Color of base coat ______________________

Color of cobwebbing acrylics ______________________

Technique

Material strained into paint gun ______________________

Pressure used ______________________

Gun distance from panel ______________________

Number of clear coats applied ______________________

Checkup Questions

1. Was a test spray made? _____ Yes _____ No
2. Was first color allowed to dry for at least 30 minutes? _____ Yes _____ No
3. How many coats of clear were applied? _____

Date Completed ____________ Instructor's Signature ______________________

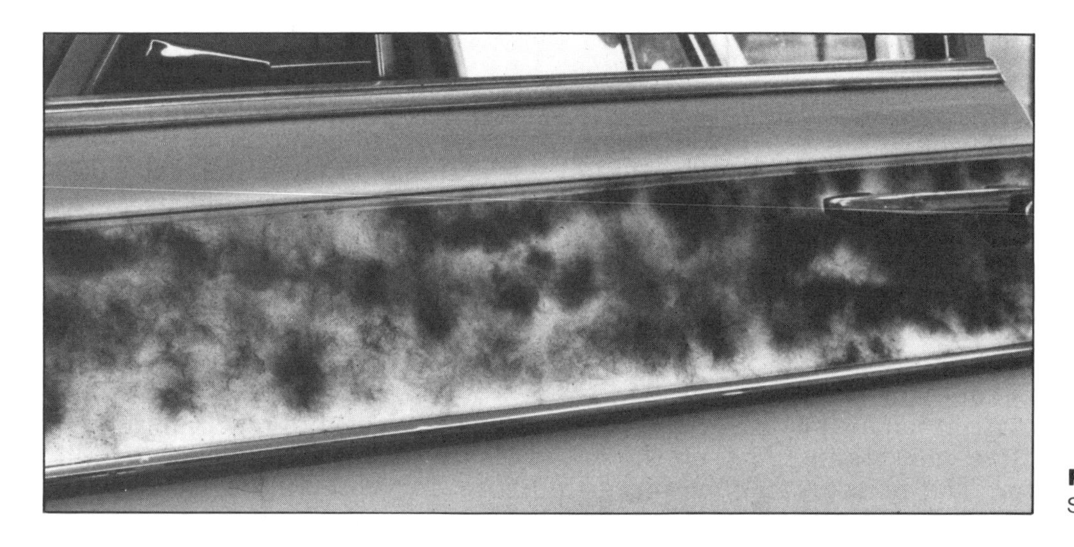

FIG 9-23
Smoke finish. (David Keown)

SMOKE FINISH

There are two methods used to apply a smoke finish (Fig. 9-23). The first uses gray or black acrylic lacquer fogged over a light base coat, and the second actually uses smoke from an oxy-acetylene torch. Both methods require that the painter begin with a base coat of an appropriately light color to contrast with the dark smoke. The base is thoroughly cleaned with wax and grease remover, wiped with enamel reducer, and tacked.

Using Paint

To apply a smoke finish with the paint method, use a dark gray or black lacquer thinned not more than one part color to three parts reducer. Holding the gun 12 to 14 inches from the panel, spray the color on the panel with quick, uneven mist coats, with the gun's pattern set wide.

The stroke must be fast to allow the dark color to form a smoke-like pattern on the panel. Swirl it so that the paint being deposited on the panel looks like smoke.

Allow the panel to dry for 10 minutes. Then apply clear, mixed one part clear to two parts thinner. This will give the smoke pattern some depth and allow it to flow a little. Two coats of clear is sufficient. More than that will result in overwetting, causing too much flowing of the material and distorting the smoke pattern.

Using Real Smoke

The second method of applying a smoke finish uses real smoke from an oxy-acetylene torch. Applying a smoke finish in this way is believed by some to be a safety hazard, but it is thoroughly safe if the refinisher uses specified oxy-acetylene procedures and follows safety precautions. This method is not recommended for student use except in the presence of an instructor, and with the instructor's approval.

Your instructor or an experienced welder should make sure the oxygen and acetylene cylinders are chained securely upright. Then he or she should install the regulators, hoses, and torch tips; check all fittings for leaks with a soap and water solution, and pressure test the system.

Oxy-acetylene Safety

Using an oxy-acetylene kit can be dangerous. It can result in burns and explosions. But it doesn't have to. A basic understanding of the materials involved and the adoption of a few simple safety rules will make handling and using this equipment and material as safe as spray painting.

Acetylene gas is extremely volatile and explosive. It is stored and transported in cylinders which also contain porous matter and acetone. These two substances absorb the gas, much as a beverage absorbs carbonation. Opening the acetylene cylinder valve allows the gas to boil out of the acetone.

Acetylene is unstable, and must never be allowed to reach, in its free state, more than 15 psi on the low-pressure side of the pressure regulator. The pressure can be more than this in the cylinder because, as noted, the acetylene is not free, having been absorbed.

When using acetylene, always make sure the cylinder is standing upright. Acetylene bottles have safety valves on them. These are called *fuse plugs*, and they are engineered to melt at 220 degrees and release the gas before it gets hot enough to explode. For this reason, never place an acetylene bottle near a grinder where sparks can hit it, or next to a water heater, or in any other place warm enough to melt the safety plug. Every shop has a pilot light somewhere, or an open flame. If a plug should melt, the gas and acetone will escape, come into contact with the pilot light or flame, and cause an explosion that could level the entire shop.

The regulators on top of the acetylene bottles are delicate and cannot take abuse. When the valve on the cylinder is open, the valve and gauges are under high pressure. Bumping or banging them could cause them to explode. Because of this pressure, when the welding outfit is not in use, the cylinder valve should be kept closed. This relieves the tension on the springs and diaphragm inside the regulator.

When using the oxy-acetylene setup, you must wear gas welding goggles and welding gloves. Tie back long hair. Wear a long-sleeved shirt and long pants that are made of heavy cotton or wool (not synthetic fabric). Wear sturdy shoes—boots are recommended—and no open toes. Do not wear clothing with grease spots, because these make the cloth more flammable.

Before setting up the oxy-acetylene station, get your panel ready. Apply the base color and allow it to dry thoroughly. Remove all masking and roll the automobile or panel into a clean, open area in the shop. Place an ABC-type fire extinguisher close by. Roll the oxy-acetylene outfit into the shop. Begin by using these steps to set the regulators:

1. Turn out the regulator adjusting screws (counter-clockwise) until they turn freely.
2. Open the oxygen cylinder valve *slowly*. Once it's "cracked," and the high-pressure gauge is at its highest reading, open the cylinder valve as far as possible.
3. Open the main valve on the acetylene a quarter to a half turn. Leave the T-wrench on the cylinder at all times.
4. Open the acetylene valve on the torch body slightly. Then turn the acetylene regulator adjusting screw inward, clockwise, watching the low-pressure gauge. When it reaches 3–5 psi (NEVER OVER 15 psi), stop turning.

5. Close the acetylene valve on the torch body.
6. Open the oxygen valve on the torch body. Turn the oxygen regulator adjusting screw in (clockwise) until the low-pressure oxygen gauge reaches 4–8 psi. Close the oxygen valve on the torch body.

Applying Smoke to the Panel

To light the torch, do not use a cigarette lighter or matches, because these may result in burns. The only tool to use is an igniter, or striker, which is made expressly for lighting welding torches. Open the acetylene valve on the torch body 1/16 turn. Aim the torch tip away from your body, away from flammable materials, and away from the cylinder. Place the igniter flint near the stream of gas, and squeeze the igniter handle to make the flint scrape and produce a spark. This will light the torch. Adjust the acetylene valve on the torch handle to produce a broad yellow flame from 3 to 5 inches long. You will note that black smoke pours off the end of the flame. Slowly add oxygen with the torch oxygen valve until the heavy soot disappears from the flame. Keeping the end of the flame 3 to 5 inches away from the painted panel, aim the smoke plume at the panel surface and the smoke will be deposited there. Move the torch in strokes similar to those used in spray painting. If insufficient smoke is applied to the panel the first time over it, additional smoke may be applied as needed.

When you get enough smoke on your panel, use these steps to shut down the oxy-acetylene outfit:

1. Shut off the oxygen valve on the torch body.
2. Shut off the acetylene valve on the torch body.
3. Turn off the acetylene cylinder valve.
4. Turn off the oxygen cylinder valve.
5. Open both torch body valves and let the gases drain from the hoses until the low-pressure gauges drop to "0."
6. Back off both regulator valves counterclockwise, until they turn freely.

Do not touch the panel. The smoke surface is very easily marred at this point. Two coats of clear, thinned one part clear to two parts thinner, are applied. This will flow the smoke into the color and leave a nice, deep smoke pattern.

Safety Rules for Using Torch to Apply Smoke Finishes

1. Oxy-acetylene equipment is not to be used by anyone who has not received instruction on torch safety and permission from the instructor.
2. Wear boots, long sleeves, and long pants. Do not wear synthetic clothing. Avoid large pockets and cuffs.
3. Always keep all cylinders upright, fastening them to a wall or chaining them to the welding cart so they cannot tip over.
4. Keep grease and oil away from all cylinders, hoses, regulators, and torches.
5. Protect cylinders from excessive heat.
6. Use only soap and water to test for leaks in an oxy-acetylene welding station. Never use matches or any other fluid.

7. Open the cylinder valve very slowly to avoid blowing the regulator's diaphragm.
8. Adjusting screws on regulators must be turned off (counterclockwise) before tank valves are opened, or diaphragms could be blown.
9. Open acetylene tank main valve one-fourth to one-half turn only. This will enable you to shut it off with one quick turn in an emergency.
10. Wear approved welding goggles to avoid damage to your eyes.
11. Wear gloves to protect your hands.
12. Do not carry matches.
13. No open bottles or cans of any kind, and no cloth or paper or any other item not needed for the job should be in the area when the torch is in operation.
14. An ABC-type fire extinguisher should be placed 5 to 8 feet from where you are working.
15. Do not attempt to light the torch with anything but a torch striker. Use of matches or lighters can result in serious burns.
16. Always turn off the torch unless you are actually holding it.
17. The tip of the torch is copper and will remain hot long after you shut it off. If the tip must be changed, use leather gloves to avoid burns.
18. If a piece of equipment is faulty, shut the outfit down. Then mark the equipment problem on the equipment with chalk and report it to your instructor immediately.

OBJECTIVE 9-A8 (manipulative)

Working alone, with a test panel painted white or some other light color, use black or very dark gray paint to apply a light, smoke-like mist to the panel. Wet it with clear. Use acrylic lacquer. Use Job Report Sheet 9-A8 and obtain instructor's approval upon completion of assignment.

Time Recommended:

1 hour

Preparation:

1. Review pages 357 through 404.
2. Study pages 404 through 407.
3. Attend class discussion on smoke finishes.
4. Discuss assignment with instructor.

Tools and Materials:

1. Practice panel, painted white
2. Tack cloth and clean shop cloths
3. Respirator
4. Suction-feed paint spray gun
5. Dark gray or black acrylic lacquer
6. Acrylic lacquer reducer

7. Grease and wax remover
8. Enamel reducer

Procedure:

1. Thoroughly clean the panel with grease and wax remover.
2. Wipe the panel down with fast-drying enamel reducer. Tack it.
3. Thin the gray or black paint one part paint to three parts reducer.
4. Adjust the air pressure to read 40 psi at the regulator and adjust spray pattern to 12 inches at 12 inch distance.
5. With the gun held to one side of the panel, start a stroke at 12 to 14 inches from the panel and move across it as swiftly as you can. If the smoke effect is not dark enough, the speed of the stroke may be decreased accordingly. Extra material may be added, if needed, by fast short bursts of the trigger at a 14-inch distance.
6. When smoke effect has been applied to the panel, clean the spray gun and mix clear lacquer one part to one and a half parts thinner.
7. Adjust pressure at the regulator to read 45 psi; set gun pattern to 6 inches at 6 inch distance.
8. Do not wait for the panel to dry. Do not tack it. Spray two coats of the clear allowing the first to flash before the second one is applied. Avoid overwetting with the clear as this may cause the smoke effect to flow into the ground coat.
9. The panel may be force dried at 165 degrees or allowed to dry overnight before compounding and polishing.

JOB REPORT SHEET 9-A8

PAINTED SMOKE EFFECTS

Student Name ______________________ Date ______________

Time Started ____________ Time Finished ____________ Total Time ____________

Specifications

Color of panel background ______________ Paint number ______________

Color used for smoke effect ______________ Paint number ______________

Type of paint material ______________________________

Technique

Spray gun psi used ____________ Distance of gun from panel ____________

Width of spray pattern ______________________________

Time between application of smoke and application of clear ______________

Checkup Questions

1. What kind of smoke effect did you create? ______________________________

   ____

2. Did you use long or short strokes? ______________________________

3. Why isn't the panel dried and tacked before the clear is applied? ______________

   ____

4. What effect did the clear produce? ______________________________

Date Completed ______________ Instructor's Signature ______________________

Working as a team with two other students and with the aid of Job Report Sheet 9-A9, you will apply smoke effects with an oxy-acetylene torch to a finished practice panel.

OBJECTIVE 9-A9 (manipulative)

Time Recommended:

3½ hours

Preparation:

1. Review pages 357 through 407.
2. Study pages 409 through 412.
3. Attend classroom lecture and discussion.
4. Study safety rules on pages 403 through 404.

Tools and Materials:

1. Panel painted white, light cream, or beige, with lacquer. Oxy-acetylene outfit and striker
2. Tack cloth
3. Fire extinguisher 5 to 8 feet from panel
4. Welding goggles and gloves
5. Spray gun
6. Clear lacquer

Procedure:

1. Place the panel in the open shop on a rack or easel, and tack it with a tack cloth.
2. Place the oxy-acetylene welding outfit 5 to 8 feet from one side of the panel.
3. Place the fire extinguisher (ABC type) on the opposite side of the panel from the torch not less than 5 feet away, or more than 8 feet away.
4. Check the torch regulator adjusting screws to make sure that they spin freely, and have no pressure on the regulator diaphragm, on both the oxygen and the acetylene.
5. Open the oxygen tank valve slowly, standing to one side to avoid facing the gauge directly. Turn the oxygen tank valve to the left. When the tank pressure gauge begins to rise continue to the left (counterclockwise) until it seats itself at full open.
6. Open the acetylene valve at the cylinder by turning it to the left (counterclockwise) slowly until it is at least one-fourth turn but not over one-half turn open.
7. Open the acetylene valve on the torch body one-fourth turn. Adjust the acetylene to read 5 psi by turning the regulator adjustment screw to the right (clockwise) with the acetylene torch valve open one-fourth turn making sure that the pressure is maintained. Close the acetylene valve on the torch body.
8. Adjust the pressure at the oxygen regulator screw by turning to the right (clockwise) until the gauge reads 10 psi nearest the oxygen hose.

9. With the torch striker in one hand and the torch in the other, open the acetylene valve on the torch approximately 1/16 turn. Point the torch away from yourself and other people, away from the panel, and away from the cylinders. Point the tip of the torch at the striker at a distance of 1 to 2 inches from the striker. Strike the flint, causing the torch to light. Slowly open the acetylene valve at the torch until the flame is at least 3 inches in length, then slowly add oxygen until the soot disappears from the end of the flame, leaving only fine smoke at the end of the flame.
10. With the torch held to one side of the panel, start a stroke as if you were spraying. Allow the smoke to be applied to the panel, but keep the end of the flame from contacting the paint. The stroke with the torch is continuous from one end of the panel to the other. The smoke pattern on the panel may vary from 2 to 3 inches in width. The next stroke must be made in a way that allows it to lap into the first stroke to keep the effect uniform.
11. When all of the panel has been smoked, close the acetylene valve at the torch, then close the oxygen valve at the torch.
12. Close the acetylene valve at the tank and open the acetylene valve at the torch until the two pressure gauges both read zero. Then, close the valve and release the spring tension on the acetylene regulator by turning the adjusting screw to the left until it spins freely with the tip of the finger.
13. Close the valve on the oxygen tank and open the oxygen valve on the torch. When both oxygen gauges read zero, close the valve on the torch and release the spring tension on the regulator by turning it to the left until it will spin freely by the tip of the finger.
14. Return the hose and torch to their place of storage and place the fire extinguisher back on its hanger.
15. Mix two parts of lacquer thinner to one part of clear and adjust air regulator to read 45 psi. Adjust spray gun to 6 inch pattern at 6 inch distance.
16. DO NOT tack or touch the panel. Spray the clear with a 50-percent overlap spraying one coat at a time, allowing each coat to flash before applying the next, until a total of four coats have been applied.
17. The panel may be force dried at 165 degrees or allowed to dry overnight before compounding and polishing.

JOB REPORT SHEET 9-A9

OXY-ACETYLENE SMOKE EFFECTS

Student Name ______________________________ Date ______________

Time Started ______________ Time Finished ______________ Total Time ______________

Specifications

Color of background panel ______________ Paint number ______________

Welding torch tip number ______________________________

Pressure of oxygen ______________ Pressure of acetylene ______________

Distance between torch flame and panel ______________________________

Techniques

Position of acetylene cylinder valve _____ ¼ open _____ ½ open

Position of oxygen cylinder valve ______________________________

Position of acetylene torch valve ______________________________

Position of oxygen torch valve ______________________________

Color of flame ______________ length of flame ______________

Distance between flame and panel ______________________________

Width of stroke ______________________________

Amount of overlap of stroke patterns ______________________________

Checkup Questions

1. How far from the panel was the welding setup? ______________
2. How far from the panel was the fire extinguisher? ______________
3. Why must a torch be lighted with a flint igniter? ______________
4. What kind of stroke pattern did you use? ______________
5. Did you need to go over the panel more than once to get enough smoke? ______

6. Why do you need to wear protective clothing, goggles, and gloves when using the oxy-acetylene outfit? ____

____

7. Why are the panels with smoke effect not tacked before the clear is applied? ____

____

8. Explain the difference that you noticed between the painted smoke effect and the real smoke effect? ____

____

Date Completed ______________ Instructor's Signature ______________________

Student Name ______________________ Date ____________

DIRECTIONS: Circle the best answer or answers to each question.

1. The sort of gun most frequently used for freehand custom work is a (an):
   A. Regular spray gun.
   B. Airbrush.
   C. Touch-up gun.

2. Trigger control on an airbrush can be used to:
   A. Do a 50-percent overlap.
   B. Reduce overspray.
   C. Control amount of material being sprayed.

3. When applying custom paint, the panel you are working on should be:
   A. Freshly waxed.
   B. Washed with soap and water.
   C. Completely rubbed out and finished.
   D. Cleaned with wax and grease remover.

4. Once the panel is cleaned, do not touch it with your hands because:
   A. Skin oil and oil from your hair will damage the base coat.
   B. Skin oil and oil from your hair will damage the paint you are going to apply.
   C. Fingerprints on a base coat will not look good and will shine through the custom work.

5. Acrylic lacquer is used for custom work because:
   A. It is inexpensive.
   B. When used over lacquer, it bonds extremely well to the base coat.
   C. It bonds extremely well with enamel.

6. When applying decals, soapy water is used to:
   A. Clean the base paint on the panel you are working on.
   B. Help you keep your hands clean.
   C. Help you move the decal around to get it in perfect position.

7. When deciding between tape stripes and painted stripes, remember this:
   A. The vinyl stripe does not expand and contract with temperature extremes.
   B. Vinyl stripes require much artistic ability to apply.
   C. It is not necessary to apply clear over paint stripes, but it is over vinyl tape stripes.
   D. Most refinishers can apply either paint or tape stripes in about the same amount of time.

8. Tape stripes:
   A. Need not follow body contours and lines.
   B. Can be applied in a straight line by pulling the tape taut before sticking it to the panel.
   C. Cannot be used to follow curves in the bodywork.

9. Paint stripes are applied:
   A. Only with a sword brush.
   B. On hot-rods.
   C. Using either pre-cut tape or freehand.

10. Stencils can be handmade by projecting the desired design onto:
    A. The panel you are going to paint.
    B. A piece of tracing paper.
    C. The shop floor.

11. Spray mastic, when used as a stencil material:
    A. Produces smooth, neat lines.
    B. Always covers well.
    C. Always peels off well.
    D. Clings to the panel well.

12. When applying a lace-type stencil effect:
    A. The paint should be applied heavily enough so that it will soak through the lace.
    B. The lace should be applied to the panel slightly damp.
    C. The paint should be very thin.

13. When applying a two-tone paint job, the first painted area must be fully masked before painting the second color.
    A. True. B. False.

14. When applying a wood-grain finish:
    A. Similar colors should be used.
    B. Make the grain using a brush with short, stiff bristles.
    C. The wood-grain top coat should flow into the base coat.
    D. It is possible to produce only one type of grain.

15. Cobwebbing involves:
    A. Careful application of actual spider webs to panels.
    B. Use of unthinned paint sprayed at relatively high pressures.
    C. Only one color.

16. To obtain the cobweb effect, an airbrush is most commonly used.
    A. True. B. False.

17. When applying a painted smoke finish:
    A. The base coat must be a dark coat.
    B. Tack the panel before applying clear.
    C. Hold the gun 12–15 inches from the panel.
    D. No clear coat is necessary.

18. When using an acetylene torch for the smoke effect:
    A. There is no need for a fire extinguisher.
    B. Soot from the torch is deposited directly onto the panel.
    C. The stroke used is similar to that used in spray painting.
    D. The smoke finish is extremely sturdy.

19. Acetylene, used to apply smoke finishes:
    A. Is extremely safe and stable.
    B. Is kept in cylinders that should be stored in an upright position.
    C. Is used at pressures exceeding 15 psi.

20. An acetylene torch:
    A. Can be lit with a cigarette lighter or a match.
    B. Is reliable and never needs to be cleaned.
    C. Should be turned off unless you are actually holding it.

Glossary

abrasive A substance used for grinding, sanding, smoothing, or polishing painted or unpainted surfaces.

abrasive coating The coating applied to sanding paper or sanding discs.

abrasive disc A disc coated with abrasive and used on a rotating sander or grinder.

acetone A solvent that will dissolve many plastics. It is extremely volatile and flammable.

acetylene A colorless, flammable gas, used with oxygen to make an oxy-acetylene torch flame.

acrylic A chemical compound used in lacquer and enamel paints for durability, and to maintain color and gloss.

acrylic resin A man-made resin used as a binder in paint.

activator A chemical that creates a reaction when mixed with another chemical. The activator mixed with polyurethane paint immediately before spraying causes the paint to harden. The catalyst or hardener used with plastic body filler is sometimes called an activator.

adhere To stick to a surface.

adhesion The ability of a substance to adhere.

adhesive A substance that sticks to something, or causes two parts to stick together.

airbrush A small spray gun, used for detail or delicate work.

air compressor A machine that compresses air used to operate air-powered equipment, driven by a gasoline engine or electric motor.

air dry To allow paint to dry at normal room temperature.

air file An air-operated straight-stroke sander, equipped with a file blade.

air filter A device that allows air to flow, but traps and holds dust or larger foreign bodies in the air.

air horns The horns on a spray gun air cap. Horns adjusted to a vertical position give a horizontal spray pattern. Horizontal horns give a vertical spray pattern.

air line A pipe or hose that conducts compressed air from a compressor to an air-operated tool.

air pressure The amount of pressure available to operate air-powered tools.

air pump A device for compressing air, usually smaller than a compressor, perhaps hand operated.

air transformer An adjustable mechanism used to reduce compressor air pressure to a lower, more stable level. May include a filter or water trap. Also called a regulator.

air washer booth A spray booth that uses a stream of running water to carry away the overspray from painting.

alkyd A chemical used in enamel paint.

alloy A metal that has been made by melting and mixing together two or more metals, or a metal and a nonmetal.

atmospheric pressure The air pressure that exists naturally on earth and varies with elevation or weather conditions.

atomization The separation of a liquid into fine droplets that are suspended in a moving air stream.

atomize To cause atomization of a liquid.

baking resin An additive used with enamel paint to prevent wrinkling when force drying is used. Also known as antiwrinkle.

banding A spray gun technique wherein the edges of a panel are painted first.

base metal The car body metal underneath the filler, primer, or paint. To "get down to base metal" means to sand, grind, or chemically strip off everything that has been applied over the original body metal.

belt sander A sanding machine that uses an endless abrasive belt to remove material very quickly from large areas.

binder A chemical that is the backbone of any paint. The binder holds the pigment particles together and makes them stick to the surface being painted.

bleed An orifice or hole for air or liquid to pass through. Also, the ability of an old paint finish to rise to the surface of new paint and change the color if not sealed first.

bleeder gun A type of spray gun used with small compressors, in which the air flows through the gun continuously and can only be shut off by disconnecting the hose.

bleeding A finish defect wherein the old paint film partially dissolves and rises to the surface of the new paint, changing the color.

blending A spray gun technique used to blend new paint into old paint so that the repaired area does not show.

blistering A finish defect where there are small bubbles in the topcoat.

bloom A finish defect where the top coat has a cloudy appearance.

blushing A finish defect in lacquer paint where there is a milky white haze on the topcoat.

body The structure of the car that encloses the driver and passengers, engine compartment, and trunk.

body filler A soft material of metal or plastic; used to fill and level small defects in body panels.

body grinder *See* disc sander.

body panels The metal or plastic sections that are welded or bolted together to form the body.

body side molding Any molding that is fastened to the side of the body and runs from front to rear.

body trim Seat covering, floor covering, or other upholstering fabric used to trim the interior of the body.

bronzing A finish defect that consists of a metallic haze on the surface.

buffing compound A fine abrasive, usually made in the form of a stick, for application to a buffing pad.

build The amount of paint built up on a panel, measured in thousandths of an inch.

bull's-eye effect A finish defect where a crack encircles a spot repair at the featheredge.

butyl acetate A lacquer solvent made from a reaction between butyl alcohol and acetic acid.

catalyst A substance that assists in a chemical reaction but does not react with the chemicals.

Centari Dupont's copyrighted name for their acrylic enamel.

chalking A condition found in old, weather-worn paint, with loose, powdery pigment on the surface and a dull finish. Also found in new paint as a defect.

checking A finish defect showing cracks in the surface, very close together and in a regular pattern.

cheese-grater file A file that is used to shape or level newly-applied plastic body filler before it completely hardens.

chipping A paint condition where small pieces of paint are knocked out of the surface by impact from flying objects, usually revealing the old finish underneath.

clear A topcoat that is transparent, like clear plastic.

closed coat A sanding paper or sanding disc with the abrasive particles packed tightly together.

coalescence The ability of atomized paint droplets to reform into a liquid.

coat, double Two coats of paint, with the second coat applied quickly, before the first coat solidifies.

coat, single One coat of paint, allowed to flash dry before the next coat is applied.

cobwebbing A spray painting technique using unthinned acrylic lacquer that results in long, stringy lines in the finish, similar to a spider's web.

color retention The ability of a paint finish to resist the elements and not change color.

compatibility The ease with which materials work or mix together. Example: Oil-base paint will not mix with water, but will mix with an oil-base solvent.

compound A paste or liquid material containing fine abrasive, used with a damp rag or buffer to smooth new lacquer finishes or remove oxidized paint on old enamel finishes.

compounding Using rubbing compound by hand or machine to rub out a finish.

compressor A machine used to compress and store air.

condensation Any liquid that has condensed from a vapor. Hot, compressed air from a compressor contains water vapor that condenses in the tank and lines when the air cools.

contaminants Foreign objects or chemicals in a paint finish.

corrosion An unwanted reaction between the surface of a metal and a chemical, resulting in coating or erosion of the metal.

coverage The ability of a paint to hide the old finish color.

cowl assembly The inverted-U-shaped structure, including the area in front of the windshield and extending down on each side of the car in front of the doors.

cracking A break in the paint film, similar to a crack in a piece of glass.

cratering A defect in the finish consisting of holes or small craters.

craters Small holes or craters in the paint film.

crazing Small cracks in a finish that look similar to crow's-feet, all interlaced and completely covering an area.

cross-grinding The technique of moving a rotary body grinder first in one direction and then in the opposite direction, to eliminate circular tracks in the surface.

crow's-feet Another name for crazing, the small cracks that cover a surface.

curing The final drying of paint, where it becomes stable and reaches full film strength.

decal A decalcomania, or loosely, any sticker, transfer, or label.

decalcomania A decoration that is loosened from its paper mounting by immersion in water, then slid off the paper into position. *See* decal.

die back A finish defect where there is loss of gloss in a topcoat after polishing.

dirt in paint Any foreign matter in a paint finish.

discing Using a disc sander.

disc sander A sanding machine using a rotating abrasive disc.

double coat Two coats of paint, with the second coat applied quickly, before the first coat solidifies.

drier A chemical mixed with enamel paint to speed up the drying time.

drop In a compressed air pipe system, a branch that goes from the main line to a work station. Also called a takeoff.

dry air booth A spray booth that uses a flow of air to pull overspray into filters, without any water.

dry film gauge A tool that will measure paint film thickness on steel body cars.

dry sanding Sanding without the use of water or other liquid.

dry spray A finish defect with pigment particles dried on top of the paint surface like particles of sand.

Duco DuPont's name for nitrocellulose lacquer, the first modern automotive finish, developed in 1924.

duct tape A wide, cloth-backed gray tape used to protect moldings and trim when sandblasting.

Dulux DuPont's name for alkyd enamel.

durability The length of time a paint finish will last in good condition.

duster gun A blow gun. A gun connected to an air hose, used for blowing dust off a car before painting.

Eerie-Dess Badger's name for their wood-grain paint.

enamel A finish that cures by chemical change.

epoxy Common name for plastic body filler.

evaporation The chemical change from a liquid to a gas. Paint is said to "evaporate" when the solvent evaporates and leaves the pigment and binder behind.

face shield A transparent shield that protects the face from grinding sparks or other flying objects.

fading The effect of sunlight and weathering that causes paint to become dull and faded.

featheredge The gradual taper from a coat of old paint down to base metal, accomplished by sanding.

featheredging The technique of sanding the edge of old paint down to base metal on a gradual taper so the repair will not show when painted.

ferrous Any substance made of iron, or containing iron.

fiberglass Any material made from woven glass cloth mixed with resin.

fifty percent overlap The amount that each successive stroke with a spray gun should cover the previous stroke path.

file board A wooden handle, with screw holes for attaching a file.

filler Any of several substances used to fill small holes and dents before priming. Formerly lead melted with a torch was the most used filler, but now a plastic paste is used that sets hard through chemical action.

finish A coating applied for protection or appearance.

finish coat The final coat of paint.

fisheye A finish defect showing small circles with spots in the middle.

flaking A finish defect where small areas of the paint film separate from the finish and fall off in flakes.

flammable Capable of igniting easily and burning.

flash A paint's first stage of drying, when the solvent evaporates and the paint film changes from a high wet gloss to a normal gloss.

flash off *See* flash.

flattening compound A chemical mixed with paint to dull its gloss and make it look older so it will better match old paint. Also used when painting instrument panels to give a non-gloss flat finish that will not reflect light.

flow The merging of sprayed paint droplets to form a smooth coat of paint.

flowing *See* flow.

flux A substance used to clean metal in preparation for brazing, soldering, or application of lead filler.

fog coat A thin coat of paint sprayed so that the color underneath can still be seen, as if through a fog.

force dry Using heat lamps to shorten drying time of a paint coat.

friction A resistance to movement of one substance along or through another substance. Air moving through a pipe is slowed because of friction between the air and the walls of the pipe.

frisket paper A self-stick paper that is used for making stencils.

frisket knife A special knife used for cutting stencils out of paper.

galvanized steel A steel that has been coated with zinc to slow down rust and corrosion.

glazing putty Putty used to smooth large areas, as opposed to spot putty, which is used in small spots. The putty comes in a tube, ready to use.

gloss The reflecting ability of a surface.

goggles Transparent lenses for eye protection, usually enclosed at the sides.

grater file A coarse file similar to a cheese grater, used to level plastic body filler.

grit Abrasive particles attached to a paper or disc backing.

grit number A number that indicates the size of abrasive grit. The higher the number, the smaller the grit size.

hardener A chemical added to enamel paint to make it cure faster.

hardness The ability of a surface or paint finish to resist abrasion or scratching.

hazing A finish defect where the top coat loses its gloss as it dries.

hiding The ability of a paint to cover and hide the old paint color.

holdout The ability of an undercoat to keep the topcoat from sinking. The ability of a paint finish to last.

hopper An open top container that feeds material through a small hole at the bottom, similar to a funnel, but larger.

humidity The amount of moisture contained in the air.

induction baking Drying painted metal bodies with an electrostatic or electromagnetic machine that causes the metal car body to heat up instead of the air or the paint. The heat then moves directly from the metal body into the paint and dries it.

infrared The type of ray put out by a heat lamp used in a paint baking or drying booth.

insoluble Not capable of being dissolved.

iridescent A finish with rainbowlike bands that change pattern and hue as the viewer changes his position. Similar to the rainbow effect seen in a soap bubble.

jitterbug A small, air-powered pad sander.

ketones A group of solvents, highly volatile and flammable.

lacquer A type of finish that forms a film by evaporation, without chemical reaction.

lacquer thinner A solvent used for thinning lacquer.

lifting A finish defect where the paint shrivels and comes loose from the surface.

line-checking Closely spaced, parallel straight-line cracks in a paint finish.

Lucite DuPont's trademarked name for acrylic lacquer.

mandrel A shaft or rod made to attach specially shaped abrasives on a body grinder.

manometer A highly sensitive instrument for measuring atmospheric pressure. Used in a spray booth to determine the force of the exhaust fans and the condition of the filters.

masking The technique of covering surfaces with tape and/or paper to prevent paint overspray.

masking paper Roll paper used for masking.
masking tape A tape used for masking.
M.E.K. Methyl-ethyl-ketone, a highly volative and flammable solvent.
metal conditioner A chemical metal cleaner that removes minor rust and corrosion, etches the surface for better paint adhesion, and leaves a film that retards rusting.
metal finishing The process of preparing a metal surface for painting.
metal-finishing marks Small scratches left from improper sanding or grinding.
metallics Metallic paints.
metallic paints Pigmented paints that have reflective aluminum, colorless metal flakes imbedded in the finish.
micro-checking A finish defect consisting of fine cracks in a paint film that look like dulling of the paint, but appear as cracks when examined with a magnifying glass.
mist coat A final coat, sprayed with thinner only or with very little color. Used to insure final flowing of the finish.
mottling A finish defect in metallic paints where the metal flakes join together to form a mottled pattern.

neutral flame A torch flame that is neither oxidizing nor carbonizing.
nib(s) Small foreign objects or dirt in a finish.
nitrocellulose A type of lacquer.
noncorrosive Any chemical that will not corrode metal.
nonferrous Not made of iron, or not containing iron.
nonferrous metal A metal other than iron.

open coat An abrasive that has been attached to its backing with spaces between the abrasive particles so that sanded material will not accumulate.
orange peel A finish defect that looks like the skin of an orange.
orbital sander A rotary sander that changes its center of rotation to avoid gouging or scratching. Some pad sanders also have orbital action instead of a back and forth action.
original finish The finish originally applied to the car body when it was manufactured.
overlap To spray paint so that each pass with the spray gun applies paint partially over the previous spray path, or over old paint.
overreduction Excessive thinning of paint by adding too much thinner or reducer.
overspray Paint spray that goes over the area being painted and lands on an unwanted area.
oxidation The chemical process of an enamel paint film combining with oxygen to become hard and dry. The process continues indefinitely, eventually forming a surface powder that must be removed along with oxidized paint to reveal fresh paint.
oxidized Chemically combined with oxygen.
oxidized paint An enamel paint finish that has reacted with oxygen over several years and taken on a chalky, dull appearance.
oxidizing flame A torch flame with excess oxygen.

packing nut A nut that compresses packing material to prevent leakage around a shaft, as on a spray gun.

paint film The total thickness of paint on a panel.

paint remover A liquid or paste that will loosen paint so it can be washed or wiped off.

particle A small part or a small piece of something.

pearlescent finish An iridescent finish made of pearl dust suspended in a binder. Its basic color is white with rainbowlike bands swirled throughout.

peeling A finish defect where the paint comes loose and exposes the old finish or metal underneath.

phenol A type of plastic used to make backup pads for disc sanders.

pigment The part of paint that gives it color, is solid, and will not dissolve in liquid.

pinholing A finish defect with small holes in the paint film.

plastic A substance soft enough to be shaped that later chemically hardens to maintain the shape.

plastic body filler A paste chemical used to fill and smooth low areas in a panel.

polisher A machine with a rotating pad for polishing paint.

polishing compound A paste or liquid material containing fine abrasive.

polishing pad A rotating pad used on a polisher.

polychromatic Showing a variety of reflected colors, as in a metallic finish, which contains aluminum flakes.

polymerization The way some chemicals dry.

polyurethane enamel A paint that sets hard when it dries from the chemical reaction of an activator that is mixed in just before spraying.

poor drying A finish defect where the paint film remains soft instead of hardening.

porcelain enamel A glassy enamel paint that is fired on by heating the painted metal to a high temperature. Also known as vitreous enamel.

power file A file driven by an air-operated, hand-held machine.

pressure An amount of force per unit area, as pounds per square inch in the U.S. System, or newtons per square meter in the metric system. The unit of pressure in the metric system is the kilopascal, which equals 1,000 newtons per square meter, or 0.1450 psi.

prewarming The technique of heating a panel with heat lamps to bring it up to room temperature before spray painting.

prime coat The first coat put on an automobile.

primer The paint used when applying a prime coat.

primer-surfacer A liquid which is a combination of primer and surfacer which both primes the surface and levels small scratches.

protective goggles *See* goggles.

psi Pounds per square inch.

putty A type of filler.

random orbital disc sander A rotary sander that randomly changes its center of rotation to avoid gouging or scratching.

reducer A liquid used to thin enamel paints.

resilient Capable of resisting damage from impact.

resin A chemical that solidifies and becomes hard and durable when its solvent evaporates. Used in paint, plastic body filler, and fiberglass bodies.

respirator A mask worn over the mouth and nose to prevent inhaling paint while spraying.

retarder A chemical added to lacquer to lengthen the drying time.

rubbing compound A paste or liquid material containing fine abrasive, used with a damp rag or buffer to smooth new lacquer finishes or remove oxidized paint on old enamel finishes.

rubbing out The technique of using rubbing compound on a finish.

rust The oxidation of iron, leaving reddish-brown stains.

rust inhibiting The ability of a chemical coating to resist rusting of the underlying iron.

sag A finish defect where the wet paint moves down the panel in small waves and then dries with the waves making ridges in the paint.

sand pot The hopper that holds and feeds the sand to a sandblaster.

sander A machine used to sand.

sanding block A hand-sanding device used to hold a piece of sanding paper.

sanding sludge The debris from wet sanding, a kind of mud composed of particles of paint, primer, filler, and metal.

sand scratches Small scratches in the base coat or base metal, that are made by the sanding or grinding abrasive and become filled when the surface is primed.

sandscratch swelling A finish defect consisting of invisible scratch impressions in the topcoat that make the finish dull.

scuff sand To sand a finish with fine grain abrasive (600A) to smooth it before compounding.

sealer The final undercoat, used to prevent the top coat from being affected by the primer, filler, or old finish.

settling The tendency of the heavier particles in a paint to settle at the bottom of a paint can or spray gun.

silicone A chemical used in polish and wax that causes finish defects if it is not removed before painting.

silicone and wax remover A liquid used with a wiping rag to remove old wax and the silicone that is in wax in preparation for painting.

single coat A coat of paint that is sprayed on, overlapping each stroke by 50 percent, and allowed to dry before the next coat is applied. On lacquer or fast-drying enamels, the time between coats may be only a few minutes. *See* double coat.

siphoning A method of moving paint from a spray gun cup to the nozzle. When the spray gun trigger is pulled, air blows across the end of a tube, creating a pressure lower than atmospheric. The atmospheric pressure above the paint in the cup then pushes paint into the tube and out into the flow of air, where it sprays from the gun.

skinning A finish defect caused by the paint outer surface drying quickly and forming a tough skin that prevents the paint from drying properly. It can also occur on paint standing in a can, from exposure to air.

solids The pigment particles and binder that solidify on the panel surface to form the paint film.

solubility The ability of lacquers to be affected by thinner long after they have dried. The high solubility of lacquer enables newly sprayed lacquer to bond tightly to an old lacquer finish because the thinner in the new lacquer dissolves some of the old finish.

solvency factor The ability of solvent to dissolve other substances. A solvent with a low solvency factor is a weak solvent.

solvent A liquid that is used to dissolve a substance. In paints, the solvent dissolves the resin base, and evaporates after it is sprayed. *See* thinner and reducer.

solvent popping A finish defect where there are bubbles in the paint film.

spark torch lighter A device that uses flint and abrasive to make a spark to light a torch.

spiderwebbing *See* cobwebbing.

spot putty Putty used for leveling or filling small areas, as opposed to glaze putty, which is used for large areas. The putty comes in a tube, ready to use.

spot repairs Body repairs done to a small area, such as repairing a small dent.

spray booth An enclosure with a filtered ventilation and exhaust system so that cars may be painted without dust getting into the paint.

spray gun A hand-held device which sprays paint when the trigger is pulled.

spray mastic A rubberlike covering that is sprayed on and cut away to make a stencil.

squeegee A flexible blade that is pulled over a surface to remove the water.

stains A finish defect where surface contamination changes or affects the color of the finish.

stencil A design cut out of paper that is placed against a car body and sprayed to put the design on the car.

straight-stroke sander An air-operated sander that moves the abrasive back and forth in a straight line.

strainer A device for separating any dried lumps of paint before putting the paint into the spray gun, to prevent clogging.

striker A spark torch lighter.

stripper Paint remover.

surface drying *See* skinning.

surform file A coarse file used to shape plastic body filler before it hardens completely.

synthetic resin A resin produced artificially instead of by plants or animals.

tack cloth A cloth impregnated with a sticky substance and used to wipe dust from a car body before painting.

tack coat A thin coat of alkyd enamel that is allowed to dry 20 or 30 minutes before applying the first full coat of paint.

tack rag *See* tack cloth.

takeoff In a compressed air pipe system, a branch that goes from the main line to a work station. Also called a drop.

thermoplastic The quality of becoming pliable when hot.

to thin paint To add solvent to lacquer or enamel.

thinner A solvent used for thinning lacquer. *See* reducer.

tinting The process of mixing in small amounts of color in the factory paint formula to make it match an aged or weathered finish.

tone A variation of a color; a color.

topcoat One or more of the color coats applied to a car.

transformer-regulator The device in the air line that reduces the pressure from the compressor. Some designs also filter the air and remove oil and moisture.

trim The parts attached to the body which are not painted. Upholstery is known as soft trim, while moldings and emblems are known as hard trim.

two-tone Two different colors on a car. Usually the top is a different color from the rest of the body.

undercoat A coat of paint sprayed on before the finish color is applied.

undercoating A coating of heavy insulating material that is sprayed onto the underside of a vehicle to protect and soundproof it.

underreduction Adding too little thinner or reducer to paint before spraying, so that the paint is too thick.

underspray Paint spray that reaches a masked area by going under masking tape that is not stuck because of dirt, oil, or water on the surface.

uniforming finish A clear sprayed finish used to smooth and blend spot repairs and provide a light protective coating which prevents buffing through the repair or weathering of the blended edge.

valve A device that can be turned on to allow liquid or air to flow out of a container or pipe.

vapor The state of a substance that has evaporated.

vaporization The act of evaporating, wherein a liquid changes to a gas.

vehicle identification number The number on a vehicle that identifies its manufacturer, year, model, engine, and serial.

vent The hole in the lid of a spray gun paint cup where atmospheric pressure and air enter.

ventilation Supplying fresh air.

vibrator A shaker for thoroughly mixing paint that is in an enclosed can.

vibrator sander A small air-operated pad sander. Also called a jitterbug.

VIN *See* vehicle identification number.

vinyl A material used for seat covers, upholstery, and top coverings.

vinyl tape A tape used with spray-on vinyl tops to imitate a seam.

viscosity A measurement of how thick or thin a liquid is.

viscosity cup A cup with a long handle and a hole in the bottom, used to measure the viscosity of paint.

viscous Thicker than other liquids, and pouring very slowly.

volatile Easily evaporating.

volatility A measure of how easily a liquid evaporates.

waterborne Carried or supported by water. Sometimes used to describe water base paints.

water spotting A finish defect caused by allowing drops of water to stand on a painted surface.

weathering Deteriorating from exposure to weather.

weather tape A wide tape used to protect glass, moldings, or trim during sandblasting. It is more durable than masking tape.

welding blanket A thick blanket used to protect car metal or glass areas from welding sparks or sandblasting sand.

wet sanding Sanding with a hose running on the sanding area to carry away the loose material and prevent clogging of the abrasive.

wet spots A finish defect with small areas where the paint does not dry, caused by finger marks or other contamination.

wood-graining A painting technique with a result that looks similar to wood. Also, a decal or transfer that is applied to large areas to make them look like wood.

wrinkling A finish defect in enamel topcoat that looks like minute furrows very close together and running in different directions.

zebra effect A finish defect caused by tilting the spray gun, resulting in alternating bands of wet and dry paint that look similar to a zebra's stripes.

zinc chromate A primer used on galvanized metal before painting.

Index

T

U

V

W

Z

CONVERSION TABLE

INCH FRACTIONS AND DECIMALS TO METRIC EQUIVALENTS

INCHES		MM	INCHES		MM	INCHES		MM
Fractions	Decimals		Fractions	Decimals		Fractions	Decimals	
—	.0004	.01	—	.4331	11	31/32	.96875	24.606
—	.004	.10	7/16	.4375	11.113	—	.9843	25
—	.01	.25	29/64	.4531	11.509	1	1.000	25.4
1/64	.0156	.397	15/32	.46875	11.906	—	1.0236	26
—	.0197	.50	—	.4724	12	1-1/32	1.0312	26.194
—	.0295	.75	31/64	.48437	12.303	1-1/16	1.062	26.988
1/32	.03125	.794	—	.492	12.5	—	1.063	27
—	.0394	1	1/2	.500	12.700	1-3/32	1.094	27.781
3/64	.0469	1.191	—	.5118	13	—	1.1024	28
—	.059	1.5	33/64	.5156	13.097	1-1/8	1.125	28.575
1/16	.0625	1.588	17/32	.53125	13.494	—	1.1417	29
5/64	.0781	1.984	35/64	.54687	13.891	1-5/32	1.156	29.369
—	.0787	2	—	.5512	14	—	1.1811	30
3/32	.094	2.381	9/16	.5625	14.288	1-3/16	1.1875	30.163
—	.0984	2.5	—	.571	14.5	1-7/32	1.219	30.956
7/64	.1093	2.776	37/64	.57812	14.684	—	1.2205	31
—	.1181	3	—	.5906	15	1-1/4	1.250	31.750
1/8	.1250	3.175	19/32	.59375	15.081	—	1.2598	32
—	.1378	3.5	39/64	.60937	15.478	1-9/32	1.281	32.544
9/64	.1406	3.572	5/8	.6250	15.875	—	1.2992	33
5/32	.15625	3.969	—	.6299	16	1-5/16	1.312	33.338
—	.1575	4	41/64	.6406	16.272	—	1.3386	34
11/64	.17187	4.366	—	.6496	16.5	1-11/32	1.344	34.131
—	.177	4.5	21/32	.65625	16.669	1-3/8	1.375	34.925
3/16	.1875	4.763	—	.6693	17	—	1.3779	35
—	.1969	5	43/64	.67187	17.066	1-13/32	1.406	35.719
13/64	.2031	5.159	11/16	.6875	17.463	—	1.4173	36
—	.2165	5.5	45/64	.7031	17.859	1-7/16	1.438	36.513
7/32	.21875	5.556	—	.7087	18	—	1.4567	37
15/64	.23437	5.953	23/32	.71875	18.256	1-15/32	1.469	37.306
—	.2362	6	—	.7283	18.5	—	1.4961	38
1/4	.2500	6.350	47/64	.73437	18.653	1-1/2	1.500	38.100
—	.2559	6.5	—	.7480	19	1-17/32	1.531	38.894
17/64	.2656	6.747	3/4	.7500	19.050	—	1.5354	39
—	.2756	7	49/64	.7656	19.447	1-9/16	1.562	39.688
9/32	.28125	7.144	25/32	.78125	19.844	—	1.5748	40
—	.2953	7.5	—	.7874	20	1-19/32	1.594	40.481
19/64	.29687	7.541	51/64	.79687	20.241	—	1.6142	41
5/16	.3125	7.938	13/16	.8125	20.638	1-5/8	1.625	41.275
—	.3150	8	—	.8268	21	—	1.6535	42
21/64	.3281	8.334	53/64	.8281	21.034	1-21/32	1.6562	42.069
—	.335	8.5	27/32	.84375	21.431	1-11/16	1.6875	42.863
11/32	.34375	8.731	55/64	.85937	21.828	—	1.6929	43
—	.3543	9	—	.8662	22	1-23/32	1.719	43.656
23/64	.35937	9.128	7/8	.8750	22.225	—	1.7323	44
—	.374	9.5	57/64	.8906	22.622	1-3/4	1.750	44.450
3/8	.3750	9.525	—	.9055	23	—	1.7717	45
25/64	.3906	9.922	29/32	.90625	23.019	1-25/32	1.781	45.244
—	.3937	10	59/64	.92187	23.416	—	1.8110	46
13/32	.4062	10.319	15/16	.9375	23.813	1-13/16	1.8125	46.038
—	.413	10.5	—	.9449	24	1-27/32	1.844	46.831
27/64	.42187	10.716	61/64	.9531	24.209	—	1.8504	47

CONVERSION TABLE (Cont'd)

INCH FRACTIONS AND DECIMALS TO METRIC EQUIVALENTS

INCHES		MM	INCHES		MM	INCHES		MM
Fractions	Decimals		Fractions	Decimals		Fractions	Decimals	
1-7/8	1.875	47.625	—	3.0709	78	—	4.7244	120
—	1.8898	48	—	3.1102	79	4-3/4	4.750	120.650
1-29/32	1.9062	48.419	3-1/8	3.125	79.375	4-7/8	4.875	123.825
—	1.9291	49	—	3.1496	80.	—	4.9212	125
1-15/16	1.9375	49.213	3-3/16	3.1875	80.963	5	5.000	127
—	1.9685	50	—	3.1890	81	—	5.1181	130
1-31/32	1.969	50.066	—	3.2283	82	5-1/4	5.250	133.350
2	2.000	50.800	3-1/4	3.250	82.550	5-1/2	5.500	139.700
—	2.0079	51	—	3.2677	83	—	5.5118	140
—	2.0472	52	—	3.3071	84	5-3/4	5.750	146.050
2-1/16	2.062	52.388	3-5/16	3.312	84.1377	—	5.9055	150
—	2.0866	53	—	3.3464	85	6	6.000	152.400
2-1/8	2.125	53.975	3-3/8	3.375	85.725	6-1/4	6.250	158.750
—	2.126	54	—	3.3858	86	—	6.2992	160
—	2.165	55	—	3.4252	87	6-1/2	6.500	165.100
2-3/16	2.1875	55.563	3-7/16	3.438	87.313	—	6.6929	170
—	2.2047	56	—	3.4646	88	6-3/4	6.750	171.450
—	2.244	57	3-1/2	3.500	88.900	7	7.000	177.800
2-1/4	2.250	57.150	—	3.5039	89	—	7.0866	180
—	2.2835	58	—	3.5433	90	—	7.4803	190
2-5/16	2.312	58.738	3-9/16	3.562	90.4877	7-1/2	7.500	190.500
—	2.3228	59	—	3.5827	91	—	7.8740	200
—	2.3622	60	—	3.622	92	8	8.0000	203.200
2-3/8	2.375	60.325	3-5/8	3.625	92.075	—	8.2677	210
—	2.4016	61	—	3.6614	93	8-1/2	8.500	215.900
2-7/16	2.438	61.913	3-11/16	3.6875	93.663	—	8.6614	220
—	2.4409	62	—	3.7008	94	9	9.000	228.600
—	2.4803	63	—	3.7401	95	—	9.0551	230
2-1/2	2.500	63.500	3-3/4	3.750	95.250	—	9.4488	240
—	2.5197	64	—	3.7795	96	9-1/2	9.500	241.300
—	2.559	65	3-13/16	3.8125	96.838	—	9.8425	250
2-9/16	2.562	65.088	—	3.8189	97	10	10.000	254.000
—	2.5984	66	—	3.8583	98	—	10.2362	260
2-5/8	2.625	66.675	3-7/8	3.875	98.425	—	10.6299	270
—	2.638	67	—	3.8976	99	11	11.000	279.400
—	2.6772	68	—	3.9370	100	—	11.0236	280
2-11/16	2.6875	68.263	3-15/16	3.9375	100.013	—	11.4173	290
—	2.7165	69	—	3.9764	101	—	11.8110	300
2-3/4	2.750	69.850	4	4.000	101.600	12	12.000	304.800
—	2.7559	70	4-1/16	4.062	103.188	13	13.000	330.200
—	2.7953	71	4-1/8	4.125	104.775	—	13.7795	350
2-13/16	2.8125	71.438	—	4.1338	105	14	14.000	355.600
—	2.8346	72	4-3/16	4.1875	106.363	15	15.000	381
—	2.8740	73	4-1/4	4.250	107.950	—	15.7480	400
2-7/8	2.875	73.025	4-5/16	4.312	109.538	16	16.000	406.400
—	2.9134	74	—	4.3307	110	17	17.000	431.800
2-15/16	2.9375	74.613	4-3/8	4.375	111.125	—	17.7165	450
—	2.9527	75	4-7/16	4.438	112.713	18	18.000	457.200
—	2.9921	76	4-1/2	4.500	114.300	19	19.000	482.600
3	3.000	76.200	—	4.5275	115	—	19.6850	500
—	3.0315	77	4-9/16	4.562	115.888	20	20.000	508
3-1/16	3.062	77.788	4-5/8	4.625	117.475	21	21.000	533.400

NOTES